Digital Humanities

SPEC KITS
Supporting Effective Library Management for Over Thirty-five Years

Committed to assisting research and academic libraries in the continuous improvement of management systems, ARL has worked since 1970 to gather and disseminate the best practices for library needs. As part of its commitment, ARL maintains an active publications program best known for its SPEC Kits. Through the Collaborative Research/Writing Program, librarians work with ARL staff to design SPEC surveys and write publications. Originally established as an information source for ARL member libraries, the SPEC Kit series has grown to serve the needs of the library community worldwide.

What are SPEC Kits?

Published six times per year, SPEC Kits contain the most valuable, up-to-date information on the latest issues of concern to libraries and librarians today. They are the result of a systematic survey of ARL member libraries on a particular topic related to current practice in the field. Each SPEC Kit contains an executive summary of the survey results; survey questions with tallies and selected comments; the best representative documents from survey participants, such as policies, procedures, handbooks, guidelines, Web sites, records, brochures, and statements; and a selected reading list—both print and online sources—containing the most current literature available on the topic for further study.

Subscribe to SPEC Kits

Subscribers tell us that the information contained in SPEC Kits is valuable to a variety of users, both inside and outside the library. SPEC Kit purchasers use the documentation found in SPEC Kits as a point of departure for research and problem solving because they lend immediate authority to proposals and set standards for designing programs or writing procedure statements. SPEC Kits also function as an important reference tool for library administrators, staff, students, and professionals in allied disciplines who may not have access to this kind of information.

SPEC Kits can be ordered directly from the ARL Publications Distribution Center. To order, call **(301) 362-8196**, fax **(240) 396-2479**, e-mail **pubs@arl.org**, or go to **http://www.arl.org/resources/pubs/**.

Information on SPEC Kits and the SPEC survey program can be found at **http://www.arl.org/resources/pubs/spec/index.shtml**. The executive summary for each kit after December 1993 can be accessed free of charge at **http://www.arl.org/resources/pubs/spec/complete.shtml**.

SPEC Kit 326

Digital Humanities
November 2011

Tim Bryson

Librarian for South Asian Studies and Religious Studies

Emory University

Miriam Posner

Mellon Postdoctoral Research Associate

Emory University

Alain St. Pierre

Humanities Librarian for European History and Philosophy

Emory University

Stewart Varner

Digital Scholarship Coordinator

Emory University

ASSOCIATION OF RESEARCH LIBRARIES

Series Editor: Lee Anne George

SPEC Kits are published by the

Association of Research Libraries
21 Dupont Circle, NW, Suite 800
Washington, DC 20036-1118
P (202) 296-2296 F (202) 872-0884
http://www.arl.org/resources/pubs/spec/
pubs@arl.org

ISSN 0160 3582

ISBN 1-59407-870-X
978-1-59407-870-5

Copyright © 2011

SPEC
Kit 326

Digital Humanities

November 2011

SURVEY RESULTS

REPRESENTATIVE DOCUMENTS

Services

Policies and Procedures

SELECTED RESOURCES

SURVEY RESULTS

EXECUTIVE SUMMARY

Introduction

The ARL escience survey in 2009 confirmed how profoundly and quickly technology has transformed research in the sciences. Research in the humanities is being transformed as well. Digital humanities is an emerging field which employs computer-based technologies with the aim of exploring new areas of inquiry in the humanities. Practitioners in the digital humanities draw not only upon traditional writing and research skills associated with the humanities, but also upon technical skills and infrastructure. A number of research institutions host digital scholarship centers or otherwise provide services to help researchers design, produce, disseminate, and maintain digital projects. These centers are often, but not always, located in libraries and incorporate library staff or services into their core programming. Other institutions provide similar services in a less centralized manner. Some services target specific disciplines; others are multidisciplinary. Some institutional initiatives, such as George Mason University's Center for History and New Media, are well established, while others are still in the planning phase.

This survey was specifically interested in digital scholarship centers or services that support the humanities (e.g., history, art, music, film, literature, philosophy, religion, etc.) The purpose of the survey was to provide a snapshot of research library experiences with these centers or services and the benefits and challenges of hosting them. It explored the organization of these services, how they are staffed and funded, what services they offer and to whom, what technical infrastructure is provided, whether the library manages or archives the digital resources produced, and how services are assessed, among other

questions. The survey was conducted between April 11 and May 13, 2011. Sixty-four of the 126 ARL members completed this survey for a response rate of 51%.

Ad Hoc Nature of Service

While a great many of the responding libraries do offer support for digital humanities, the survey indicates that they are still developing systematic policies and staffing models for this type of project. In many cases, libraries are piecing together resources from many departments to meet demand as it arises. A number of respondents described their digital humanities support as "a work in progress" or "in development."

Libraries are likewise developing staffing procedures to meet patrons' needs. While some libraries have staff dedicated to digital humanities, others call on IT staff and librarians as needs arise. Respondents repeatedly described librarians' roles in digital humanities projects as "ad hoc." A number of respondents indicated that their institutions were waiting to determine the full level and complexity of demand before fully staffing support for digital humanities.

Major Trends

While most respondents provide services supporting digital humanities projects, only five (8%) reported that their library hosts a center specifically dedicated to the field. Almost half of the respondents (30 or 48%) provide ad hoc services, and almost a quarter (15 or 24%) host a digital scholarship center that provides services to a number of disciplines including humanities. Only four (6%) reported that no digital scholarship services are offered at their institution, although one of these commented that service was scheduled to start in the fall of 2011.

Project Staffing

Most library staff support is improvised and depends on the needs of the specific project and the availability of related services in units outside the library. Only 18 respondents (35%) indicated they have any dedicated staff for DH projects, and while one of these reported 16 permanent staff available to support researchers, the majority have fewer than five. Dedicated staff is most often a digital scholarship or digital humanities librarian. Technologists, such as programmers and developers, are the next largest category. These 18 libraries also call on subject librarians, support staff, and others depending on project need.

Subject librarians are dedicated project staff at only three libraries, but this category is the most likely to be called upon on an ad hoc basis, followed closely by technologists. In comments about other categories of available library staff, about half mentioned including a metadata specialist, followed by media, preservation, and communication specialists. A few also mentioned design, instructional, repository, archivist, and scanning specialists.

Services and Support

The survey responses suggest that there is a strong desire for digital humanities projects to be closely affiliated with the library. For example, some respondents stated that they only support projects that use library collections, while others indicated that they want library staff to participate as partners in projects. This participation most commonly takes the form of high-level support such as consultations and project management for DH projects. Less frequently, there is technical support such as web development, encoding, and systems administration. Beyond that, support takes the form of traditional library activities such as instructional services, metadata support, and resource identification.

Hardware and Software

The responding libraries provide a variety of hardware and software to support DH projects. Scanners are provided almost universally, and well over half of the libraries provide image, video, and audio editing stations. Most of the libraries provide bibliographic management applications and content management

systems. A majority also provides GIS software and data analysis tools. In many cases these tools are available for self-service by researchers, though a few respondents pointed out that staff use the tools to support DH projects. A slim majority of respondents (25 or 52%) reported that their libraries provided dedicated space to use these tools for digital humanities projects. The size of this space ranges from 100 to 6,000 square feet and averages 1204 square feet. In most cases (16 or 70%), some part of the space is securable for working with sensitive datasets.

Service Users

A large majority of respondents (47 or 98%) reported that faculty may use digital humanities support services, while slightly fewer—though still a substantial majority—provide services to graduate students (41 or 85%) and post-doctoral or other affiliated researchers (37 or 77%). About two-thirds of the respondents (31 or 65%) provide services to undergraduate students. More than a quarter offers services to nonaffiliated researchers, particularly if they are collaborating with an affiliated faculty member.

Libraries employ a variety of methods to advertise their digital humanities support services. Respondents rely on communications from subject liaisons more than any other method, but library websites are also widely used. Half of the responding libraries use publications in print or electronic form to market services. Library staff also attend events, send direct email, and use social media to spread the word about these services.

Project Workspace

Library staff meet with researchers in a variety of spaces to plan or consult on DH projects. Staff offices are the most popular meeting spaces by far; 94% of respondents (45) meet with scholars there. Library staff also commonly meet with researchers in scholars' own offices and in a variety of library meeting spaces. Coffee shops are popular, too.

Funding Sources

Most respondents report that funding for DH projects from a combination of the library operating budget and grants. About half report funding from academic departments, library IT, or special one-time funds, and about a third receive funding from endowments. About three-fourths of the respondents reported that researchers do not usually bring funding with them. In some case because they are still in the grant writing stage of their project.

While formal policies governing library support for DH projects are currently rare (only six libraries reported having a written document), libraries are developing mechanisms for managing these projects. Sixteen respondents described proposal processes that help determine whether a project warrants support based on academic criteria, such as research significance and audience, as well as more practical concerns such as resource availability and existing workload. Proposals tend to be reviewed and approved by library management or, in some cases, a library committee.

Policies and Procedures

Even when formal policies and proposal processes are absent, about half of those who responded to the survey use a Memorandum of Understanding, or MOU, to define the roles and responsibilities of those working on the project. Specifically, MOUs often define the scope of work, deliverables, timeline, costs (and who pays them), deposit agreement (when items will be placed in the library collection), downtime, and hours of operation.

Sustainability

The majority of respondents (27 or 59%) indicated that their libraries preserve digital humanities projects produced in-house. However, comments suggested that many libraries' preservation strategies are selective or evolving: in a number of cases, preservation workflows are "in-process" or "under discussion." Those libraries that preserve digital humanities projects adopt a range of sustainability strategies. Most commonly, libraries create projects that adhere to widely accepted standards for metadata. They also commonly preserve digital projects in repositories and create projects using widely supported platforms. A number of libraries (18 or 51%) develop grant proposals to ensure sustainability, while some work with project planners to incorporate sustainability costs

into project cost estimates (37%) or audit projects for long-term sustainability (31%).

Partnerships

Partnerships, both intra-institutional and inter-institutional, are very common in the digital humanities. Three-fourths of the responding libraries have partnered with other units in their institutions, frequently with university-wide technology services. University departments and various centers and offices were also common partners. Partnerships with other institutions were less common (56%), though respondents demonstrated a level of diversity within those partnerships. Other universities were the most common partners but non-profits and community groups were well represented.

Assessment

Most of the responding libraries do not perform a formal assessment of the effectiveness of their digital humanities services. Of those that do, the primary measures were level of demand and web analytics. A slight majority of those that did assessments made or plan to make adjustments as a result of them—some technical, some logistical, and some programmatic.

Emerging Practices and Procedures

As mentioned above, library-based support for the digital humanities is offered predominantly on an ad hoc basis. However, as demand for services supporting the digital humanities has grown, libraries have begun to re-evaluate their provisional service and staffing models. Many respondents expressed a desire to implement practices, policies, and procedures that would allow them to cope with increases in demand for services. A number of these models exhibit characteristics that are noteworthy either for their uniqueness or success. This section will examine noteworthy emerging practices and procedures.

Library-hosted Digital Humanities Centers

Although not prevalent, a number of research libraries are hosting dedicated digital humanities centers. At this point it is difficult to say whether dedicated digital humanities centers will become more common than the more generalized digital scholarship centers as the field of digital humanities matures. Future surveys might explore the advantages and disadvantages of hosting dedicated digital humanities centers with respect to more generalized approaches or approaches that target specific fields in the digital humanities.

Staff Contributions

It is striking that many of the technical skills required for digital humanities projects are ones commonly possessed by professionals working in traditional fields of librarianship. To be specific, the survey results indicate that metadata librarians, archivists, special collections librarians, preservation specialists, and subject librarians are routinely called upon to serve on teams executing digital humanities projects. This gives credence to the belief that libraries have more to offer for digital humanities projects than just their collections. In fact, one is tempted to conclude that libraries will continue to support the digital humanities not only by acquiring staff with novel skill sets, but also by relying upon skills that have long been required in traditional librarianship.

Service Formalization

As mentioned above, libraries have typically provided digital humanities services on a provisional basis. As demand for such services has grown, however, libraries have found it increasingly difficult to maintain this service model. A number of respondents indicated in their survey responses a desire to formalize their service models in order to manage both growth in demand and customer expectations. A number of libraries have begun using Memoranda of Understanding (MOUs) as a way of formalizing the scope of services they provide.

Project Sustainability

As digital humanities projects have grown in size, complexity, and number, libraries have had to devote increasingly more attention to the sustainability of the projects they support. A number of respondents acknowledged the importance of sustainability, and a few noted that their preservation workflows are "in process" or "under discussion." One strategy adopted by many libraries is to sustain or preserve only some projects, but not all. Another is to adhere to widely accepted platforms and metadata standards when creating a project.

Challenges and Opportunities

The survey revealed that at this stage in the evolution of digital humanities partnerships, there are still many challenges that need to be addressed. The general lack of policies, protocols, and procedures has resulted in a slow and, at times, frustrating experience for both library staff and scholars. This points toward the need for libraries to coordinate their efforts as demand for such collaborative projects increases. Additionally, support for digital humanities suffers from the perennial library issues of underfunding and understaffing. While scholars have traditionally used grant funds to pay for hardware, software, and labor, respondents to the survey reported that it is uncommon for scholars to come to the library with grant funds in hand for a digital humanities project.

It is clear that creative solutions will need to be found as money for still-emerging initiatives remains elusive. Libraries may find it valuable to present their support of digital humanities projects not as a new service, but as a way to more efficiently utilize scarce resources in the support of faculty projects. For example, deans and provosts are often inundated with funding requests for projects that start from scratch. They may be interested in a library-based initiative that could provide a foundation for such work and efficiently coordinate resource allocation by procuring hardware and software for the initiative as a whole and not just for individual projects. Similarly, granting agencies frequently receive applications for exciting projects that will have a hard time surviving reality if there is no dedicated technology support available to the scholar. Furthermore, explicitly involving the library from the beginning of a project should help scholars create more realistic sustainability plans, which are increasingly being required by grants.

SURVEY QUESTIONS AND RESPONSES

The SPEC survey on Digital Humanities was designed by **Tim Bryson**, Librarian for South Asian Studies and Religious Studies, **Miriam Posner**, Mellon Postdoctoral Research Associate, **Alain St. Pierre**, Humanities Librarian for European History and Philosophy, and **Stewart Varner**, Digital Scholarship Coordinator, at Emory University. These results are based on data submitted by 64 of the 126 ARL member libraries (51%) by the deadline of May 13, 2011. The survey's introductory text and questions are reproduced below, followed by the response data and selected comments from the respondents.

Scholars and librarians share a common interest in creating, converting, and finding information in digital formats, for analyzing or manipulating this information, and for sharing, disseminating, or publishing it. A number of research institutions host digital scholarship centers or otherwise provide services to help researchers design, produce, disseminate, and maintain digital projects. These centers are often, but not always, located in libraries and incorporate library staff or services into their core programming. Other institutions provide similar services in a less centralized manner. Some services target specific disciplines; others are multidisciplinary.

This survey is specifically interested in digital scholarship centers or services that support the humanities (e.g., history, art, music, film, literature, philosophy, religion, etc.) The purpose of this survey is to provide a snapshot of research library experiences with these centers or services and the benefits and challenges of hosting them. The survey explores the organization of these services, how they are staffed and funded, what services they offer and to whom, what technical infrastructure is provided, whether the library manages or archives the digital resources produced, and how services are assessed, among other questions.

BACKGROUND

1. Which of the following statements best describes services that support digital humanities projects at your institution? N=63

The library provides ad hoc services that support digital humanities projects	30	48%
The library hosts a digital scholarship center that supports multiple disciplines, including the humanities	15	24%
Services for digital humanities projects are hosted outside the library	7	11%
The library hosts a digital scholarship center that is specifically dedicated to the humanities	5	8%
The library hosts digital scholarship services but not for humanities projects	2	3%
Digital scholarship services are not offered at my institution	4	6%

Comments

The Library Provides Ad Hoc Services that Support Digital Humanities Projects

As a single check box I must say that the bulk of services rest outside the Libraries. However, that is not to say that the Libraries does not host content and provide services, we do.

Digital humanities projects are supported both by the Libraries and by separate entities on our campus.

Our new facility, the Taylor Family Digital Library, has a host of services that will support Digital Humanities projects, including hardware and software, consultation and presentation practice rooms, display opportunities and space for presenting exhibitions and seminars, etc. It is just in the process of opening, so we don't have our formal program in place yet.

The campus IT organization has also made a recent modest investment in digital humanities support services.

The library is considering consolidating DH services into a center, but it has not happened yet.

The main support for digital humanities is provided through the Institute of Digital Arts and Humanities (IDAH). IDAH sponsors faculty fellows to work on projects for a year, providing some software development and grant proposal writing support, and the library (through the Digital Library Program, DLP) supports those projects on a more or less ad hoc basis

There are also some services hosted outside the library.

We offer a set of repository and publishing services to the university community. We do not offer services specifically tailored to humanities faculty, but they are among our users.

The Library Hosts a Digital Scholarship Center that Supports Multiple Disciplines

It is work in progress.

Our center supports multiple disciplines, but has several programs targeted toward the digital humanities.

Some projects are also hosted outside the library.

The libraries are currently working to build Digital Libraries through Special Collections and an Institutional Repository. Both will serve the Humanities, as well as other disciplines.

The Libraries' digital repository, RUcore, along with the Scholarly Communication Center, provides services supporting the humanities and other disciplines, including digital exhibits, online journals, and digital collection archiving.

The unit in the library that supports digital humanities is "Digital Library Services" but this has broader concerns (i.e., digitizing library collections, ETDs, etc.). There is a separate "Humanities Digital Workshop" that more specifically supports digital humanities, and exists outside the library physically and organizationally, with which we collaborate.

We are imminently hosting a digital scholarship center for humanities, social sciences, and interdisciplinary research. It will be fully operational this summer.

We have multiple centers for digital scholarship services on campus: In addition to the library's new digital scholarship center, there are two other institutes that provide fellowships, forums, and other funding for students and faculty doing digital scholarship.

Within the Libraries' Center for Digital Scholarship (CDS) is a partnership called the Institute for Digital Research in the Humanities which has three partners: the Libraries, the Hall Center for humanities research, and the College of Liberal Arts and Science. It is one of several CDS programs.

Services for Digital Humanities Projects are Hosted Outside the Library

The library has a Digital Collections Department that works with Digital Humanities and the University Press on digital scholarship projects.

The projects managed by the Center for Bibliographic Studies and Research are hosted outside of the campus library.

The Library Hosts a Digital Scholarship Center that is Specifically Dedicated to the Humanities

The Digital Humanities Center focuses on helping patrons use our digital humanities resources and to create digital resources for individual or small group research projects. However, we also assist in the creation of some digital content that is aimed for a broader audience, and work closely with departments charged with larger scale digital projects. We are also becoming a place where patrons can bring a project idea, do some small-scale testing for proof of concept, and then get referred to those dedicated production departments. In addition to the Digital Humanities Center, we also offer digital humanities support through the Center for Digital Research and Scholarship and the Center for New Media Teaching and Learning, both of which are units within the University Libraries/Information Services. There is a Faculty Drop-by Center for the Center for New Media and Teaching and Learning.

We have a number of small units that do support digital scholarship in all disciplines, but my unit is specifically devoted to the Humanities. We are hoping to create a DSC consortium and a New Media Production Lab open to faculty and students.

Digital Scholarship Services are not Offered at My Institution

Currently in development; official launch this fall.

PROJECT STAFFING

2. Please indicate which categories of library staff provide services that support digital humanities projects and whether these staff are dedicated to such services or are called on an ad hoc basis to meet demand. N=51

	N	Dedicated Staff	Ad hoc
IT staff	46	7	39
Subject librarian	44	3	43
Digital scholarship/humanities librarian	39	13	28
Support staff	38	5	33
Undergraduate student assistant	29	3	26
Graduate student assistant	24	4	21
Other staff category	17	5	15
Number of Responses	51	18	50

Please specify the other staff category. N=20

Dedicated Staff

Digital Repository Manager; production team (programmers, web developers) supporting digital humanities projects within CDRS; educational technologists, programmers, and web developers supporting digital humanities projects within CCNMTL.

DLS has a Director, Metadata, Digital Access and Digital Projects Librarians who support digital humanities projects as they arise and also in-house digitization.

Grant-funded Post-Doc.

Metadata and other librarians who are not "subject librarians."

We have one grant funded programmer working full-time on a single DH project.

Ad hoc

Developers, Content Lead.

Digitization staff.

From campus: campus GIS specialist, Center for Digital Humanities staff; from in the library: Digital Library Program staff, metadata librarians, archivists and Special Collections staff; scholarly communication specialists; CLIR Postdoctoral Fellows.

Instruction.

Instructional services, technical services, library communications staff.

Librarians and staff in the MPublishing wing of the library.

Metadata services.

Metadata, design, media production, logistics, web.

Non-IT non-librarian specialist exempt project or production management staff, Metadata librarians.

Other librarians depending on project—cataloguers, preservation specialists, etc.

Part-time librarians.

Preservation staff, Metadata staff.

Special Collections—not sure if dedicate students to this.

Special collections/archives curators or archivists and metadata librarian.

We have a unit (DCAPS) that focuses full-time on supporting the library's digital scholarship initiatives but not limited to digital humanities.

3. **If you indicated above that dedicated staff support digital humanities projects, please enter the number of permanent staff who provide these services. N=13**

Number of permanent staff

Minimum	Maximum	Mean	Median	Std Dev
0.50	16	4.31	2	5.19

4. **If library staff are called on an ad hoc basis to support digital humanities projects, please briefly describe how many of each staff category typically work on a project and under what circumstances they are called (e.g., to help resolve a specific technical question or to collaborate on an entire project). N=44**

1–2 Digital librarians; 1-2 Subject librarians; 1-2 IT staff; 1 Preservation librarian; 1 Metadata/Bibliographic librarian; New Media specialist; any number of student assistants. Teams are put together based on perceived or anticipated outcome; each is expected to contribute in his/her own area of expertise to project outcomes.

2–3 librarians, 1 support staff.

3 FTE librarians provide ad hoc assistance to collaborate on entire projects 4 FTE IT support staff help to resolve specific technical questions and supervise students .50 FTE support staff provides assistance variable student assistance

At least one staff member will remain stuck to a project as a project liaison though that is not necessarily their only position. Technical staff will also generally stick to a project though they will likely have multiple projects going.

At this point, there has not been enough consistent throughput to speak authoritatively about the "typical" contributions of the Subject librarians. As the English Literature specialist, I have worked principally as a consultant on digital projects. The University Press, which is housed in the library's MPublishing wing, publishes an imprint called digitalculturebooks, dedicated to the digital humanities and new media studies. Furthermore, the MPublishing wing includes several units dedicated to digitization and digital dissemination of humanities material. The infrastructure for HathiTrust, and much of its administrative staff, is housed at the U-M Library. The Digital Library Publishing Services unit of library IT has long been a leader in digital archiving. The recent addition of a unit called the Digital Media Commons (including a 3D lab, 3D printers, Media conversion labs, performances spaces, and a top-tier audio recording studio) to the library will be increasingly used for digital humanities projects.

Currently there isn't a lot of digital humanities activity here. It's *very* ad hoc; there have only been a couple of projects so far. We have a relatively new Digital Initiatives and Open Access department in the libraries, whose staff does have DH expertise, but we work overwhelmingly on digital library services as opposed to DH services.

Depends on the project and specialties needed.

Developers: 2. Content Lead: 1. Role varies depending on the project.

Digital scholarship/humanities librarians (i.e., digital projects librarians) perform project management throughout the lifecycle of an initiative. These staff also provide similar services to digital projects in non-humanities disciplines. Subject librarians (mostly in the past) have helped to develop project ideas and speak to user needs for a set of materials. IT staff provide technical (hardware and software) support, mostly to the Carolina Digital Library and Archives staff who then use these tools to assist faculty, but occasionally to faculty directly. Graduate and undergraduate student assistants provide digitization support, metadata creation support, and writing of contextual material. Instructional services staff consult on usability, interface design, and issues related to integration of data with web-based tools. Technical services staff consult on metadata implementation, and create collection-level MARC records for digital projects. Library communications staff provide public relations support.

Five to six staff on average get involved/collaborate, typically: an archivist or curator (to help select objects and define scope of support, etc.), IT support staff (to structure the project), head of digital library initiatives, head of special collections, a metadata librarian (to consult about metadata structure or crosswalking), a student assistant (for scanning objects).

In my department, staff and students are called on an ad hoc basis to help create digital finding aids that are posted on lib guides. In my capacity as Humanities Librarian and Subject Specialist I have selected some materials for digitization for the Digital Libraries of the Caribbean and possible FSU Digital Library Collections. I have asked staff and students to review microfilm and print holdings to identify potential additions to such collections.

In the number above [16 permanent staff], I am including all members of the Libraries Digital Program staff and the Preservation and Reformatting staff devoted to digitization projects. If I were to add the staffs of the Center for New Media in Teaching and Learning and the Center for Digital Research and Scholarship, we could add another 50 staff. All of these 66 staff support digital projects. Not all of them are humanities projects, but we could certainly count at least 50 percent of their time as dedicated to such, given the fact that the majority of materials scanned, at least, are of a historic character. When we speak of individual researchers' projects at the Digital Humanities Center, the number of staff involved is usually one (DHC head or graduate assistant), most frequently in a consulting or training role, but occasionally, where some more advanced technical skills are required, the DHC head may get involved in such areas as processing of files, markup, or database creation. When tasks are of a larger scale, involving the Libraries Digital Program, Preservation, CCNMTL, or CDRS, as many as 4 to 5 may be involved, here in a production capacity (even where materials may ultimately be sent out of house for parts of the process).

It all depends on the project.

It depends on the size of the project. Digital Initiatives Librarian and/or the Digital Projects Librarian plus support staff.

IT Staff for technical support; undergrad students for scanning, OCR, ORC editing; Head, Digital Initiatives for collection creation, metadata creation, project management, uploading, marketing; Support Staff for web pages, uploading, maintenance.

IT staff have been called in to establish web server space and support software and hardware needs related to the publishing of digital scholarship and providing access to web-based projects. Subject librarians have been called in to provide subject specific support in a team working on digital scholarship—for instance to teach students to use a bibliographic tool that we then adapt to create data files, etc. Staff members with expertise in digital sound and imaging have been brought in to work with students on individual projects.

Librarians work with a scholarly society outside of the library as a librarian editor and metadata consultant to scholars who contribute content; with faculty as needed on their digital projects; staff supply support on the same projects that librarians are involved with.

Often the projects are imaging projects so image management specialists will be involved, then there are generally some technical aspects to get the material online (programming/designing interface).

One or two people collaborate on a digitization committee.

Please note that we are just rolling out this suite of services and are still figuring out the staffing needs. The number of staff involved in a single project can range from quick reference questions to intensive subject expertise, programming, and metadata support. Subject librarians: 1 (may collaborate fully on project; may provide quick reference or collection support). Support staff: 1 or 2 (may collaborate fully on project; may troubleshoot as needed). Other staff: metadata librarians (1–2); Digital Library Program staff (1–2); archivists and other Special Collections staff (1–2); CLIR Postdoctoral Fellows (1); scholarly communication specialists (1).

Project management (project by project); digitization lab staff; Fedora support; support of DLP infrastructure. Software development dedicated to faculty DH projects typically happens in IDAH.

Projects generally include a project leader, one of the two dedicated staff, plus other specialists representing digital imaging, data archiving, metadata services, audio/video expertise, technology, or preservation services.

Projects range from publishing digital journals and (currently one) monograph to online archives with scanning, design, and funding needs. Draws on a range of skills, from subject librarians, special collections librarians, cataloguers, digital library programmers, media specialists, etc.

Several librarians collaborate with a campus digital humanities group. This effort is in the early stages here.

Special Collections/digital scholarship librarian to oversee the entire project. Subject librarian to consult with the faculty member. Metadata librarian to develop metadata scheme and review metadata. IT librarian for project management. IT staff member to configure systems, set up accounts, upload content. Web Services staff member to configure search and browse interfaces.

Subject librarians are involved when their liaison group has specific projects—this number varies. Metadata librarians involved in all projects as required. Digital Initiatives Coordinator and Institutional Repository Services Librarian involved as required. IT librarians and programmers involved as required.

Subject librarians or librarians and library IT staff from other areas (government documents, digital media production, preservation, etc.) are frequently called in for short time periods to address a certain technical or content-related issue. Less frequently, they will collaborate as partners throughout the time span of the project.

Teams are formed surrounding specific projects, which would usually consist of one or two IT staff, relevant subject librarians, one support staff member, and student assistants depending on voucher or grant funding.

The ad hoc help is called upon fairly regularly for specific projects that require more input of time and expertise.

The Digital Library Center has two core functions: service and production. The service group (1 librarian, 1 programmer dedicated to digital work but technically in the IT department, and 2 staff) provides support and collaborates on digital humanities projects.

Typically, assign a metadata librarian, developer (IT), subject specialist, and user-interface specialist (web).

Varies widely depending on project. Typically, 1–2 in each category above will work on a project.

We are at the beginning of this service/facility and wanted to avoid "staffing up" until such time as we knew the level of activity we would have. A typical circumstance for now follows a path something like this: faculty member contacts or is referred to the Associate Dean, discussion of project leads to recommendations about what types of consultations with which library faculty/staff would be appropriate, separate meetings occur with these consultants, faculty member continues with project (libraries can provide training and ongoing consultation). Thus far, this approach has worked well. We do have a place holder for a dedicated faculty position as the program grows. In the model we follow, which interested humanities faculty helped build, the individual faculty member is responsible for "doing" the project.

We are dependent on library IT staff for all of our system maintenance and any programming or web services that we require.

We have a metadata team consisting of 3 librarians, 3 professional staff, a graduate assistant, and a number of undergraduate student assistants. This team works closely with a librarian and a professional staff in the IT division who support digital projects. None of these staff and faculty are specifically dedicated to digital humanities projects, but all of them support humanities faculty and resources that come through our services. One of our librarians has a particular interest in digital humanities, and so tends to be the point person for any special DH-related projects that come to us.

We have five librarians, one IT professional, and varying numbers of support staff and student assistants who engage with projects according to the needs of the projects. These staff members represent two teams: Research Enterprise and Scholarly Communication, and Archives and Special Collections.

We have metadata specialists who assist with metadata projects from time to time and subject librarians who assist with outreach.

We have one (or maybe two) librarians who provide digital humanities support services, but these services are usually only on a discussion level and not necessarily on a doing level.

We have several librarians and library staff whose job descriptions include support of digital humanities projects, but they will be called together based on the student or faculty query. The Digital Content Creation and Metadata librarians will be brought in to collaborate on a mass digitization project and/or one that involves ContentDM archive. Several other librarians, such as the Mathematics and Engineering librarians, who currently lead projects on metadata and digital libraries, are brought in as needed for their respective expertise. And I, as the English and Digital Humanities Librarian, consult with students and faculty to refer them to the correct personnel and resources on campus who can help them.

We have two librarians (Fine Arts and Humanities) and two staff members who assist when faculty bring a digital humanities project to us. The librarians help with content and copyright questions. The staff help with technical support and actually do the digitization using scanners, photo, or multimedia equipment.

We have worked with scholars to acquire materials for a project, to extract data or files from a database, to assist with technical questions, and to put material into the Institutional Repository. We provide information for grant applications and sometimes matching funding.

We host linguistic corpora that require ongoing server maintenance and ad hoc technical troubleshooting. Around this dataset we have co-hosted various events requiring various staff involvement, including PR. Other efforts include text markup, course design, and data management, each of which typically engage the Digital Information Division.

We typically launch pilot projects with the collaboration of multiple people across several departments, and use these to develop grant proposals for more ambitious DH endeavors. A seed project typically involves participants from the Department of Digital Scholarship and Programs, Cataloging and Metadata Services, Web and Emerging Technologies, and our special collections units.

We usually create a team of relevant experts that could include people from Preservation (includes our digitization unit), Metadata/Cataloging Services, Special Collections or Subject Bibliographers, and Library IT staff. Typically the team will persist throughout the project unless some staff are only needed on an ad hoc consulting basis. We may work with Campus IT or Divisional IT staff as well, so roles are defined at the beginning of the project depending on what is needed.

5. **What is the title of the position that has primary responsibility for managing/coordinating these services?**

6. **To whom does this person report?**

   N=48

Primary Responsibility	Reports to	Comments
A group: Director, Centre for Scholarly Communication, Director, Centre for Arts and Culture, Technology Officer, TFDL	Vice Provost, Libraries and Cultural Resources	
Again, these are ad hoc, typically involving Associate Dean.	Dean of Libraries	To date our efforts here have been ad hoc and opportunistic.
Associate Dean for Library Technology	Dean	
Associate Librarian	Dean of Libraries	No single person in charge. Team approach. A given project may fall more in one Associate Librarian's areas than another.
Associate Librarian for Digital Services and Co-director for the Institute for Digital Research in the Humanities.	Assistant Dean, Collections and Scholar Services	There is also a faculty co-director who reports to the Chair of Anthropology in the College of Liberal Arts and Sciences.
Associate University Librarian for Digital Initiatives and Open Access	University Librarian	Again, the AUL for DIOA does not have formal responsibility for this. But if a humanities scholar is thinking about a digital project, that's who will probably do the initial consult with the scholar.
Associate University Librarian for Digital Library Systems	University Librarian	
Co-Director, Digital Library Development Center	Library Director	

Primary Responsibility	Reports to	Comments
Co-Director, IDAH	Vice Provost for Research	Coordinator of DH support does not report through the library, which can cause issues as the person responsible for bringing in faculty projects has no responsibility for the work that is actually done on those projects in the DLP.
Diffuse	Mostly through Collections.	
Digital Initiatives Coordinator	Acting Associate University Librarian for Information Resources	Staff time commitment to digital humanities (as opposed to other digital scholarship services) has not been quantified.
Digital Initiatives Librarian	Head, Bibliographic Services	
Digital Library Center, digital services librarian (currently serving as interim director.)	Permanent chair of department once hired, currently Associate Dean for Technology & Support Services	
Digital Library Production Head (Manages/Coordinates all Digital Services, not just Humanities)	The Associate Dean of Special Collections	
Digital Projects Librarian	Associate Directory for Information Technology	
Digital Scholarship Coordinator	The Chief Technology Strategist	
Director of Digital Library Services	Associate Dean for Library Technologies	
Director of Digital Research & Scholarship	Deputy University Librarian	
Director of Scholarly Technology	AUL Digital Initiatives and Content Management	
Director of the Digital Library	Library AD for Organizational Development	
Director, Center for Digital Scholarship	University Librarian	
Director, Digital Library Technology Services	Dean of Libraries	
Director, Wired Humanities Projects	Dean of the Libraries	When I put 3 down for permanent staff, that's deceiving. Two of us are sort of permanent, and we are each half time. The third, a graduate assistant, is quarter time. But we manage about 12 work-study students and volunteer undergraduates.
English and Digital Humanities Librarian	Dean of the University Library	My title has more or less designated me as the coordinating point person for digital humanities services, but there are a host of library staff and other campus personnel who actively coordinate digital humanities projects and activities.

Primary Responsibility	Reports to	Comments
For small projects: Head of the DHC; for larger library projects: Director of the Libraries' Digital Program	Head of DHC reports to Director for History and Humanities (who reports to Associate University Librarian for Collections & Services); Director of LDPD reports to Deputy University Librarian and Associate Vice President for Digital Programs and Technology Services	CCNMTL and CDRS projects are overseen by the directors of those two groups. Services are not yet tightly coordinated, so each group serving digital humanities operates somewhat independently. We plan for more coordination in the future as we bring on new leadership for the Humanities & History division.
Head of Digital Library Initiatives	Senior Associate University Librarian	
Head of Digital Library Services	Deputy Director	
Head of Digital Scholarship and Programs	Deputy University Librarian	
Head of Special Collections, Archives and Digital Scholarship	Associate University Librarian for Collections	
Head, Desktop & Network Services	AUL for LIT	
Head, Digital Collections	Associate University Librarian for Special Libraries	
Head, Digital Humanities Center	Associate Dean for Public Services	
Head, Digital Initiatives	Associate Dean of Libraries for Collection & Technology Services	
Head, Digital Publishing Group in the Carolina Digital Library and Archives	Head, Carolina Digital Library and Archives	The Carolina Digital Library and Archives (CDLA) is the unit within the UNC Library that is charged with primary outward-facing support for digital humanities work. The Library Systems department provides core infrastructure for these initiatives, and since early 2010, oversees any local development (programming) work. However, many others throughout the library provide support for digital humanities work as well. Also, the CDLA, Library Systems, and the library in general collaborate on digital projects in disciplines other than the humanities.
Head, Digital Scholarship Lab	Associate Director for Research and Learning Services	
Head, Research Enterprise and Scholarly Communication	Associate University Librarian	

Primary Responsibility	Reports to	Comments
Head, Scholarly Communication and Digital Services	Associate Dean	We provide support for digital scholarship to humanities researchers. The Scholarly Communication and Digital Services department provides lecture recording, conference, journal, and repository services that help researchers from across campus produce, disseminate, and maintain the digital products of their creative endeavors.
Librarian for Digital Research and Scholarship	Head of Collections, Research, and Instructional Services (unit head under the AUL for Academic Services)	Please note that we are just rolling out this suite of services and are still figuring out the staffing needs. The number of staff involved in a single project can range from quick reference questions to intensive subject expertise, programming, and metadata support.
Manager, Instructional Support Services	Associate Dean for Support Services	
Metadata Librarian	Head of the Scholarly Resources Integration Department	
N/A	N/A	Although there is significant ad hoc Digital Humanities activity in the library, there is no centralized approach to Digital Scholarship as an object of study in itself. AULs for Publishing and Library IT are ultimately the hierarchical leaders for most DH work, but such work is seldom imagined strictly in terms of Digital Humanities (especially inasmuch as the term is viewed as nebulous, or a moving target).
No one position		
No position currently exists.		
Subject Librarian	Department Head of Information Services	
There is no primary position.		
Varies		
Varies by project/program		Distributed, at the moment, to some extent.
		Responsibility is shared across library departments including collections, rare books & manuscripts, and IT.

7. Please indicate which of the following types of services your library offers users who are engaged in digital humanities projects. Check all that apply. N=49

Project Development and Support N=47

Initial project development consultations	46	98%
Digital project management	43	92%
Grant writing to support digital humanities research	26	55%
Outreach and marketing	23	49%
Other activity, please describe	14	30%

Assistance with identification of materials for the collection/project.

Assistance with system specifications, coordination with the Library Systems department.

Co-write grant if library is a partner. Referral to appropriate digital tools and services.

Digital curation of resources from prior/existing digital humanities projects. Facilitation of interdepartmental and inter-institutional collaboration.

Except for the first of these, the Libraries would take on those tasks only when it had become a full- edged Libraries Digital Project, CCNMTL, or CDRS project. Only the first, and to minor degree the third, would apply in the case of individual patron DHC projects.

Most projects are internal, based on the library's special collections.

Ongoing consultations as project proceeds.

Scanning, OCR, uploading, PhotoShop editing, archiving, maintenance.

Seed grants. Connections to special collections for shared projects that utilize manuscripts. Assistance with long-term data management. We are willing to support grant writing activities, but thus far have not assumed this role. We do provide supporting statements for grant seekers.

Skills workshops for faculty and/or students (typically in conjunction with other campus units). Our new research commons, which includes digital humanities lab space and a library sandbox, may help us to add to/refine this list of services.

Small grants to projects; coordination of teams to support projects.

Training, hosting, facilitating connections with other resources on campus.

We include digital asset management, i.e., SIP agreements, and are building digital preservation capacity.

We offer metadata/description services, preservation services, and electronic journal publishing services as well.

Technology and Design N=47

Website development	40	85%
Data conversion	35	75%
Software coding and development	34	72%
Graphic design	31	66%
Usability testing	25	53%
Text encoding	24	51%
Hardware and software procurement	22	47%
AV editing	19	40%
Other activity, please describe	15	32%

Any and all of these services are available dependent on project and partnership agreements (cost-recovery, for a fee, part of a grant, etc.)

Copyright, digitization, metadata, publishing.

Current work is all done in connection with the UF Digital Collections and the Digital Library of the Caribbean. Work not connected is outside of the scope of support from the current staff.

Discovery interface.

Education in theory and practical use/application.

Imaging.

Metadata analysis and development.

Metadata creation, digitization.

Once again, in their fullest sense, at least, these would normally apply only for full- edged LDPD, CCNMTL, or CDRS projects. DHC projects might involve some small level of programming, but would instead tend to rely on preexisting software tools.

Open source software installation, configuration, and XML markup.

Our new research commons, which includes digital humanities lab space and a library sandbox, may help us to add to/refine this list of services. Most of our previous technology and design work would have been done within or in partnership with the Digital Library Program.

Provision of server space (on servers we already own); installation and maintenance of free, open-source software such as WordPress, Omeka, Archon.

Referral to services outside the Libraries for services not provided.

Software development where DLP infrastructure is concerned. Text encoding consultation.

The Libraries are prepared to provide these services as we are able.

Preservation and Education N=47

Digital asset preservation and access	42	89%
Instruction in technologies	32	68%
Acquisition of primary and secondary resources for use in digital projects	31	66%
Other activity, please describe	8	17%

Advising on metadata standards and curation/preservation for physical and digital materials.

Again, actual digital preservation is still in development but we are already committed to it for various projects and assets.

Digital asset preservation and access is a developing service. We also participate in funding and providing nationally recognized digital humanities speakers with our partners.

Library instruction in use of mature digital humanities projects.

Many of these are in preliminary stages of development.

Preservation would only apply to the large-scale projects. The other two would be more likely to be functions handled by the DHC.

Some preservation assistance is given by another unit in the College of Education (Center for Advanced Technology in Education). But we also have a unit in the library with which we may be joining forces soon.

Work within the library as a whole to develop support for these activities, and to ensure library staff have skills in these areas.

8. **Which of the following terms describe the role of the librarian in your library's support for digital humanities? Check all that apply. N=50**

Consultant	37	74%
Scholarly collaborator	34	68%
Project manager	30	60%
Resource manager	26	52%
Research assistant	9	18%
Other term, please specify	12	24%

Co-PI.

Collaborator. We are building institutions and collections to support Digital Humanities. New ideas and assistance selecting materials is welcome.

Curator.

Digital Asset Manager.

Digital Librarian.

Educator.

Here, once again, the mix will vary by the group and scale of project. LDPD projects would involve playing roles 2, 3, and 5. CCNMTL and CDRS 1, 2, 3, 4, 5. DHC primarily 1 and 5.

It is less "scholarly collaborator" but we are moving in that direction.

Partner.

Some of our student staff provide research assistance.

Steward for digital content when needed. Instructor for techniques useful to digital humanities.

To clarify, the metadata librarian consults, the Head of Digital Library Initiatives and Head of Special Collections are both librarians and manage or consult, but "the role of the librarian" for us really depends what librarian and what project and what skills are needed.

9. **In which of the following ways does library staff contribute expertise to digital humanities endeavors? Check all that apply. N=49**

Strategizing on: N=43

Creation of tools for use in the digital humanities	33	77%
Marketing/outreach	20	47%
Customer intelligence	13	30%
Other, please describe	11	26%

Assessment of the viability of various initiatives and development of multi-disciplinary partnerships. We do very little tool creation, but we do assist in the adoption of tools.

CCNMTL and CDRS in particular are involved in this area, and occasionally LDPD.

Curation life-cycle planning.

Funding opportunities.

Installation/configuration of tools for use in the digital humanities.

Librarians are leading DH, not schools.

Organization of materials, presentation, interactivity.

Resource acquisition.

See dcaps.library.cornell.edu for examples.

Selection of objects for projects.

Sustainable business models, including open access.

Instruction on: N=39

Tools or techniques used in digital humanities research	36	92%
Pedagogical use of digital object collections	26	67%
Other, please describe	7	18%

Development of digital collections, digital curation, digital preservation, usability.

DHC plays the primary role here.

Management of rights and access.

Mark-up, XML.

Metadata and other technical standards.

Our library also has another unit engaged in these services.

What is the digital humanities/digital cultural heritage. Copyright, licensing, access issues.

Services related to: N=48

Application of specialized metadata or ontologies	41	85%
Scanning and/or OCR	43	90%
Selection of resources for digitization or some other inclusion in a digital humanities project	40	83%
Tagging (TEI, etc.)	32	67%
GIS, geotagging	26	54%
Other, please describe	8	17%

Again, we do some of this and some other library units also do this, and we are collaborating, increasingly. The GIS ad hoc support comes from the InfoGraphics lab in the Geography department. This is not centralized.

DHC is most likely to be involved in 1, 3, and 4, CCNMTL, CDRS, and LDPD in all.

GIS is primarily with the GIS librarian, outside DLS but we have done some FGDC encoding and geotagging, etc.

Note: some of this work is done in conjunction with other campus units.

Providing a space for collaborators to create digital products.

Several of these are in initial stage of development only.

Use of relevant software.

Visualization, publishing, interoperability, APIs, search engine optimization.

Assistance with: N=45

Identifying potential partners for digital humanities projects	39	87%
Conceiving or writing project proposals	37	82%
Shepherding projects through development	37	82%
Grant support	27	60%
Other, please describe	6	13%

All areas where faculty need support.

Concept development of projects.

Grant support in the libraries is limited but we have experience with grant writing and have assisted with this. There may be a dedicated position in the future.

Much of this work is done in conjunction with a campus steering group for digital research in humanities, arts and architecture, social and information sciences.

These have been done by CCNMTL, CDRS, and LDPD, but not DHC.

We are hoping to develop internal fellowships for course releases for faculty who wish to work with us, and for graduate students with projects that are a good fit with our expertise. But, currently, we lean mostly on external funding (mainly NEH).

Consultation on: N=47

Preservation management	43	92%
Sustainability	39	83%
Usability	37	79%
Accessibility	36	77%
Other, please describe	8	17%

Database design and architecture, graphic design, web interactivity, metadata, ontologies, encoding.

For the items in this category, the library frequently assumes responsibility for these things rather than simply advising a faculty member on ways he or she could do it themselves.

Metadata strategies and standards.

Plan to implement other categories of consultation in the coming year.

There is a dedicated assessment coordinator in the library, outside DLS who works through committees but there is overlap in personnel with DLS.

These have been done by CCNMTL, CDRS, and LDPD, but not DHC.

We get help on this from other library units, currently, although we have relied on some of our own expertise here, too.

We prefer the term "life cycle management."

Education about: N=47

Copyright issues	46	98%
Open access issues	42	89%
Ethical issues	18	38%
Other, please describe	4	9%

Copyright review and education on intellectual property and permissions. These have been done mostly by CCNMTL, CDRS, and LDPD, but not DHC (except for some minimal beginning advice on copyright).

There are dedicated specialists in open access in the Medical Library (separate organization) but here again, we are gaining expertise; Digital Access Librarian is an attorney.

This is all done only on an as-needed basis. Moral rights, privacy rights, cultural and documentary heritage rights, academic faculty rights (AAUP), informed consent, requirements from the institutional review board, and their relation to responsibilities in terms of cultural heritage/trust institutions. Permissions-based models to support varied rights and responsibilities.

We get help on this from other library units, currently, although we have relied on some of our own expertise here, too.

10. **Does your library encourage/facilitate/promote cross-, trans-, or inter-disciplinary projects? N=47**

Yes	39	83%
No	8	17%

If yes, please briefly describe the strategies used to support such projects (such as identifying potential research partners, hosting cross-disciplinary symposia or events, tracking research projects with a cross-disciplinary potential). N=34

At this point, the library chie y encourages interdisciplinary projects through outreach and referral. We have hosted the annual TEI conference. Our librarians attend and present at conferences, unconferences, THATcamps, etc. We have cross-institutional digital projects like the Text Creation Partnership and the HathiTrust. All of these activities turn up projects with cross-disciplinary potential, which are then shared through liaisons of various orders (including subject specialists as well as staff in MPublishing and the Digital Media Commons).

Bringing people together in common fora are the most prominent strategy. A recent "jump start" workshop brought together participants from various disciplines and provided an opportunity for them to talk about their interests.

Cross-disciplinary projects are always encouraged. Recently we hosted a Digital Humanities Days event complete with speakers and demonstrations. More recently we started supporting a website where digital humanities computing tools will be implemented and made available. Finally, we have started digitizing simple texts and plan to integrate text mining interfaces into our catalog.

Host a digital humanities discussion group, monthly "brown bag lunch" meetings and online discussion list. Host and co-host symposia related to digital humanities in a variety of disciplines. Create an atmosphere for idea generation and people connection across disciplines. Actively participated in first digital humanities course offered.

Host various scholarly events with guest speaker.

Hosting cross-disciplinary symposia or events.

Identifying faculty partners, grant writing support, hosting events.

Identifying potential partners (both in the institution and beyond). Tracking projects. Contributing specific local collections as appropriate.

Identifying potential partners locally and externally.

Identifying potential partners.

Identifying potential research and service partners (both within and external to the Libraries). Hosting cross-disciplinary events (especially for graduate students). Urging open access to materials we host online for use and reuse by others. I am not sure there are any clear proactive strategies here, but the Libraries are certainly open to such projects. The interdisciplinarity tends to rise out of the projects themselves as they are presented.

Identifying potential research partners, certainly. We are also in the middle of an NEH Digital Humanities Start-Up Grant; its subject addresses in part the role of the library in interdisciplinary research.

Identifying potential research partners, fostering communication, bringing forward information and contacts.

Interdisciplinary teams; cross-institutional initiatives.

Liaison librarians work with faculty members and staff members in other departments to organize symposia or events on interdisciplinary themes. Librarians solicit contributions to an institutional repository. Librarians organize conferences and events to educate cross-disciplinary audiences about copyright, scholarly communication, and open access issues. The libraries recently initiated the creation of a Faculty Senate Library subcommittee on Scholarly Communication. Librarians host educational sessions on tools for scholarly communication and tracking scholarly production.

Library frequently hosts events, brings in relevant partners from other disciplines on any projects.

Most often, these include work between departments within the library; recently our library liaisons also provide feedback from their subject areas, which help identify interest/need throughout our campus.

Our Dean assigns us projects that tend to have a theme or regional focus (e.g., Mesoamerica; Northwestern Tribal

Legacies; or East Asian cultures) involving resources that can be tapped by faculty and students in a wide array of disciplines. Some faculty come to us with projects, and we reach out to additional people to create multidisciplinary networks.

Participate in campus steering group for digital research in humanities, arts and architecture, social and information sciences. Training subject specialists to think in terms of interdisciplinary and cross-disciplinary research and bring related subject experts on board to support this kind of research. Hosting cross-disciplinary events to showcase this kind of scholarship. Marketing for our research commons and related library spaces will emphasize cross-disciplinary potential.

Several librarians are named investigators on grants and active research partners in cross-disciplinary projects in humanities, archives, and LIS. The library also has co-hosted symposia on digital humanities work and digital libraries research.

The answer now is really no, but we have made a proposal to the university for a center that would promote inter-disciplinary digital projects.

The library encourages faculty to work together on projects that have broad application. We provide the technical services to facilitate completion of the projects.

The library space itself takes advantage of the fact that it is a common ground and the staff attempt to bring diverse scholars in with programming.

Tracing research projects.

UF supports a digital collection/services/asset and content management system with over 500 digital collections (including the Institutional Repository and the Digital Library of the Caribbean) and from many dozens of partners of all types (libraries, archives, museums, universities, NGOs, publishers, etc). These are all ongoing projects with various specific specifics supports. With so many collections and partners, especially with the Digital Library of the Caribbean as a central project and one that is an international collaborative, cross-, trans-, and inter-disciplinary projects are an emergent occurrence.

Unfortunately, I'd say we are more reactive than proactive (participate in grant proposals, co-sponsor symposia, serve on curricula committees).

We actively seek partnerships on campus that cover the range of needs identified in a given project. We seek support and encourage collaboration with partner groups who strengthen the suite of services provided for a given project or faculty member's work. For instance, the library works with the Baker-Nord Center for the Humanities to identify projects where partnerships are appropriate, i.e., Humanities projects that require infrastructure support, research and subject support, preservation and work ow support, etc. In May we are also jointly hosting a Digital Humanities event with Cleveland State University featuring speakers from George Mason's Center for History & New Media.

We are involved in one multi-institutional, cross-disciplinary project as a result of responding to a call regarding a national data preservation project, not a local project. Much activity still relies on personal networks at this stage.

We are open to helping faculty deposit research content that might be utilized by different disciplines.

We collaborate formally and hold regular meetings with other centers outside of the library but within the university to make sure that we're aware of projects seeking support across disciplinary boundaries. Our lecture series and programs for graduate students (including fellowships) are interdisciplinary.

We do symposia or events. Our Digital Scholarship Center is called cyberinfrastructure Center that is basically infrastructure and services to ALL disciplines. We submit grants.

We host a local meeting of the New Media Consortium and other cross-disciplinary events.

We offer fora to enable researchers from all disciplines to share knowledge and collaborate.

Work in this area has been informal to date. We would like to start up more formal programs to increase awareness of digital projects that will allow interested faculty to more easily find areas of common interest.

HARDWARE AND SOFTWARE

11. What hardware does the library offer to support digital humanities projects? Check all that apply. N=47

Scanners	45	96%
Image editing stations	36	77%
Video editing stations	30	64%
Audio editing stations	30	64%
Large-scale monitors	23	49%
Visualization tools	14	30%
Gaming consoles	5	11%
Other hardware, please describe	17	36%

3D printers. A "virtual reality cave."

Digital cameras.

Digitization robots for books.

Individual workstations without peripherals where patrons can access markup, OCR, database, web publishing, and other tools.

Laptops, wall-mounted monitors, wall-size rear projection screens in lab space.

Large format printers, storage.

Library provides a hosting environment through its institutional repository, as well as a separate instance of the repository for a specific humanities project.

Microfilm scanner.

SmartBoard, two HD projection systems with Egan Walls, 65 inch multi-touch monitor.

The libraries have a great deal of equipment available for all faculty, staff, and students for self-service use, and the Digital Library Center has staffed/supported equipment that can be used by faculty/staff as appropriate with support.

The library provides scanning and image editing services so we do not directly support such hardware for direct use by faculty partners.

These types of hardware are used by staff throughout the library in their support of digital humanities projects; it has not been our policy to provide these services to our patron. It is considered a service provided by the library.

To this point, these are tools our staff works on for the collaborator; we do not have dedicated scanners, etc. for outside collaborators.

Video cameras, audio recorders, audio recording studio, video recording studio, dedicated usability lab.

We are currently researching more hardware, but have not purchased anything, yet.

We plan to offer all of these in a near future.

We provide video conferencing equipment in a large meeting room. Providing visualization tools is a future service we will offer. We also have substantive wireless networking services and a small wired training lab.

12. **What software does the library offer to support digital humanities projects? Check all that apply. N=46**

Bibliographic management software	40	87%
Content Management Systems	36	78%
GIS	29	63%
Data analysis tools	23	50%
TEI	19	41%
Project management software	16	35%
Data visualization software	11	24%
3D rendering platforms	9	20%
Concept/mind mapping software	8	17%
Other software, please describe	16	35%

All of these are available in different forms in the libraries. None are promoted as "digital humanities" specific. Some of these are often best served by software that is available at no cost for academics (pivotal tracker for project management, etc.), so the libraries offer them via consultation and not as a paid service.

Collaborate with Scholars Portal to develop data tools, for geographical health informatics and statistical data (under development).

CONTENTdm for housing collections, managing metadata, handling OCR, etc.

Digital library/institutional repository software (DSpace).

Graphic design and production, XML editor.

Graphic design software.

Multimedia authoring tools/platforms (Pachyderm, Omeka, etc.)

Repository and specialized microsites/virtual research environments.

Software to support audio, video, and image editing.

Some of the areas not checked include software that we might seek out elsewhere on campus or off campus. Some of our work in virtual environments is done by a contractor off campus using equipment and software at the university where she studies (in Texas), or by collaborators at the Smithsonian in DC.

Textual analysis, qualitative analysis, and powerful indexing tools.

Usability testing software, Open Journal System, repository systems, multimedia publishing software.

We are currently testing several Mac-based applications.

We can provide data visualization or concept/mapping software but have not yet done so for a specific project.

We offer Oxygen XML editor which is used by many for TEI encoding.

Web archiving service; an electronic publishing service; a suite of digital preservation services.

SERVICE USERS

13. **Who may use the services that support digital humanities projects? Check all that apply. N=47**

Faculty	47	98%
Graduate students	41	85%
Post-doctoral or other researchers affiliated with your library or institution	37	77%
Undergraduates	31	65%
Researchers not affiliated with your library or institution	14	29%
Other user category, please describe	11	23%

Depending on the project, this could include many partners from libraries, archives, museums, etc.

Librarians and library staff.

Much of the software and services are available to customers on a walk-in basis; more specialized consultation/ collaboration is available to university affiliates.

Our GIS scanner/large scale printer is available to all users; but all other services are restricted to library-sponsored projects.

Researchers from other institutions working in partnership with a university researcher.

Service infrastructure is currently under development.

Students require faculty sponsor.

These are offered as services we perform, not generally as resources people are able to access directly (not a public service per se).

Walk in, non-affiliates.

We may make strategic partnerships with people from outside the institution but only where there is also a faculty member involved.

We would like to develop the resources to be able to offer post-docs.

14. **How do they find out the services are available? Check all that apply. N=48**

Communications from library subject liaisons	41	85%
Library website	37	77%
Print or electronic publications	24	50%
Events	23	48%
Email	20	42%
Orientations for newcomers	18	38%
Social media, such as Facebook or Twitter	14	29%
Use of your institution's communications office	10	21%
Other method, please describe	18	38%

At this point, quite informally, through conversation at meetings and Open Access Week events.

CDLA staff participate in campus events, such as those offered by the Institute for the Arts and Humanities.

Coordinator in College of Arts and Sciences.

Faculty using our collections ask for the help of curators in developing projects. Or faculty may approach library administrators asking for help in formulating grant proposals which have library components.

Library communications office.

Participation in campus steering group for digital research in humanities, arts and architecture, social and information sciences. Ongoing collaborations with other campus units.

Presentation at faculty council and Senate meetings. We run workshops for graduate students on scholarly communications.

Separate website for the Institute for Digital Research in the Humanities.

Simple word of mouth. Our services are edgling at best.

These services are not currently promoted because of the limited staffing available to support them and because "digital humanities" is not yet well known by a critical mass of researchers in context with the work they are doing on the campus. The Center for the Humanities will be hosting a fall forum that will include the digital humanities and will increase this awareness rapidly.

University-wide interdisciplinary committees, symposia.

We do not advertize yet since we're not ready.

Word of mouth from other customers; inquiry based on other library projects/products.

Word of mouth; interdepartmental channels; programs (Freedman Fellows program).

Word of mouth. (4 responses)

PROJECT WORKSPACE

15. **Where do library staff met with researchers to plan/consult on digital humanities projects? N=48**

Library staff member's office	45	94%
Researcher's office	35	73%
Library group study room	18	38%
Digital scholarship/humanities center conference room	13	27%
Other space, please describe	19	40%

Campus coffee shops, faculty center, neighborhood establishments. Will soon be able to meet in our new research commons, library cafe.

Campus meeting rooms, library technology office.

Coffee shop.

Conference rooms in the library.

Conference Rooms in the TFDL. We work with the scholars wherever they might be in the library, depending on the stage of research.

Digital Library Services office.

Instructional Support Services has a suite of offices and workrooms within the library.

Library conference rooms, especially those equipped with large monitors for collaborative viewing of digital objects or comparator sites.

Library meeting room.

Library meeting rooms.

Library meeting spaces. Hall Center for the Humanities (research center) meeting spaces.

Library space allocated for using hardware and software described below is general space allocated for digital media services and digital libraries. There are two studios for users (small, 8 x 8 feet), there is another room with a scanner (8 x 12 feet), and a larger room to store, organize, scan, and process materials that is approximately 12 x 24 feet.

Library staff meeting rooms (not public).

Meeting space in the main library.

MPublishing meeting room. Digital Library Production Services meeting room.

Multimedia Lab.

Over lunch.

There are a number of meeting rooms in the library staff are free to reserve for consultations.

We are hoping to improve our spaces, making them more visible, more welcoming, with users, support staff, and lab equipment in closer proximity, too.

16. Is there dedicated library space allocated for using the hardware and software that is available to support digital humanities projects? N=48

Yes	25	52%
No	23	48%

If yes, please estimate the square footage of the dedicated library space. N=20

Minimum	Maximum	Mean	Median	Std Dev
100	6000	1204	800	1392.14

Is any part of this space secured/securable (e.g., as mandated by the federal government when working with certain datasets)? N=23

Yes	16	70%
No	7	30%

FUNDING SOURCES

17. What is the source of funding for digital humanities projects? Check all that apply. N=48

Library operating budget	43	90%
Grants	38	79%
Library IT budget	30	63%
Academic departments	24	50%
Special one-time funds	24	50%
Endowments	14	29%
Central operating budget	5	10%
Central IT budget	4	8%
Other source of funding, please describe	7	15%

At some points university IT funds, special one-time funds, grants, and endowments may be pursued for such projects.

Capital campaign gift funded the construction and initial technology, along with a one-time payment for the raised oor from the Office of Information Technology.

College of Liberal Arts budget and the Hall Center for the Humanities are equal funding partners with the libraries.

Donations.

Multi-institutional partnerships.

Sponsorships, donations.

This applies to a combination of libraries around the university.

18. Do researchers typically come to a project having already secured funding necessary to accomplish the goals of their digital projects? N=46

Yes	11	24%
No	35	76%

Comments

Yes

Half of the time.

Mostly, yes, but on occasion proposals are generated after initial discussion.

Or they are doing small-scale projects that don't require significant funding.

Yes, but that is more of a projection of how we would like things to go once we open our research commons. We would like the library to become involved in digital projects as early as possible so that we can advise on funding needs. The library will not typically provide funding unless the project furthers/builds upon existing library collections. Increasingly, experienced digital researchers understand the need to come up with their own funding. The library will need to help educate scholars who are newer to digital research and scholarship.

No

A mixture. Researchers come to the library at many stages, but usually they have not already secured funding.

Often they come to us when they are in the middle of writing a grant, so before funding is secured but contingent on it coming in order for a project to start.

Sometimes researchers approach the library when preparing grant proposals.

That is not a requirement.

These researchers typically do not have a deep understanding of the level of funding that would be required to perform the work they have in mind.

This will vary.

Through IDAH, we assist with developing prototypes and writing proposals to fund further work. There have been instances where faculty come to us with funding but it is not typical.

We are working hard to change this.

We work with researchers to provide the technical specifications they will need to complete their grant proposals.

We've only had once instance of this occurring. Wish it happened more!

Other

Sometimes.

Varies.

19. Does your library have a policy or written statement describing the ways in which it supports digital humanities projects? N=49

Yes	6	12%
No	43	88%

20. Is there a formal process for reviewing or developing proposals and allocating resources for digital humanities projects? N=47

Yes	16	34%
No	31	66%

If yes, please briefly describe the process. N=15

After discussions on the front-line level, librarians submit a project proposal form, signed by one of the divisional directors, and submit it to the Libraries' Digital Program Division. The division considers the feasibility and priority of the project, meets with the proposers to agree to any needed modifications, and then implements the project, usually in conjunction with the Preservation and Reformatting Department or outside vendors, in accordance with its budgetary and staff resources.

Currently, scholars work with librarians to produce a proposal which is submitted to the Digital Systems Division for approval and planning.

Digital initiatives advisory group sets priorities which we submit for approval by library administration.

For projects involving deposit of content in a local of system-wide repository, a faculty member contacts his or her subject librarian about a potential project. The subject librarian completes a proposal form for the Libraries' Digital Scholarship Program Working Group to review. The proposal is evaluated according to established criteria concerning its research significance, the target audience, the availability of resources, and the availability of other, external services to meet the faculty's needs. If librarians on the working group can not fit the project into their existing workload, the proposal is reviewed by the Libraries' Leadership Council for further allocation of resources.

Freedman Fellows Program: annual award program for which eligible faculty submit proposals. Proposals are received, reviewed, final selections are made and awards are announced.

IDAH fellowships.

Projects generally come to Head, Digital Initiatives. Each project is "costed out" as much as possible in conjunction with our Systems Department. Then it is presented to the Dean's Advisory Group (DAG) for final approval. Occasionally, projects will come directly from DAG.

Proposals come in via a web form; evaluated by a library committee.

The library has a steering committee and proposal process for internal digitization activities and that structure informs the process of undertaking a digital humanities project but there is no direct formal process for deciding on such projects. Often they run on a timeframe that cannot accommodate going through a formal approval process (e.g., upcoming grant deadline) but the internal library process helps ensure the right questions are asked and people consulted.

The Library Technology Council, made up of key administrators and the chairs of key committees related to digital library work (in general, beyond just the humanities) accepts and vets proposals. This iteration of the model is new in the last year and is still under development.

There is a formal pipeline administered by the campus steering group for digital research in humanities, arts and architecture, social and information sciences, of which the library is a part. Within the library, there is a project pipeline administered by the Digital Library Program. There are also less formal means by which projects can come to the attention of the library and receive support.

There is a formal process for all digital projects, including digital humanities projects.

There is a formal process for reviewing and awarding seed grant funds. We also informally consult and allocate some resources directly as the Libraries.

This is developing, but we have an online form that subject and Special Collections librarians will fill out in an interview with faculty, but also that is available for internal library digital projects. This is viewed more as a "communication tool" to help inform faculty about aspects of developing digital projects, and raise concerns, i.e., with digital projects using in-copyright material.

We have a form for faculty to submit with detailed questions about project proposals; it is used to get an idea of what types of projects people would like to do with us. Most of these are in the digital humanities, but the form is not specific to this domain. After a faculty member fills out the form, we have an internal discussion to decide whether we can commit to supporting the project or not.

Additional Comments

Dependent on support being requested and potential sources of funding, there may be a variety of processes that apply.

There are various library committees that are working to identify project priorities, financial and equipment needs, and possible sources of funding to pursue for such projects. These committees have drafted their own mission statements and policies. They are not yet ready for public consumption.

This is currently under review.

21. Does your library use any document, such as a statement of work or operating agreement, to clarify the scope of services that will be provided for the project? N=46

Yes	23	50%
No	23	50%

If yes, please briefly describe the contents of that document. N=22

Agreements such as this are generally at institution level (i.e., when we work with other organizations). They outline roles, scope of work, time frame, responsibilities, costs (if any) and expenses; level of service to be provided. It's a memorandum of understanding.

Drawing up memoranda of understanding is a recent development, and is not always used depending on the project. The MOU is used when we are developing specialized microsites, but special image digitization projects typically don't utilize them, although in some cases special external contracts are in force (for example when developing a collection for contribution to ARTstor).

For any project in which we collaborate with a faculty member for deposit of content in a local of system-wide repository, we require a memorandum of understanding and a deposit agreement. The MOU outlines the responsibilities of all project participants and establishes a time line for all project steps. The deposit agreement ensures that the faculty member has the rights to make the material available on the web.

For some projects we create an MOU (memo of understanding) or we spell out a work statement in a grant application. This could include staff percentages, work to be undertaken, timelines, and budgets.

For some projects, we develop an MoU describing the scope of work and any digital preservation commitments. We also share an SLA (service level agreement) covering downtime, hours of operation, etc. for projects that we host.

If part of the proposal process.

Instructional Support Services has a work order form which specifies the work to be done, the schedule, and any costs incurred.

It is an agreement that indicates we will retain and preserve digital assets, but not necessarily a complete digital project (because technologies change, etc.)

Our department has developed project intake forms for audio production, video production, and geospatial services.

Project plan template with information on all standards, definition of the project, expected timelines, deliverables, project costs, etc.

Sometimes Memorandums of Agreement/Understanding are used.

Strategic plan under development.

The document(s) required vary by project (MOU, grant letter of support, project proposal form, etc.) All work to date has been bundled with the digital collections and so follows those processes.

The library develops a Memorandum of Understanding with the scholar.

The library has drawn up a Memorandum of Agreement with digital project partners on occasion. For example, we have an agreement with a group of faculty who are externally funded to teach courses based in a digital cultural mapping pedagogy. The MOA states the arrangements by which those faculty can request maps from library collections to be digitized for use in these courses. There is a bounded period of time during which the arrangement holds.

These documents vary depending on the type of project. Sometimes, a memorandum of understanding is all that is necessary. Often, however, a legally binding contract is used, which lays out the duties of each partner and stipulates the rights situation.

This has been done haphazardly, for some initiatives and not others, and for those that do use it in many different forms. One key item they typically cover is what base funding can support and what grant funds are needed for, most importantly for how an initiative will be sustained over time.

This would be specified in grant proposals for grant-funded projects.

Varies by document. Outlines contributions from library, i.e., which services will be provided by library, any equipment to be purchased, funding to be provided, timelines, etc.

We create a basic Project Charter specifying the scope of the work to be done, the timeline, budget, and who will be involved.

We develop a project charter for any significant partnership.

We have developed Memorandum of Understanding (MoU) documents for some projects.

Additional Comments

Agreements are under development by the co-directors who have been working together since fall 2010. The Libraries does have a partnership agreement used for its projects.

Some projects have them, but there is no set policy. We have them for our DLP projects although I don't know how they are actually used.

Sometimes, depending on the nature of the project and partners.

Sometimes.

The Libraries have focused human resources on consultation thereby limiting the scope of engagement, but this is not formalized and is subject to change over time.

This is not currently done in the Digital Humanities Center. At CDRS, there is a requirements-gathering discussion where a service agreement is created spelling out roles and responsibilities for project partners.

22. Does your library preserve all digital humanities project resources that are produced in-house?
    N=46

Yes	27	59%
No	19	41%

Comments

Yes

Again, this is in-process. We currently have active Fedora installations and are working on developing work ows for ingest of assets.

Assets not platforms.

Most digital humanities projects are maintained on servers and sustainable open source platforms.

Once we commit to the project (time, budget, personnel), we expect to provide for the preservation of the collection.

We also use the state's consortial digital archiving system.

Yes, BUT there are occasions when a digital humanities project may not warrant preservation. The library is working to define the circumstances in which we may opt not to preserve a digital resource once it has been completed.

No

Large-scale projects are preserved, and we have an Institutional Repository which is capable of preserving certain outputs and file types. Many smaller DH projects are undoubtedly underway that use library resources but do not involve library staff in a significant way.

Not for all projects. Some projects for the Special Collections Research Center are archived.

Only selective projects created at the DHC are saved. However, LDPD as well as CCNMTL and CDRS project are saved, as a rule.

Some (not all).

Some projects go into our repository software, and so are preserved. Others are more ephemeral, such as web exhibits.

The library intends digital preservation; however, the library is currently in discussions about its digital preservation strategy.

This is an enormous issue for us at the moment. In the past we have implicitly (though not explicitly) assumed the library would provide long term preservation support over both the data used in and applications built by digital humanities projects. However, we are now looking to more clearly outline when this will be a service we provide and when it will not. When we do preserve the output, we employ many of the strategies listed in the 2nd part of this question (that one only answers if one checked 'yes' for this first part).

To date we have been preserving the results of production, but we have explicitly (and in writing/email) indicated that we cannot commit to preserving all websites or online exhibits or collections assembled for more than a couple years.

We do NOT attempt to preserve "all DH project resources," but we do have a sustainability strategy, applicable to those we commit to preserve and those we do not.

We preserve some projects for deposit in UCIspace @ the Libraries. We do not preserve the output from GIS or faculty using available scanning or video imaging equipment. We also deposit some projects at UC system wide like Merritt.

Other

Depends on the nature of the content created.

Repository infrastructure is in developmental stage.

If yes, and your library has a strategy for ensuring the sustainability of these resources, which strategies does your library use? Check all that apply. N=35

Work within widely accepted standards for metadata, etc.	34	97%
Preserve digital projects in repositories	29	83%
Create projects using widely supported platforms	29	83%
Develop grant proposals to support project sustainability	18	51%
Work with project planners to incorporate sustainability costs into initial cost estimates for projects	13	37%
Audit projects for long-term sustainability	11	31%
Other strategy, please describe	5	14%

cIRcle (Institutional Repository) does preserve digital projects.

Digital initiatives support has become a core service and supported by library operating funds.

Ensure materials are created in sustainable formats or normalize to multiple formats to ensure support, retain hardware for retro conversion as needed.

Include library's Preservation Officer on the digital library council, which discusses and tracks library-supported digital projects.

This question is problematic as different levels of preservation may be assigned to different resources, so "all" may not be equally preserved. Example: not all file formats may be migrated and preserved, and a item may be deposited in multiple formats, only one or two of which we would commit to migrating and preserving. It is a negotiated process to determine scope of what will be preserved, not a uniform outcome.

23. Has the library partnered with other units in your institution to provide digital humanities services? N=48

Yes	36	75%
No	12	25%

If yes, please identify the partner and briefly describe the nature of the partnership and how it was cultivated. N=36

Academic department (funding).

Academic Technology Services: they have project management expertise and the campus GIS expert—cultivated through collaboration on particular projects. Institute for Digital Research and Education-Humanities, Arts and Architecture, Social and Information Sciences (IDRE-HASIS):campus steering group for digital research, teaching, and scholarship—cultivated by invitation when the group was created. Center for Digital Humanities: CDH hosts humanities Moodle instance and provides instructional support—cultivated through conversations with digital humanities liaison librarian and the CDH senior fellows program which had awarded fellowships to librarians in the past.

As noted above, CCNMTL and CDRS, while not directly part of the Libraries, frequently partner with librarians or groups on humanities related projects, in addition to acting on faculty requests made directly to them.

Campus Teaching and Learning Centre: collaboration over many years to produce videos that are marketed by the university press, collaboration on training sessions and defining technology requirements for teaching. Information Technologies: infrastructure support. Individual faculty members as projects require.

Center for Latin American Studies for the Digital Library of the Caribbean. This has been a long-term collaboration for preservation and access and continued to grow in need in relation to making rare materials usable by providing contextual and instructional resources to complement them and new ways to use the materials. Harn Museum and Florida Museum of Natural History, for access, dissemination, and preservation. See all partners here: http://ufdc.u . edu/partners.

Collaborated with History Department to create Medieval and Early Modern Data Bank (medieval price data).

Collaboratory for Research for Computing in the Humanities.

College of Arts and Sciences eTech Office: they provide technology support to faculty in the college, including things such as accounts on a Drupal CMS.

College of Arts and Sciences; Baker Nord Center for Humanities; Research Computing and Academic Technology.

College of Humanities: written in as consultants on a gaming research grant—cultivated from liaison librarian relationships. Mexican-American Studies: collaboration with faculty to identify historic materials for digitization, faculty member provided some materials—cultivated from liaison librarian relationships. Various campus units: collaboration with faculty and Library Special Collections on digital exhibits, digitization, and programming.

Consultation with the Canadian Homeless Research Network on the "Homeless Hub" [http://www.homelesshub.ca/default.aspx] and the Gender and Work Database [http://www.genderwork.ca/]. Librarians were co-applicants on the

Sagittarius Project, an initiative to digitize literary resources for teaching and learning for use by Canadian high schools. Archives partnered with PhD students in the History Department on the Portuguese-Canadian History Project and with PhD students from the Music Department on the Mariposa Digital Archives Project.

Digital Humanities Initiative. The dean was a founding partner and encouraged broader collaboration by librarians.

English department; worked together to provide funding.

Grants writing with departments.

Here are some examples: Library & Cornell Society for the Humanities: http://goldsen.library.cornell.edu/. Collaboration with Arts & Sciences: https://con uence.cornell.edu/display/grantsas/Grants+Program+for+Digital+Collections+in+Arts+and+Sciences. Collaboration with the University Press: http://signale.cornell.edu/, https://con uence.cornell.edu/display/grantsas/Grants+Program+for+Digital+Collections+in+Arts+and+Sciences.

Humanities Computing and/or Campus IT Scholarly Computing units. We have an informal understanding about what types of projects each unit should be involved in so often projects come to us through referral from another IT department or vice versa. The library tends to focus more on the collections involved, the archiving, and the metadata components of a project, whereas other campus IT units might focus on the classroom use of what is being developed, the staffing to create the resource, and multi-media support.

Hyperstudio, consulting and project concept development.

I don't think there have been significant formal partnerships. In some cases, however, librarians have worked with faculty members in academic departments to identify materials, digitize them, and create web pages and finding aids to promote their use.

IDAH, University IT Services (UITS).

Instructional Media Services, a division of University IT, helps with checkout of hardware; other divisions of UIT have been helpful in planning and setting up some services as well as helping faculty understand the full spectrum of multimedia production services that are available on campus. We are currently collaborating with the Geography Department to develop our geospatial information services.

Modern Language and Cultures Department: partnered to house a film clips database to support language instruction. Philosophy: partnered with a professor to create online visual mapping of seminal works in philosophy. English: partnered with faculty members to teach digital humanities labs.

On an ad hoc project-by-project basis, for example history department structured a public history course syllabus around production of a digital humanities project and had the students enrolled in the course do scanning and metadata production for objects that went into both our ongoing repository and into their course-generated portal.

Our own Special Collections and Oral History Research Program. We also partner with several department on campus, not necessarily humanities.

The Libraries have partnered with the Hall Center for the Humanities (a university research center) and with the College of Liberal Arts and Sciences. The partnership was cultivated through an 18 month task force that recommended the partnership to the current partners. The task force was chaired by a faculty member from the college and a librarian. The Libraries and the Hall Center initiated the task force.

The library worked with the Graduate School of Library and Information Science (GSLIS) to develop and support the public instance of a text-mining software, MONK. Researchers at GSLIS approached the library about supporting this digital humanities tool for text mining, and an agreement was reached to transfer the tool from the researchers' servers to the library's servers. We also worked together to establish Shibboleth authentication for 12 other institutions in the Committee of Institutional Cooperation consortium. Now MONK is available to all users as a digital humanities tool for research through the library.

There are many other faculty-driven centers offering DH services at the university. The library provides space to two of them (IATH and SHANTI) and, in both cases, was instrumental in their creation. Partnerships with these and other centers are sustained as projects move uidly between them.

UNC Press: on print on demand and a digital publishing platform with annotation capabilities. Faculty in English, History, American Studies, African-American studies, Latin American studies, Journalism and Mass Communication, Religious Studies, Comparative Literature, and the Center for the Study of the American South: on individual projects. Faculty from these and other disciplines serve on the Editorial Board for Documenting the American South (a agship digital humanities initiative), which helps to cultivate relationships, as does word of mouth from successful relationships. With the School of Information and Library Science, we provide field experience to students to work on digital humanities projects while simultaneously teaching them about how such projects are designed and run.

University Press: to publish a digital humanities monograph.

We are partnering with our art museum, our museum of natural and cultural history, our InfoGraphics lab in Geography, our Social Sciences Instructional Lab, the Yamada Language Center. Most partnerships have arisen around specific projects, specific resources.

We collaborate with the campus's Information Technology Division to host our local repository. We also work with the California Digital Library, as they host a variety of digital services our faculty may use, such as ArtStor, an electronic publishing service, and a web archiving service.

We have long-standing collaborative relationships with the Academic Technologies unit of central IT and the Multimedia Learning Center, a small faculty support unit within the college of arts and sciences. New relationships are being developed with other school IT units, with particular focus on the IT group in the college of arts and sciences.

We have ongoing regular meetings with the Humanities Digital Workshop, part of Arts & Sciences. We are currently collaborating with them on a library, IMLS-funded digital project, and are in discussions with them about creating a digital collaborative space in which internal library resources (DLS) would be co-located with HDW.

We have partnered with research computing.

We have worked with faculty in English, History, and Jewish Studies.

Work with academic departments and IT in School of Arts & Sciences and campus museum.

Yes, more as sub-contractor (we served as key scanning facility, for example).

24. **Has the library partnered with other institutions to provide digital humanities services? N=48**

Yes	27	56%
No	21	44%

If yes, please identify the partner and briefly describe the nature of the partnership and how it was cultivated. N=26

Afghanistan Centre at Kabul University: collaboration, digitization, and hosting—cultivated through personal librarian relationships. USAIN Historical Agricultural Documents: collaboration, digitization, hosting—relationships with Cornell/liaison librarians.

Asian community: gathering data/submissions.

Columbia has produced at least three major collaborative digital projects: the Advanced Papyrological Information System, the Digital Scriptorium, and the Jay Papers. Ultimately these partnerships brought in a broad number of US libraries holding papyri, medieval manuscripts, and papers of John Jay. Only one, I believe, was set up on a consortial basis, Digital Scriptorium, which began out of a partnership between manuscript librarians at Berkeley and Columbia. Those librarians subsequently worked through their library links to engage other partners. In the other cases, I believe, the faculty sponsor behind APIS reached out to papyrologists at other US institutions, while the Jay Papers project was able to take advantage of the libraries that had contributed papers to a print editorial project that had been going on at Columbia for some years.

Currently creating colloquia with Cleveland State University to provide an event where regional digital humanities activities can be discussed and considered in a larger context. Provide a Scholarly Communications Lecture series which brings in high profile contributors to the Digital Humanities and Library profession.

Digital Library of the Caribbean. This has been a long-term collaboration for preservation and access and continued to grow in need in relation to making rare materials usable by providing contextual and instructional resources to complement them and new ways to use the materials. See all partners here: http://dloc.com/dloc1/partners.

HathiTrust includes over 50 partner institutions (http://www.hathitrust.org/community) and the Text Creation Partnership includes over 150 partner institutions (http://www.lib.umich.edu/tcp/eebo/status.html).

In process of joining Project Bamboo.

In recognition of the sesquicentennial of the start of the American Civil War, members of the Association of Southeastern Research Libraries (ASERL) Civil War and the American South collaborated to provide a central portal to access digital collections from the Civil War Era (1850–1865) held by members.

Northwestern is a partner in the Mellon-funded Bamboo Technology Project.

Not on a programmatic basis, but we partner with other institutions on a project-by-project basis.

Oklahoma Arts and Humanities Council: historical projects. National Endowment for the Humanities: historical projects. Osage Tribal Museum (Oklahoma).

Other universities and consortia.

SAHARA, developed by the Society of Architectural Historians in collaboration with ARTstor and two other academic institutions.

Synergies, national project to bring SSH journals online. SSHRC-funded project on Knowledge Synthesis, currently at the Letter of Intent stage. Working with individual faculty members with research grants (English, Computer Science).

The library is working with the German institution Herzog August Bibliothek, Wolfenbüttel, to create the Emblem Books digital archive drawing upon our collection of rare Emblem Books from the Rare Books and Manuscript Library.

They vary on a project-by-project basis.

This also happens frequently, and is generally more oriented toward tool development than toward "service provision" in other senses of the word. A recent example would be a Library of Congress-funded collaboration between UVa Library's Scholars' Lab and the Center for History and New Media at George Mason to extend and develop scholarly plug-ins for Omeka.

USC: funding for the Shoah Archive.

Via the Bamboo Initiative.

We are a member of CARLI and rely on their Digital Collections services, which include a statewide license for CONTENTdm.

We are also partnering with the Catholic Research Resources Alliance.

We are collaborating with UC Berkeley and others on The Bamboo Technology Project to develop applications and a shared infrastructure for humanities research. This is a Mellon-funded project which grew out of a planning project that engaged faculty, librarians, and technologists from 115 different institutions to define scholarly technology needs in the humanities.

We have some national and international partnerships, e.g., Central Michigan University (a digital library project); a research center in Zacatecas, Mexico (a digital dictionary project); the University of Warsaw (more lexical database work). We largely have collaborations on specific projects. We have also helped organize symposia (Oaxaca, Warsaw, Vienna). We have run summer institutes (Eugene, Oregon and Oaxaca, Mexico). Our director has a Fulbright Specialist designation intended to cultivate partnerships in Europe, such as with an ethnological museum in Berlin. It may also take her back to Warsaw.

We partnered with the Missouri History Museum on a state-funded grant, and now on an IMLS funded project.

We worked with a number of other schools on a text encoding project. The goal was to share resources and I believe the partnering scholars maintained the relationship.

Worked with NJ Historical Commission and many institutions around the state to develop the New Jersey Digital Highway (archive of materials on NJ History). Worked with Women's Project of New Jersey to develop New Jersey Women's History site. Collaborations typically arise out of existing relationships or grant projects.

ASSESSMENT

25. **Has there been any assessment of the effectiveness of the digital humanities services? N=49**

Yes	12	25%
No	37	75%

If yes, what measures are used to assess the effectiveness of these services? Check all that apply. N=12

Demand (e.g., services provided relative to demand, increase in demand)	8	67%
Web analytics (e.g., number of hits on web-facing projects)	8	67%
Publications (e.g., research publications or web projects published citing or based on these services)	5	42%
Financial (e.g., funding targets reached, good grant funding record)	3	25%
Media coverage (e.g., non-research publications about the program)	3	25%
Other measure, please describe	4	33%

A survey of users made as part of the planning process for a new Digital Humanities Center.

Faculty compliments.

Responses by users.

Survey and focus groups to understand user needs and expectations.

Additional Comment

There has not been an assessment yet, but that is planned for the end of the first year.

26. Were any changes made to the services offered as a result of the assessment? N=11

Yes	6	55%
No	5	45%

If yes, please briefly describe up to three changes that were made. N=6

Expansion of hours, deployment of scanners at many more places across the university, new focus in the DHC program on notes and resource management programs.

For our Freedman Fellows Program we have not only reshaped how it functions (project support and partnering from education) but will reshape the program again in coming years.

Made modifications to projects.

Many, based on annual usability studies, quarterly/midyear/annual reports for specific grants, etc.

Migrating content to new formats; updating or replacing software; experimenting with improved web interactivity. We have identified some additional areas that could benefit from more attention, but we are shorthanded and underfunded, making some desired changes nearly impossible.

Small changes, informally over time. This has been much more of an evolution rather than a formal study and response.

27. Overall, how would you assess the effectiveness of your library's digital humanities services? N=36

Because our program is ad hoc, and serves the entire faculty of the university, support for humanities has not been an intentional focus, and the spectrum of services is quite broad, including special project support but also substantial ongoing digitization services for courses, research, and as an extension of services in other special libraries. Use and demand is strong, but it is difficult to assess a specific impact on digital humanists/the humanities.

Given that we don't have a systematic support structure for digital humanities services, we're doing pretty well. There's a website for one of our projects (http://digilib.bu.edu/mission/), and we've consulted on some others. We are in the midst of significant growth right now in all aspects of library services; a lot more should happen in the next couple of years.

Good.

Improving. We are ramping up for a launch of our new research commons and will develop a new suite of services in the process. New hires related to this space and services will have assessment as one piece of their responsibilities.

It could be a lot better.

It has been mixed. While the work has been outstanding we have had trouble with scope creep and not working very efficiently because everything was ad hoc.

It is too new to easily assess. An early indicator of success is the turnout for the first "digital jump start" workshop. We had over 30 participants which is a good number for a faculty workshop.

It needs to be expanded and strengthened. It needs to combine forces with other library units and other campus-wide units to maximize resources and centralize expertise. We are in the process of trying to do this.

Needs work. Needs clearer direction and more and better communication amongst the units providing support. The collaboration with IDAH particularly needs work. It is problematic to have a division of labor where one group that does not report through the library makes project decisions that have such a strong impact on a unit in the library.

Our ad hoc, idiosyncratic services suffer from lack of a unifying theme. Poor advertising keeps, for the most part, our expertise in a closet. However, when we are engaged outcomes have been uniformly positive.

Our primary strengths are in the STEM disciplines, but we have met expressed needs in the humanities disciplines.

Our service is growing. As we begin to get more grant funding for digital humanities projects, we are little by little establishing a digital humanities program in the library. I would assess our program as being in its starting phase, but on the right track for growth.

Over the last year, we have acquired additional software that should provide more accurate statistics on the use of our collections for effective assessment going forward.

Services have been effective in responding to faculty and institutional needs that have been identified; however, more outreach and planning could reach a much larger audience for these services.

Still in developmental stage.

Still new, but promising.

The digital humanities services are bundled with the digital collection services, which makes each more successful and in all are extremely successful.

The faculty who have been involved are very satisfied at this point.

The library has highly skilled personnel to support the different aspects of digital humanities research, including digitization software and hardware tools, metadata application, resource acquisition, and copyright issues. But at the moment, it is still a somewhat fragmented set of services and we do not actively coordinate on each project. Rather, people are brought in based on researchers' knowledge of them or referrals from someone like me.

The quality is excellent though the scope is somewhat limited.

The services are less than effective because it really has not been in existence for very long, less than six months.

The services are still in a development stage but we are encouraged.

They are in transition and should be much more robust in the next year.

Too soon to tell whether we will be more than marginally effective until we seen publications and get a sense about sustained web traffic (ongoing demand) which might warrant longer term preservation of the products.

Very effective in the sense of building faculty relationships and being seen as a leader. Much less effective in terms of sustainability, systematic prioritization of work, and appropriate choice of technology used. We are at a crossroads in our plans for these services going forward, and are currently actively planning how we can maintain this type of service, while also providing some reasonable level of long-term support for selected outcomes of these activities.

We already have a popular and well-appreciated Digital Humanities Center where patrons can get assistance with digitization, bibliographic and resource management, and small-scale individual research projects. We have a Libraries' Digital Program that has produced an number of first-class resources for humanities scholars. We have a Center for New Media that does an excellent job of supporting instructional needs in the humanities and in creating curricular-related resources. We have a fairly new Center for Digital Research and Scholarship that does excellent job supporting faculty research and developing a repository for material produced at the university. We are looking forward to providing a larger and more robustly equipped center for patrons to come for front-line help, and an active planning process is in place to implement such an enhanced facility in the 2012–2013 academic year, bringing it up to par with the recently opened Digital Social Science Center and Digital Science Center. Another area where we look to improve services would be in developing a smoother path for transition from the front-line, fairly ad hoc project work that individual patrons undertake in the DHC to the kinds of full-blown, fully supported projects created by our Libraries Digital and other programs.

We are at the beginning of our engagement with digital humanities services. As a result, we don't have grounds for assessing our overall effectiveness. That being said, we have many improvements and adaptations to make which will be driven by campus demand.

We are coming to the end of a major planning and strategy effort to formulate a new Digital Library Program that will include digital humanities support. Assessment will be part of that program moving forwards.

We are just beginning but are moving in interesting directions.

We are meeting a well-defined need on the campus where other units have been less successful or disinterested. In six years of programmatic activity we have helped, directly, 29 faculty, hundreds of undergraduate students and provided $100,000 in grants.

We are tracking projects and inquiries, but have made no formal assessment. While I believe that we are providing very high quality service to those who have found us, we have not yet reached a critical mass of those we could support. However, we are kept busy by the projects we are working on.

We have a rich history of initiatives in digital humanities, several of them involving broad collaboration. Currently, we are in the process of assessing our service infrastructure and opportunities for more closely collaborating with faculty.

We have knowledgeable staff and students who perform technical tasks in support of these projects. We maintain a variety of equipment and software options that can be used to meet the needs of the individual project.

We haven't done a formal and rigorous study since the creation of the Scholars' Lab four years ago, but anecdotally our DH services have been very successful in all of the measures you list above. We also frequently hear that the library's support for DH is a major factor in faculty recruitment and retention, and in the recruitment of top-notch graduate students. We're often cited locally for having created a vibrant graduate student community, and for changing the tenor of partnerships with faculty—emphasizing library staff as true intellectual partners on digital projects.

We want to do much more but are limited by our capacity; we can't really do outreach because we are already more or less at capacity and still get inquiries. Projects take longer than they should to go to completion due to multiple projects, other library responsibilities, and still limited technical infrastructure. But we are also taking specific steps to better follow-up on corrections, manage capacity, etc.

Weak.

INSTITUTION PROVIDES DIGITAL SCHOLARSHIP SERVICES

28. You indicated that digital scholarship services are located outside the library. Which of the following best describes how the services are provided. N=7

The institution hosts a digital scholarship center dedicated to the humanities	3	43%
The institution supports digital scholarship in a decentralized manner	3	43%
The institution hosts a multidisciplinary digital scholarship center that supports the humanities	0	—
Other service method, please describe	1	14%

Humanities and Fine Arts offers seed grants in Digital Humanities through the Digital Humanities initiative. There is also a DH lab. See: http://www.umass.edu/hfa/grants/hfafunding/frs/digitalhumanities.html.

29. Do library staff play any role in providing theses services? N=7

Yes	4	57%
No	3	43%

If yes, please briefly describe which staff participate and the role(s) they play. N=4

Called on for cataloging services for the English Short Title Catalog.

Library staff, especially subject librarians, may advise faculty and graduate students about services offered by the (University of Washington) Simpson Center for the Humanities.

Not formal or systematic, but library staff are occasionally consulted for assistance and/or advice on format transfers, rights issues, and arrangement and access issues.

The library will digitize library materials for the Press and for Digital Humanities projects. These digitized materials are usually hosted on the library server, but can also be hosted elsewhere.

ADDITIONAL COMMENTS

30. Please enter any additional information that may assist the authors' understanding of your library's support for digital humanities projects. N=20

As stated earlier, we are in the early stages of offering these services. We consciously went with a "policy lite" approach to get things off the ground. The design and outfitting of the space and the services offered were guided by participating faculty from African American Studies, Art, English, Gender and Race Studies, History, Modern Languages and Classics, Music, and Women's Studies. The faculty who have been involved are very satisfied and pleased at this point.

At our institution, the projects are all very different and funding is limited. So our approach to digital humanities is informal and varied. There isn't a central coordinator role.

I think the primary strengths of the digital humanities initiative is our partnership representing the libraries, research, and faculty as well as incorporating the program into the Center for Digital Scholarship.

It is difficult to draw a line between humanities and other digital library services. We are developing most services as part of our RUcore repository platform, including support for video, audio, and data, and a full suite of digitization services through our Digital Curation Lab. These services support all disciplines, and are used by humanities researchers, but we do relatively little "target marketing" to the humanities only. At Douglass Library, we have the Margery Somers Foster Center which conducts multimedia training and outreach, in conjunction with digital multimedia production facilities in the Sharon Fordham Lab (video and audio creation and editing). This is probably the closest we come to a "humanities" center.

Our approach is not to differentiate digital humanities projects vs sciences. We're trying to start with sciences since we may get grants. Then, it will trickle down to humanities. Our university administration is supportive of these efforts, specially the new cyberinfrastructure Center.

Our Dean is very supportive of the direction we are taking to improve our library's digital humanities offerings. We are also trying to think even more broadly, beyond the humanities, although we do feel that the humanities are an important target. The Wired Humanities Project was founded in the late 1990s when "humanities computing" was getting off the ground. Fortunately, we had the support of a few administrators who understood this new "interdiscipline" and the potential for winning external funding for faculty projects. Our unit is now in its third home on campus, having been born as a spinoff of another research center (on gender), then being given a temporary home in a language center, and now finally having a home (less than a year) in the library, where the Dean is very aware of the growing research-library role in providing digital humanities services. Our success at winning federal grants has helped keep us alive through drastic budget cuts and other obstacles. Fortunately, the field (now called "digital humanities") has caught on with lending agencies. The availability of grants in DH has caught the attention not only of administrators but of more and more faculty and graduate students, too, making our job much easier. In fact, we need to consolidate and expand to meet the growing interest/demand.

Our Digital Humanities Center is still very new and establishing a strategic plan, mission, and vision. Our faculty members are exploring digital scholarship in a variety of ways and have involved the library staff as collaborators in every project so we envision playing an important role in Humanities Scholarship.

Our library is still very much developing its digital humanities services in terms of defining what our services will be, implementing marketing and outreach, and training staff. But with two recent hires for a visual media digitization coordinator and a digital humanities specialist for Library IT, we are quickly building a team of specialized personnel who are dedicated to assisting researchers with digital humanities projects.

Support of DH projects at IU has developed organically over several years, but until very recently there hasn't been a sustained effort to communicate and work together. In addition to the Digital Library Program (http://www.dlib.indiana. edu/) and IDAH (http://www.indiana.edu/~idah/), the university's institutional repository, IUScholarWorks (http:// scholarworks.iu.edu/) and the University IT Services (http://uits.iu.edu/), particularly the Advanced Visualization Lab (http://www.avl.iu.edu/) also provide services of various sorts to humanities faculty.

The CBSR works with individuals and organizations in California, nationally, and internationally to identify potential partners and projects and manage projects.

The demand started out small and could be managed on an ad hoc basis. As demand has increased we have scrambled to meet demands just as the library itself has demanded more digital know-how. We are preparing to launch a new research center which should allow us to work more efficiently.

The focus of our Digital Library Program includes the humanities as major partners, but is not limited to their needs solely. Digital Humanities support also available from various IT service points, and from the campus Humanities Center.

The institution supports digital scholarship in a decentralized manner. Library staff serve as members of the initiative.

The library staff in Digital Collections work with the Digital Humanities staff on grant proposals and the Digital Collections Librarian is on the board of the Digital Humanities Center.

This is new area that is not yet a distinct service within umbrella of digital initiatives. We have a few projects that are digital humanities, more in the queue, but are still staffing up to handle the projects in hand. More structure, policy development, and procedural solutions will occur in next 12 to 18 months.

This response relates to: The Chung Collection, The Malcolm Lowry Collection digitization project, Global Encounters Project, and 2010 UBC Olympic & Paralympics Project.

We are actively planning to collaborate with some of the colleges to provide a more coordinated and substantive support for digital humanities, social sciences, and arts projects.

We have concerns about our ability to keep up with demand once our new research commons is open. We anticipate that, at least initially, demand with outstrip our capacity, both in terms of services and infrastructure.

We hope to develop a strategic direction regarding digital humanities services in the next few years.

We're very much struggling with the appropriate level of service we should be providing. To what degree should we move beyond providing the raw materials (primary and secondary sources) upon which new digital research is done, into being partners in the actual implementation of that research (for example, with technology support)? Faculty have a frequently blurry line between their research activities and their service activities: to what degree is it the library's role to support the latter? Where are the lines between 'digital humanities' and 'scholarly communication' and 'digital libraries'? We have many activities in the latter two areas that weren't reported in this survey, as they are not necessarily humanities based.

RESPONDING INSTITUTIONS

University of Alabama

University of Alberta

University of Arizona

Boston University

Brigham Young University

University of British Columbia

University of Calgary

University of California, Irvine

University of California, Los Angeles

University of California, Riverside

Case Western Reserve University

University of Chicago

University of Colorado at Boulder

Columbia University

Cornell University

Dartmouth College

Emory University

University of Florida

Florida State University

George Washington University

Georgia Institute of Technology

University of Guelph

University of Hawaii at Manoa

University of Illinois at Urbana-Champaign

Indiana University Bloomington

Johns Hopkins University

University of Kansas

University of Kentucky

Library of Congress

Louisiana State University

University of Louisville

McMaster University

University of Massachusetts, Amherst

Massachusetts Institute of Technology

University of Miami

University of Michigan

Michigan State University

University of Missouri

National Agricultural Library

New York University

University of North Carolina at Chapel Hill

North Carolina State University

Northwestern University

University of Notre Dame

Ohio University

Ohio State University

Oklahoma State University

University of Oregon

University of Pennsylvania

Purdue University

Rice University

University of Rochester

Rutgers University

University of South Carolina

Southern Illinois University Carbondale

Temple University

Texas Tech University

University of Utah

Vanderbilt University

University of Virginia

University of Washington

Washington University in St. Louis

University of Western Ontario

York University

REPRESENTATIVE DOCUMENTS

Mission/Purpose

UNIVERSITY OF ALABAMA
Alabama Digital Humanities Center
http://www.lib.ua.edu/digitalhumanities

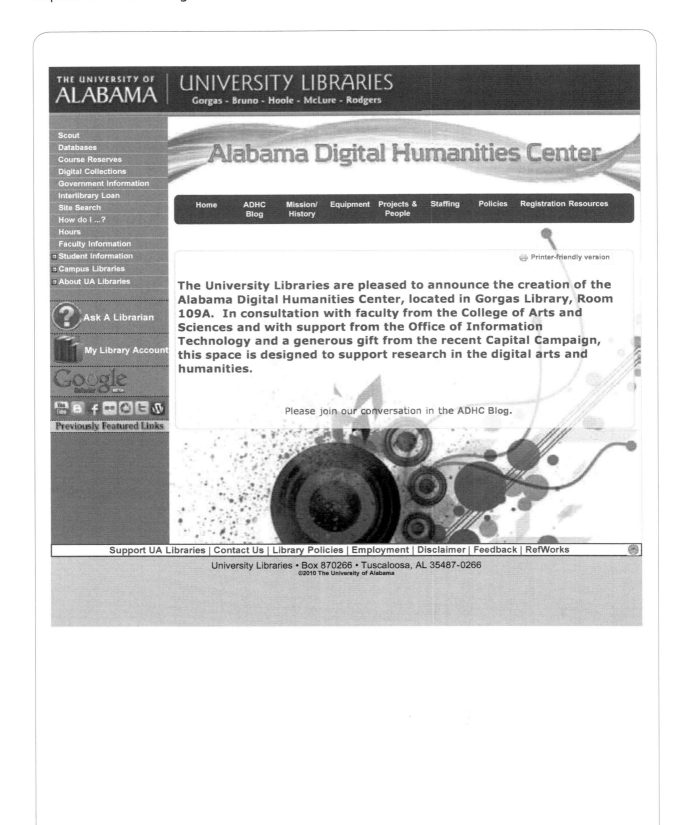

THE UNIVERSITY OF
ALABAMA | **UNIVERSITY LIBRARIES**
Gorgas - Bruno - Hoole - McLure - Rodgers

Scout
Databases
Course Reserves
Digital Collections
Government Information
Interlibrary Loan
Site Search
How do I ...?
Hours
Faculty Information
Student Information
Campus Libraries
About UA Libraries

Ask A Librarian

My Library Account

Google Scholar

Previously Featured Links

Alabama Digital Humanities Center

Home | ADHC Blog | Mission/History | Equipment | Projects & People | Staffing | Policies | Registration Resources

Mission/History

Printer-friendly version

Our mission is to:

- **Encourage** and **engage** faculty and graduate students in art, humanities, and performing arts digital research.
- **Support** exploration and application of technology to arts and humanities research and teaching.
- **Provide** a venue for collaborative development and hosting of research projects.
- **Foster** interdisciplinary approaches to digital research questions.
- **Feature** prominent digital scholars in colloquia.
- **Facilitate** new research agendas.
- **Participate** in international standards and best practices.
- **Conduct** research on digital humanities research.
- **Enhance** collaboration among library faculty and scholars.
- **Provide** opportunities to collaborate on grant funding or seeking other sources of financial support.

A pictorial history of Gorgas Room 109A

In the beginning...

...there was a room, and it was unused, having served as office space and storage.

A Cyberinfrastructure for Research and Learning in a Digital Culture
http://www.bu.edu/dioa/cyberinfrastructure/

CASE WESTERN RESERVE UNIVERSITY
Freedman Center
http://library.case.edu/ksl/freedmancenter/

Print This Page   Email This Page   A A A Font Size

CASE WESTERN RESERVE
UNIVERSITY est. 1826

Freedman Center

Home
Digital Library
Language Learning
Multimedia Services
Special Programs
Training
Who We Are
Contact Us

FC Related Sites
College of Arts & Sciences
Kelvin Smith Library
Instructional Technology & Academic Computing
Modern Languages & Literature

Freedman Center

The Samuel B. & Marian K. Freedman Digital Library, Language Learning, and Multimedia Services Center

The Freedman Center is a partnership between the College of Arts and Sciences and the Kelvin Smith Library. Established in 2005, with over 2,700 square feet of highly functional workspace and state-of-the-art equipment, the Freedman Center harnesses the power of modern technology and combines it with the driver of academic creativity.

The Freedman Center consists primarily of three service areas, but also offers special programs:

* Digital Library Services
* Language Learning Services
* Multimedia Services
* Special Programs

For the College of Arts and Sciences the Freedman Center is evidence of the College's commitment to the evolution of education and the integration of information technologies in its curriculum and research practices. For the Kelvin Smith Library, the Freedman Center is the culmination of a ten-year vision for a center that provides faculty, students, and staff with the ability to utilize both analog and hardcopy information sources in digital works, presentations, and research.

Helpful staff is on hand to guide you through your project and teach you how to use the latest technology whether you are creating a PowerPoint presentation or full media CD-ROMs and interactive DVDs. You will not only walk away with a completed project, but with the skills to do it again.

The Freedman Center also houses workstations with language learning capabilities. Users have access to region-free technology that allows them to view any foreign language DVD, VHS tape, and television broadcast. The Freedman Center offers many tools to support classroom learning. Modern Language faculty can post assignments for their students and can track both student usage and attendance. The Center also offers the Pimsleur Comprehensive Series for language learning, a world-renowned instructional program that features fourteen languages including Japanese, Russian, and Portuguese.

To learn more about the capabilities of the Freedman Center, please continue.

RSS Feeds

FC News Blog

Apr 29, 2011
Freedman Fellows 2011 Announced
The Freedman Center is very happy to announce the winners of the 2011 Freedman Fellows Program. The ...

Mar 31, 2011
Freedman Fellows Program 2011
Freedman Fellows Program 2011 The Samuel B. and Marian K. Freedman Digital Library, Language Learnin...

Mar 12, 2010
Freedman Center Fellow Program 2010
The Freedman Center is pleased to announce the 2010 Freedman Fellows Program for faculty. The Freedm...

Apr 30, 2009
Freedman Fellows 2009 Announced
The Freedman Center is very happy to announce the winners of the 2009 Freedman Fellows Program. The...

Other Blogs
KSL Reference & Instruction
ITS News 222

KSL Home | BlackBoard | Site Map | Privacy | Contact Us | OhioLink | Libraries of Case | Browser Requirements

Kelvin Smith Library | 11055 Euclid Avenue | Cleveland, OH 44106-7151 | 216-368-3506

CASE WESTERN RESERVE UNIVERSITY
Freedman Center Mission and Vision
http://library.case.edu/ksl/freedmancenter/whoweare/mission.html

CASE.EDU: HOME | DIRECTORIES | SEARCH   Print This Page   Email This Page   A A A Font Size

Freedman Center > Who We Are > Mission and Vision

Home
Digital Library
Language Learning
Multimedia Services
Special Programs
Training
Who We Are
Contact Us

FC Related Sites
College of Arts & Sciences
Kelvin Smith Library
Instructional Technology & Academic Computing
Modern Languages & Literature

Mission and Vision

The Mission of the Samuel B. and Marian K. Freedman Digital Library, Language Learning, and Multimedia Services Center is to bring together in one place a variety of technological resources in order to support and sustain learners and create new ways of teaching and learning. The Freedman Center is an innovative partner with faculty, students, and staff in providing full-service digital library, language learning, and multimedia services so that members of the Case community can achieve/accomplish their research, scholarly, and artistic goals.

The Freedman Center sees itself as the crossroads of physical and virtual space, where information from a multitude of disciplines across time, in a variety of languages and formats, is available to faculty, students, and staff, and can be moved seamlessly from one format to another, for purposes of teaching, research, and learning.

The Freedman Center supports an innovative research library system and a dynamic Case community and strives to be the world's most cutting-edge center for the generation of new materials and methods of teaching and learning. This goal is accomplished by:

* Serving as a model information service provider committed to excellence;
* Providing collections of physical, virtual, and technological resources, and using them to maximum advantage;
* Leveraging resources to make available high quality technology services and to support the Case community in their effective use;
* Serving as a laboratory with its own research agenda;
* Developing innovative ways of creating, managing, using, sharing and preserving information in response to a changing information environment;
* Developing opportunities and forming partnerships for the purposes of exploring new ways to use technology to support teaching, research and learning;
* Educating the Case community about Copyright;
* Becoming a center and resource on campus for electronic publication.

RSS Feeds

FC News Blog

Apr 29, 2011
Freedman Fellows 2011 Announced
The Freedman Center is very happy to announce the winners of the 2011 Freedman Fellows Program. The ...

Mar 31, 2011
Freedman Fellows Program 2011
Freedman Fellows Program 2011 The Samuel B. and Marian K. Freedman Digital Library, Language Learnin...

Mar 12, 2010
Freedman Center Fellow Program 2010
The Freedman Center is pleased to announce the 2010 Freedman Fellows Program for faculty. The Freedm...

Apr 30, 2009
Freedman Fellows 2009 Announced
The Freedman Center is very happy to announce the winners of the 2009 Freedman Fellows Program. The...

Other Blogs
KSL Reference & Instruction
ITS News 222

KSL Home | BlackBoard | Site Map | Privacy | Contact Us | OhioLink | Libraries of Case | Browser Requirements

Kelvin Smith Library | 11055 Euclid Avenue | Cleveland, OH 44106-7151 | 216-368-3506

COLUMBIA UNIVERSITY
Digital Humanities Center
http://library.columbia.edu/indiv/dhc.html

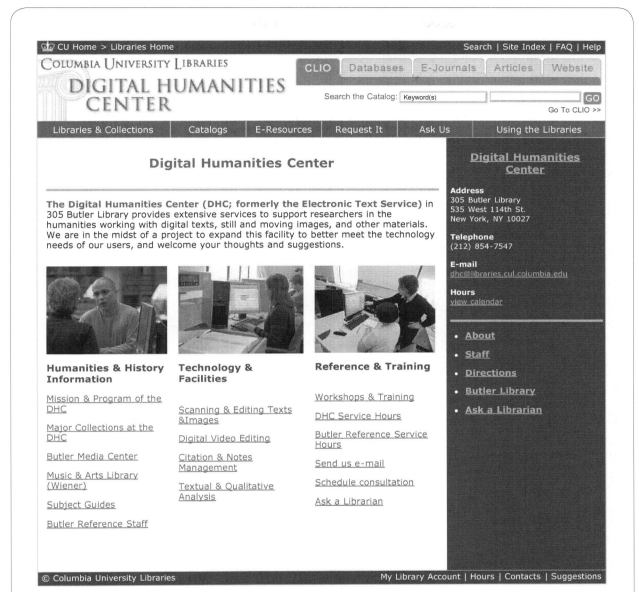

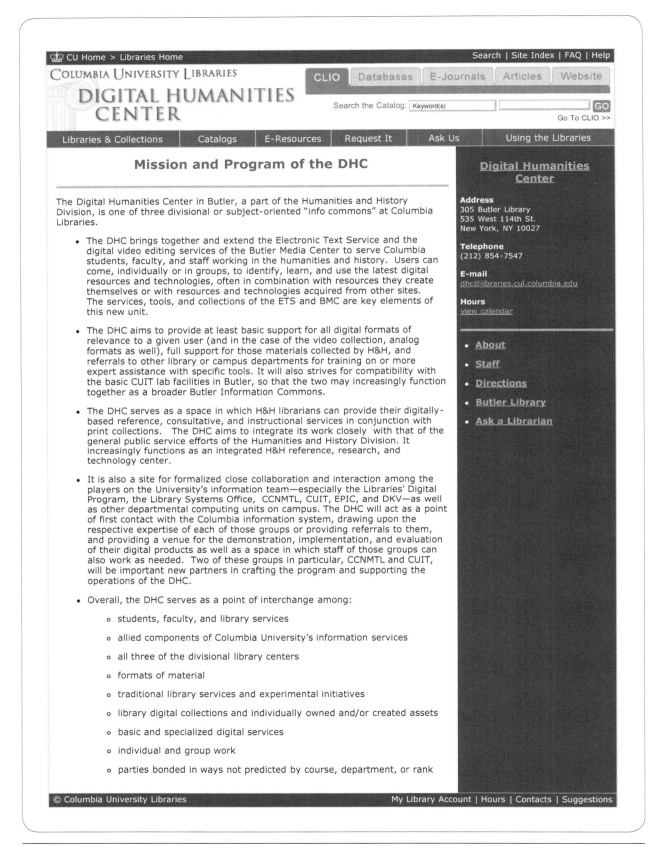

Mission and Program of the DHC

The Digital Humanities Center in Butler, a part of the Humanities and History Division, is one of three divisional or subject-oriented "info commons" at Columbia Libraries.

- The DHC brings together and extend the Electronic Text Service and the digital video editing services of the Butler Media Center to serve Columbia students, faculty, and staff working in the humanities and history. Users can come, individually or in groups, to identify, learn, and use the latest digital resources and technologies, often in combination with resources they create themselves or with resources and technologies acquired from other sites. The services, tools, and collections of the ETS and BMC are key elements of this new unit.

- The DHC aims to provide at least basic support for all digital formats of relevance to a given user (and in the case of the video collection, analog formats as well), full support for those materials collected by H&H, and referrals to other library or campus departments for training on or more expert assistance with specific tools. It will also strives for compatibility with the basic CUIT lab facilities in Butler, so that the two may increasingly function together as a broader Butler Information Commons.

- The DHC serves as a space in which H&H librarians can provide their digitally-based reference, consultative, and instructional services in conjunction with print collections. The DHC aims to integrate its work closely with that of the general public service efforts of the Humanities and History Division. It increasingly functions as an integrated H&H reference, research, and technology center.

- It is also a site for formalized close collaboration and interaction among the players on the University's information team—especially the Libraries' Digital Program, the Library Systems Office, CCNMTL, CUIT, EPIC, and DKV—as well as other departmental computing units on campus. The DHC will act as a point of first contact with the Columbia information system, drawing upon the respective expertise of each of those groups or providing referrals to them, and providing a venue for the demonstration, implementation, and evaluation of their digital products as well as a space in which staff of those groups can also work as needed. Two of these groups in particular, CCNMTL and CUIT, will be important new partners in crafting the program and supporting the operations of the DHC.

- Overall, the DHC serves as a point of interchange among:

  o students, faculty, and library services

  o allied components of Columbia University's information services

  o all three of the divisional library centers

  o formats of material

  o traditional library services and experimental initiatives

  o library digital collections and individually owned and/or created assets

  o basic and specialized digital services

  o individual and group work

  o parties bonded in ways not predicted by course, department, or rank

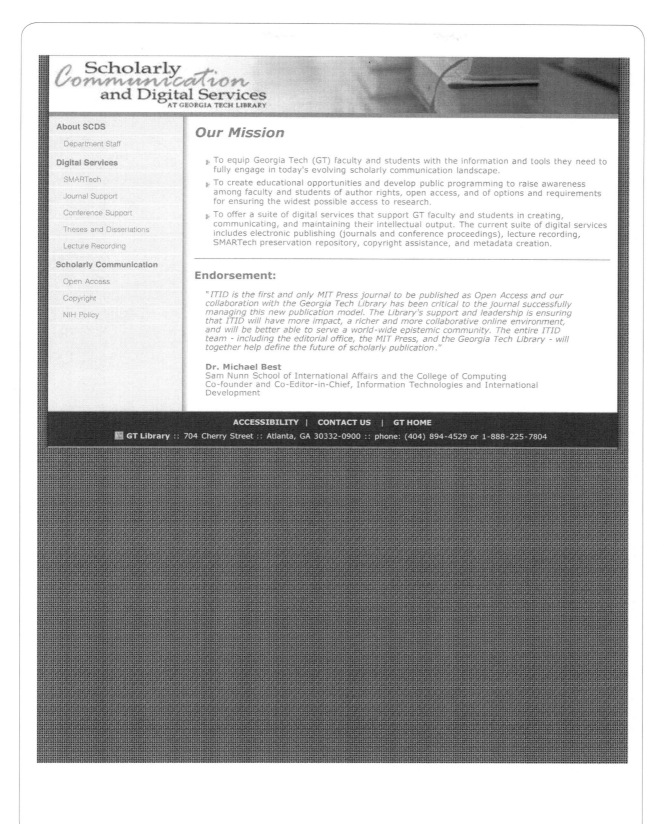

Scholarly Communication and Digital Services
AT GEORGIA TECH LIBRARY

About SCDS

Department Staff

Digital Services

SMARTech

Journal Support

Conference Support

Theses and Dissertations

Lecture Recording

Scholarly Communication

Open Access

Copyright

NIH Policy

Our Mission

- To equip Georgia Tech (GT) faculty and students with the information and tools they need to fully engage in today's evolving scholarly communication landscape.
- To create educational opportunities and develop public programming to raise awareness among faculty and students of author rights, open access, and of options and requirements for ensuring the widest possible access to research.
- To offer a suite of digital services that support GT faculty and students in creating, communicating, and maintaining their intellectual output. The current suite of digital services includes electronic publishing (journals and conference proceedings), lecture recording, SMARTech preservation repository, copyright assistance, and metadata creation.

Endorsement:

"ITID is the first and only MIT Press journal to be published as Open Access and our collaboration with the Georgia Tech Library has been critical to the journal successfully managing this new publication model. The Library's support and leadership is ensuring that ITID will have more impact, a richer and more collaborative online environment, and will be better able to serve a world-wide epistemic community. The entire ITID team - including the editorial office, the MIT Press, and the Georgia Tech Library - will together help define the future of scholarly publication."

Dr. Michael Best
Sam Nunn School of International Affairs and the College of Computing
Co-founder and Co-Editor-in-Chief, Information Technologies and International Development

ACCESSIBILITY | CONTACT US | GT HOME

GT Library :: 704 Cherry Street :: Atlanta, GA 30332-0900 :: phone: (404) 894-4529 or 1-888-225-7804

INDIANA UNIVERSITY BLOOMINGTON
Institute for Digital Arts and Humanities
http://www.indiana.edu/~idah/

Kyou   Email   Blackboard   Enroll & Pay
KU Home   A-Z ▼

Institute for Digital Research in the Humanities

IDRH Home   About IDRH   Calendar   CoLang 2012   Digital Humanities Seminar   Representing Knowledge Conference   Seed Grants
News and Announcements

About IDRH

The Institute for Digital Research in the Humanities provides resources and training in the practices and tools of the digital humanities, facilitating interdisciplinary academic collaborations and innovative externally-funded research.

The Institute is supported through a partnership of the University of Kansas Libraries, the Hall Center for the Humanities and the College of Liberal Arts and Sciences.

Goals

The goal of the Institute for Digital Research in the Humanities is to prepare and support faculty and graduate students as they explore and use computing technology to advance humanistic scholarship across disciplines. The IDRH will enhance the possibilities that digital technologies present to humanities research by:

1. Providing opportunities for faculty and graduate students to learn about the use of technology for humanistic inquiry, and stimulating ongoing discussions about relationships between technologies and human experience;
2. Supporting the development or novel use of digital tools and practices for innovative humanities research, including collaborative and interdisciplinary research;
3. Assisting scholars to explore new and emerging models of digital research, publishing, and peer-review;
4. Providing a knowledge base and the training for faculty to successfully pursue external grant awards, particularly in computationally-assisted research;
5. Working with faculty, departmental leadership, promotion and tenure committees, and KU administration to generate a series of dialogues about the transformation occurring in humanities scholarship, and the implications for digital research contributions and their evaluation; and
6. Providing a forum for scholarly innovation, as well as for discussions between faculty, departmental leadership, promotion and tenure committees, and KU administration about the implications of the transformations in digital scholarship on their evaluation.

IDRH Co-Directors

Arienne Dwyer
Dr. Arienne M. Dwyer is an Associate Professor of Linguistic Anthropology, and an affiliate in with Linguistics and Indigenous Nations Studies. She works in language documentation and technology, and is currently directing three NSF-sponsored research projects. She is Co-Director (with Professor Carlos Nash) of the upcoming Co-Lang: Institute for Language Research, to be held at KU in June and July of 2012.

Brian Rosenblum
Brian Rosenblum is Associate Librarian for Digital Scholarship at the University of Kansas Libraries, where he has administrative, production and outreach responsibilities in support of a variety of digital initiatives and publishing services. Prior to joining KU Libraries' digital initiatives program in 2005 Brian worked at the Scholarly Publishing Office at the University Library, University of Michigan, where he helped develop numerous electronic journals and digital scholarly projects. In 2003-04 Brian was a Fulbright Scholar in the Czech Republic. He was a Keeler Family Intra-University Professor at the Spencer Museum of Art during the Fall 2010 semester.

About IDRH

Goals

People

Contact

Arienne Dwyer
Co-director,
Institute for Digital Research in the Humanities
Associate Professor,
Anthropology
☎ 785-864-2649
email: anthlinguist AT ku DOT edu

Brian Rosenblum
Co-director,
Institute for Digital Research in the Humanities
Associate Librarian,
KU Libraries
☎ 785-864-8883
✉ brianlee@ku.edu

Past IDRH Events

THATCamp Kansas
(September 2011)

Digital Jumpstart Workshops
(March 2011)

New Scholarly Texts, New Scholarly Practices: A Discussion with Kathleen Fitzpatrick
(February 2011)

Related Links

KU Libraries Center for Digital Scholarship

IDRH Partners

KU Libraries

Hall Center for the Humanities

College of Liberal Arts and Sciences

University of Miami Digital Scholarship and Programs: Overview

In the University of Miami Libraries' Department of Digital Scholarship and Programs, scholars, technologists, librarians, and archivists collaboratively explore creative applications of digital media and web technology to the future of research, teaching, and learning. The department leads initiatives that result in sustainable creative tools for digital scholarship, make unique materials available on the web, and facilitate the meaningful use of new media in scholarly research.

Digital Scholarship

In 2010, the University of Miami Libraries and the College of Arts and Sciences received a grant from the Andrew W. Mellon Foundation to rebuild the technical and organizational infrastructure for the Cuban Theater Digital Archive (CTDA, http://scholar.library.miami.edu/archivoteatral/), a unique digital collection of Cuban theater materials. The CTDA is a resource for teaching, learning, and research in Cuban theater and performance as well as in related fields; a community repository for important Cuban theatrical materials; and a forum to foster scholarly communication in this field. The department of Digital Scholarship and Programs is leading the development of a technical platform to support the CTDA for scholars and students in the College of Arts and Sciences, and is interested in similar strategic partnerships across the university community and beyond to expand the impact of contemporary scholarship on the web. A beta version of the new system will be made available on the web in late 2011.

Digital Reproduction

The department of Digital Scholarship and Programs houses a Digital Production Lab specializing in the conversion of unique materials held in the university's archives and special collections to digital format. Trained in digital imaging and audio and video conversion, the lab's technicians reproduce print and visual materials, audio recordings, and videos, in digital format for purposes of long-term preservation and accessibility on the web. Many of these unique materials can be browsed and searched online in the University of Miami Libraries' Digital Collections (http://merrick.library.miami.edu/).

New Media

To support the use of new media by scholars, librarians, and archivists, the Department of Digital Scholarship and Programs provides extensive outreach in its areas of expertise. This includes consultations to faculty on using new media in teaching and research, workshops, and the development of open source software for program needs.

NORTHWESTERN UNIVERSITY

Digital Collections Department

http://www.library.northwestern.edu/about/library-administration/departments-offices/digital-collections

ASK A LIBRARIAN   HOURS   OFF-CAMPUS ACCESS   FAQ   CONTACT

Try our new search tool...

more for Friday, October 28

Find Materials   Libraries & Collections   Research & Instruction   Services   News & Events   About

Home » About » Library Administration » Departments & Offices » Digital Collections

DEPARTMENTS & OFFICES

Academic Liaison Services
Administrative Services Division
Acquisitions and Rapid Cataloging
Bibliographic Services
Business & Finance
Circulation Services
Collections Services Division
Digital Collections
  Overview
  Staff
  Digitization Services
  Equipment Checkout
  Digital Image Library
  Training and Media Lab
E-Resources & Collection Analysis
Library Technology Division
Personnel Office
Preservation
Public Services Division
Reference Department
Resource Sharing and Reserve
Special Libraries Division
Oak Grove Library Center

RELATED NEWS

Upcoming Workshops
Upcoming workshops and presentations sponsored by Digital Collections
Commedia dell'Arte Website Launches
Interact with Fava Masks online!
New Digital Tool
Search collection finding aids online using the Archival and Manuscript Collections Portal
New equipment and checkout procedures from Digital Collections
New audio, photo and video equipment available to faculty, graduate students and staff from the Digital Collections department.

more news

Digital Collections Department

Digital Collections Department advances the University's teaching and research mission by providing digitization services and support to Northwestern faculty and graduate students. We partner with other Library and University departments to provide these services and to undertake special digitization projects that bring Northwestern's unique and rare collections to researchers around the world. While digital content production is at the heart of the Digital Collections Department, we are also firmly committed to instruction, training and user support.

Within the Marjorie I. Mitchell Digital Media Center, Digital Collections-2E Production provides digitization services, including audio and video streaming, slide scanning, audio production and special projects, for Northwestern faculty, staff and graduate students. In addition, the Kirtas scanning initiative digitizes out-of-copyright books from the Library's collections, including brittle books, ensuring broad access to their contents.

The Digital Collections-2E Digital Media Lab provides production equipment and instruction on various hardware and software applications. Though it is primarily a Mac lab, the Library's only public optical character recognition text scanner (running on a Windows PC) is also available here. The most common training and production requests in the lab are for video editing, audio editing, DVD burning, text scanning and slide scanning. Instruction is available to faculty, staff and graduate students who wish to explore new modes of research and presentation.

Digital Collections Department staff also works with the Digital Library Committee to identify and manage digital library projects. Eighteen digital library projects are currently available through the Digitized Collections page.

HOURS

Digital Collections
Fall Quarter
(09/20/2011 - 11/27/2011)
Mon-Fri: 8:30 AM - 5:00 PM
Thanksgiving Break Hours:
11/23 8:30 AM to 5:00 PM.
11/24 to 11/25 Closed.
11/26 10:00 AM to 2:00 PM.
11/27 10:00 AM to Midnight.
Click here for future dates

LOCATION

Level 2, East Tower
Main Library
1970 N. Campus Drive
Evanston, Illinois 60208

CONTACTS

Digital Collections
+1 (847) 467 1080
digitalcollections@northwestern.edu

COLLECTIONS & EXHIBITS

ARTstor
Digital Image Library (MDID)
Digitized Collections
Northwestern BOOKS

QUICKLINKS

Guide to Streaming Media
Image Request Form
RealPlayer Troubleshooting
Scholarly Resources and Technology Series
Special Libraries Division
Streaming Request Form

CONTACT   DISCLAIMER   POLICY STATEMENTS   NU CAMPUS EMERGENCY INFORMATION

Library Home | Northwestern Calendar: PlanIt Purple | Northwestern Search

NORTHWESTERN UNIVERSITY

Northwestern University Library   1970 Campus Drive   Evanston, IL 60208-2300   Evanston: 847.491.7658   Fax: 847.491.8306   library@northwestern.edu

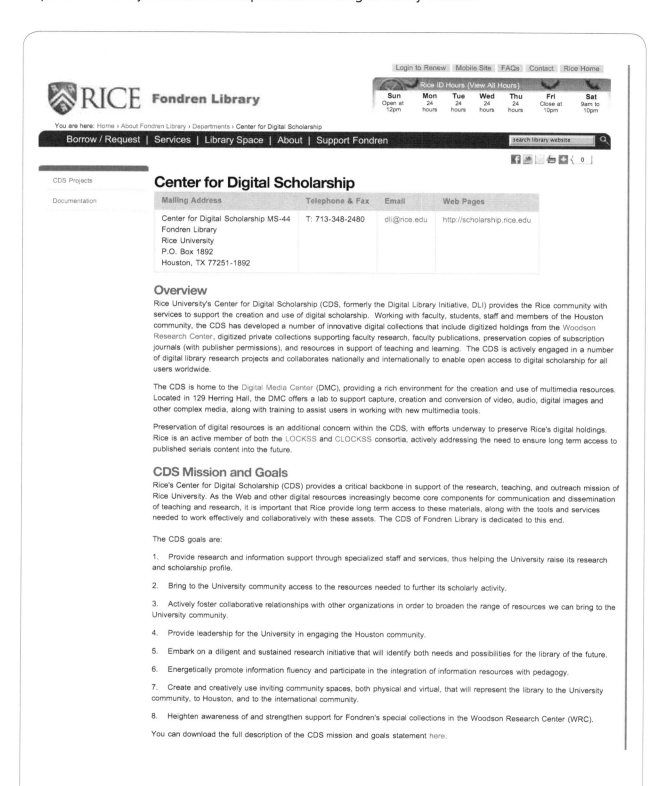

Center for Digital Scholarship

Mailing Address	Telephone & Fax	Email	Web Pages
Center for Digital Scholarship MS-44 Fondren Library Rice University P.O. Box 1892 Houston, TX 77251-1892	T: 713-348-2480	dli@rice.edu	http://scholarship.rice.edu

Overview

Rice University's Center for Digital Scholarship (CDS, formerly the Digital Library Initiative, DLI) provides the Rice community with services to support the creation and use of digital scholarship. Working with faculty, students, staff and members of the Houston community, the CDS has developed a number of innovative digital collections that include digitized holdings from the Woodson Research Center, digitized private collections supporting faculty research, faculty publications, preservation copies of subscription journals (with publisher permissions), and resources in support of teaching and learning. The CDS is actively engaged in a number of digital library research projects and collaborates nationally and internationally to enable open access to digital scholarship for all users worldwide.

The CDS is home to the Digital Media Center (DMC), providing a rich environment for the creation and use of multimedia resources. Located in 129 Herring Hall, the DMC offers a lab to support capture, creation and conversion of video, audio, digital images and other complex media, along with training to assist users in working with new multimedia tools.

Preservation of digital resources is an additional concern within the CDS, with efforts underway to preserve Rice's digital holdings. Rice is an active member of both the LOCKSS and CLOCKSS consortia, actively addressing the need to ensure long term access to published serials content into the future.

CDS Mission and Goals

Rice's Center for Digital Scholarship (CDS) provides a critical backbone in support of the research, teaching, and outreach mission of Rice University. As the Web and other digital resources increasingly become core components for communication and dissemination of teaching and research, it is important that Rice provide long term access to these materials, along with the tools and services needed to work effectively and collaboratively with these assets. The CDS of Fondren Library is dedicated to this end.

The CDS goals are:

1. Provide research and information support through specialized staff and services, thus helping the University raise its research and scholarship profile.

2. Bring to the University community access to the resources needed to further its scholarly activity.

3. Actively foster collaborative relationships with other organizations in order to broaden the range of resources we can bring to the University community.

4. Provide leadership for the University in engaging the Houston community.

5. Embark on a diligent and sustained research initiative that will identify both needs and possibilities for the library of the future.

6. Energetically promote information fluency and participate in the integration of information resources with pedagogy.

7. Create and creatively use inviting community spaces, both physical and virtual, that will represent the library to the University community, to Houston, and to the international community.

8. Heighten awareness of and strengthen support for Fondren's special collections in the Woodson Research Center (WRC).

You can download the full description of the CDS mission and goals statement here.

RICE UNIVERSITY
Center for Digital Scholarship
http://fondrenlibrary.rice.edu/about/departments/CDS/digital-library-initiative/

The following are a few of the digital collections that are part of the Digital Library Initiative:

- Rice Digital Scholarship Archive (RDSA) for housing several digital collections
- TIMEA (Travelers in the Middle East Archive)
- Our Americas Archive Partnership (OAAP)
- The Connexions project
- The Shoah Archive at Rice
- Advanced Placement Digital Library (APDL)
- Learning Science and Technology Repository (LESTER)
- Rice University Theses and Dissertations
- The Rice Institute Pamphlets
- Digital Research Tools (DiRT) wiki

Our Team

- Geneva Henry
- Sid Byrd
- Ying Jin
- Nadalia Liu
- Monica Rivero
- Lisa Spiro
- Jane Zhao

Physical Address: 6100 Main Street, Houston, Texas 77005

Mailing Address: MS-44, P.O. Box 1892, Houston, Texas 77251-1892

Phone: 713-348-5698 | © 2011 Rice University | Maps + Directions

Accessibility   Contact   Libstaff

RUTGERS UNIVERSITY
Scholarly Communication Center
http://www.scc.rutgers.edu/scchome/

Scholarly Communication Center

We provide State of the Art Conference/Teaching/Training Facilities

**Welcome to the Scholarly Communication Center
in the Rutgers University Libraries.**

The SCC, a department of Technical and Automated Services, supports the development and integration of scholarly / scientific / educational information into the mainstream through a wide range of innovative digital services:

- State-of-the-art conference, teaching, and training facilities
- Digital project research and development
- Humanities and Social Science Data Services
- Digital information services
- Hosted Digital Projects

For additional information about using SCC facilities or developing digital content, contact Rhonda Marker, Head, SCC.

Digital Projects Highlights

RUcore
RUcore -the Rutgers Community Repository- is a digital repository for the significant intellectual property of Rutgers University-its libraries, faculty and their collaborators.

New Jersey Digital Highway
A portal to information about New Jersey from the collections of public information providers in New Jersey: libraries, museums, archives, historical societies, public broadcasting, schools, and more.

New Jersey Environmental Digital Library
The NJEDL is an online library of environmental literature and multimedia related to New Jersey. The collection includes documents and reports, scientific studies, photographs, videos, maps, and more.

Medieval and Early Modern Databank
The MEMDB provides an expanding library of information on European History circa 800-1815 C.E.

Eagleton Public Opinion Polls
Providing access to survey data from Eagleton's quarterly statewide polls on matters of political and social interest.

Navigation menu (left sidebar):
- Search SCC
- More About Search SCC
- SCC Home
- About The SCC
- Event Facilities
- Data Services
- Digital Services
- Digital Projects
- Hours, Directions & Contacts
- Book Room
- Library Home
- Rutgers Homepage

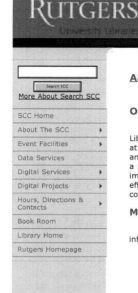

About the Scholarly Communication Center

http://www.scc.rutgers.edu/scchome/about/aboutus.cfm

RUTGERS
University Libraries

Search SCC

More About Search SCC

- SCC Home
- About The SCC
- Event Facilities
- Data Services
- Digital Services
- Digital Projects
- Hours, Directions & Contacts
- Book Room
- Library Home
- Rutgers Homepage

About the Scholarly Communication Center

Overview

The Scholarly Communication Center (SCC) represents a major commitment of the Rutgers University Libraries to the publishing and integration of electronic resources into the mainstream of intellectual activity at Rutgers University. Networked access to scholarly information and computer-based methods for research and teaching are central to all activities in the modern university. The Scholarly Communication Center plays a major role in providing the tools and platforms for digital libraries and publishing unique materials that are important for the Libraries and the Rutgers community as a whole. The SCC seeks to establish collaborative efforts with academic departments and other institutions to deliver electronic information to all the communities served by Rutgers University.

Mission

The mission of the Scholarly Communication Center (SCC) is to promote access to scholarly and scientific information by:

- developing and providing open access to digital content and services;
- deploying digital technology to identify, collect and preserve the intellectual assets of Rutgers University, its scholars, and the State of New Jersey;
- facilitating and supporting teaching and training by creating and maintaining a technology-rich learning environment.

The SCC mission is developed in accordance with the **Rutgers University Libraries' Digital Library Initiative**.

Frequently Asked Questions

Q. How do I book the SCC facilities?
A. To book the SCC facilities call **Bill Puglisi, Program Coordinator** (732-932-7129, x174).

Before contacting the program coordinator, please do the following:

- Visit the **Event Facilities** web page to see which of our facilities best meet your events needs.
- Visit the **New Brunswick Libraries Room Use Schedule** web site to see if the facilities that determine if the room(s) that meet(s) your need(s) is / are available on the day of your event.
- Please be explicit when stating the needs of your event. If you know that you need a certain software title or browser plugin and you do not see it listed on the event facilities web page, please state that you need it on this form.

RUTGERS
University Libraries

LOGIN HERE ①   ASK A LIBRARIAN   HOURS & DIRECTIONS   SEARCH SITE   SITE INDEX   FACULTY SERVICES   MY ACCOUNT

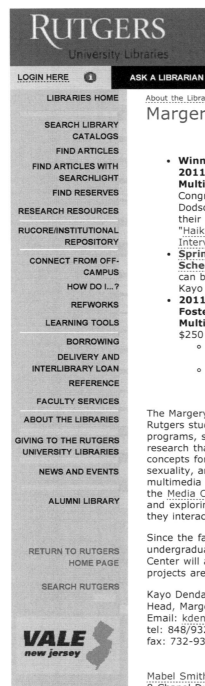

LIBRARIES HOME

SEARCH LIBRARY CATALOGS

FIND ARTICLES

FIND ARTICLES WITH SEARCHLIGHT

FIND RESERVES

RESEARCH RESOURCES

RUCORE/INSTITUTIONAL REPOSITORY

CONNECT FROM OFF-CAMPUS

HOW DO I...?

REFWORKS

LEARNING TOOLS

BORROWING

DELIVERY AND INTERLIBRARY LOAN

REFERENCE

FACULTY SERVICES

ABOUT THE LIBRARIES

GIVING TO THE RUTGERS UNIVERSITY LIBRARIES

NEWS AND EVENTS

ALUMNI LIBRARY

RETURN TO RUTGERS HOME PAGE

SEARCH RUTGERS

VALE new jersey

About the Libraries: Libraries & Digital Centers:

Margery Somers Foster Center

Kayo Denda leading an interview workshop

- **Winning videos for the 2011 Undergraduate Multimedia Award**. Congratulations to Tiffany Dodson and Mimi Zander for their projects "Cameo" and "Haiku" and "Inked: an Interview with Alison Bechdel"
- **Spring 2011 Workshop Schedule** (additional sessions can be arranged by contacting Kayo Denda)
- **2011 Margery Somers Foster Undergraduate Multimedia Award** (Two $250 awards)
  - Award Application Overview and Form
  - Award Brochure [PDF]

The Margery Somers Foster Center of Rutgers University Libraries strives to enable Rutgers students to build their leadership skills. Through the Foster Center's creative programs, students have the opportunity to engage in critical analysis and innovative research that enhances their academic experience. The programs also explore concepts for better understanding into alternative accounts of race, gender and sexuality, and power dynamics. Additionally, the Foster Center cultivates students' multimedia skills by utilizing the library resources, in particular the media resources at the Media Center and the capabilities of the Sharon Fordham Multimedia Laboratory, and exploring the dimensions of new media, and media technologies and cultures, as they interact with gender.

Since the fall of 2010, the Foster Center is offering two pilot workshops to Rutgers undergraduate students, one in multimedia skills, and one in interview practices. The Center will also sponsor two Undergraduate Multimedia Awards. The center's past projects are available here.

Kayo Denda
Head, Margery Somers Foster Center & Women's Studies Librarian
Email: kdenda@rci.rutgers.edu
tel: 848/932-5023
fax: 732-932-6777

Mabel Smith Douglass Library
8 Chapel Drive

RUTGERS
University Libraries

LOGIN HERE
LIBRARIES HOME

SEARCH LIBRARY CATALOGS
FIND ARTICLES
FIND ARTICLES WITH SEARCHLIGHT
FIND RESERVES

RESEARCH RESOURCES

RUCORE/INSTITUTIONAL REPOSITORY

CONNECT FROM OFF-CAMPUS
HOW DO I...?
REFWORKS
LEARNING TOOLS

BORROWING
DELIVERY AND INTERLIBRARY LOAN
REFERENCE

FACULTY SERVICES

ABOUT THE LIBRARIES

GIVING TO THE RUTGERS UNIVERSITY LIBRARIES

NEWS AND EVENTS

ALUMNI LIBRARY

RETURN TO RUTGERS HOME PAGE

SEARCH RUTGERS

VALE
new jersey

ASK A LIBRARIAN   HOURS & DIRECTIONS   SEARCH SITE   SITE INDEX   FACULTY SERVICES   MY ACCOUNT

About the Libraries: Libraries and Centers: Sharon A. Fordham Multimedia - Resource Laboratory:

Sharon A. Fordham
Multimedia Resource Laboratory

Statement of Purpose and General Terms of Use

The Sharon A. Fordham Multimedia Lab, based at the Douglass Library, has twelve computers intended for both the creation and manipulation of multimedia projects. It is a library resource, intended for use by members of the Rutgers University Community including students, faculty, administrators and staff. The lab is not an instructional space, cannot be reserved for ongoing classes, and is not configured to support instruction sessions for classes. It is a lab for individual users to create multimedia projects and materials in support of the academic programs at Rutgers University.

Recognizing that the lab is a shared resource for the Rutgers community, and that working with digital multimedia materials requires extraordinary computing and time resources, Rutgers University Libraries has developed specific policies and guidelines to help ensure access to these resources to the broader community as necessary. These specific guidelines include the Sharon A. Fordham Multimedia Lab User Responsibilities [PDF], and the Rutgers University Libraries Copyright and Fair Use Statement [PDF] which are available for review at the lab, upon request and online.

For more information, please contact Jane Sloan, jsloan@rci.rutgers.edu

Welcome

A Thank You to Sharon A. Fordham

Fordham Lab Resources

Last updated September 2008; February 2009; July 2010
URL: http://www.libraries.rutgers.edu/rul/libs/fordham/terms_use.shtml
Website Feedback | Privacy Policy
Copyright © 2011, Rutgers, The State University of New Jersey   (Further Copyright Information)

UNIVERSITY OF SOUTH CAROLINA
Center for Digital Humanities
http://cdh.sc.edu/

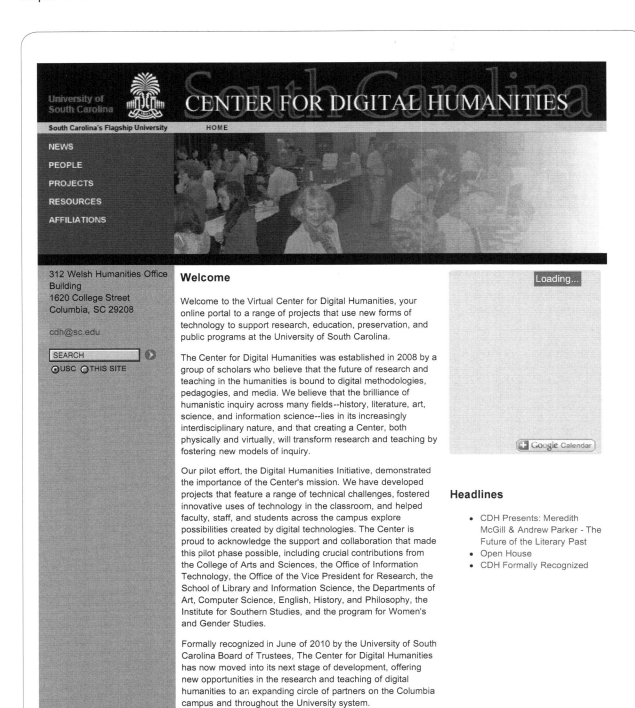

University of
South Carolina

South Carolina's Flagship University

CENTER FOR DIGITAL HUMANITIES

HOME

NEWS

PEOPLE

PROJECTS

RESOURCES

AFFILIATIONS

312 Welsh Humanities Office
Building
1620 College Street
Columbia, SC 29208

cdh@sc.edu

SEARCH
USC   THIS SITE

Welcome

Welcome to the Virtual Center for Digital Humanities, your online portal to a range of projects that use new forms of technology to support research, education, preservation, and public programs at the University of South Carolina.

The Center for Digital Humanities was established in 2008 by a group of scholars who believe that the future of research and teaching in the humanities is bound to digital methodologies, pedagogies, and media. We believe that the brilliance of humanistic inquiry across many fields--history, literature, art, science, and information science--lies in its increasingly interdisciplinary nature, and that creating a Center, both physically and virtually, will transform research and teaching by fostering new models of inquiry.

Our pilot effort, the Digital Humanities Initiative, demonstrated the importance of the Center's mission. We have developed projects that feature a range of technical challenges, fostered innovative uses of technology in the classroom, and helped faculty, staff, and students across the campus explore possibilities created by digital technologies. The Center is proud to acknowledge the support and collaboration that made this pilot phase possible, including crucial contributions from the College of Arts and Sciences, the Office of Information Technology, the Office of the Vice President for Research, the School of Library and Information Science, the Departments of Art, Computer Science, English, History, and Philosophy, the Institute for Southern Studies, and the program for Women's and Gender Studies.

Formally recognized in June of 2010 by the University of South Carolina Board of Trustees, The Center for Digital Humanities has now moved into its next stage of development, offering new opportunities in the research and teaching of digital humanities to an expanding circle of partners on the Columbia campus and throughout the University system.

Please feel free to explore the virtual Center and to contact me should you have any questions.

Sincerely,

Loading...

Google Calendar

Headlines

- CDH Presents: Meredith McGill & Andrew Parker - The Future of the Literary Past
- Open House
- CDH Formally Recognized

David Lee Miller

Founding Member and Director, Center for Digital Humanities
Carolina Distinguished Professor of English and Comparative
Literature

Mission

The Center for Digital Humanities at South Carolina supports
innovations in the use of digital technology for research,
teaching, and public outreach in the Humanities and related
disciplines. Our primary mission is to collaborate with faculty in
developing research proposals for external funding, but we
supplement this core objective with efforts to promote
awareness of digital technologies among humanities faculty, to
initiate courses and curricula in the digital humanities, and to
provide students with opportunities for hands-on experience
working with sponsored projects.

Goals

The Center's goals stem directly from its mission. We believe
that the Humanities are entering a period of major innovation,
and our goal is to help place faculty at South Carolina in the
forefront of disciplinary change. We seek as well to provide
graduate and undergraduate students in a wide range of fields
with skills they will need in an era of rapid technological
growth. To achieve these goals, the Center is dedicated to
creating the technical and human infrastructure necessary to
support interdisciplinary collaboration on digital research
projects.

| RETURN TO TOP | USC LINKS: | DIRECTORY | MAP | EVENTS | VIP | SITE INFORMATION |

312 Welsh Humanities Office Building, Columbia, SC 29208 • cdh@sc.edu

© University of South Carolina Board of Trustees

UNIVERSITY OF VIRGINIA
Scholars' Lab
http://www2.lib.virginia.edu/scholarslab/

SEARCH: [   ] [Go]

SCHOLARS' LAB
Works in Progress

ABOUT US
BLOG
PROJECTS
CONTRIBUTORS
ALUMNI PROJECTS
FEED

About Us

Searching for the real Scholars' Lab home page, with info about our digital resources, rooms and equipment, and consultative services? **Find it on the UVA Library website.**

About this Blog

The **Scholars' Lab** was established in 2006 at **UVA Library** as a site for innovation in the humanities and social sciences. The idea was to combine the resources and expertise of the Library's successful *Electronic Text* (Etext) and *Geospatial and Statistical Data* (GeoStat) centers with that of UVA's *Research Computing Support Group* in a physical space that promotes collaboration and experimentation. Now we're extending the conversations that happen in our offices and in the Lab to a wider forum.

This blog will trace the activities of our **Graduate Fellows in Digital Humanities** and staff, in collaboration with scholars from a variety of disciplines and fields. Over the coming months, we'll be inviting our Fellows, grad student consultants, **Scholars' Lab faculty and staff**, visiting scholars, and UVA collaborators to share this blog and make it their own.

Digital Research and Scholarship at UVA Library

The **Scholars' Lab** caters to the research, digitization, and online editing needs of faculty and students in the humanities and social sciences. Staffed with friendly, expert consultants from UVA Library's **Digital Research and Scholarship** department and ITC's **Research Computing Support Group**, the Scholars' Lab is the perfect place to take your digital humanities scholarship and social science research to the next level. **UVA Library** also plays host to **IATH**, **VCDH**, and **SHANTI**.

The Scholars' Lab has two sister spaces which (together with the **Digital Curation Services** department) make up the Library's network of support for digital research, scholarship, and production. These are the **Research Computing Lab** in Brown Science and Engineering Library and the **Digital Media Lab** in the Robertson Media Center of Clemons Library.

Collaborate, Iterate, Discuss

If you just can't get enough of the **SLab**, please come and visit our bright, airy space on the 4th floor of Alderman Library! The Scholars' Lab was designed for both collaborative and solo work, with room for small, collaborative groups and larger classes. We regularly host **events** such as talks, workshops, and brown-bag lunches on topics of interest in humanities computing and social science research. Our regular "Digital Therapy" luncheons are a fun opportunity to meet like-minded folks and hear more about our **graduate fellowships** in digital humanities. Drop by or us **send us a message**! We're eager to partner with you on projects large and small.

About
Here we trace works in progress and research interests of faculty, staff, student consultants, and graduate fellows affiliated with the Scholars' Lab at the University of Virginia Library.

Needless to say, their opinions are their own. The real Scholars' Lab home page is elsewhere.

Categories
Praxis Program
Digital Humanities
Announcements
Geospatial and Temporal
Visualization and Data Mining

Archives
October 2011
September 2011
August 2011
July 2011
More...

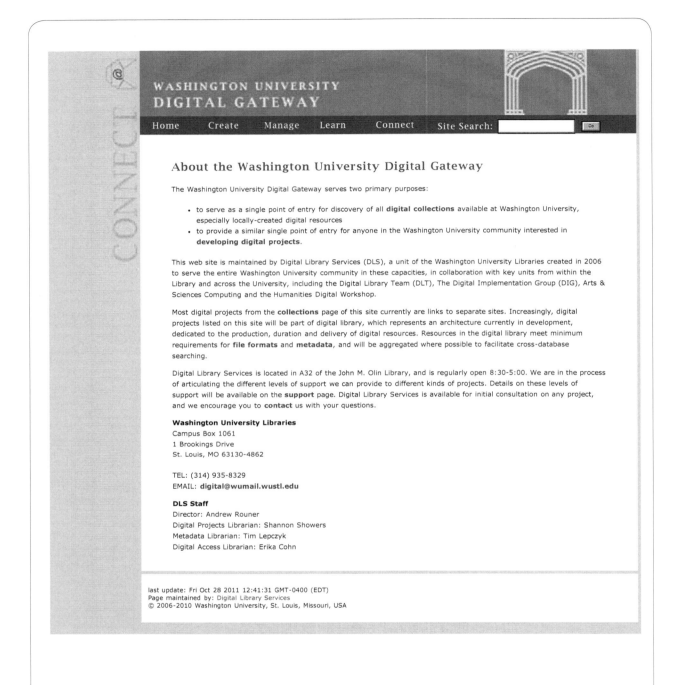

WASHINGTON UNIVERSITY
DIGITAL GATEWAY

Home   Create   Manage   Learn   Connect   Site Search: [   ] Go

About the Washington University Digital Gateway

The Washington University Digital Gateway serves two primary purposes:

- to serve as a single point of entry for discovery of all **digital collections** available at Washington University, especially locally-created digital resources
- to provide a similar single point of entry for anyone in the Washington University community interested in **developing digital projects**.

This web site is maintained by Digital Library Services (DLS), a unit of the Washington University Libraries created in 2006 to serve the entire Washington University community in these capacities, in collaboration with key units from within the Library and across the University, including the Digital Library Team (DLT), The Digital Implementation Group (DIG), Arts & Sciences Computing and the Humanities Digital Workshop.

Most digital projects from the **collections** page of this site currently are links to separate sites. Increasingly, digital projects listed on this site will be part of digital library, which represents an architecture currently in development, dedicated to the production, duration and delivery of digital resources. Resources in the digital library meet minimum requirements for **file formats** and **metadata**, and will be aggregated where possible to facilitate cross-database searching.

Digital Library Services is located in A32 of the John M. Olin Library, and is regularly open 8:30-5:00. We are in the process of articulating the different levels of support we can provide to different kinds of projects. Details on these levels of support will be available on the **support** page. Digital Library Services is available for initial consultation on any project, and we encourage you to **contact** us with your questions.

Washington University Libraries
Campus Box 1061
1 Brookings Drive
St. Louis, MO 63130-4862

TEL: (314) 935-8329
EMAIL: **digital@wumail.wustl.edu**

DLS Staff
Director: Andrew Rouner
Digital Projects Librarian: Shannon Showers
Metadata Librarian: Tim Lepczyk
Digital Access Librarian: Erika Cohn

last update: Fri Oct 28 2011 12:41:31 GMT-0400 (EDT)
Page maintained by: Digital Library Services
© 2006-2010 Washington University, St. Louis, Missouri, USA

Services

EMORY UNIVERSITY
Digital Scholarship Commons
http://web.library.emory.edu/disc

DISC > ABOUT

Emory University's Digital Scholarship Commons (DiSC) offers faculty members and graduate students the space, expertise, and project management assistance they need to develop innovative multidisciplinary projects. Located in the Research Commons of the Robert W. Woodruff Library, DiSC will be formally launched in October 2011 with funding from the Andrew W. Mellon Foundation.

Whether working solo or as part of a group, DiSC patrons can:

▶ Build projects using the latest digital scholarship tools and software

▶ Partner with DiSC staff to add depth and insight to works of scholarship

▶ Connect with a community of scholars

▶ Reflect on the possibilities and challenges of these new technologies

DiSC employees hold advanced degrees in a variety of disciplines, and Emory Libraries' subject liaisons are available to assist DiSC patrons with their projects.

Among the help available to faculty and graduate students at the Digital Scholarship Commons is assistance with:

▶ Electronic text encoding

▶ Geographic information systems (GIS)

▶ Statistical analysis

▶ Scanning and graphics

UNIVERSITY OF FLORIDA
Digital Collection Services
http://digital.uflib.ufl.edu/digitalservices/

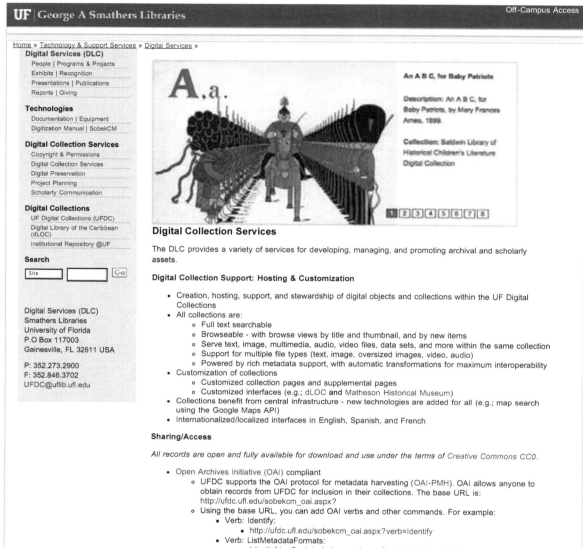

Digital Collection Services

The DLC provides a variety of services for developing, managing, and promoting archival and scholarly assets.

Digital Collection Support: Hosting & Customization

- Creation, hosting, support, and stewardship of digital objects and collections within the UF Digital Collections
- All collections are:
    - Full text searchable
    - Browseable - with browse views by title and thumbnail, and by new items
    - Serve text, image, multimedia, audio, video files, data sets, and more within the same collection
    - Support for multiple file types (text, image, oversized images, video, audio)
    - Powered by rich metadata support, with automatic transformations for maximum interoperability
- Customization of collections
    - Customized collection pages and supplemental pages
    - Customized interfaces (e.g.; dLOC and Matheson Historical Museum)
- Collections benefit from central infrastructure - new technologies are added for all (e.g.; map search using the Google Maps API)
- Internationalized/localized interfaces in English, Spanish, and French

Sharing/Access

All records are open and fully available for download and use under the terms of Creative Commons CC0.

- Open Archives Initiative (OAI) compliant
    - UFDC supports the OAI protocol for metadata harvesting (OAI-PMH). OAI allows anyone to obtain records from UFDC for inclusion in their collections. The base URL is: http://ufdc.ufl.edu/sobekcm_oai.aspx?
    - Using the base URL, you can add OAI verbs and other commands. For example:
        - Verb: Identify:
            - http://ufdc.ufl.edu/sobekcm_oai.aspx?verb=Identify
        - Verb: ListMetadataFormats:
            - http://ufdc.ufl.edu/sobekcm_oai.aspx?verb=ListMetadataFormats
        - Verb: ListSets:
            - http://ufdc.ufl.edu/sobekcm_oai.aspx?verb=ListSets
- URI's provide unique and constant links ready for bibliographic citation
- Records for all collections and items:
    - available as METS/MODS, MARCXML, and qualified Dublin Core
    - all formats are accessible online
    - a batch record feed in MARCXML is available here
    - all records and feeds include thumbnail icons. Catalogs can show the thumbnails along with records to greatly assist patrons in browsing and reviewing materials
    - RSS feeds for all items and all new items
- Worldwide reach via Google, Google Scholar, and other search engines
- Rooted in providing Open Access to archival and scholarly assets
- Notification tools for new content alerts via RSS
- Increase archival and scholarly assets' audience and access
- Image zoom and pan viewing capabilities

- Ability to serve a variety of organizational options for objects including:
  - hierarchical groupings allowing collocation by Area, topic, and geographical hierarchies for College, Department
  - monographic, page-turning functionality
  - multiple files connected to one descriptive record
  - one item, one record
  - mapping between various versions of a single work
  - journal volume, issue, title organization
- Broad, internationally applied description methods using METS/MODS Metadata
- Ability to apply controlled vocabularies and name headings

Scholarly Publications & Rights management

- Journal hosting with Open Journal System (OJS) at FCLA with all journals digitally preserved in FDA
- Authors remain the copyright holders
- Library requests right to distribute content
- Assist with understanding copyright status of work
- Creative Commons licensing capabilities
- Assist with mandatory deposit of electronic-only publications to the Library of Congress

Digitization of materials held by the Libraries

- Digitization equipment operated within a color managed environment for artifactual fidelity:
  - large format scanner for maps
  - slide scanner
  - open book scanner for fragile objects
  - high speed sheet feed scanner
  - flat bed scanners
  - digital photography studio for large or 3-D objects
- Digitization experts
- Software Suite - the Digitization Toolkit
  - Customizable Software Toolkit for contributing digitized materials
  - Digitization manual
  - Presentation about the Toolkit
- Publishing
  - Convert traditional publications into digital publications
  - Provide a means for born digital publication
- *For other materials: CITT Faculty Media Lab (pricelist)*

Digital Curation & Stewardship

- Internships (internship policy; available internships; internships with partners: Samuel Proctor Oral History Program)
- Content Knowledge & Outreach
- Collection Support & Processing
- Metadata Coordination
- Preservation & Archiving
  - Bit level archiving
  - Multiple redundant data back-ups provided
  - Migration of various formats supported
  - Ability to archive all format types
  - System interoperability
- Training on technologies for digital stewardship
- Digital curation for data sets
- Digital curation for digital scholarly works (following established guidelines to support evaluation)
- Digital humanities (speculative computing) project collaboration and supports; see example projects:
  - Curated online exhibits: by scholars and students with scholarly review
  - Digital Library of the Caribbean : Teaching Materials Collection: graduate humanities students developed materials as part of coursework)
  - Arts of Africa: curated online collection from library and museum materials, with related physical exhibit
  - Digital Vodou: curated scholarly archive of primary and research materials
  - Supporting interns, fellows, and visiting scholars
  - Collaborative support on projects (speculative; reflective; interpretive; analytical) and to support existing research enhanced with technology

Authors and Patrons

- myUFDC
  - self-submittal system for the UF Institutional Repository
  - user tools for saving searches, creating and sharing collections, and many others
- reference support by email, phone, and mail for all collections

Standards Compliant

- METS Metadata
- Digitization standards followed:
  - High resolution TIFFs or A/V for archiving
  - JPEG2000 format for viewing

Digital Collection Development, Project Management, and Post-Development Tools & Services

- Funding: Grants and assistance locating other funding opportunities
- Project Development Resources
  - Copyright and permissions
  - Digital Collection development template
  - Sample Operational Workflow for digitization (draft)
  - Information for potential partners
- Evaluation:
  - Online usage statistics provide usage counts overall, by collection, and by item
  - Annual usability studies
  - User feedback
- Promotion:
  - Collection Findable through main UFDC site, which is already optimized for search engines; through the UF Catalog; through WorldCat
  - Promoted through the UFDC Blog; through RSS feeds; through press releases and training classes
  - Development of promotional materials (brochures, exhibits, slideshows)
- Additional
  - Assistance available for loading to external sites (YouTube, Flickr) for promotion
  - New technologies benefit all when implemented

Last modified: Thursday September 22 2011 lnt

Share and bookmark:

Staff web | Staff Directory | Conduct in the library | Contact us | Privacy policy

Send suggestions and comments to ufdc@uflib.ufl.edu.

Digital Content Creation Services

Digital Content Creation offers the following services in support of the digitization of Library holdings:

- Project planning and consultation
- Full-book digitization
- Digitization of maps, images, letters, archival material, slides, microfiche, microfilm, filmstrips, and three dimensional objects
- Optical character recognition (OCR)
- OCR correction
- Color managed workflow
- Image processing
- PDF creation

Our partners include Digital Library Initiatives and Content Access Management.

Digital Content Creation also offers digital consulting and production services to campus faculty, staff, and graduate students through the Library's Scholarly Commons.

Equipment

- Digital cameras and copystands
- Large format Graphtec CS610 Pro scanner (for originals up to 42" wide)
- Epson GT 15000 flat bed scanner 11 x 17 with sheet feeder
- Plustek OptiBook A300 flat bed scanner 11 x 17 (book friendly)
- Wilkes & Wilson ScanStation FS300 microfiche scanner
- Nikon SuperCool Scan 4000 microfilm and slide scanner

Contact Us

UNIVERSITY OF NORTH CAROLINA AT CHAPEL HILL

Carolina Digital Library and Archives | Services

http://cdla.unc.edu/index.html?page=services

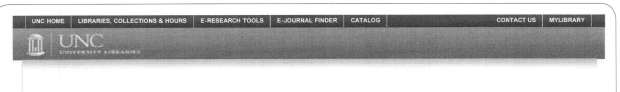

CAROLINA DIGITAL LIBRARY
AND ARCHIVES

CDLA Home
About Us
Services
Our Portfolio
Newsletter
Contact Us

Digital Publishing
Digital Production Center
Carolina Digital Repository

SERVICES

🖨 print this page

The Carolina Digital Library and Archives serves UNC Library staff, UNC faculty and other faculty affiliates, as well as other organizations by way of formal partnerships. Many of our services can be provided at no cost to you, but others require external support. Please contact us to discuss your ideas and needs. We look forward to working with you!

» Services by Function
» Services by Technology

Services by Function

DIGITIZATION

The CDLA's Digital Production Center maintains a wide range of equipment for the conversion of analog paper and photographic media to digital form. In this facility, we produce more than 1.5 million image files per year. We also provide knowledgeable referrals to other services for formats we do not have the ability to convert (such as microfilm, audio, and video), and for collections of material that would benefit from outsourcing of digitization.

DIGITAL PROJECT PLANNING AND MANAGEMENT

We offer a wide range of digital project planning and management services for placing library collections online and facilitating UNC faculty's digital research. CDLA staff will work with you to refine your ideas, explore technical and funding possibilities, and facilitate UNC Library collaboration on initiatives when appropriate. We can consult on rights issues and technology selection, as well as the formal articulation of functional requirements. For projects that are seeking grant funding, we can provide assistance with the writing of a proposal, helping to ensure the proposal document has the best chance of funding success. Once in-house, grant, or private support is obtained in support of a digital project, we can oversee or assist with the management of the many tasks necessary to produce high-quality digital resources. We can provide web and user experience design, workflow management, quality control, and general project management services, including day to day oversight of work done in support of a particular digital initiative.

DIGITAL COLLECTION DEVELOPMENT

CDLA staff use our expertise in digital data and online user experience to assist UNC affiliates with the collecting of digital resources in support of your collection, research, or instruction goals. Our current focus in this area is on the archiving of faculty research output into the Carolina Digital Repository.

CONSULTING

Even if the CDLA or the UNC Library isn't a partner on your digital initiative, we're happy to provide consulting in our areas of expertise, to help you ensure your work is as productive as it can be. We're here to provide feedback on your plans and documentation, point you to helpful resources, or simply bounce ideas off of.

PROFESSIONAL TRAINING

The CDLA is committed to increasing knowledge of digital library practice within UNC and the profession as a whole. We provide formal and informal support to those who aspire to work in this field, or who wish to become more involved in digital library efforts. We maintain a close relationship with the UNC School of Information and Library Science to help train the next generation of librarians, archivists, and information professionals.

Services by Technology

CAROLINA DIGITAL REPOSITORY

The Carolina Digital Repository is a repository for material in electronic formats produced by members of the University of North Carolina at Chapel Hill community. Its chief purpose is to provide for the long-term preservation of these materials. More information about CDR services can be found here.

CONTENTDM

CDLA staff provide assistance with creating and maintaining digital collections in the UNC Library's CONTENTdm digital asset management system. We can offer you support at all steps of this workflow, from the first project idea, to public launch, to ongoing additions to an online collection over time.

SCRIBE

We run 3 Scribe digitization stations provided by the Internet Archive for the mass digitization of bound paper materials. Digitized materials quickly appear online at the Internet Archive Ebook and Texts Archive.

Home | Hours | Search This Site | UNC Home | Privacy Policy

Website comments or questions: Carolina Digital Library and Archives
Suggestions on Library Services? Give us your feedback.
URL: http://cdla.unc.edu/index.html?page=services
This page was last updated Thursday, June 18, 2009.

UNIVERSITY OF VIRGINIA
What is the Scholars' Lab?
http://www2.lib.virginia.edu/scholarslab/about/

GIS Utilities

ERDAS IMAGINE

ArcView GIS

Street Map

Image Analyst

3D Analyst

Spatial Analyst

ArcGIS

ArcCatalog

ArcMap

ArcScene

ArcToolbox

Spatial Analyst

Geostatistical Analyst

3D Analyst

Graphics and Presentations

Adobe Photoshop

Adobe ImageReady

Microsoft PowerPoint

GeoExpress View (Mr. SID viewer)

Dreamweaver

Network Utilities (E-Mail, HomeDir, etc.)

Corporate Time for the Web

Exceed

Home Directory

Internet Explorer

Mulberry

Mozilla

Secure CRT

Secure FX

WinZip

Statistical Utilities

Access XP

Amos

Excel XP

Intercooled Stata

Lisrel/Prelis

Maple

Minitab

R

SAS

S-Plus

SPSS

Stat Transfer

Stata

Text Encoding, Scanning, and Word Processing

ABBYY FineReader OCR

Adobe Acrobat Professional

Acrobat Distiller

Microsoft Word

NoteTab

OmniPage Professional OCR

oXygen XML Editor

University of Virginia Library

PO Box 400113, Charlottesville, VA 22904-4113

ph: (434) 924-3021, fax: (434) 924-1431, library@virginia.edu

Libraries | Depts./Contacts | U.Va. Home | ITC

Website Feedback | Search | Questions? Ask a Librarian | Hours | Map | Policies | Press | Jobs

© 2007 by the Rector and Visitors of the University of Virginia

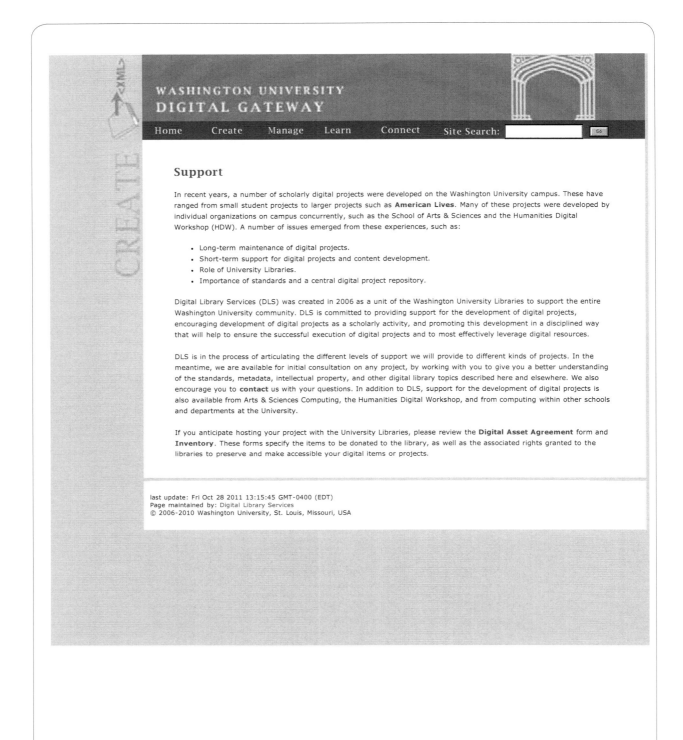

WASHINGTON UNIVERSITY DIGITAL GATEWAY

Home   Create   Manage   Learn   Connect   Site Search: [   ] [Go]

Support

In recent years, a number of scholarly digital projects were developed on the Washington University campus. These have ranged from small student projects to larger projects such as **American Lives**. Many of these projects were developed by individual organizations on campus concurrently, such as the School of Arts & Sciences and the Humanities Digital Workshop (HDW). A number of issues emerged from these experiences, such as:

- Long-term maintenance of digital projects.
- Short-term support for digital projects and content development.
- Role of University Libraries.
- Importance of standards and a central digital project repository.

Digital Library Services (DLS) was created in 2006 as a unit of the Washington University Libraries to support the entire Washington University community. DLS is committed to providing support for the development of digital projects, encouraging development of digital projects as a scholarly activity, and promoting this development in a disciplined way that will help to ensure the successful execution of digital projects and to most effectively leverage digital resources.

DLS is in the process of articulating the different levels of support we will provide to different kinds of projects. In the meantime, we are available for initial consultation on any project, by working with you to give you a better understanding of the standards, metadata, intellectual property, and other digital library topics described here and elsewhere. We also encourage you to **contact** us with your questions. In addition to DLS, support for the development of digital projects is also available from Arts & Sciences Computing, the Humanities Digital Workshop, and from computing within other schools and departments at the University.

If you anticipate hosting your project with the University Libraries, please review the **Digital Asset Agreement** form and **Inventory**. These forms specify the items to be donated to the library, as well as the associated rights granted to the libraries to preserve and make accessible your digital items or projects.

last update: Fri Oct 28 2011 13:15:45 GMT-0400 (EDT)
Page maintained by: Digital Library Services
© 2006-2010 Washington University, St. Louis, Missouri, USA

Policies and Procedures

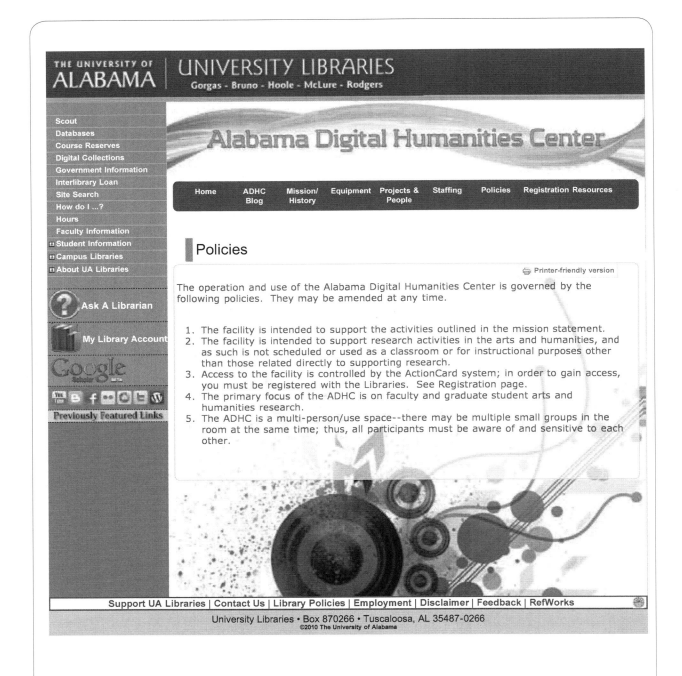

Columbia University *Libraries Digital Program*

Collection Digitization & Exhibition Program Procedures

Path: <u>Digital Library Projects</u> : <u>Collection Digitization</u> : **Procedures**

	[Complete Digital Project List A–Z]
Specific Project Tracks	**Applicable Documentation**

A. "Digital Project" Track. For projects that
 	
1. typically involve a complete collection or a significant part of a collection
2. involve more than ca. 150 simple images
3. will be of significant research or curricular value
4. will require and interface with more than simple browse functionality (e.g., specialized searching, browsable indexes)
5. involve content with complex relationships, (e.g., multipage documents, an image of a puppet linked to information about plays, productions, character types, and specific actors).
 	
(See section E below for audio-video preservation and access projects)
	Digital Project Track
	
	• Project proposal form: <u>doc</u> / <u>pdf</u>
	
	• <u>Project proposal procedures</u>
	
	• *Examples*
	   o <u>CUL Digitization Program Wiki</u>
	   o <u>Bunraku Collection</u>
	   o <u>NY Real Estate Brochures</u>

B. "Brick & Mortar + Online Exhibition" Track. For projects that 1. will be a physical exhibition accompanied by a simultaneous online version; or it 2. will be an online version of a past physical exhibition	**Online Exhibition Track** • Exhibition planning form: <u>doc</u> / <u>pdf</u> • <u>Exhibition planning checklist</u> • *Example* o <u>Plimpton Exhibition</u>
C. "Brick & Mortar Only" Track. For projects that 1. will make use of the Exhibition Support Software's features for organizing & planning the exhibition, generating pick lists, labels, etc.	**Brick & Mortar Only Exhibition Track** • Exhibition planning form: <u>doc</u> / <u>pdf</u> • <u>Exhibition planning checklist</u>

D. "Online (E-Only) Gallery" Track. For projects that
 	
1. typically will involve 150 or fewer simple images
2. is a sample or selection from one or more collections
3. no complex searching or browsing is required
4. involves chiefly objects that are simple, single part items **
5. has an unexpected, near-term deadline for presenting the content on the Web
6. will be adequately-served by Omeka software features and functionality
 	
**** *Textual / manuscript works:* If an otherwise gallery-oriented project also include one or more complete textual or manuscript works (e.g., <u>the Korean Independence Outbreak Movement</u>), the textual works should be digitized separately, presented in our ebook reader, and linked to from the exhibition display.
	Online Gallery Track
	
	• Gallery planning form: <u>doc</u> / <u>pdf</u>
	
	• <u>Gallery planning checklist</u>
	
	• *Examples*
	   o <u>Ambedkar</u>
	   o <u>Melting Pot</u>
	   o <u>Dramatic Museum Realia</u>
	   o <u>Butler 75</u>
	   o <u>Burroughs</u>
	   o <u>Wilbert Webster White</u>

E. Audio-Video Digitization Project	• <u>Project profile form</u>

Proposal Template for New Digital Collections & Projects

Subject Specialist/PI and Digital Services

Title:	*Project Title*
Date needed by & reason:	*Class, exhibit, donor request, no deadline*
Source of funds:	*Departmental endowments, donor, grant, etc.*
Holding Institution:	*UF Materials, digital acquisition/archiving*
Departmental priority:	
Project abstract:	*250-500 words covering the theme/subject area and purpose.*
Quantity / Scope of the project:	*Size and scope of what is being proposed for digitization.* *Type of material: photos, books, audio, video, etc* *Type of content: color pages, black and white, audio interviews, music* *Media Format: reel to reel, from microfilm, from slides, etc.* *Size: in inches for page size to determine if large format equipment is needed; and/or length in minutes for audio/video* *Uniqueness* *Condition: brittleness, preservation needs* *Copyright status* *Metadata available (catalog record, spreadsheet, none, etc.). Is there a title, author, and date for each item? If not, is there a finding guide with this information?*
Journals/Serials:	*Included in the exchange program?*
Copyright status:	*Public domain, permissions on file, etc.*
Connection to Existing Collections:	*How does this collection enhance existing library collections, departments or research at UF?*
Audience for the digital project:	*Which departments, colleges, and particular researchers at UF and in the state of Florida, in the region, worldwide?*
Possible partners:	*What other libraries or groups may be digitizing it or in partnering (local museums, public libraries, publishers, community groups)?*

	Is any of the material already digitized and online from potential partners?
Workload impact for your and other departments:	*Will Special Collections need to create a finding aid?* *Will Cataloging need to catalog materials? If so, how much will be original cataloging?* *Will the materials need Conservation work?* *What will the impact be for your department?*
How will users interact with the collection?	*In answering this, please explain any special needs for this project that are not supported by the current UF Digital Collections System. Please also explain any desires related to additional functionality. How would the project being proposed benefit from being mapped, in motion, data mined, etc?*
Resource commitment; initial and ongoing:	*Digital collection management requires collection creation, ongoing curation, and patron and partner assistance.*

Digital Services

Processing resources required:	*If internal, staff impact and OPS costs. Estimated processing timeline.* *If external, staff impact, OPS costs, vended costs, and shipping. Estimated processing timeline.*
Digital storage costs:	*Ongoing storage costs using the DataSpace model (2x the first year's costs to cover perpetual storage).*
Other requirements and impacts:	*Other requirements in terms of digital collection functionality (programming and web support), development scheduling changes, production scheduling changes, etc.*
New non-MARC collections	*Estimated requirements developed in collaboration with Cataloging for all records to be included in record feed to MANGO.*

The Co-Director will contact the applicant regarding the committee's decision.

- If IDAH and the applicant agree to work together, the applicant will work regularly with IDAH staff on iterations of the grant proposal or, if the project does not involve a grant application, on the workplan.
- IDAH staff will determine the costs to be charged for its work based on the finalized workplan, and these costs will be reflected in the proposal budget if the project is to be grant-supported.
- If the project is to be grant-supported and IDAH is not the unit submitting the proposal, the Co-Director must sign off on the proposal and budget before the applicant routes the budget and submits the proposal to the Office of Research Administration. If the Co-Director does not sign off on the final proposal and budget, IDAH cannot guarantee its participation if the applicant obtains the grant.

NOTE: The projects of current and past IDAH fellows will take priority when IDAH is considering collaborating on new projects. Since current IDAH fellows are working closely with IDAH staff on an ongoing basis, they do not need to submit a written proposal to the Co-Director.

COLLABORATE

Stay in touch

IDAH offers email updates regarding

- Upcoming brownbags
- IDAH Fellowship news
- Grants and Funding Opportunities

Click here to sign-up for IDAH e-mails, or here to manage your current subscriptions.

Site navigation

- Home
- Directory
- News and events
- Grants and funding opportunities
- Fellowships
- Collaborate

Syndicate

Click here for the IDAH RSS

Contact us

Herman B. Wells Library E170
1320 E. 10th St.
Bloomington, IN 47405
(812) 855-0829

UNIVERSITY OF MIAMI ⚘ LIBRARIES

Proposal for a Digital Initiative

Please complete the following questions. Thank you!

1. Project Leader

   - *Name:*
   - *Department:*
   - *Address:*
   - *Phone Number:*
   - *Email Address:*

2. Project Title:

3. Abstract of the project (a one paragraph description of project scope):

4. What are the desired goals of the project? (Please provide itemized list of deliverables):

5. Does the digital content in this project in any way represent materials that are currently available via the world wide web?

6. How will this project be funded? (Library, other UM Department or grant):

7. Please provide an outline of participants and their respective levels of engagement:

8. What resources can you provide for the project?

9. Who are the primary and secondary audiences for the project?

10. What will the access points for the project be?

University of Miami Libraries - Proposal for New Digital Initiatives – Digital Initiatives Team – 8/11/06   1

11. For projects with a digitization component, please provide the following information:

- *How many items will be digitized?*
- *What format is the content currently in?*
- *What is the desired output format?*
- *Have the materials been cataloged or inventoried in any way?*
  - *(If yes, please provide inventory list as attachment)*
- *What condition are the materials in?*

12. What is the intellectual property status of project content? Who is the rightful copyright holder?

13. What is the proposed timeline for this project?

14. How does this project support the teaching, learning, and research goals of the University of Miami?

15. If available, please provide the following:

- *Samples of project-related content*
- *A current CV*
- *Letters of support from relevant departmental representatives, administrators, or scholars*

Return this completed form to:

Kyle Rimkus
Digital Projects Librarian
kyle@miami.edu

University of Miami Libraries
Otto G. Richter Library
1300 Memorial Drive
Coral Gables, FL 33146

(305) 284 - 6221

University of Miami Libraries - Proposal for New Digital Initiatives – Digital Initiatives Team – 8/11/06   2

RICE UNIVERSITY
Guidelines for Digital Projects
http://library.rice.edu/about/departments/CDS/documentation

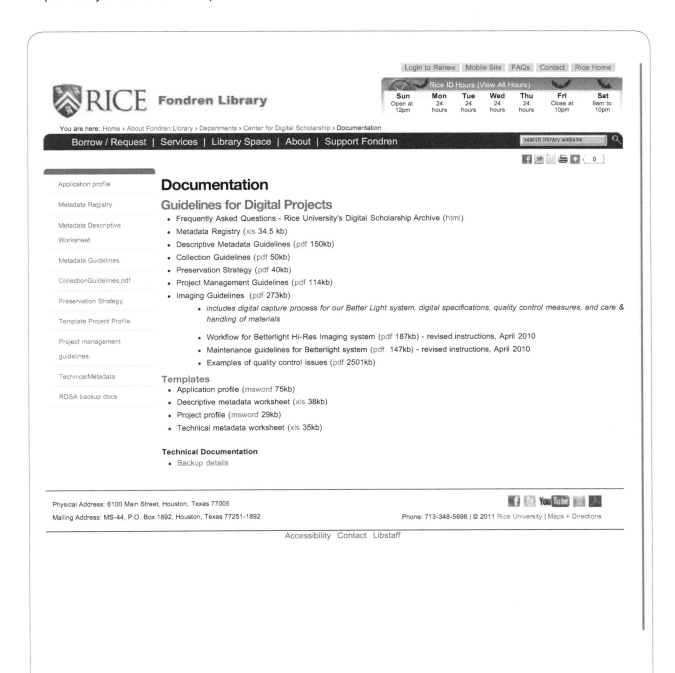

Digital Library Initiative

Rice University

Application Profile

for the Insert Digital Project Name here

authored by

dli at rice.edu

Version 1.0, Insert date

Table of Contents

Introduction

[Provide any background information that will orient a reader for the specific project. This may include history, collection description or scope and or a project overview.]

Purpose

[Purpose statement for guidelines, intended audience (for example technical and subject users)]

Version

[Date of guidelines, contributors or expected review or revision schedule]

Project Overview

[Provide scope of project, important goals, milestones, timeframe and or stakeholders]

Collection Description

[Provide scope include broad description of material types and size of collection]

2

Standards

Metadata format and structure should be prepared according to the Dublin Core Metadata Best Practices, published by the Collaborative Digitization Program (CDPDCMBP), (http://www.cdpheritage.org/). Use qualifiers as needed.

Guidelines for the creation of bibliographic metadata

The below list is a starting sample set of elements and qualifiers. Individual projects should customize this list to meet the information needs and specific collection characteristics.

element.qualifer

Provide data value description. Note any data standards. Denote if optional or mandatory entry. Denote if multiple values allowed. Provide number of examples as beneficial to illustrate options.

Example:

| Note: | Insert notes as needed. |

contributor

Recommended to use qualifier to denote roles. Some example roles may include: author, editor, publisher, photographer, composer, performer, transcriber, illustrator, etc.

Example:

Note: Proper names -- The latest version of CDPDCMBP recommends using the creator element to denote primary entities responsible for creating the content of the resource and the contributor element to denote any secondary persons making intellectual contributions. This is a recent change from prior versions of CDPDCMBP. The current DSpace configuration is based on earlier versions and as a consequence, only data in the contributor field is used to generate the author browse and search function. Data in the creator field serves as display only. Therefore all proper names for an artifact will use the contributor element with roles denoted by a qualifier (e.g. contributor.author; contributor.editor; etc). At some future date, when the configuration of Dspace is updated to reflect the newer guidelines, then a mass conversion of contributor to creator element may take place.

coverage

insert guidelines here

Example:

date.issued

Use standard: Date and Time Formats (W3C-DTF) http://www.w3.org/TR/NOTE-datetime. Single date value only.

Example:

3

> Note: DSpace configuration uses the qualified element date.issued to generate the browse and search functionality and requires data to be in the W3CDTF format which does not allow for approximate dates or a range of date values. Given the nature of some archival materials, actual creation dates may not be known and therefore need to be approximated or given in range values. Therefore, we will use the qualified element date.original to capture the date of the original artifact in free text format

date.original

Original date of artifact. Free text field. May include textual description

Example:

Approximately 1925

Circa 1800

after 1867 January 5

1942-1998, predominant 1975-1991

Undated

description

insert guidelines here

Example:

format

insert guidelines here

Example:

identifier

Unique identifier per item based on specific project naming conventions.

Example:

Identifier.uri

Assigned by DSpace system as persistent identifiers for web access to DSpace item. (DSpace item is the page containing metadata and digital objects). DSpace identifier standard is based on CNRI's Handles system (http://www.handle.net/)

Example:

language.iso

Original language from examination of text. Multiple values allowed. Use controlled vocabulary terms from the ISO 639-1 language code (alpha-2 code) http://www.loc.gov/standards/iso639-2/php/English_list.php

Example: en

> Note: Though CDPDCMBP recommends using 3-digit language code, DSpace is actually configured for the 2-digit language code.

4

publisher

Electronic publisher. Boilerplate entry.

Example: Digital version published by Rice University, Houston, Texas

relation.qualifier

usually used with qualifier. See CDPDCMBP for possible qualifiers. insert guidelines here

Example:

rights

Url link to appropriate license. Select appropriate license from Creative Common Licenses at http://creativecommons.org.

Example: This work is licensed under a Creative Commons attribution 2.5 License. http://creativecommons.org/licenses/by/2.5/

> Note: The DLI general practice is to recommend the use of creative commons licenses. See http://creativecommons.org/. Individual projects must evaluate the proper copyright determination and note any intellectual property issues.

source

insert guidelines here

Example:

title

insert guidelines here

Example:

type

Digital manifestation of resource. Typical values are Text or Image. Controlled vocabulary terms from the DCMI type vocabulary at http://dublincore.org/documents/dcmi-type-vocabulary/

> Note: element and qualifier are usually populated automatically in batch processing

5

Digital Projects

PROJECT CHARTER

PROJECT NAME
CommonWealth / Postcolonial Studies @ Emory

PROJECT OBJECTIVE
To update a valuable resource about postcolonial studies and build a community of scholars on the subject.

AUDIENCE
Scholars, students, public, educators

TEAM MEMBER ROLES AND RESPONSIBILITIES

Project Initiator
Lends scholarly vision to project. Supervises graduate student researchers. Participates in ongoing development of project.

Scholarly Contributor
Contributes to the discussion about how the site is organized, presented, and contextualized.

Librarian Consultant, Primary
Advises on copyright, metadata, usability, and searchability. Advises on South Asian history, literature, and religion.

Project Manager
Arranges meetings. Ensures good communication and adherence to timelines. Keeps track of progress. Removes roadblocks.

Librarian Consultant, Secondary
Advises on copyright, metadata, usability, and searchability. Advises on Anglophone literatures and women's studies.

Manager, Software Engineering Team
Helps identify the technical scope of the project. Consults on platform portability. Identifies software engineers to work on project (if any). Works with the software engineers (if any) to ensure on-time and in-scope delivery. Addresses technical roadblocks.

TIMING AND CONSTRAINTS

1. DiSC will provide engineering assistance for the project throughout its development.
2. The project's development will be completed within one year of funding, by 31 August 2012.
3. Limited support for the project will be available in the second year, but active development should be completed within the first year.

4. We will implement the agreed-upon scope of the project.
5. Neither DiSC nor the Library assumes responsibility for sustaining the project beyond the two years of this agreement.
6. The project should be well-documented, including the documentation required for ongoing support, and the documentation preserved by the project manager. The documentation will be provided to the project initiator.

COMMUNICATION
Project members will make every effort to keep in regular contact by email or other electronic means. The preferred means of communication will be email.

DEADLINES
Project members will make every effort to attend meetings as arranged. If unable to attend, they will communicate this to the project manager as soon as possible.

Project members will jointly establish and attempt to meet self-imposed deadlines, in part through providing the project manager with lists of commitments, so that reminders will be sent out as a matter of routine.

FINANCIAL ARRANGEMENTS
Requests for reimbursement must be accompanied by receipt and submitted in writing to the DiSC Coordinator. Reimbursements will not exceed the amount approved for the project, regardless of actual expenses.

DISSEMINATION
Any and all project members may use the project as an example in presentations, papers, interviews, and other media opportunities. They may describe and discuss the project on their web sites. The name of the project should be used widely; wherever possible, publications, presentations, etc. should mention the names of the other project members who were directly involved.

For presentations or papers where this work is the main topic, all team members who worked directly on this subproject should be co-authors. Any member can elect at any time not to be listed, but may not veto publication.

For presentations or papers that spin off from this work, only those members directly involved need to be listed as co-authors. The others should be mentioned if possible in the acknowledgments, credits, or article citations.

All project participants may list the project on their curriculum vitae, and should attempt to describe their contributions honestly and comprehensively.

In accordance with grant requirements, the project initiator will provide a brief description of the project to provide to the Mellon Foundation.

PORTABILITY / SUSTAINABILITY OF PLATFORMS

The project team will work with Emory IT to deploy CommonWealth in the current Proof-of-Concept (POC) WordPress installation. Should the POC not be approved for continued development, DiSC will provide the project initiator with advice / assistance transitioning the site to another appropriate platform.

During Summer 2012, the team will review the platform for its suitability for the intended task.

FUTURE PHASES

In addition to PDFs or other formats for presentation, project members will keep safe and distribute regularly all native files generated for the project: Photoshop, Illustrator, Flash, InDesign, and any other data files or source files. These files will be unflattened and editable. Where copyright restrictions do not apply, fonts should also be included in shared files.

Local projects should also make provisions for regular backup of all project files, including versions of files in progress.

PROFESSIONAL DIGNITY

We will strive to maintain a tone of mutual respect whenever we write or meet; we will strive to forgive lapses if they occur.

We will attempt to keep communications transparent, for example, by copying everyone involved in any given discussion and by directly addressing any questions or concerns that may arise with each other.

We will participate in an assessment program and attempt to measure the efficiency of our communication.

GOODWILL

We will strive to be a group working toward different parts of a larger, coherent, and important whole — one that promises to exceed the sum of its parts.

DRAFT PROJECT CHARTER

PROJECT NAME

Lynchings in Georgia (1875–1930)

PROJECT OBJECTIVE

To develop and deploy an online resource documenting lynchings in Georgia

AUDIENCE

Scholars, public, schools, educators

TEAM MEMBER ROLES AND RESPONSIBILITIES

Project Manager
Arranges meetings, ensures good communication and adherence to timelines, keeps track of progress, removes roadblocks

Senior Software Engineer
Helps to build and implement the software

Digital Humanities Consultant.
Help conceptualize possibilities for the resource. Brainstormer!

Project Initiator
Stays involved in the development process, lends scholarly vision to project.

Scholarly Contributor
Contributes to the discussion about how the resource is organized, presented, and contextualized.

Manager, Software Engineering Team
Helps identify the technical scope of the project. Helps form high-level technical strategy for implementing the project. Work with the software engineers to ensure on-time and in-scope delivery. Addresses technical roadblocks.

Lead Developer
Works to implement technical aspects of the project.

Librarian Consultant
Advises on copyright, metadata, usability, and searchability. Advises on southern history.

TIMING AND CONSTRAINTS

*The project will be completed within one calendar year from its start date

*We will implement the agreed-upon scope of the project.

*Limited support for the project will be available in the second year, but active development should be completed within the first year.

*DiSC will provide engineering assistance for the project throughout the year.

*Neither DiSC nor the Library assumes responsibility for sustaining the project beyond the two years of this agreement.

The project should be well-documented, including the documentation required for ongoing support, and the documentation preserved by the project manager. The documentation will be provided to the project initiator.

FINANCIAL ARRANGEMENTS

*Requests for reimbursement must be submitted in writing to the DiSC Coordinator.

*Reimbursements will not exceed the amount approved for the project, regardless of actual expenses.

DISSEMINATION

Project members may use any of it as examples in presentations, papers, interviews, and other media opportunities. They may post any of it to their web sites. Wherever possible, they should mention the names of the other project members who were directly involved, as well as the name of the project.

No project participants will publish datasets or distribute the data for purposes other than this project.

For presentations or papers where this work is the main topic, all team members who worked directly on this subproject should be co-authors. Any member can elect at any time not to be listed, but may not veto publication.

For presentations or papers that spin off from this work, only those members directly involved need to be listed as co-authors. The others should be mentioned if possible in the acknowledgments, credits, or article citations.

All project participants may list the project on their curriculum vitae, and should attempt to describe their contributions honestly and comprehensively.

*In accordance with grant requirements, the project initiator will provide a brief description of the project to provide to the Mellon Foundation.

DEADLINES

Project members will make every effort to attend meetings as arranged and to keep in regular contact by email or other electronic means.

Project members will jointly establish and attempt to meet self-imposed deadlines, in part through providing the project administrator with lists of commitments, so that reminders will be sent out as a matter of routine.

FUTURE PHASES

In addition to PDFs or other formats for presentation, project members will keep safe and distribute regularly all native files generated for the project: photoshop, Illustrator, Flash, InDesign, and any other data files or source files. These files will be unflattened and editable. Where copyright restrictions do not apply, fonts should also be included in shared files.

Local projects should also make provisions for regular backup of all project files, including versions of files in progress.

PROFESSIONAL DIGNITY

We will strive to maintain a tone of mutual respect whenever we write or meet, and to forgive lapses if they occur.

We will attempt to keep communications transparent, for example, by copying everyone involved in any given discussion and by directly addressing with each other any questions or concerns that may arise.

We will participate in an assessment program and attempt to measure the efficiency of our communication.

GOODWILL

We will strive to be a group working toward different parts of a larger, coherent, and important whole — one that promises to exceed the sum of its parts.

The University of Florida Digital Collections (UFDC) hosts more than 300 outstanding digital collections, containing over 7 million pages of unique manuscripts and letters, antique maps, rare children's literature books, theses and dissertations, newspapers, historic photographs, oral histories, and more. The University of Florida Digital Collections (UFDC) enables users to find unique and rare digitized materials held at the University of Florida and partner institutions.

With UFDC, remote and local researchers have free, open access to the full content of the resource. This is a constantly growing collection of resources. The search box above searches across all the digital resources in all the collections. By clicking on the icons below, you can view and search individual collections.

Arts, Humanities and Social Sciences Collections

Arts Collections
The Arts Collection Group includes collections of arts, from performing arts to graphical arts to comics and also includes architecture and landscape design as well as the psychology in art collection.

Baldwin Library of Historical Children's Literature
Rare English and American 19th century children's literature from the Baldwin Library of Historical Children's Literature in the Department of Special Collections at the University of Florida.

History and Heritage Collections
History and heritage collections include the history of florida, the historical role that Florida has played in the greater history of the U.S., and the general history of the United States.

Literature Collections
The literature collections include great literature and children's literature as well as general literary studies collections.

Social Sciences Collections
Humanities collections ncludes information about general studies of humanities, as well as social movements and the study of people's place in their society. This currently includes two collections about religion and two collections relating to women's studies.

Science and Technology Collections

Herbarium Collections
The 'University of Florida Herbarium Specimen Collections' provides digital images for selected specimens from the Florida Museum of Natural History / University of Florida Herbarium.

Sciences Collections
The sciences collections includes natural and earth sciences, herbarium collections, wetlands research, as well as food and agricultural sciences and sciences and technologies.

Map Collections

Aerial Photography: Florida
Historical aerial photographs dramatically document changes in Florida's land use. The initial Aerial Photography: Florida collection was funded by two Florida Library Service and Technology Assistant grants from the Florida Department of State.

Map and Imagery Collections
Map and imagery collections includes maps of Florida and the world, both historic and contemporary, as well as aerial photographs of Florida.

FLORIDA COLLECTIONS

Florida Digital Newspaper Library
The Florida Digital Newspaper Library, hosted by the University of Florida Libraries, provides access to the news and history of Florida.

Florida Law Collections
Florida Law currently holds the Journal of the Florida House of Reprentatives and a Florida Water Law collection. Planned additions include the Laws of the Florida Territory and the Early Florida Constitutions, as well as a variety of general texts on Florida laws, the legislative process, and government.

Florida Photograph Collections
Historic and contemporary photographs visually document Florida and the University of Florida. This collaborative collection was created with content from several schools within the University of Florida, the Matheson Historical Center Collection, SWFLN, and many other smaller archives, libraries, and museums.

Living in Florida: Its Cities and People
These collection groups tell the stories of the people that lived in Florida and the cities they built.

Oral History Collections
The Oral History Collections comprise the digital holdings of both the Matheson Museum (Gainesville, Florida) and the Samuel Proctor Oral History Program at the University of Florida. Together, the Collections document life in Gainesville, across Florida, the Caribbean and other locales.

WORLD COLLECTIONS

African Studies Collections
The Africana Collection support the past, ongoing and future needs of University of Florida's Center for African Studies, one of the most active and well regarded such centers in the United States of America and the only United States Department of Education Title VI Center for African Studies in the American southeast.

Asian Collections
This digital collection draws from the Asian Studies Collections at the University of Florida, and includes rare resources on Chinese Art History.

Digital Library of the Caribbean
The Digital Library of the Caribbean (dLOC) is a cooperative digital library for resources from and about the Caribbean and circum-Caribbean. dLOC provides access to digitized versions of Caribbean cultural, historical and research materials currently held in archives, libraries, and private collections.

Judaica Collections
The Judaica Digital Collections draw from the Isser and Rae Price Library of Judaica at the University of Florida which, with holdings of 90,000 volumes, is the largest Jewish studies research collection in the southeastern United States. Initial materials selected for digitization are unique and rare items, and more will be added as the Judaica Digital Collections continue to grow.

UNIVERSITY OF ILLINOIS AT URBANA-CHAMPAIGN
MONK
https://monk.library.illinois.edu/cic/public/

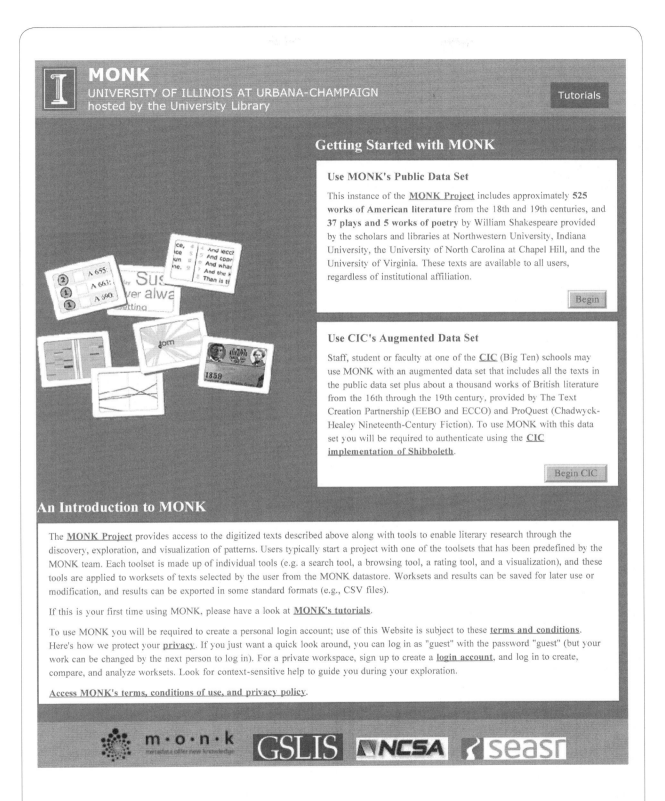

MONK
UNIVERSITY OF ILLINOIS AT URBANA-CHAMPAIGN
hosted by the University Library

Tutorials

Getting Started with MONK

Use MONK's Public Data Set

This instance of the **MONK Project** includes approximately **525 works of American literature** from the 18th and 19th centuries, and **37 plays and 5 works of poetry** by William Shakespeare provided by the scholars and libraries at Northwestern University, Indiana University, the University of North Carolina at Chapel Hill, and the University of Virginia. These texts are available to all users, regardless of institutional affiliation.

Begin

Use CIC's Augmented Data Set

Staff, student or faculty at one of the **CIC** (Big Ten) schools may use MONK with an augmented data set that includes all the texts in the public data set plus about a thousand works of British literature from the 16th through the 19th century, provided by The Text Creation Partnership (EEBO and ECCO) and ProQuest (Chadwyck-Healey Nineteenth-Century Fiction). To use MONK with this data set you will be required to authenticate using the **CIC implementation of Shibboleth**.

Begin CIC

An Introduction to MONK

The **MONK Project** provides access to the digitized texts described above along with tools to enable literary research through the discovery, exploration, and visualization of patterns. Users typically start a project with one of the toolsets that has been predefined by the MONK team. Each toolset is made up of individual tools (e.g. a search tool, a browsing tool, a rating tool, and a visualization), and these tools are applied to worksets of texts selected by the user from the MONK datastore. Worksets and results can be saved for later use or modification, and results can be exported in some standard formats (e.g., CSV files).

If this is your first time using MONK, please have a look at **MONK's tutorials**.

To use MONK you will be required to create a personal login account; use of this Website is subject to these **terms and conditions**. Here's how we protect your **privacy**. If you just want a quick look around, you can log in as "guest" with the password "guest" (but your work can be changed by the next person to log in). For a private workspace, sign up to create a **login account**, and log in to create, compare, and analyze worksets. Look for context-sensitive help to guide you during your exploration.

Access MONK's terms, conditions of use, and privacy policy.

m·o·n·k   GSLIS   NCSA   seasr

NEH Digital Humanities Start-up grant.

» "James Dusenbery Journal"
Supported by private funding.

» "Main Street, Carolina"
Supported by the C. Felix Harvey Award to Advance Institutional Priorities at the University of North Carolina at Chapel Hill and NEH Digital Humanities Start-up grant.

» Scribe Digitization Program
Established in December 2007, the Scribe Digitization Program is a partnership between the UNC University Library, and the Open Content Alliance. The Scribe (a high-speed scanner) and associated software applications developed by the Internet Archive facilitate high-volume conversion of bound materials to digital format. All books digitized by the UNC Library are hosted by the Internet Archive and are freely available online. As of June 2009, over 4,000 titles have been digitized as a part of this program.

» Southern Oral Histories Transcript Digitization
This project entails digitizing approximately 2,600 oral history transcripts (about 95,000 8.5" x 11" typescript sheets) and includes Optical Character recognition (OCR) processing resulting in the creation of text-searchable PDF versions of oral history transcripts. Digital production and text processing for this project is done with the high-speed Fujitsu 5900C sheet-fed scanner and ABBYY FineReader OCR software. Digitized materials from this project will be used by the UNC Library's Southern Historical Collection in developing an online collection of oral history transcripts.

» University Research Council Small Grant Program (for developing a new digital scholarly edition).

» William R. Ferris Collection
Supported by the University Library of the University of North Carolina at Chapel Hill.

» "World War I Postcards from the Bowman Gray Collection"
Supported by the University Library of the University of North Carolina at Chapel Hill.

» "The Mini Page Archive, 1969-2007"
Supported by private funding.

Research Projects

We have and are currently building humanities computing research programs with a number of scholars at the University of Oregon and elsewhere. Our foci represent a broad spectrum of humanities fields: Medieval Europe, Early Mesoamerica, Digital Art Annotation, applying GIS to early maps, and Indigenous Languages.

While our grasp is broad, we have approached all of our work with collaboration and persistence in mind. It takes a long time to develop fundable projects in the humanities and even longer to secure the funding. We have benefited from extraordinary investment of time and funding from both individuals and units of the University of Oregon including the Center for the Study of Women in Society, the Vice President for Research, the College of Arts and Sciences, the Yamada Language Center, the Knight Libraries, the Jordan Schnitzer Museum of Art, and the Museum of Natural and Cultural History.

What we have done and continue to do is the result of close work with scholars over time, and sifting through what can be crafted into fundable projects. For humanities computing this has meant chasing ever advancing and complex technologies to fashion projects that are interesting not just to the scholars involved but represent competitive new ideas to such major funding providers as the National Endowment for the Humanities.

Research Areas

Digital Mesoamerica
Gender in Medieval Europe
Indigenous Language Dictionaries
Digital Art Annotation
Historical Geography

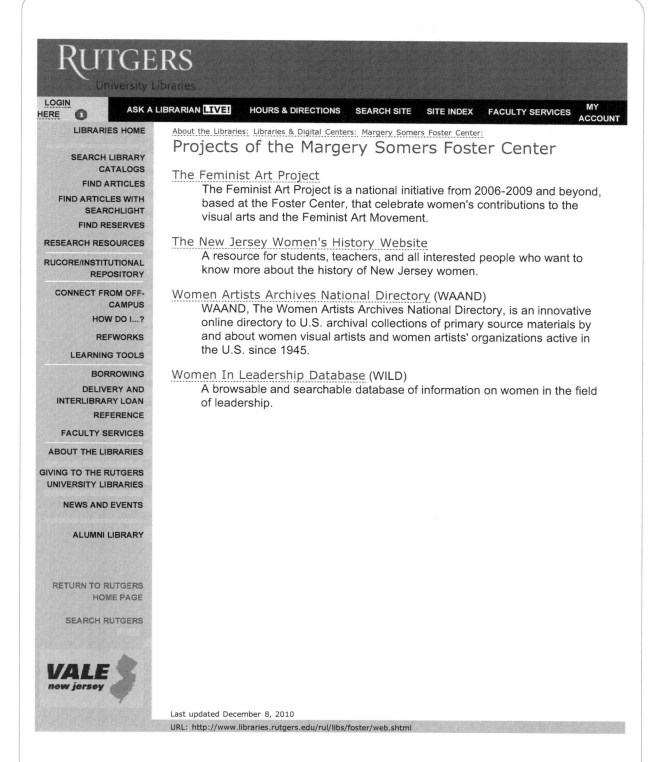

RUTGERS
University Libraries

LOGIN HERE | ASK A LIBRARIAN LIVE! | HOURS & DIRECTIONS | SEARCH SITE | SITE INDEX | FACULTY SERVICES | MY ACCOUNT

LIBRARIES HOME

SEARCH LIBRARY CATALOGS

FIND ARTICLES

FIND ARTICLES WITH SEARCHLIGHT

FIND RESERVES

RESEARCH RESOURCES

RUCORE/INSTITUTIONAL REPOSITORY

CONNECT FROM OFF-CAMPUS

HOW DO I...?

REFWORKS

LEARNING TOOLS

BORROWING

DELIVERY AND INTERLIBRARY LOAN

REFERENCE

FACULTY SERVICES

ABOUT THE LIBRARIES

GIVING TO THE RUTGERS UNIVERSITY LIBRARIES

NEWS AND EVENTS

ALUMNI LIBRARY

RETURN TO RUTGERS HOME PAGE

SEARCH RUTGERS

VALE new jersey

About the Libraries: Libraries & Digital Centers: Margery Somers Foster Center:

Projects of the Margery Somers Foster Center

The Feminist Art Project
The Feminist Art Project is a national initiative from 2006-2009 and beyond, based at the Foster Center, that celebrate women's contributions to the visual arts and the Feminist Art Movement.

The New Jersey Women's History Website
A resource for students, teachers, and all interested people who want to know more about the history of New Jersey women.

Women Artists Archives National Directory (WAAND)
WAAND, The Women Artists Archives National Directory, is an innovative online directory to U.S. archival collections of primary source materials by and about women visual artists and women artists' organizations active in the U.S. since 1945.

Women In Leadership Database (WILD)
A browsable and searchable database of information on women in the field of leadership.

Last updated December 8, 2010
URL: http://www.libraries.rutgers.edu/rul/libs/foster/web.shtml

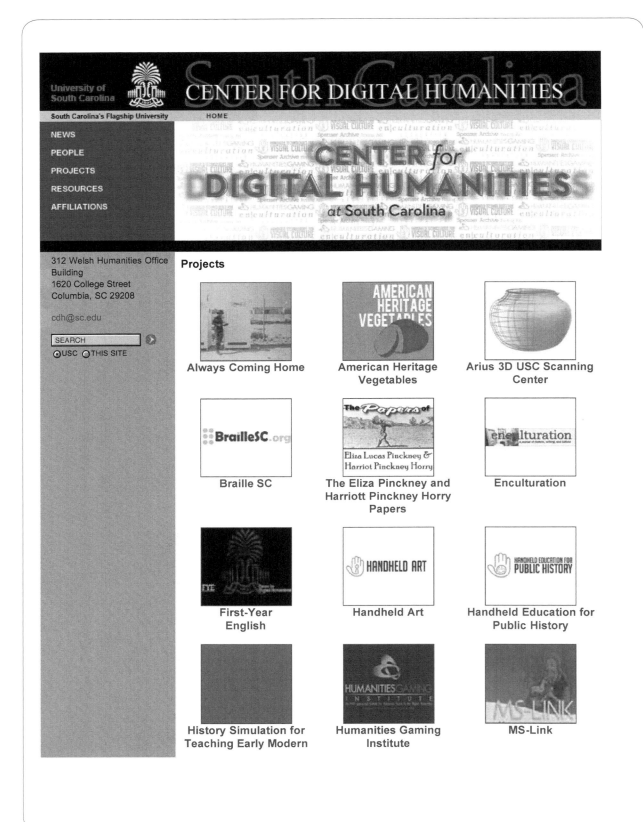

UNIVERSITY OF SOUTH CAROLINA
Center for Digital Humanities | Projects
http://cdh.sc.edu/projects.html

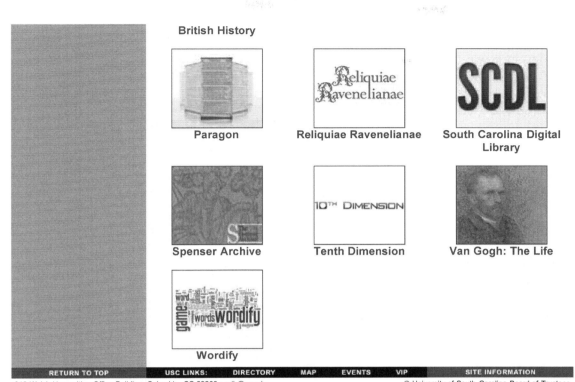

British History

Paragon

Reliquiae Ravenelianae

South Carolina Digital Library

Spenser Archive

Tenth Dimension

Van Gogh: The Life

Wordify

RETURN TO TOP   USC LINKS: DIRECTORY   MAP   EVENTS   VIP   SITE INFORMATION

312 Welsh Humanities Office Building, Columbia, SC 29208 • cdh@sc.edu

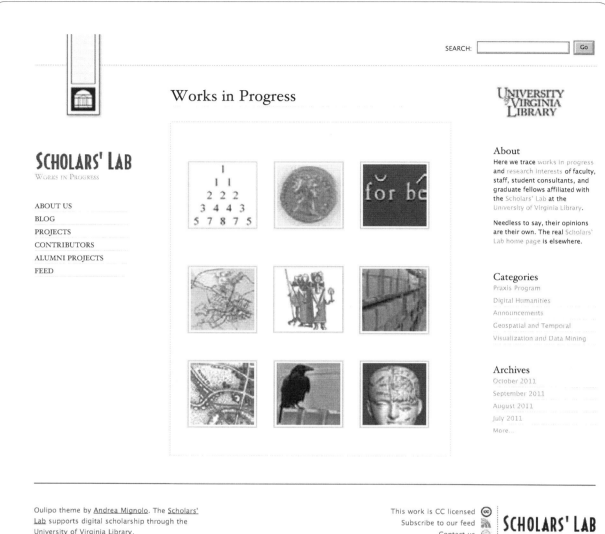

Fellowships

CASE WESTERN RESERVE UNIVERSITY
Freedman Fellows Program—Overview
http://library.case.edu/ksl/freedmancenter/specialprograms/fellows/

CASE.EDU: HOME | DIRECTORIES | SEARCH   Print This Page   Email This Page   A A A Font Size

CASE WESTERN RESERVE
UNIVERSITY   EST 1826

Freedman Center

Home	
Digital Library	
Language Learning	
Multimedia Services	
Special Programs	
Training	
Who We Are	
Contact Us	

FC Related Sites

College of Arts & Sciences

Kelvin Smith Library

Instructional Technology & Academic Computing

Modern Languages & Literature

Freedman Center > Special Programs > Freedman Fellows

Freedman Fellows Program -- Overview

The Samuel B. and Marian K. Freedman Digital Library, Language Learning, and Multimedia Services Center is a partnership between the College of Arts and Sciences and the Kelvin Smith Library. For the College of Arts and Sciences the Freedman Center is evidence of the College's commitment to the evolution of education and the integration of multimedia technologies and digital tools in its curriculum. For KSL the Freedman Center is the culmination of a ten-year vision for a center that provides faculty, students, and staff with the ability to utilize both analog and hardcopy information sources in digital works and presentations.

Since it's inception in 2005, the Freedman Fellows Program has awarded $100,000, supported 29 faculty proposals, and 300+ graduate and undergraduate students have used multimedia technologies as a part of their learning at Case Western Reserve.

The Freedman Fellows Program is further evidence of the commitment of both the College of Arts and Sciences and the Library to revolutionizing education at Case Western Reserve University. We are proud to announce a further commitment on the part of the Samuel B. and Marian K. Freedman Family of $250,000 over five years to support this important and innovative program. When the commitment is completed the interest on the donated sum will be used to fund future Freedman Fellows Program awards, specifically: ensure the use of multimedia technology in the curriculum of classes and in the work done by students at Case Western Reserve; ensure the use of multimedia technology in the research conducted at Case Western Reserve: specifically Digital Humanities research as coordinated with the Baker-Nord Center; and finally a commitment to Institutional Memory--that is, a commitment of materials to Digital Case, the Digital Library for Case Western Reserve University.

* 2011 Freedman Fellow Program
* Previous Award Recipients

For more information please contact Tom Hayes, Freedman Center Managing Librarian and Head of Digital Library Programs.

Freedman Center Home | Freedman Fellows Program Home | Previous Award Information

RSS Feeds

FC News Blog

Apr 29, 2011
Freedman Fellows 2011 Announced
The Freedman Center is very happy to announce the winners of the 2011 Freedman Fellows Program. The ...

Mar 31, 2011
Freedman Fellows Program 2011
Freedman Fellows Program 2011 The Samuel B. and Marian K. Freedman Digital Library, Language Learnin...

Mar 12, 2010
Freedman Center Fellow Program 2010
The Freedman Center is pleased to announce the 2010 Freedman Fellows Program for faculty. The Freedm...

Apr 30, 2009
Freedman Fellows 2009 Announced
The Freedman Center is very happy to announce the winners of the 2009 Freedman Fellows Program. The...

Other Blogs
KSL Reference & Instruction
ITS News 222

KSL Home | BlackBoard | Site Map | Privacy | Contact Us | OhioLink | Libraries of Case | Browser Requirements
Kelvin Smith Library | 11055 Euclid Avenue | Cleveland, OH 44106-7151 | 216-368-3506

Freedman Center > Special Programs > Freedman Fellows > Freedman Center Fellow Program 2011

Freedman Fellows Program 2011

The Samuel B. and Marian K. Freedman Digital Library, Language Learning, and Multimedia Services Center is pleased to announce the 2011 Freedman Fellows Program for full-time faculty. The Freedman Center is a partnership between the College of Arts and Sciences and the Kelvin Smith Library.

In 2011, the Freedman Fellows Program will identify and support scholarly projects that meet all of the following conditions, i.e., the projects are: (1) currently underway, (2) involve some corpus of data that is of scholarly or instructional interest (e.g., data sets, digital texts, digital images, databases), (3) involve the use of digital tools and processes, and (4) have clearly articulated project outcomes.

The Freedman Fellows Program supports and facilities a variety of digital scholarship activities, such as:

* Scholarly endeavors using emerging digital tools and processes such as the use of data-mining, text-analytic techniques, GIS [geospatial information systems], and data visualization;

* Digital Humanities scholarship by encouraging the use of new technologies in faculty research through assistance with research design, visualization and presentation strategies.

* Digital Case in experimenting with digital tools for storing, preserving, analyzing and making accessible digital resources;

* The use of emerging technologies for dissemination and publication of scholarship; and for use of digital scholarship resources in teaching and learning.

Freedman Fellows will receive an award of $3,000 to support the expenses related to innovative scholarly or creative projects that meet the Freedman Fellows 2011 criteria. Guidelines as to how awards may be spent are available online. Proposals are due before midnight on **Monday, April 18, 2011**.

Award Criteria

Freedman Fellows serve as a model for campus faculty for how to successfully integrate new digital processes and tools in their scholarship and teaching. These new approaches to scholarship create bold visions of what is possible for scholarly outcomes, enhance understanding, create opportunities for formulating original questions, and fundamentally re-define how scholars work. Fellows must be full-time faculty who are motivated by excellence and the desire to be leaders in their disciplinary programs. Former Freedman Fellows are encouraged to apply. Award criteria and further information on the Freedman Fellows Program are available at the Freedman Fellows website. To be successful, applications must describe a corpus of data (digital texts, digital images, processed data, databases, etc.), include discussion of the project's impact with regard to scholarly or teaching goals, identify potential users or uses, describe the intended use of digital tools and processes, demonstrate current project planning, and articulate a project outcome (including a statement regarding the intended use of the award). In addition, the proposal must include a statement that addresses copyright concerns (detailed information is provided on the Freedman Fellows website). While there is a preference given to projects that are humanities-based, projects that are not solely humanities-oriented will be considered if they are compelling in their application of emerging digital tools and resources for scholarship, research and/or teaching.

Application Process

Application information is available at the Freedman Fellows Program website, as is a list of individual questions that should be addressed in the submitted proposal. Proposals shall not exceed three (3) pages and must include a 100-word abstract at the outset describing the project. Proposals are due before midnight on **Monday, April 18, 2011**.

A committee of faculty and staff will review all proposals and make final selections. Freedman Fellows will be announced no later than Friday, April 22, 2011.

Expectations of Fellows

Freedman Fellows are expected to participate in periodic meetings with not only their project groups (which will be created to meet project needs) but with Freedman Fellow colleagues to provide updates on their projects and to contribute as a group to the development of models, services and practices for support of scholarship, research and teaching at CWRU. The first such meeting will take place on Friday, May 6. Details are available on the Freedman Fellows Program website. Freedman Fellows are expected to confer with Departmental Chairs or Departmental Assistants in setting up accounts for their $3,000 award. Guidance as to the manner in which the award may be used, as well as additional information is available in the FAQ section of the Freedman Fellows Program site. Freedman Fellows will be expected to participate in a colloquium (tentatively scheduled for October 2011) that addresses digital scholarship and future directions for digital scholarship at CWRU.

Questions regarding the Freedman Fellows Program and application process are welcome. Please contact Thomas Hayes (Thomas.Hayes@case.edu) or by phone at **216-368-6513** for further information.

Left navigation

- Home
- Digital Library
- Language Learning
- Multimedia Services
- Special Programs
- Training
- Who We Are
- Contact Us

FC Related Sites
- College of Arts & Sciences
- Kelvin Smith Library
- Instructional Technology & Academic Computing
- Modern Languages & Literature

RSS Feeds

FC News Blog

Apr 29, 2011
Freedman Fellows 2011 Announced
The Freedman Center is very happy to announce the winners of the 2011 Freedman Fellows Program. The ...

Mar 31, 2011
Freedman Fellows Program 2011
Freedman Fellows Program 2011 The Samuel B. and Marian K. Freedman Digital Library, Language Learnin...

Mar 12, 2010
Freedman Center Fellow Program 2010
The Freedman Center is pleased to announce the 2010 Freedman Fellows Program for faculty. The Freedm...

Apr 30, 2009
Freedman Fellows 2009 Announced
The Freedman Center is very happy to announce the winners of the 2009 Freedman Fellows Program. The...

Other Blogs
KSL Reference & Instruction
ITS News 222

INDIANA UNIVERSITY BLOOMINGTON

Institute for Digital Arts and Humanities | Fellowships

http://www.indiana.edu/~idah/index.php?option=com_content&view=category&layout=blog&id=36&Itemid=56

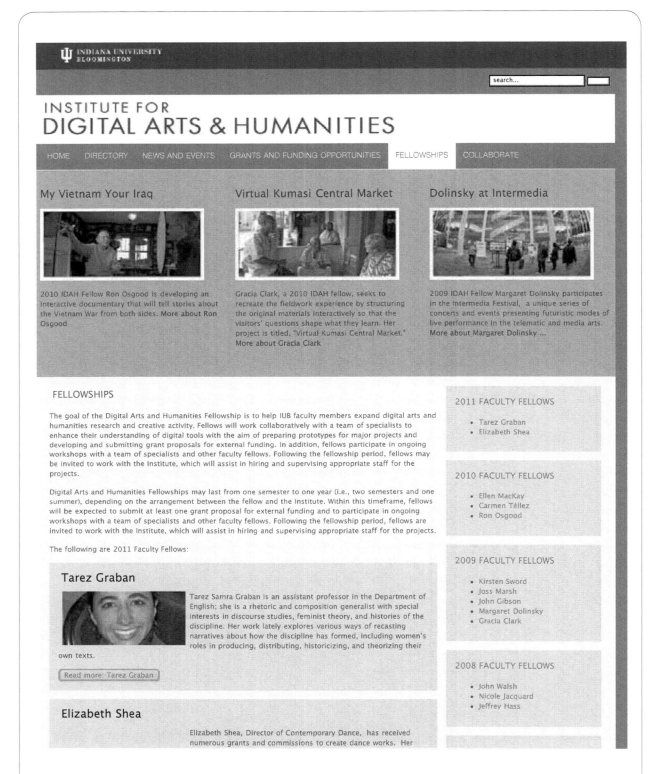

INDIANA UNIVERSITY BLOOMINGTON

search...

INSTITUTE FOR
DIGITAL ARTS & HUMANITIES

HOME   DIRECTORY   NEWS AND EVENTS   GRANTS AND FUNDING OPPORTUNITIES   FELLOWSHIPS   COLLABORATE

My Vietnam Your Iraq

2010 IDAH Fellow Ron Osgood is developing an interactive documentary that will tell stories about the Vietnam War from both sides. More about Ron Osgood

Virtual Kumasi Central Market

Gracia Clark, a 2010 IDAH fellow, seeks to recreate the fieldwork experience by structuring the original materials interactively so that the visitors' questions shape what they learn. Her project is titled, "Virtual Kumasi Central Market." More about Gracia Clark

Dolinsky at Intermedia

2009 IDAH Fellow Margaret Dolinsky participates in the Intermedia Festival, a unique series of concerts and events presenting futuristic modes of live performance in the telematic and media arts. More about Margaret Dolinsky ...

FELLOWSHIPS

The goal of the Digital Arts and Humanities Fellowship is to help IUB faculty members expand digital arts and humanities research and creative activity. Fellows will work collaboratively with a team of specialists to enhance their understanding of digital tools with the aim of preparing prototypes for major projects and developing and submitting grant proposals for external funding. In addition, fellows participate in ongoing workshops with a team of specialists and other faculty fellows. Following the fellowship period, fellows may be invited to work with the Institute, which will assist in hiring and supervising appropriate staff for the projects.

Digital Arts and Humanities Fellowships may last from one semester to one year (i.e., two semesters and one summer), depending on the arrangement between the fellow and the Institute. Within this timeframe, fellows will be expected to submit at least one grant proposal for external funding and to participate in ongoing workshops with a team of specialists and other faculty fellows. Following the fellowship period, fellows are invited to work with the Institute, which will assist in hiring and supervising appropriate staff for the projects.

The following are 2011 Faculty Fellows:

Tarez Graban

Tarez Samra Graban is an assistant professor in the Department of English; she is a rhetoric and composition generalist with special interests in discourse studies, feminist theory, and histories of the discipline. Her work lately explores various ways of recasting narratives about how the discipline has formed, including women's roles in producing, distributing, historicizing, and theorizing their own texts.

Read more: Tarez Graban

Elizabeth Shea

Elizabeth Shea, Director of Contemporary Dance, has received numerous grants and commissions to create dance works. Her

2011 FACULTY FELLOWS
- Tarez Graban
- Elizabeth Shea

2010 FACULTY FELLOWS
- Ellen MacKay
- Carmen Téllez
- Ron Osgood

2009 FACULTY FELLOWS
- Kirsten Sword
- Joss Marsh
- John Gibson
- Margaret Dolinsky
- Gracia Clark

2008 FACULTY FELLOWS
- John Walsh
- Nicole Jacquard
- Jeffrey Hass

INDIANA UNIVERSITY BLOOMINGTON
Institute for Digital Arts and Humanities | Fellowships
http://www.indiana.edu/~idah/index.php?option=com_content&view=category&layout=blog&id=36&Itemid=56

choreography has been chosen for performance by the World Dance Alliance, the National Dance Association, the American College Dance Festival Association, the International Computer Music Association, Regional Dance America and for other national and international venues.

Read more. Elizabeth Shea

WHAT CAN IDAH DO FOR YOU?

What are the Digital Arts and Humanities?

What Roles Does IDAH Play?

What is the Scope of IDAH's Technical Assistance?

What Kinds of Faculty Fellowship Projects can IDAH Support?

What is the IDAH Brown Bag Series?

FELLOWSHIPS

Stay in touch

IDAH offers email updates regarding

- Upcoming brownbags
- IDAH Fellowship news
- Grants and Funding Opportunities

Click here to sign-up for IDAH e-mails, or here to manage your current subscriptions.

Site navigation

- Home
- Directory
- News and events
- Grants and funding opportunities
- Fellowships
  - What can IDAH do for you?
- Collaborate

Contact us

Herman B. Wells Library E170
1320 E. 10th St.
Bloomington, IN 47405
(812) 855-0829

UNIVERSITY OF KANSAS
IDRH co-sponsors three HASTAC Scholars
http://idrh.ku.edu/

KU INSTITUTE FOR DIGITAL RESEARCH IN THE HUMANITIES — The University of Kansas

Search KU Web | keyword/name

Kyou   Email   Blackboard   Enroll & Pay
KU Home   A-Z

Institute for Digital Research in the Humanities

IDRH Home   About IDRH   Calendar   CoLang 2012   Digital Humanities Seminar   Representing Knowledge Conference   Seed Grants
News and Announcements

The Institute for Digital Research in the Humanities provides resources and training in the practices and tools of the digital humanities, facilitating interdisciplinary academic collaborations, innovative research, and external funding opportunities.

IDRH co-sponsors three HASTAC Scholars

The Institute for Digital Research in the Humanities and the Center for Digital Scholarship are pleased to sponsor three KU graduate students as participants in the 2011-2012 HASTAC Scholar's program.

Founded in 2002, HASTAC (Humanities, Arts, Science and Technology Advanced Collaboratory) is a network of individuals and institutions that come together to share, collaborate, and learn through online forums, blogs, conferences, social media and other channels of communication. Every year institutions from around the world support graduate and undergraduate students as HASTAC Scholars with small scholarships.

"HASTAC Scholars report on the work happening on their campuses and in their region to an international audience....The HASTAC Scholars also orchestrate a regular discussion on the HASTAC web site. Open to all, these expansive forums initiate rich insights and deep exchanges on timely issues related to digital media and learning and the digital humanities more broadly."

This year's KU Scholars are the first from KU to participate in the HASTAC program. Congratulations to all three, and please follow their work at the links below!

Avery Dame (American Studies):
I'm currently a Master's Candidate in American Studies at the University of Kansas. My interests include queer representation in media, online communities, and comics studies. My thesis is a critical reading of how the five best-connected trans male vloggers manage being both public trans figures and private individuals. I also currently serve as assistant editor of the journal *American Studies*.
*Follow Avery's HASTAC blog: **http://hastac.org/users/adame***

Natalie Pennington (Communication Studies):
I'm a doctoral student at the University of Kansas in the department of Communication Studies. My research is focused on interpersonal communication through social media sites. From how we manage our impressions online, to how we seek out social support from our networks, if its about how we communicate through Facebook, I'm interested!
*Follow Natalies's HASTAC blog: **http://hastac.org/users/natpen***

Kenton Rambsy (English):
Kenton Rambsy is a graduate student in Literature and Theory at the University of Kansas. His research interests include self-education and political thought in African American autobiographical and fiction narratives. He is the Project Digital Initiative Coordinator and Blog Editor for the Project on the History of Black Writing (HBW) at the University of Kansas (Lawrence).

Contact

Arienne Dwyer
Co-director,
Institute for Digital Research in the Humanities
Associate Professor,
Anthropology
☎ 785-864-2649
email: anthlinguist AT ku DOT edu

Brian Rosenblum
Co-director,
Institute for Digital Research in the Humanities
Associate Librarian,
KU Libraries
☎ 785-864-8883
✉ brianlee@ku.edu

Past IDRH Events

THATCamp Kansas
(September 2011)

Digital Jumpstart Workshops
(March 2011)

New Scholarly Texts, New Scholarly Practices: A Discussion with Kathleen Fitzpatrick
(February 2011)

Related Links

KU Libraries Center for Digital Scholarship

IDRH Partners

KU Libraries

Hall Center for the Humanities

College of Liberal Arts and Sciences

Digital Library Fellows: Request for Proposals

University of Miami Libraries

Overview

The University of Miami Libraries are initiating the second cycle of the Digital Library Fellows program to create innovative new electronic scholarly content by awarding grants to faculty interested in developing digital resources.

The Libraries will provide funding and technological support to UM faculty for the creation and online delivery of scholarly electronic resources. The Libraries are seeking projects that will have a significant impact on teaching, learning, and research, and encourage projects which include student participation.

Projects will result in open access on-line resources designed to have long-term relevance to UM faculty and students. To ensure long-term access to resources created, all digital content will be produced in strict adherence to state-of-the-art digital preservation standards and technical specifications.

Eligibility

The competitive Digital Library Fellowships are open to full-time, regular (tenured or tenure track) University of Miami faculty interested in developing innovative digital resources. The fellowship is limited to Coral Gables campus faculty.

Funding

Up to two Fellowships will be awarded with a maximum of $15,000 for one year. The earliest project start date is March 1, 2008. Later start dates are possible, but all projects must be completed by March 1, 2009.

Project Selection

Selected projects will result in the creation of scholarly, internet-based digital resources that meet the following criteria:

- Represents a new and innovative type of resource or provides access to a traditional resource in new ways;

- Generates a new user experience which would not be possible via access to a print resource;

- Contributes to the teaching and learning at the academic level of content relevant to the University of Miami student body as well as the international scholarly community.

Proposal Format

The proposal must include the following parts:

- A one paragraph abstract of the project;

- A two to three page narrative describing the proposal;

1

Digital Library Fellows:
Request for Proposals

- A current CV of the applicant;

- A detailed project budget;

- An outline of participants and their respective levels of engagement;

- A realistic time line for the accomplishment of stated project goals;

- Letters of support from the applicant's departmental Chair and Dean.

Proposal Tips

Writing the Narrative. The narrative section should describe both the relevance of the project to the University of Miami as well as its plan of implementation, and include a detailed description of how the digital content created by the project would be used in teaching and research. Projects that make use of digital images, audio, video, or text are particularly encouraged, and the narrative should specify whether the content to be presented already exists in a digital form or needs to be converted from an analog format.

Copyright Control. A proposal burdened by intellectual property issues will not be awarded funding. All applicants should carefully review the UM Libraries Digital Initiatives Copyright Guidelines [http://merrick.library.miami.edu/digitalprojects/copyright.html], and make sure that they resolve or adequately plan for the resolution of any potential copyright problems in their proposals before applying.

Sound Budgeting. Strong preference will be given to projects with realistic budget proposals. Applicants should consider carefully the work to be done, the tools required to complete the work, and the wages paid to project workers, as these often make up the majority of a given project's budget. While budgeting for student workers, on the undergraduate and/or graduate level, is strongly encouraged, applicants are strongly discouraged from including budget allocations which will contribute funds to their own salaries.

Library Participation. Applicants are encouraged to craft proposals which would support the University of Miami Libraries mission to advance innovation in information technology and scholarly communication. For more information on these objectives, visit the Mission Statement [http://www.library.miami.edu/about/mission/mission_program_objectives.html] page on the UM Libraries website.

Work Space. Work space for student workers and work stations for new projects will not typically be made available to Digital Fellows. Applicants are encouraged to collaborate with their departments to provide office space and work stations to project contributors when possible. For projects working directly with locally held archival materials, some space may be made available in the Libraries on a temporary basis.

Consultations. Faculty with questions about project plans or the proposal process are welcome to speak to Kyle Rimkus (<kyle@miami.edu>, 305-284-6221), Digital Projects Librarian, before applying.

Review Procedures

A committee of internal and external reviewers made up of administrators and experts in the field of digital projects will review each proposal and select those that best meet the stated goals of the Digital Library Fellows program.

Award Criteria

Recipients will be expected to share their experiences with other faculty through a forum sponsored by the Libraries, as well as authoring a final written report, and acknowledging the Libraries in any publications, printed materials, or websites that result from the grant.

2

Digital Library Fellows:
Request for Proposals

Fellows are expected to work closely with the Libraries in developing a detailed timetable and plan of work in order to ensure successful completion of their projects, and to develop a presence on the Libraries Digital Initiatives website [http://merrick.library.miami.edu/].

Intellectual Property Rights

Working with Legacy Materials. Digital Fellowship applicants must ensure that they hold valid rights to publish the materials in their proposals in an open access on-line format. In practice, this means that Fellows work with materials in the public domain, own copyright to the materials in question, or allocate funds to purchase permission from the respective copyright holder to publish the materials online. For more information on the University of Miami Digital Initiatives copyright policy, visit the Copyright Guidelines [http://merrick.library.miami.edu/digitalprojects/copyright.html] page on our website.

Creating new Intellectual Content. Intellectual property rights for content produced during Digital Fellowships, including digital files, software, hardware, or other innovations, are governed by the policies outlined in the "Patent and Copyright" section of the UM Faculty Manual [http://www6.miami.edu/UMH/CDA/UMH_Main/0,1770,2460-1;2998-3,00.html].

Previous Recipients

Past Digital Fellows have included:

- *Robin Bachin*, Associate Professor of History, who created a digital archive and contextual narrative that examined the variety of elements that have shaped Travel, Tourism, and Urban Growth in Greater Miami [http://scholar.library.miami.edu/miamidigital/].

- *Kim Grinfeder*, an Assistant Professor in the School of Communication, who developed a rotational object video prototype that captures movement of three-dimensional objects from a 360 degree angle.

- *Lillian Manzor*, Associate Professor of Spanish, who developed and launched the Cuban/Latino Theater Archive [http://scholar.library.miami.edu/archivoteatral/], an interactive, multimedia, bilingual web resource for the study and research of Cuban theater and performing arts.

Important Dates

The deadline for the submission of proposals is December 14, 2007.

Contact

Submit all applications, and address all questions to:

Kyle R. Rimkus
Librarian Assistant Professor
Digital Projects Librarian
University of Miami Libraries
Otto G. Richter Library
1300 Memorial Drive
Coral Gables, FL 33146
email: <kyle@miami.edu>
tel: (305) 284 - 6221

3

UNIVERSITY OF VIRGINIA
UVA Library Graduate Fellowship In Digital Humanities
http://www2.lib.virginia.edu/scholarslab/about/fellowship.html

Grants

Dashboard » Arts & Sciences Grants Program

Browse ▾ Log In

» Grants Program for Digital Collections in Arts and Sciences

 ## Grants Program for Digital Collections in Arts and Sciences

⚙ Tools ▾

6 Added by Eric D. Robinson, last edited by Fiona C. Patrick on Oct 05, 2011 (view change)

Goals of the Program

The program aims to support collaborative and creative use of resources through the creation of digital content of enduring value to the Cornell community and scholarship at large. Application process *does not require any expertise* - all you need is a **good idea** as the Library's visual resources team will guide you through the application process. The program, funded by the College of Arts of Sciences and coordinated by the Cornell University Library, was developed by the Arts & Sciences Visual Resources Advisory Group. Information about the Cornell University Library's visual resources services is available at: http://images.library.cornell.edu

Examples of proposals that are within the scope of the grants program include:

- Creating new digital collections that are based on resources regularly used in teaching or research, including lecture notes, slides, photographs, printed documents, and manuscripts.
- Digitizing collections that are already held by the Cornell University, which are instrumental in supporting learning, teaching, and research at Cornell (Final selection of materials will be subject to ability to clear copyright, if required.) View selected examples of sample collections.
- Converting materials held by other cultural institutions, and that will support teaching and research at Cornell - especially combining dispersed resources to create new and enriched ones (Final selection of materials will be subject to ability to clear copyright, if required.).

For examples of projects within the context of the grants program, see the 2010 awards listed below.

The emphasis is on building a library of resources to support a range of scholarly activities in the College of Arts and Science and at Cornell in general rather than creating teaching applications or custom-designed web sites for a specific course. The digital collections created through this grants program will become a part of Cornell University Library's digital library.

Individual project awards will be in the range of **$5,000-$25,000** in the form of digital collection development services and systems provided by the Library, collaboration planning, and wages or summer stipends for research assistants. Collaborative projects that combine internal and external funding and other special programs are welcome.

For more information or an initial assessment of a project idea, please email dcaps@cornell.edu or call 255-1830

Proposal Selection Criteria

The grant program is open to Cornell faculty in the **College of Arts and Sciences**. The Library particularly encourages projects that:

- Increase the availability, and consequently the use of a collection of demonstrated scholarly significance
- Identify collections from the Cornell University that are important and should be accessed online by a large community

- Demonstrate strong interest within the academic community for access to the collection
- Contribute significantly to the existing digital collections such as the ones included in the Cornell University Library's digital library.
- Support the College's subject strengths

Application Process

Express initial interest by **February 17, 2012** by sending an email to dcaps@cornell.edu. In a paragraph please include the following information - description of collection, document types (photographs, monographs, manuscripts, slides, etc.) and estimated collection size.

Staff from the Library's Digital Consulting and Production Services (DCAPS) will contact and assist applicants with the full proposal application process - including copyright issues, budgets, technology options. Full proposals due by **March 30, 2012.**

Download full proposal application (.doc)

The Proposal Review Committee, comprised of members of the Arts & Sciences Visual Resources Advisory Group, will evaluate proposals and make their recommendations.

Important Dates for 2012 Program

Stage	Date
Express initial interest by	February 17, 2012
Proposals due	March 30, 2012
Awards announcements	May 2012
Planning & Implementation Begins	August 2012

2011 Awards

Annetta Alexandridis, Classics/Art History - Greek and Roman Coin Collection
Collaborators: Verity Platt, Classics
Cornell's coin collection is listed among the most important numismatic collections in the United States. Online availability of 1,500 coins from the ancient world with detailed descriptions will enable the integration of these coins in teaching and learning at Cornell and elsewhere. Because the coins are too valuable and risky, currently they can be used only for small-group classes. The potential is enormous.

David Bathrick, German Studies/Theater - Kluge Online,
Collaborators: Dr. Rainer Stollmann, University of Bremen(Germany), University of Bremen Library, Dr. Michael Jennings (Princeton University)
We will significantly expand the existing Muller-Kluge online collection, which is one of the most visited collections hosted by the Library. The website consist of interviews between West German filmmaker Alexander Kluge and the East German playwright Heiner Muller < http://muller-kluge.library.cornell.edu/en/. The new site will will incorporate Kluge interviews with Hans Magnus Enzenberger and Oskar Negt. This initiative also involves a partnership and will enable Cornell to have access to Princeton's Kluge Research Collection.

Katsuya Hirano, History/Asian Studies - Japanese Woodblocks from the William Elliot Griffis Collection
Collaborators: Daniel McKee, Japanese Bibliographer, CUL
These 17th century Japanese woodblock printed books represent Japan's initial attempts to understand the west and modernize itself. They are therefore of great importance in understanding the formation of modern Japan. These books, many of which are

rare or even unique in US collections, have great appeal to historians, art historians, and scholars of cultural politics.

Tim Murray, Society for the Humanities/Comparative Literature & English - Experimental Television Center (ETC)
The funding will enable the digitization and preservation of the Experimental Television Center (ETC) video collection, which is a prominent video art collection. This project will provide an invaluable resource to students and faculty studying the history of the contemporary media arts and will be used in History of Art and Visual Studies, Comparative Literature, Art, Music, American Studies, Latino Studies, Asian American Studies, and Theatre, Film and Dance.

Karen Pinkus, Italian and Comparative Literature - Divine Comedy Image Archive, Fiske Dante Collection
Collaborators: Marilyn Migiel, Italian Literature, William Kennedy, Comparative Literature, Patrick Stevens, Curator, Fiske Dante Collection
The Divine Comedy, the chief epic poem in Italian literature, may be described as compulsory study for any student specializing in Italian literature. Italian Studies programs will be the initial beneficiaries of the DCIA, but interdisciplinary approaches such as art history, visual studies and the history of the book will also find the DCIA a significant resource. The Divine Comedy Image Archive will offer scholars a large and diverse repository of images accessible for research and publication and will be accompanied with English/Italian descriptions and transcriptions.

Steve Pond, Music - Hip Hop Collection
Collaborators: Katherine Reagan, Curator of Rare Books and Manuscripts; Bonna Boettcher, Music Library
Founded in 2007, Cornell's hip hop collection is the largest archive on early hip hop culture in the United States. Faculty from the Departments/Programs of History, English, Africana Studies and Music have all incorporated elements of the archive into their research or teaching. This initial project will digitize flyers and preserve original recordings to set the stage for a future larger national grant with other partners aimed and enhancing access to and preserving the early history of hip hop culture.

2010 Awards

2010 awards were announced in May 2010 and the projects are in progress. See the Cornell Chronicle story about the initiative.

FACULTY NAME	DEPARTMENT	PROPOSAL SUMMARY	SITE	PROJECT TYPE
Janice Kanemitsu

Dan McKee | Asian Studies

Asia Collections/CUL | Japanese Theater Manuscripts - nineteenth century woodblock printed, heavily illustrated books on the Japanese theater. 20 Volumes/1600 pages | | Digitization and online delivery |
| Annetta Alexandridis | Classics/Art History | Cornell's plaster cast collection that once consisted of ca. 600 casts of statues and inscriptions (made in the 19th century mainly from Greek and Roman, but also from Egyptian, Near Eastern, European Medieval and Renaissance objects), and several hundred casts of medallions and gem stones. | | Digitization and online delivery |
| Howard Howland | Representing CAPE (Cornell Association of Professors Emerti) | Update "Contributions to Cornell history: Portraits and Memorabilia" by Elizabeth Baker Wells (Olin Ref LD 1371.WD 45) This book of 265 pages was published in 1984 with a supplement published about 10 years later. It lists about 2000 plaques, pictures, sculptures, and other objects of artistic and historical interest scattered around the Cornell campus. *It is an invaluable record of the University's historical and artistic artifacts.* | | Digitization, OCR for Database Development |
| Kath March

Bronwen Bledsoe | Anthropology

South Asia Collection/CUL | Nepali Texts
Nepali textbooks to be of interest to scholars in the politics, language/linguistics, sociology, religious studies, agricultural and international economic development studies, and of course, education. They are visually interesting, part of everyday and popular culture, and ripe for application to timely | | Digitization and online delivery as PDF. ~200 titles, 25,000 pages |

		academic problems in virtually any field.	 Nepali Texts	
David Bathrick	German Studies	Müller: Kluge - interviews between West German writer and film maker Alexander Kluge and the East German playwright Heiner Müller		Additional video content integrated into existing web delivery platform

Contacts

For more information, please email dcaps@cornell.edu or call 255-1830.

DCAPS (Digital Consulting & Production Services)
175 Kroch Library
http://dcaps.library.cornell.edu

For general assistance with **Visual Resources & Digital Support Services**
http://images.library.cornell.edu
email vrhelp-l@cornell.edu

Visual Resources Support for A&S Faculty

Information about imaging, metadata creation, online access, and visual resource support services are available at
https://confluence.cornell.edu/x/CRAMC

Grants Program Poster

Click for the full poster

Institute for Digital Research in the Humanities

IDRH Home   About IDRH   Calendar   CoLang 2012   Digital Humanities Seminar   Representing Knowledge Conference   Seed Grants

News and Announcements

Seed Grants

The deadline for the 2012 Seed Grant competition is February 8, 2012.

*See **Full Guidelines and Application Form** for more details.*

The IDRH Digital Humanities Seed Grants are intended to encourage KU faculty and academic staff to plan or pilot a collaborative project using digital technologies, which should in turn result in a more competitive subsequent external funding application. The digital humanities use "digital media and technology to advance the full range of thought and practice in the humanities, from the creation of scholarly resources, to research on those resources, to the communication of results to colleagues and students" (Cohen 2011).

Description: Projects should be for the initial stages of digital research in the humanities, and include a commitment to apply within a year for external funding. Seed grants may be used to create pilot projects, develop ideas via a workshop, attend workshops, support project-related travel, hold a substantial planning or brainstorming session, or similar activities. Projects can include, but are not limited to:

- text analysis and data-mining techniques;
- data visualization techniques;
- applying of Geographic Information Systems to humanities research;
- examining the emerging multimedia and multimodal technologies in the humanities
- collaborative work via Internet sites and tools (e.g. commons-based peer production)
- development of new digital tools for analyzing and making available digital resources
- new digital models of publication and dissemination of scholarship
- digital technology for research and teaching

Outcomes: IDRH Seed Grants should result in pilot projects, plans, or prototypes that will be used to pursue subsequent external funding. Successful applicants may be asked to present their project as part of the Hall Center for the Humanities Faculty Seminar in Digital Humanities.

Eligibility: KU full-time humanities and social science faculty.

Anticipated funding levels: Up to $15,000.

Please refer to the 2011 Seed Grant Proposal Guidelines (PDF) for more information. (Guidelines subject to change for future grant rounds.)

Funded Projects

2011

Project Title: Digital Resources for Second Language Acquisition Research: an Annotated Longitudinal Corpus of Learner German

Description: This project aims to annotate, analyze, and make publicly available a digital longitudinal corpus of writing samples collected from American learners of German at dense time intervals over several semesters. This project will advance the digital humanistic scholarship by applying a new annotation schema developed specifically for learner language, evaluating the output of this annotation, and publishing the corpus and studies afforded by this annotation. This international project will combine the PI's language acquisition expertise and the collaborator's computational linguistics expertise.

P.I.: Nina Vyatkina, Assistant Professor, Germanic Languages and Literatures

Award: $15,000

Awarded May 2011

Contact

Arienne Dwyer
Co-director,
Institute for Digital Research in the Humanities
Associate Professor,
Anthropology
785-864-2649
email: anthlinguist AT ku DOT edu

Brian Rosenblum
Co-director,
Institute for Digital Research in the Humanities
Associate Librarian,
KU Libraries
785-864-8883
brianlee@ku.edu

Past IDRH Events

THATCamp Kansas
(September 2011)

Digital Jumpstart Workshops
(March 2011)

New Scholarly Texts, New Scholarly Practices: A Discussion with Kathleen Fitzpatrick
(February 2011)

Related Links

KU Libraries Center for Digital Scholarship

IDRH Partners

KU Libraries

Hall Center for the Humanities

College of Liberal Arts and Sciences

UNIVERSITY OF MASSACHUSETTS AMHERST

Digital Humanities Grants

http://www.umass.edu/hfa/grants/hfafunding/frs/digitalhumanities.html

UMassAmherst

Search UMass Amherst | Go

College of
HUMANITIES
and **FINE ARTS**

About | Students | Faculty | Alumni | Staff | News & Events | Grants | Dean's Office | Give Online | Contact

Find Funding

HFA Funding

University Funding

External Funding

Resources

Grants Calendar

Grant Writing

Campus Support

Recent Activity

FAQ

Digital Humanities Grants

Request for Proposals: Seed grants in Digital Humanities

Description

The College of Humanities and Fine Arts (CHFA) is offering seed grants to help faculty develop and launch new research projects in the Digital Humanities. Proposals for these grants will reflect the contemporary use of technology for research and scholarly activity in the Humanities and Fine Arts. Applications that propose to use grant funds in one's own teaching will not be considered; however, research projects on pedagogy are welcome. Successful proposals will describe innovative projects that show promise of eventually gaining external funding. For example, the CHFA seed grants might be used for "proof of concept" or pilot projects that would enhance applications for external funding. The review of proposals and recommendations for recipients will be made by the directors of the Digital Humanities Initiative, in consultation with the dean.

Applicants may apply for grants up to $10,000; larger amounts will be considered only in exceptional circumstances. Applications should include the following sections:

1) Description of the Project
2) Significance of the Project within one's field of study
3) Statement of Innovation, specifying the contribution of the project to the digital humanities
4) Proposed External Sponsor and Timeline for application
5) Detailed Budget, including equipment needed
6) Proof of willingness to cooperate from any collaborators (on or off campus). An email asserting a willingness to cooperate is sufficient.

Application

Applications should not exceed five pages, single-spaced, and are due November 5, 2010. Please attach a short c.v. and a copy of the RFP (or program description) for the intended externally sponsored grant that will come out of this seed funding. Send completed applications as an attachment (pdf or Word) to Kate Freedman at kfreedma@history.umass.edu.

Successful applicants will be expected to become active members in the Digital Humanities Initiative and will gain access to its facilities and support structures. The Digital Humanities Initiative is composed of core HFA faculty whose research projects directly engage the use of digital tools for analysis, as a site of study, or as a forum for engaging scholarly and public audiences in research findings. The Initiative provides lab space (in Herter Hall adjacent to the Translation Center) for those working on such projects, a collaborative research group to help develop successful proposals, and a seminar series open to interested faculty on ongoing digital research projects. Any faculty member who seeks sponsored funding for a digital humanities project may put a sponsored grant through the Initiative, thus gaining access to the lab, support staff, and collaborative mentorship. In return, a faculty member with an active project in the Initiative becomes a core member and contributes to the expanding and defining of the group's goals.

Back to Faculty Research Support

Back to HFA Funding

This page is maintained by the **College of Humanities and Fine Arts**.
© 2011 University of Massachusetts Amherst • **Site Policies**

Promotional Materials

The **DHC** brings together **PEOPLE, TECHNOLOGY,** and **INFORMATION RESOURCES** in an environment where researchers can work with multimedia resources in consultation with humanities librarians and technology specialists.

THE DHC FEATURES

* Windows and Mac workstations
* Flatbed, film, and large-format book scanners
* Digital video editing workstations
* Library research and technology workshops
* A help desk for research and technology questions
* One-on-one consultations with research librarians and technology experts
* A wide range of specialized software

www.columbia.edu/library/dhc

SERVICES

- Help using the Libraries' digital primary- and secondary-source collections
- In-depth consultations on research and technology projects
- Support for digitizing texts and images by scanning or reprocessing
- Editing and publishing texts and images using DreamWeaver, oXygen, Adobe Creative Suite, and word-processing software
- Digital video editing using FinalCut Pro, iMovie
- Citation management using EndNote, RefWorks, Zotero
- Research notes management using FileMaker Pro, Adobe Acrobat
- Textual and qualitative analysis using NVIVO and other tools
- Access to a collection of essential electronic text resources that are accessible on-site only

The Digital Music Lab @ The Music & Arts Library (Dodge 701)

www.columbia.edu/library/musiclab

The Digital Music Lab offers Mac workstations for creating and editing digital audio and music notation, digital pianos, and expert assistance from library staff.

STAFF

Subject specialist librarians from the Libraries' History & Humanities Division are available at the DHC to work with you on your research projects or dissertation.

Technology consultants will help you identify and use the tools available at the DHC. Consultations with librarians from other humanities libraries on campus are also available.

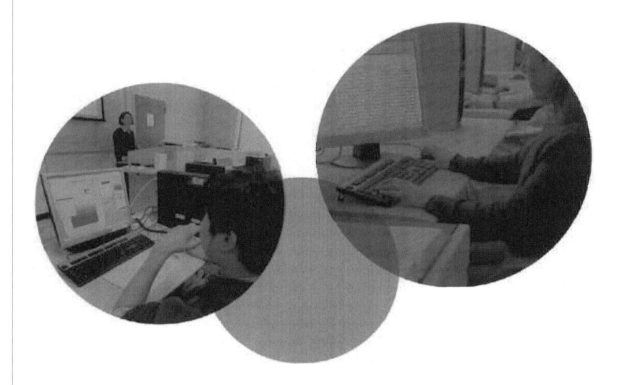

HOURS

www.columbia.edu/library/hours

CONSULTATIONS & RESEARCH ASSISTANCE

Request a research consultation at
www.columbia.edu/library/ask

For a technology consultation, e-mail
dhc@libraries.cul.columbia.edu

Walk-in assistance is available daily at the DHC.

WORKSHOPS

www.columbia.edu/library/dhc/workshops

* Course-related and research methods workshops

* Citation management software: EndNote, RefWorks, Zotero

* Qualitative analysis and database programs: NVIVO and Filemaker Pro

* Scanning techniques

* Adobe Photoshop and Advanced Google

* Digital video editing

For a wide range of software tutorials go to Lynda.com at
http://www.lynda.com/portal/columbia

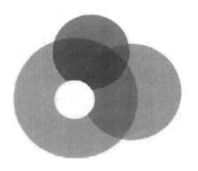

DIGITAL HUMANITIES CENTER

COLUMBIA UNIVERSITY LIBRARIES

www.columbia.edu/library/dhc
dhc@libraries.cul.columbia.edu
212 854 7547

BUTLER LIBRARY
Room 305
535 West 114th Street
New York, NY 10027

EDITOR: JENNIFER RUTNER PHOTOS: CHRIS TAGGART DESIGN: REED SEIFER

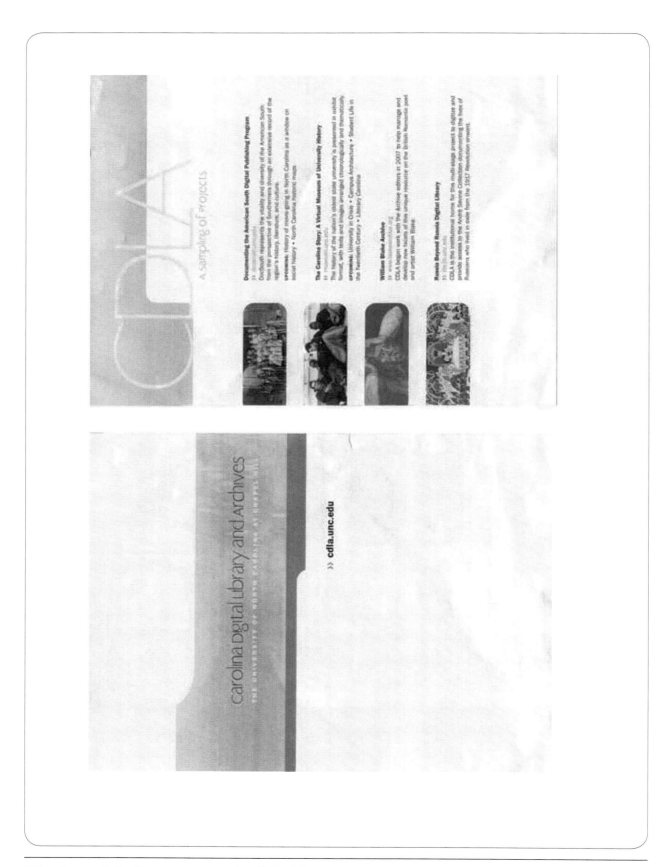

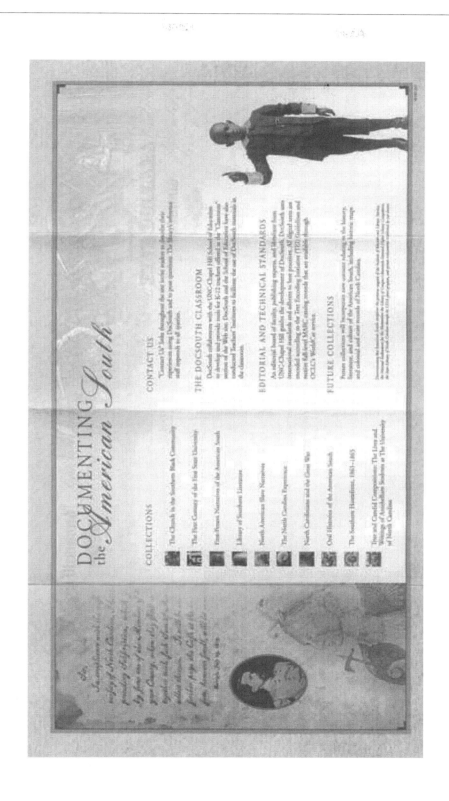

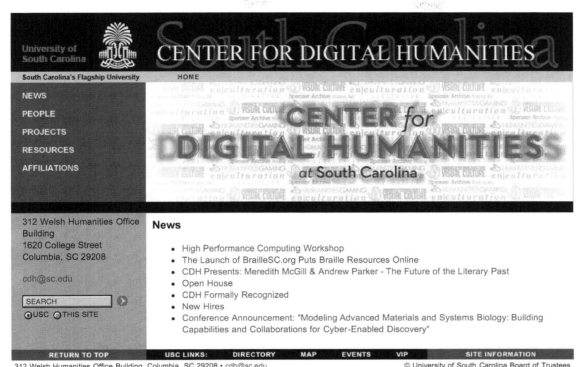

University of
South Carolina

CENTER FOR DIGITAL HUMANITIES

South Carolina's Flagship University

HOME

NEWS

PEOPLE

PROJECTS

RESOURCES

AFFILIATIONS

CENTER *for*
DIGITAL HUMANITIES
at South Carolina

312 Welsh Humanities Office
Building
1620 College Street
Columbia, SC 29208

cdh@sc.edu

SEARCH

○ USC ○ THIS SITE

News

- High Performance Computing Workshop
- The Launch of BrailleSC.org Puts Braille Resources Online
- CDH Presents: Meredith McGill & Andrew Parker - The Future of the Literary Past
- Open House
- CDH Formally Recognized
- New Hires
- Conference Announcement: "Modeling Advanced Materials and Systems Biology: Building Capabilities and Collaborations for Cyber-Enabled Discovery"

RETURN TO TOP   USC LINKS: DIRECTORY   MAP   EVENTS   VIP   SITE INFORMATION

312 Welsh Humanities Office Building, Columbia, SC 29208 • cdh@sc.edu

© University of South Carolina Board of Trustees

Repositories

CORNELL UNIVERSITY
Rose Goldsen Archive of New Media Art
http://goldsen.library.cornell.edu/

INDIANA UNIVERSITY BLOOMINGTON
IUScholarWorks Repository
https://scholarworks.iu.edu/dspace/

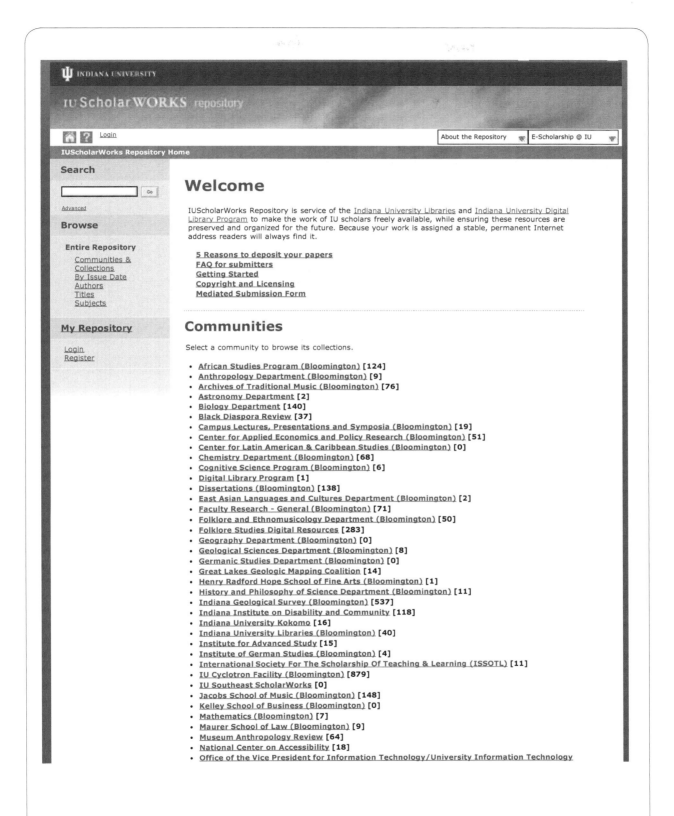

INDIANA UNIVERSITY

IU Scholar WORKS repository

Login | About the Repository ▾ | E-Scholarship @ IU ▾

IUScholarWorks Repository Home

Search

[ ] Go

Advanced

Browse

Entire Repository
- Communities & Collections
- By Issue Date
- Authors
- Titles
- Subjects

My Repository

Login
Register

Welcome

IUScholarWorks Repository is service of the Indiana University Libraries and Indiana University Digital Library Program to make the work of IU scholars freely available, while ensuring these resources are preserved and organized for the future. Because your work is assigned a stable, permanent Internet address readers will always find it.

5 Reasons to deposit your papers
FAQ for submitters
Getting Started
Copyright and Licensing
Mediated Submission Form

Communities

Select a community to browse its collections.

- **African Studies Program (Bloomington) [124]**
- **Anthropology Department (Bloomington) [9]**
- **Archives of Traditional Music (Bloomington) [76]**
- **Astronomy Department [2]**
- **Biology Department [140]**
- **Black Diaspora Review [37]**
- **Campus Lectures, Presentations and Symposia (Bloomington) [19]**
- **Center for Applied Economics and Policy Research (Bloomington) [51]**
- **Center for Latin American & Caribbean Studies (Bloomington) [0]**
- **Chemistry Department (Bloomington) [68]**
- **Cognitive Science Program (Bloomington) [6]**
- **Digital Library Program [1]**
- **Dissertations (Bloomington) [138]**
- **East Asian Languages and Cultures Department (Bloomington) [2]**
- **Faculty Research - General (Bloomington) [71]**
- **Folklore and Ethnomusicology Department (Bloomington) [50]**
- **Folklore Studies Digital Resources [283]**
- **Geography Department (Bloomington) [0]**
- **Geological Sciences Department (Bloomington) [8]**
- **Germanic Studies Department (Bloomington) [0]**
- **Great Lakes Geologic Mapping Coalition [14]**
- **Henry Radford Hope School of Fine Arts (Bloomington) [1]**
- **History and Philosophy of Science Department (Bloomington) [11]**
- **Indiana Geological Survey (Bloomington) [537]**
- **Indiana Institute on Disability and Community [118]**
- **Indiana University Kokomo [16]**
- **Indiana University Libraries (Bloomington) [40]**
- **Institute for Advanced Study [15]**
- **Institute of German Studies (Bloomington) [4]**
- **International Society For The Scholarship Of Teaching & Learning (ISSOTL) [11]**
- **IU Cyclotron Facility (Bloomington) [879]**
- **IU Southeast ScholarWorks [0]**
- **Jacobs School of Music (Bloomington) [148]**
- **Kelley School of Business (Bloomington) [0]**
- **Mathematics (Bloomington) [7]**
- **Maurer School of Law (Bloomington) [9]**
- **Museum Anthropology Review [64]**
- **National Center on Accessibility [18]**
- **Office of the Vice President for Information Technology/University Information Technology**

Services [77]
- Rob Kling Center for Social Informatics (Bloomington) [50]
- Scholarship of Teaching and Learning [1]
- School of Education (Bloomington) [36]
- School of Health, Physical Education, and Recreation (Bloomington) [40]
- School of Library and Information Science (Bloomington) [40]
- School of Optometry [2]
- School of Public and Environmental Affairs (Bloomington) [1]
- The Medieval Review [3225]
- Traditional Arts Indiana [11]
- Trickster Press [1408]

OHIO STATE UNIVERSITY
Knowledge Bank Center
https://kb.osu.edu/dspace/

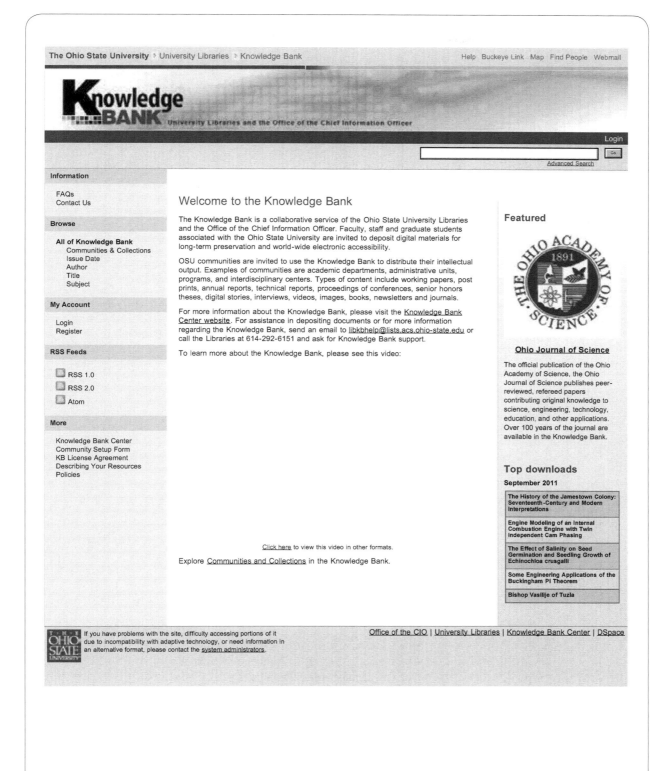

RICE UNIVERSITY
digital scholarship archive
http://scholarship.rice.edu/

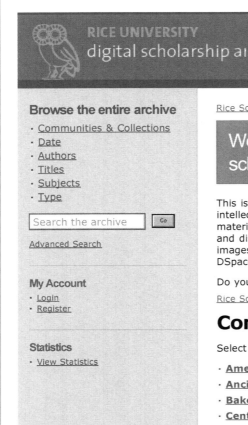

Home | FAQ | Contact Us

RICE UNIVERSITY
digital scholarship ar

Browse the entire archive
- Communities & Collections
- Date
- Authors
- Titles
- Subjects
- Type

Search the archive [Go]

Advanced Search

My Account
- Login
- Register

Statistics
- View Statistics

Rice Scholarship Home ▶

Welcome to Rice University's digital scholarship archive

This is Rice's institutional repository, a web site where the university's intellectual output is shared, managed, searched, and preserved. Most materials come from Rice faculty members' research, electronic theses and dissertations, and digitized collections of rare or unique books, images, musical performances, and manuscripts. The archive runs on DSpace, an open source software package.

Do you have questions about this archive? Read our FAQ.

Rice Scholarship Home ▶

Communities in the archive

Select a community to browse its collections.

- **Americas Archive** [1297 items]
- **Ancient Rome** [2532 items]
- **Baker Institute** [7 items]
- **Center for Technology in Teaching and Learning** [23 items]
- **Dean of Undergraduates** [6 items]
- **Digital Library Information** [1 items]
- **Fondren Library** [254 items]
- **George R. Brown School of Engineering** [1780 items]
- **History of Rice University** [51 items]
- **Indigenous Australian languages** [2 items]
- **JCDL Doctoral Consortium** [14 items]
- **Museum of Houston** [855 items]
- **Rice Ephemera Archive** [4523 items]
- **Rice University Commencement Programs and Ephemera** [313 items]
- **Rice University Electronic Theses and Dissertations** [7340 items]
- **Rice University General Announcements** [86 items]
- **Rice University Historical Images and Key Documents** [19 items]
- **Rice University News Publications** [7659 items]
- **Rice University Presidential Speeches** [6 items]
- **Rice University Press** [0 items]
- **Rice University Undergraduate Research** [2 items]
- **Rice University Yearbooks** [20 items]

- **School of Architecture** [26 items]
- **School of Humanities** [83 items]
- **Shepherd School of Music** [2315 items]
- **TIMEA - Travelers in the Middle East Archive** [1994 items]
- **The Rice Institute Pamphlet** [637 items]
- **Wiess School of Natural Sciences** [25 items]
- **Woodson Research Center** [2189 items]

Rice Scholarship Home ▶

Search the archive

Enter some text in the box below to search the archive.

 Go

Home | FAQ | Contact Us

Managed by the Center for Digital Scholarship at Fondren Library, Rice University

Home · About Us · Site Search

Open Source Projects · Developers' Area · Contact Us · Version 5.2.1

RUcore
Rutgers University Community Repository

Search RUcore   Faculty Portal   Collections   Collaborations

»RUcore   »**About RUcore**

About RUcore

RUcore –the Rutgers Community Repository– is a digital repository for the significant intellectual property of Rutgers University- its libraries, faculty and their collaborators.

RUcore's mission statement:

Rutgers Community Repository (RUcore) is a repository of digital research and educational materials created and used by the University community and its strategic collaborators. The goal of the Rutgers University Community Repository is to advance research and learning at Rutgers, to foster interdisciplinary collaboration, and to contribute to the development of new knowledge through the archiving, preservation, and presentation of digital resources. Original research products and papers of the faculty and administrators and the unique resources of the libraries will be permanently preserved and made accessible with tools developed to facilitate and encourage their continued use.

What are RUcore's policies?

What are RUcore's services?

RUcore's developing collection includes

- Primary source materials-manuscripts, photographs, maps, and multimedia, from the libraries' special collections.
- Resources about New Jersey, from the state's libraries, museums, archives and historical societies from the New Jersey Digital Highway collection.
- Electronic theses and dissertations, in collaboration with the Rutgers University graduate schools.
- Faculty and Departmental publications: pre-prints, postprints, presentations, technical reports, etc.

Learn more about current or developing collections

SELECTED RESOURCES

Libraries in the Digital Age

Academic Library Research: Perspectives and Current Trends. ACRL Publications in Librarianship no. 59. Chicago: Association of College and Research Libraries, 2008.

Association of College and Research Libraries. "Changing Roles of Academic and Research Libraries." *Association of College and Research Libraries*, November 2006. http://www.ala.org/ala/mgrps/divs/acrl/issues/value/changingroles.cfm.

Boyack, Kevin W., Brian N. Wylie, and George S. Davidson. "A Call to Researchers: Digital Libraries Need Collaboration Across Disciplines." *D-Lib Magazine* 7, no. 10 (October 2001). http://www.dlib.org/dlib/october01/boyack/10boyack.html.

Council on Library and Information Resources. *Library as Place: Rethinking Roles, Rethinking Space*. Washington, DC: Council on Library and Information Resources, 2005. http://www.clir.org/pubs/abstract/pub129abst.html.

———. *No Brief Candle: Reconceiving Research Libraries for the 21st Century*. Washington, DC: Council on Library and Information Resources, 2008. http://www.clir.org/pubs/abstract/pub142abst.html.

Crane, Gregory, and Alison Jones. "Text, Information, Knowledge and the Evolving Record of Humanity." *D-Lib Magazine* 12, no. 3 (March 2006). http://www.dlib.org/dlib/march06/jones/03jones.html.

Greenstein, Daniel, and Suzanne E. Thorin. *The Digital Library: A Biography*. Washington, DC: Digital Library Federation/Council on Library and Information Resources, 2002. http://www.clir.org/pubs/abstract/pub109abst.html.

Marcum, Deanna, and Amy Friedlander. "Keepers of the Crumbling Culture." *D-Lib Magazine* 9, no. 5 (May 2003). http://www.dlib.org/dlib/may03/friedlander/05friedlander.html.

Mitchell, Marilyn. *Library Workflow Redesign: Six Case Studies*. Washington, DC: Council on Library and Information Resources, 2007. http://www.clir.org/pubs/abstract/pub139abst.html.

Pradt Lougee, Wendy. *Diffuse Libraries: Emergent Roles for the Research Library in the Digital Age*. Washington, DC: Council on Library and Information Resources, 2002. http://www.clir.org/pubs/abstract/pub108abst.html.

Digital Humanities and the Library

Digital Librarians Initiative. *Role of Librarians in Digital Humanities Centers.* White Paper. Emory University Library, August 2010. http://docs.google.com/Doc?docid=0AZbw4Qx_a5JPZGM2OWdrdzZfMTMycW RncHJwbWo&hl=en.

Draxler, Bridget. "Digital Humanities Symposium: The Scholar, the Library and the Digital Future." *HASTAC*, February 2011. http://hastac.org/blogs/bridgetdraxler/digital-humanities-symposium-scholar-library-and-digital-future.

Edwards, Richard. "Creating the Center for Digital Research in the Humanities." University of Nebraska-Lincoln, July 18, 2005. http://cdrh.unl.edu/articles/creatingcdrh.php.

Fister, Barbara. "Getting Serious About Digital Humanities (Peer to Peer Review)." *Library Journal* May 27, 2010. http://www.libraryjournal.com/article/CA6729325.html?nid=2673&source=title&rid=#r eg_visitor_id#.

Hockey, Susan. "Living with Google: Perspectives on Humanities Computing and Digital Libraries." *Literary and Linguistic Computing* 20, no. 1 (March 1, 2005): 7–24.

Kamada, Hitoshi. "Digital Humanities: Roles for Libraries?" *College & Research Libraries News* 71, no. 9 (October 2010): 484–85.

Kretzschmar, William A., and William Gray Potter. "Library Collaboration with Large Digital Humanities Projects." *Literary and Linguistic Computing* 25, no. 4 (December 1, 2010): 439–45.

New York Public Library. "Digital Humanities and the Future of Libraries (Multimedia Conference Proceedings)." June 16, 2011. http://www.nypl.org/events/programs/2011/06/16/digital-humanities-and-future-libraries.

Nowviskie, Bethany. "A Skunk in the Library." June 28, 2011. http://nowviskie.org/2011/a-skunk-in-the-library/.

Ramsay, Stephen. "Care of the Soul." *Literatura Mundana* October 8, 2010. http://lenz.unl.edu/wordpress/?p=266.

Rydberg Cox, Jeffrey A. *Digital Libraries and the Challenges of Digital Humanities.* Chandos Information Professional Series. Oxford: Chandos Publishing, 2006.

Siemens, Lynne, Richard Cunningham, Wendy Duff, and Claire Warwick. "A Tale of Two Cities: Implications of the Similarities and Differences in Collaborative Approaches Within the Digital Libraries and Digital Humanities Communities." *Literary and Linguistic Computing* 26, no. 3 (2011): 335–48.

Sukovic, Suzana. "Beyond the Scriptorium: The Role of the Library in Text Encoding." *D-Lib Magazine* 8, no. 1 (January 2002). http://www.dlib.org/dlib/january02/sukovic/01sukovic.html.

Vinopal, Jennifer. "Why Understanding the Digital Humanities Is Key for Libraries." *Library Sphere* February 2011. http://vinopal.org/2011/02/18/whyunderstanding-the-digital-humanities-is-key-for-libraries/.

Digital Humanities: Infrastructure and Evolution

American Council of Learned Societies. *Our Cultural Commonwealth: The Report of the American Council of Learned Societies Commission on Cyberinfrastructure for the Humanities and Social Sciences.* New York: American Council of Learned Societies, 2006.

Archer, Dawn. "Digital Humanities 2006: When Two Became Many." *Literary and Linguistic Computing* 23, no. 1 (April 1, 2008): 103–08.

Borgman, Christine L. *Scholarship in the Digital Age: Information, Infrastructure, and the Internet.* Cambridge, Mass.: MIT Press, 2007.

Council on Library and Information Resources. *Working Together or Apart: Promoting the Next Generation of Digital Scholarship.* Washington, DC, March 2009. http://www.clir.org/pubs/reports/pub145/pub145.pdf.

Flanders, Julia. "The Productive Unease of 21st-century Digital Scholarship." *DHQ: Digital Humanities Quarterly* 3, no. 3 (Summer 2009). http://digitalhumanities.org/dhq/vol/3/3/000055/000055.html.

Fraistat, Neil. "The Question(s) of Digital Humanities." Maryland Institute for Technology in the Humanities February 7, 2011. http://mith.umd.edu/thequestions-of-digital-humanities/.

Kirschenbaum, Matthew G. "What is Digital Humanities and What's it Doing in English Departments?" *ADE Bulletin* 150 (2010): 55–61.

McCarty, Willard, and Matthew Kirschenbaum. "Institutional Models for Humanities Computing." *Literary and Linguistic Computing* 18, no. 4 (November 1, 2003): 465–89.

Smith Rumsey, Abby. "Report of the Scholarly Communication Institute 8: Emerging Genres in Scholarly Communication." Scholarly Communication Institute, University of Virginia Library, July 2010.

Svensson, Patrik. "The Landscape of Digital Humanities." *DHQ: Digital Humanities Quarterly* 4, no. 1 (Summer 2010). http://digitalhumanities.org/dhq/vol/4/1/000080/000080.html.

Zorich, Diane M. *Digital Humanities Centers: Loci for Digital Scholarship.* Council on Library and Information Resources, November 2008. http://www.clir.org/activities/digitalscholar2/zorich.pdf.

Digital Humanities: Staffing and Support

Barribeau, Susan. "Enhancing Digital Humanities at UW-Madison: A White Paper." University of Wisconsin at Madison, 2009. http://dighum.wisc.edu/facultyseminar/index.html.

Blackwell, Christopher, and Thomas R. Martin. "Technology, Collaboration, and Undergraduate Research." *DHQ: Digital Humanities Quarterly:* 3, no. 1 (Winter 2009). http://digitalhumanities.org/dhq/vol/3/1/000024/000024.html.

Blustain, Harvey, and Donald Spicer. *Digital Humanities at the Crossroads: The University of Virginia.* ECAR Case Studies. Boulder, Colorado: Educause, 2005. net.educause.edu/ir/library/pdf/ers0605/cs/ecs0506.pdf.

Burgess, Helen J, and Jeanne Hamming. "New Media in the Academy: Labor and the Production of Knowledge in Scholarly Multimedia." *DHQ: Digital Humanities Quarterly* 5, no. 3 (Summer 2011). http://digitalhumanities.org/dhq/vol/5/3/000102/000102.html.

Greenberg, Hope, Elli Mylonas, Scott Hamlin, and Patrick Yott. "Supporting Digital Humanities Research: The Collaborative Approach." Northeast Regional Computing Program, March 2008. net.educause.edu/ir/library/pdf/NCP08094.pdf.

Kirschenbaum, Matthew G., Bethany Nowviskie, Tom Scheinfeldt, and Doug Reside. "Collaborators' Bill of Rights." Maryland Institute for Technology and the Humanities, January 22, 2011. http://mith.umd.edu/offthetracks/recommendations/.

Kirschenbaum, Matthew. "Done: Finishing Projects in the Digital Humanities." *DHQ: Digital Humanities Quarterly* 3, no. 2 (Spring 2009). http://digitalhumanities.org/dhq/vol/3/2/000037/000037.html.

McCarty, Willard. "Humanities Computing: Essential Problems, Experimental Practice." *Literary and Linguistic Computing* 17, no. 1 (April 1, 2002): 103–25.

Nichols, Stephen G. "Time to Change Our Thinking: Dismantling the Silo Model of Digital Scholarship." *Ariadne* no. 58 (January 30, 2009). http://www.ariadne.ac.uk/issue58/nichols/.

Ruecker, Stan, and Milena Radzikowska. "The Iterative Design of a Project Charter for Interdisciplinary Research." In *Proceedings of the 7th ACM Conference on Designing Interactive Systems-DIS '08*, 288-94. Cape Town, South Africa, 2008. http://dl.acm.org/citation.cfm?id=1394476.

Siemens, Lynne. "'It's a Team If You Use "Reply All"': An Exploration of Research Teams in Digital Humanities Environments." *Literary and Linguistic Computing* 24, no. 2 (June 1, 2009): 225–33.

Siemens, Lynne, Ray Siemens, Richard Cunningham, Teresa Dobson, Alan Galey, Stan Ruecker, and Claire Warwick. "INKE Administrative Structure, Omnibus Document." *New Knowledge Environments* 1, no. 1 (2009). http://journals.uvic.ca/index.php/INKE/article/view/546/245.

Spiro, Lisa. "Examples of Collaborative Digital Humanities Projects." Blog. *Digital Scholarship in the Humanities* June 1, 2009. http://digitalscholarship.wordpress.com/2009/06/01/examples-of-collaborative-digital-humanities-projects/.

Warwick, Claire, Isabel Galina, Melissa Terras, Paul Huntington, and Nikoleta Pappa. "The Master Builders: LAIRAH Research on Good Practice in the Construction of Digital Humanities Projects." *Literary and Linguistic Computing* 23, no. 3 (2008): 383–96.

Data Preservation and Stewardship

ARL/NSF Workshop on Long-Term Stewardship of Digital Data Collections. Association of Research Libraries, September 2006. http://www.arl.org/pp/access/nsfworkshop.shtml.

Cantara, Linda. "Long-Term Preservation of Digital Humanities Scholarship." *OCLC Systems and Services* 22, no. 1 (2006): 38–42.

Kirschenbaum, Matthew G., Richard Ovenden, and Gabriela Redwine. *Digital Forensics and Born-Digital Content in Cultural Heritage Collections.* Council on Library and Information Resources, December 2010. http://www.clir.org/pubs/abstract/pub149abst.html.

Maron, Nancy, K. Kirby Smith, and Matthew Loy. *Sustaining Digital Resources: An On-the-Ground View of Projects Today.* Ithaka Case Studies in Sustainability. Ithaka S+R, July 2009. http://www.ithaka.org/ithaka-s-r/research/ithaka-case-studies-in-sustainability/report/SCA_Ithaka_SustainingDigitalResources_Report.pdf.

Nowviskie, Bethany, and Dot Porter. "Graceful Degradation Survey Findings: Managing Digital Humanities Projects Through Times of Transition and Decline?" Digital Humanities 2010 Conference Abstract, June 2010. http://dh2010.cch.kcl.ac.uk/academic-programme/abstracts/papers/html/ab-722.html.

Sustainable Economics for a Digital Planet: Ensuring Long-Term Access to Digital Information. Washington, DC: Blue Ribbon Task Force on Sustainable Digital Preservation and Access, February 2010. http://brtf.sdsc.edu/biblio/BRTF_Final_Report.pdf.

Zorich, Diane M. *A Survey of Digital Cultural Heritage Initiatives and Their Sustainability Concerns.* Washington, DC: Council on Library and Information Resources, June 2003. http://www.clir.org/pubs/reports/pub118/contents.html.

Guides to Digital Humanities Projects, Tools, and Methods

arts-humanities.net: Guide to Digital Humanities and Arts
http://arts-humanities.net/

CUNY Digital Humanities Resource Guide
http://commons.gc.cuny.edu/wiki/index.php/The_CUNY_Digital_Humanities_Resource_Guide

Digital Humanities Questions & Answers
http://digitalhumanities.org/answers/

Digital Humanities Now
http://digitalhumanitiesnow.org/

Digital Research Tools Wiki (DiRT)
https://digitalresearchtools.pbworks.com/w/page/17801672/FrontPage

Duke University Libraries Digital Humanities Research Guide
http://guides.library.duke.edu/content.php?pid=129864&sid=1114048

Harvard Library Digital Humanities Café
http://guides.hcl.harvard.edu/digitalhumanities

UCLA Library Digital Humanities Research Guide
http://guides.library.ucla.edu/digitalhumanities

Warwick, Claire, Melissa Terras, and Julianne Nyhan, eds. *A Practical Guide to the Digital Humanities.* London: Facet Publishing, 2011.

Aspects of Language and Culture

CHANDLER & SHARP PUBLICATIONS IN ANTHROPOLOGY

GENERAL EDITORS: L. L. Langness and Robert B. Edgerton

Aspects of Language and Culture

Carol M. Eastman

University of Washington

CHANDLER & SHARP PUBLISHERS, INC.

11A COMMERCIAL BOULEVARD, NOVATO, CA 94947

Previously published and copyrighted materials are reprinted with the kind permission of authors, publishers, or copyright owners as listed below:

Figure 2, p. 42. From *Language and Its Structure: Some Fundamental and Linguistic Concepts* by Ronald W. Langacker. Reprinted by permission of Harcourt Brace Jovanovich, Inc. ● Figures 7, 8, and 10, pp. 91, 93, and 93. From Stephen A. Tyler, *Cognitive Anthropology* (Holt, Rinehart and Winston, 1969). Adapted and reprinted by permission of Stephen A. Tyler and the publisher. Copyright © 1969 by Holt, Rinehart and Winston, Publishers. ● Table 4, p. 96. From "The Diagnosis of Disease Among the Subanun of Mindanao" by Charles O. Frake. Reproduced by permission of the American Anthropological Association from *American Anthropologist* 63:118, 1961. ● Table 5, p. 102. From James P. Spradley, *You Owe Yourself a Drunk: An Ethnography of Urban Nomads*, p. 74. Copyright © 1970 by Little, Brown and Company (Inc.). Reprinted by permission. ● Table 6, p. 103. From James P. Spradley, *You Owe Yourself a Drunk: An Ethnography of Urban Nomads*, p. 76. Copyright © 1970 by Little, Brown and Company (Inc.). Reprinted by permission. ● Figure 11, p. 106. From Jerry A. Fodor, Jerrold J. Katz, *The Structure of Language: Readings in the Philosophy of Language* © 1964. Reprinted by permission of Prentice-Hall, Inc., Englewood Cliffs, New Jersey. ● Figure 12, p. 128. From "On Sociolinguistic Rules: Alternation and Co-Occurrence" by Susan Ervin-Tripp, in *Directions in Sociolinguistics: The Ethnography of Communication*, edited by John J. Gumperz and Dell Hymes. Copyright © 1972 by Holt, Rinehart and Winston, Publishers. Reprinted by permission of Holt, Rinehart and Winston, Publishers.

Library of Congress Cataloging in Publication Data

Eastman, Carol M.   1941–
  Aspects of language and culture.

  (Chandler & Sharp publications in anthropology)   Bibliography: p.
  Includes index.
  1. Language and culture.   2. Linguistics.
I. Title.
P35.E2   301.2'1   74-28741
ISBN: 0-88316-514-7

FOURTH PRINTING, 1985

Book Designed by Joseph M. Roter

Composition by Hansen & Associates Graphics

CONTENTS

Figures

Tables

PREFACE

This book is intended to be a short and general survey of linguistic approaches, methods, and theories used in the anthropological context. My purpose in writing this volume has been to show how linguistics has influenced the field of anthropology and has provided theories and methods used in the analysis of man in relation to culture.

Five areas in which linguistics or linguistic influences figure prominently in anthropological inquiry were chosen for discussion. Each area is reviewed in a separate chapter examining the issues and problems at hand.

As a survey of "Language and Culture," this book naturally relies heavily on the major works in that area of study. Throughout the following pages are extensive quotations from important works in the field. I have used direct quotations especially in cases where the idea under discussion is that of the person quoted—in order to insure that the idea is presented, as far as possible, as originally intended. Though I have relied heavily on other works, I accept the responsibility for my interpretations of them.

A continual merging, separation, and renewed merging of linguistic and anthropological theory and method may be seen in each area of linguistic anthropology surveyed in this book. It has been my hope that the views presented in the following pages of various linguistic approaches in anthropology might facilitate a wider understanding of aspects of the study of language and culture from both a theoretical and practical standpoint.

I am indebted to my student Douglas Paterson for reading and commenting extensively at various stages on the work in progress. I also wish to acknowledge Lew Langness, Bob Edgerton, Ronna Brown, Michael Graves, and John Jacobsen for their helpful comments. I thank Robert C. Dunnell, David Spain, and Jay Miller for many conversations about the ideas included here and also for the loan of a number of books, and Ellen Welsch for doing the Index.

Seattle, Washington   Carol M. Eastman
September 1975

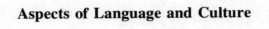

Aspects of Language and Culture

Introduction

The description of data was the major task of linguistics for a large part of this century. The linguistic scientists developed a method of descriptive linguistics which provided techniques for identifying the significant units of languages—phonemes and morphemes. It was hoped that such descriptions would be observationally adequate—that they would reflect the observable facts of the data. Further, it was hoped that languages so described could then be compared. Descriptive linguistics was an attempt to solve the nineteenth-century linguist's problem of ensuring that the linguistic data used to classify languages could be used systematically, thus also ensuring accurate classification. Ethnographers interested in cross-cultural comparison and culture classification also developed a descriptive method, using many of the notions of linguistics in order to produce ethnographies which contained an accurate description of the observed facts.

Along with the goal of descriptions which are observationally adequate, there arose an interest in understanding the nature of the phenomena described. The goal of structuralism became one of seeking descriptive adequacy, that is, of accounting for what underlies linguistic and cultural behavior. Structuralism approaches language and culture as logical systems reflecting the unconscious logical structure of the mind, which is assumed to be organized in a certain way. This organization constrains all human thought, and both language and culture are assumed to be related to thought as constrained by the structure of the mind. Thus, the structural analysis of linguistic and cultural phenomena such as mythology and kinship purports to reveal an understanding of the underlying common structure of human consciousness. A theory which could account for this commonality of human consciousness would be one that is explanatorily adequate. As yet, this goal is unattained by any theory; but progress is being made toward descriptively adequate analyses of linguistic and cultural phenomena which do seem to account for certain intuitions about language and about culture.

1

The transformationalist approach to language views language as a reflection of the mind. The view of the transformationalist is that the mind plays an "active role in determining the character of acquired knowledge" (Chomsky 1972:99). Language, in this view, is acquired knowledge, and the goal of transformational/generative grammar is to develop a model of language acquisition to reflect the role played by the mind.

Chapter 1, "Anthropological Linguistics," presents the basic ideas of descriptive linguistics from which many of the analogies in the study of culture discussed later in the book have been drawn. This chapter describes the methodology developed for the description of languages encountered by the anthropologist or linguist in the field. The goals of descriptive linguistics are similar to those of descriptive ethnography—in terms of the adequacy of the description.

Chapter 2, "Structuralism and Transformationalism," is a discussion of the trend away from descriptivism (both ethnographic and linguistic) and its stress on noting differences among languages and cultures, and the trend toward a concern with seeking generalizations which are universally applicable cross-culturally and cross-linguistically.

Chapter 3, "The Comparative Method," examines synchronic versus diachronic studies of language and culture, and the development and use of various systems of language and culture classification.

Chapter 4, "Language and Culture," considers the relationship of language to culture and culture to language, and the question as to what the studies of language and culture might have to say about the nature and process of thought. This chapter addresses itself to research concerned with the linguistic worldview problem. Does language structure the way we see the world, or does the way we see the world structure our language? What is the relationship between language and thought? How do language and thought reflect reality? The study of meaning from both the anthropologist's and the linguist's point of view is examined. This investigation touches on the development of ethnoscience in anthropology and the position of semantics in the field of linguistics.

In Chapter 5, "Sociolinguistics," the relatively new area of sociolinguistics is examined in terms of its methodology and its subject matter. Sociolinguistics examines both linguistic activity as such and linguistics as part of culture, both to be fully understood only in the context in which they take place. The discussion cites studies exemplifying the broad range of possible sociolinguistic data and offers proposals for a sociolinguistic methodology.

Chapter 1 Anthropological Linguistics

1.0 Introduction

The methods and techniques of describing languages in the field for the purpose of learning them as tools for gathering ethnographic data may, for our purposes, be termed ANTHROPOLOGICAL LINGUISTICS. This meaning encompasses linguistic description as done by the descriptive-linguistic method. For many years (mainly 1933–1957) these methods and techniques of describing unwritten languages were the sole methods and theories of the field of linguistics. The goal was to describe the data adequately and uniformly.

Descriptive linguistics, emphasizing the discovery of structures internal to language, grew out of nineteenth-century general linguistics, which placed an emphasis on historical study. It was hoped that grammars might be produced which would allow languages to be compared with each other.

In examining the descriptivist approach to linguistics in this chapter, we will look at the steps that the anthropological or descriptive linguist takes in describing his corpus of linguistic data adequately. Toward the end of the chapter, we will examine the notions of *etic* and *emic*, which grew out of descriptive linguistics. We will also look at Zellig Harris's approach to descriptive linguistics, which he termed *structural*; and we will discuss the distinction that the Swiss linguist Ferdinand deSaussure made between language as a system (*langue*) and language as speech (*parole*), which influenced the development of *structuralism* in linguistics and in anthropology. The ideas developed by Zellig Harris in his structural linguistics, the etics and emics of Kenneth Pike, and Ferdinand deSaussure's *langue* and *parole* serve as a transition from anthropological/descriptive linguistics to transformationalism and structuralism in both anthropology and linguistics as taken up in Chapter 2.

3

1.1   Phonetic Transcription and Phonemic Analysis

Before the turn of the century, American anthropological linguistics was pursued under difficult conditions. The field worker was required to deal with unwritten languages, and to carry out an analysis of a particular unwritten language on the basis of data elicited from informants in the field. The situation was, and in some areas still is, that of the first person to land on Mars who finds that he must learn to communicate in Martian and pave the way for others to do so as well. This necessity is in contrast to the situation in Europe around the turn of the century. There, linguistics dealt with the written form of basically related languages, and linguistic study could build upon a large body of linguistic literature already in existence for a long time. In America, in the 1890s and early 1900s, a method was needed for learning and describing the hitherto unsystematically studied languages of the native North American for both practical and scholarly ends.

Beginning at the turn of the century, American descriptive linguistics was developed largely under the influence of Franz Boas (*Handbook of American Indian Languages*, 1911) and took shape in the work of his student, Edward Sapir (*Language: An Introduction to the Study of Speech*, 1921). Both Boas and Sapir developed their notions of linguistic analysis through fieldwork on American Indian languages in the Pacific Northwest.

1.11   PHONETIC TRANSCRIPTION

The first step in linguistic analysis is that the linguist record the data he elicits from an informant who is a native speaker of the language to be described. To do so he must be able to write down the sounds he hears. The recording of data as perceived sounds is known as PHONETIC TRANSCRIPTION. A phonetic transcription is a record of *all* the sounds heard in speech. Such a transcription should be as detailed as possible.

In Boas and Sapir's day, the method of transcription used employed a set of both simple and complex symbols agreed upon to represent certain sounds. Boas and his students used a system which may be seen in the grammars contained in the *Handbook of American Indian Languages* and in other publications of the Bureau of American Ethnology around that time.

Later, however, the idea that there should be one and only one symbol per sound gained prevalence. This idea gave rise to what is known as IPA or the International Phonetic Alphabet. Most descriptive linguists are guided by this method of transcription, which has been set forth in *The Principles of the International Phonetic Association* (1949) (see Table 1).

Once the linguist has transcribed the data from an informant (as in Table 1, for example), it is his task to state as part of his description of the language what the sounds of that language are. He prepares a chart of phonetic symbols representing

Table 1.
Sample Transcriptions

Narrow Phonetic Transcription	[pʰǽdi: kʰék= pʰǽti kʰék= békʰ ɜ ʳz mǽ:n bék mí ə̆ kʰék ǽz fǽsd ǽz yú: kʰǽn]
Phonemic Transcription	/pæti kek pæti kek bek ɜ ʳz mæn bek mi ə kek æz fæst æz yu kæn/
Orthographic Representation	Patty cake, patty cake, baker's man, Bake me a cake as fast as you can.
	´ stress [ ] phonetic transcription / / phonemic transcription h aspiration = an unreleased sound ɜʳ an *r*-colored mid-front vowel as in *bird* v voicing ə schwa, a mid-central vowel : length

the various sounds, and notes where they are produced in the mouth and how they are produced. Table 2 illustrates some consonants arranged on such a chart (see Section 1.12 below).

Sapir noticed that the phonetic elements which a linguist transcribes do not necessarily coincide with what a native speaker of the language perceives the sounds to be. For example, in Table 1 observe that the English word *cake* is transcribed as [kʰek=], that is, with two different *k* sounds, [kh] and [k=]. If asked, a native speaker of English would say that the initial and final sounds of *cake* are the same sound, [k].

Language speakers and hearers do not speak and hear phonetic elements, but rather select and combine certain phonetic elements as distinctive sounds for their language. In Sapir's view, it is not enough in a description of a language to transcribe phonetic elements and then list them in the sound system. To be able to write down what is heard is not to be able to describe what part of that which is heard the speaker needs and uses in speech. Somehow the distinctive phonetic elements of a language must be ferreted out from the total phonetic data recorded in a phonetic transcription. Sapir used the term PHONEME for the phonetically distinct units of sound in language.

Sapir was not the first linguist to use the term *phoneme*. The phoneme had figured previously in the writings of some European linguists.[1]

Sapir's view that a speaker hears phonemes rather than phonetic elements in interpreting speech arose from his own experience in the field as he attempted to teach speakers of American Indian languages to carry out phonetic transcriptions of their own languages. He was trying to teach individuals to write down the sounds they use, the sounds they speak and hear.

Frequently, in their transcriptions, good students would consistently write sounds different from those they actually used. What occurred may be shown by an English example. If the word *pin* is spoken, its phonetic transcription (that is, the written representation of what is actually heard) would be more like [pʰin], with the [ʰ] representing the puff of air which a non-native English speaker hears after the /p/. However, a native English speaker would be more likely to write *pin*, linking the initial sound of the word with the final sound in the English word *sleep*. If asked what common sound do the words *pin* and *sleep* have, he would say /p/. Phonetically, the two words share no identical sound—the initial sound in *pin* is an aspirated /p/, [pʰ], the final sound in *sleep* is an unaspirated /p/, [p⁼]. This situation with /p/ in English parallels that with /k/ as seen in the example on p. 5. What is shared in *pin* and *sleep* and what is common about the two /k/ sounds in *cake* is a phoneme, that is, the feeling that there is a /p/, not a [pʰ], in *pin*, a /p/, not a [p⁼], in *sleep*, and two /k/'s in *cake*.

According to Sapir, languages have constraints that prevent a speaker from recognizing phonetic distinctions which do not correspond to the pattern of his language. Aspiration does not correspond to the pattern of the sound system of English, so English does not distinguish sounds that differ in that feature. The sound pattern of English for the speaker in the example above is such that the word *pin* has the same sound initially as *sleep* does finally and *happen* does medially. Yet, a speaker of another language might hear two or three different sounds where the English speaker utters the English /p/ in these three words.

---

[1]For a review of the history of phonemics beginning with Baudouin deCourtenay's *Versuch einer Theorie der Phonetischen Alternationen* (1895), see Kenneth L. Pike (1967:34).

1.12   PHONEMIC ANALYSIS

With the idea that the phonemes of a language must be discovered and described and that the listing of all the sounds of a language serves the sole purpose of gathering and transcribing data, it became necessary, if American linguistics were to develop as a rigorous science, to search for discovery procedures that could be applied to phonetically transcribed data mechanically and that would determine the distinctive sound units in the data.

Leonard Bloomfield, in his book *Language* (1933), suggested that the study of sounds in language be broken down into pure phonetics and phonology (practical phonetics). PHONOLOGY is "the study of significant speech sounds," and the PHONEME is the "minimum unit of distinctive sound feature" (1933:78–79) made up of certain distinctive acoustic features occurring in "lumps or bundles." The study of distinctive sound features of a language is called PHONEMICS. Phonology includes, as well, the study of the nondistinctive phonetic sounds (that is, nonphonemic sounds) in a language.

Both the gross acoustic, or phonetic, features (everything we hear) of the sounds of a language *and* the significant, or phonemic, sound features (what we say we hear) are required in a scientific description of a language. In his description of a language, the linguist must provide a statement of all the sounds that occur in the language (phonetics), as well as a statement of which sounds are distinctive among all the sounds that occur in the language (phonemics).

H. A. Gleason's *An Introduction to Descriptive Linguistics* (1961) provides the discovery procedures needed in order for the linguist to select out phonemes from a corpus of transcribed phonetic data.

Gleason saw the phoneme as a basic unit of linguistic expression. He defined it as a "class of sounds which: (1) are phonetically similar and (2) show certain characteristic patterns of distribution in the language or dialect under consideration" (1961:261).

Once the linguist has a phonetically transcribed corpus of data from one or more informants, he may use certain procedures to determine the phonemic status of classes of sounds in his transcription. He may test to see whether phonetically similar sounds which occur in his transcription occur in *free variation* or whether they occur in *complementary distribution*.

Phonetic similarity refers to the point of articulation and the manner of articulation of a sound. Sounds may be described phonetically as if viewed on two axes. They may be described on a horizontal axis according to their POINT OF ARTICULATION, that is, where they are produced in the mouth; and they may be described vertically according to their MANNER OF ARTICULATION, that is, how they are made in the mouth. Table 2 illustrates the point and manner of articulation of some of the consonant sounds of English. The labels are phonetic labels describing the features of sounds along two axes. The terms along the horizontal axis indicate *where* in the mouth the sound is made. BILABIAL refers to a sound made with both lips; LABIODENTAL, to one made with the teeth and the lips; ALVEOLAR, to one made at the alveolar ridge; and so forth—moving from the front to the back of the mouth. The terms on the vertical axis indicate *how* the sound is made. STOP refers to a sound made by stopping the flow of air before the sound is released, FRICATIVE indicates that there is some occlusion in the passage of air but no total stoppage, and so forth.

Table 2 illustrates that certain sounds in English are phonetically similar in that they have the same point and manner of articulation (for example, /p/ and /b/ and /t/ and /d/). Because of their similarity, these sounds may be known as SUSPICIOUS PAIRS. As such, they require special attention by the linguist as possible members of a single phoneme. A number of such sounds that we distinguish in English are not differentiated as separate phonemes in some languages.

Table 2.

Some Consonant Sounds in English Defined Phonetically in Terms of Point and Manner of Articulation

		Point of Articulation			
		Bilabial	*Labiodental*	*Alveolar*	*Velar*
Manner of Articulation	*Stop*	p b		t d	k g
	Fricative		f v	s z	
	Nasal	m		n	ŋ

If it appears, in a language a linguist is describing, that phonetically similar sounds are not distinguished, the sounds are said to be in FREE VARIATION and to constitute one phoneme. To a native speaker it does not make any difference which of the similar sounds is used. In English, if a speaker were to repeat the word *tea* over and over again, he might vary the class of features or sounds used in pronouncing the initial /t/, but he would never go as far as to use the phonetically similar /d/. He might articulate the /t/ at the alveolar ridge (alveolar point of articulation) or he might articulate it with his tongue touching his teeth (dental point of articulation), but that difference in point of articulation is not distinctive for English. English has only one /t/ phoneme; thus, for English alveolar and dental [t] are said to be in free variation.

On the other hand, for an English speaker to pronounce *tea* with the phonetically similar sound /d/ in initial position would not be judged acceptable by a native speaker. The fact that "dea" is not an acceptable pronunciation for the English word *tea* is an indication that, despite phonetic similarity, the phonetic [t] and [d] are not in free variation and are therefore likely to be assigned to different phonemes.

Further, we are able to show that English has a minimal pair or a number of minimal pairs that illustrate the distinctiveness of /t/ and /d/. A MINIMAL PAIR is a pair of words which differ in only one sound. Minimal pairs are used as evidence for phonemic distinctiveness despite phonetic similarity. In English, the words *tin* and *din* form a minimal pair differentiating /t/ and /d/; that is, an English speaker recognizes them as two different words—*tin* is not a variant pronunciation for *din* and vice versa.

The class of sounds defined as a phoneme may be found to be in COMPLE-MENTARY DISTRIBUTION, that is, each set of features or class of sounds occurs in a context in which other phonetically similar classes of sounds cannot occur. "Two elements are said to be in complementary distribution if each occurs in certain environments in which the other never occurs" (Gleason 1961:80).

An environment in which sounds occur in complementary distribution is called a MUTUALLY EXCLUSIVE ENVIRONMENT. In English, for instance, in the word *spin* the sound /p/ after /s/ is pronounced without aspiration, whereas in *pin* the initial /p/ is aspirated. An English speaker perceives that *spin* and *pin* both have the sound or phoneme /p/ even though the phonetic features he hears differ, [p=] versus [pʰ]. In English, [p=] and [pʰ] are in complementary distribution: unaspirated [p] never occurs initially before a vowel and aspirated [p] never occurs after /s/. Their environments are mutually exclusive.

A set of features or a class of sounds which are phonetically similar and occur in complementary distribution *or* free variation with respect to another set or class is said to be an ALLOPHONE of the phoneme. In the example just given, aspirated /p/ (phonetically [pʰ]) may be said to be an allophone of the phoneme /p/. The unaspirated /p/ (phonetically [p=]), as in *sleep*, is another allophone of the phoneme /p/. Allophones are phonetic elements, phonemes are phonemic elements. The phoneme /p/ may occur phonetically as both [p=] and [pʰ]. A phoneme is an abstract representation realized in speech through its allophones.[2]

The terms under discussion here—free variation, complementary distribution, suspicious pairs, mutually exclusive environment, minimal pair, phonetic similarity, point and manner of articulation, and allophone—are all part of the terminology used in carrying out a phonemic analysis. The search for these particular sound situations is the type of discovery procedure which Bloomfield thought necessary for linguistics to become a rigorous science. The terms refer to sound situations discoverable through mechanically applicable procedures whereby a linguist may define the significant sounds of a language. They also have been a stumbling block to many beginning linguists. Since the period of

---

[2]For further details on phonemes and their allophonic forms, see Gleason (1961:Chapter 16).

dominance of descriptive linguistics—in general, from 1933 (Bloomfield's *Language*) through 1955 (Gleason's *An Introduction to Descriptive Linguistics*) —many of the concepts developed within the methodology of phonemic analysis have been extended to broader areas of inquiry, especially in the field of anthropology. This extension will be seen to be the case throughout this book.

We have seen, then, that a linguist in the field, working within a descriptive linguistic framework, begins his description of a language with a PHONEMIC ANALYSIS.

The steps in a phonemic analysis are:

1. Prepare a *phonetic transcription*. Transcribe a sample of utterances from the speech of one or more native informants; that is, gather a corpus or body of data. In keeping with the principles set forth by the International Phonetic Association, use one symbol per sound transcribed, including appropriate diacritical markings.

2. Tabulate all the sounds in the corpus according to their point of articulation and manner of articulation; that is, classify the sounds as they are physically made. For example, the bilabial stop /b/ is articulated at the lips and the flow of air is stopped: the point of articulation is termed *bilabial*, the manner of articulation is termed *stop*. List suspicious pairs, "pairs of sounds which seem to be phonetically similar and hence possible allophones of the same phoneme" (Gleason 1961:275).

3. Frame a generalizing hypothesis; for example, if [p] and [b] are in complementary distribution, perhaps [t] and [d] are also, because they, too, share the point and manner of articulation.

4. Test the hypothesis by tabulating the distribution of each sound in a suspicious pair. If [t] and [d] may be shown to occur in the same environment (for example, before *in* in *tin* and *din*, medially in *la‗er* as in *latter* and *ladder*, and finally in *fee‗* as in *feet* and *feed*) and if a native speaker makes a distinction between them (that is, *tin* is a different word from *din*, *latter* from *ladder*, and *feet* from *feed*), then the sounds belong to separate phonemes, that is, to /t/ and /d/ respectively.

Phonemic analysis is a process whereby a phonetic transcription is mechanically refined to a transcription representing the significant classes of sounds in a particular language. A phonemic transcription presents a corpus of data composed of sounds distinguished by a native speaker of a particular language. A /p/ phoneme in language *X* does not represent the same class of sounds as a /p/ phoneme in language *Y*.

1.2 Morphology and Syntax

It is obvious that sound is not the only distinctive part of language. We all know that sounds occur in certain acceptable configurations and that those configurations convey meaning. Sound is used in various ways to express ideas. How to describe the meaningful arrangement of sound and how to state what is the meaningful arrangement of sound as found in a corpus is the next procedural concern of the descriptive linguist.

As seen in the preceding section, Bloomfield recognized the need for developing a rigorous methodology for American linguistic science. As part of this rigor, descriptivists developed an inclination to examine only the objectively verifiable aspects of language. For the analysis of sound, such rigor worked well. The descriptive linguists next attempted to adapt phonemic methodology to the analysis of combinations of phonemes.

Ironically, Sapir, who is largely responsible for introducing the phoneme to American linguistics, believed the proper area of study for linguistics to be the universality of language and the relationship of language to thought. The descriptivists influenced by Bloomfield steered clear of any attempt to relate language to thought and stressed instead a need to describe the differences between languages rather than the similarities among them. Sapir was interested in what he called an "intuitive formal completeness" of language, which the linguist could not hope to understand without appealing to other fields such as psychology and philosophy. It is only recently that anthropologists and theoretical linguists have begun to examine language in relation to thought once again.

Bloomfield, in accord with Sapir and Boas, maintained that ideally linguistics consists of the study of sounds (phonetics) and then the study of meaning (semantics) (1933:74). However, Bloomfield held that descriptive linguistics could not provide a way to link sound and meaning and still be scientific. Bloomfield classified linguists as either mentalists or mechanists. He was a mechanist, and the method he was instrumental in developing for a mechanical analysis of language is that presented in his book *Language* (1933). The mechanistic view holds that a scientist can deal only with observable fact. Phonemic analysis deals only with that which can be observed from a corpus of transcribed phonetic data. Once the descriptive linguist has discovered the phonemes in his data through phonemic analysis, his remaining task is to describe how the phonemes are used in the language. Again, the methodology developed requires that only those facts be described which are observable from the data by employing certain discovery procedures. Still, the goal is an adequate description of a representative corpus of linguistic data.

1.21   MORPHOLOGY

Boas observed that human speech is composed of three parts which roughly correspond to the parts in the descriptive analysis of a language: phonology, morphology, and syntax. He stated, in an objective discussion of languages, three points have to be considered: first, the constituent phonetic elements of the language; second, the groups of ideas expressed by phonetic groups; third, the methods of combining and modifying phonetic groups (1911:35).

In the grammars written by the linguists of Boas's period, first there appeared a statement of the sounds of the language, followed by a discussion of such processes as prefixation and suffixation, along with examples of words and their meanings.

Sapir, too, believed that a grammar should contain not only a description of the phonetic elements of a language, but also should describe the relationships of elements in words and sentences. These views of Boas and Sapir combined into a single concept of GRAMMATICAL PROCESSES, which in later descriptivism came to be known as morphology and syntax. They contended that a grammar should describe both the sounds and grammatical processes of a language.

Bloomfield, on the other hand, combined morphology (word formation) and syntax (the order of words in a sentence) in what he called SEMANTICS. To Bloomfield, semantics had two parts (paraphrased from Bloomfield):

1. GRAMMAR—a statement of the meaningful arrangement of forms in the language
   a. SYNTAX—a statement of the order of occurrence of forms in a sentence
   b. MORPHOLOGY—a list of the forms in the language which co-occur in sentences
2. LEXICON—a list of the total stock of morphemes in the language along with a list of their glosses (that is, their translated equivalents in the language of the investigator)

Descriptions of languages on Bloomfield's model became known as item (form) and arrangement analyses, wherein forms (phonemes, morphemes, lexical items) are stated along with their arrangement (as parts of speech, sentence types, constructions) in the order of their occurrence in a corpus of data. Semantics, as defined by Bloomfield to include grammar (morphology and syntax) and a lexicon (total stock of morphemes in a language), has the purpose of decribing what phonetic forms mean (1933:162).

According to Bloomfield, a MORPHEME may be defined as "a linguistic form which bears no partial phonetic-semantic resemblance to any other form" (161). A morpheme is a unique correspondence of sound and meaning. The English word *bird* contains one morpheme, #bird#, *singing* contains two, #sing# and #ing#. As a matter of convention, morphemes are enclosed in crosshatches, # #.

Bloomfield provides the following example (161): although the sentence *Poor John ran away* contains four words, it has more than four morphemes, namely, #poor#, #John#, #run#, #past tense#, #away#.

It was Gleason who referred to the morpheme as a basic unit of linguistic expression along with the phoneme. Phonemes and morphemes are the basic units of *expression* in language, as distinct from *content* in language. Descriptive linguistics is particularly concerned with linguistic expression rather than content. We speak by using phonemes and morphemes arranged in various orders. PHONEMICS and MORPHEMICS are methods of analyzing data such that a language's sounds and sound combinations may be described.

Gleason defined the morpheme as "the smallest unit which is grammatically pertinent" and also as "the smallest meaningful units in the structure of the language" (1961:53). A morpheme is composed of one or more phonemes.

As phonemes have variant forms known as allophones, morphemes have variant forms termed ALLOMORPHS: "an allomorph is a variant of a morpheme which occurs in certain definable environments" (62). Allomorphs may be conditioned by the environment in which they occur. That is, the variant of a morpheme in a given speech situation may depend on the sounds with which it occurs.

The morpheme #plural# in English is an example of a morpheme with both phonologically and morphologically conditioned allomorphs. The plural morpheme occurs phonologically as /s/ after voiceless stops such as /p/, /t/, and /k/ (*cat*, *cats*), as /z/ after vowels, voiced stops, laterals, and nasals such as /b/, /d/, /g/, /l/, /r/, /a/, /e/, /m/, and so forth (*bed*, *beds*; *sofa*, *sofas*; *car*, *cars*), and as /ə z/ after sounds such as /č/, /f/, /v/, /j/, /z/, /s/ (*witch*, *witches*; *nose*, *noses*).

The sounds /s/, /z/, and /ə z/ are phonologically conditioned allomorphs of the #plural# morpheme in English, since their phonological environment (the sounds with which they occur) determines which allomorph will be used.

There are other forms of the #plural# morpheme in English as well, for example, *child*, *children*; *goose*, *geese*; *shrimp*, *shrimp*. These plural forms are not phonologically conditioned, but are allomorphs of the morpheme since they have a common range of meaning with the other allomorphs (that is, they are all plural). Such allomorphs are morphologically conditioned. The word *boys* has two morphemes, #boy# and #plural#; the word *geese* has two morphemes, #goose# and #plural#.

Just as phonemes are discoverable in a descriptive framework through phonemic analysis, morphemes may be identified in a corpus of data through morphemic analysis. To a descriptive linguist, morphemic analysis represents the next higher level of structure in a language after phonemic analysis (Gleason 1961:66). A tenet of descriptive linguistics is: "Each higher level of structure is best stated in terms of the units of the preceding level" (66). Thus, morphemes should be stated in terms of phonemes.

MORPHEMIC ANALYSIS is the process of identifying morphemes by means of comparing phonemically transcribed utterances which show contrast in both expression (sound) and content (meaning). "Two elements can be considered the same morpheme if (1) they have some common range of meaning, (2) they are in complementary distribution conditioned by some phonological feature" (80).

Thus, *children*, *cats*, *shrimp*, and *geese* may all be analyzed as having two morphemes each, each having the morpheme #plural# in common with the others, but having different root morphemes:

children	=	#child# + #plural#
shrimp	=	#shrimp# + #plural#
cats	=	#cat# + #plural#
geese	=	#goose# + #plural#

Despite different phonetic shape, by reason of a common range of meaning, the plural morpheme may be identified in each form.

On the other hand, in *cats*, *dogs*, and *witches*, the differing forms of the plural are accounted for by both a common range of meaning and occurrence of the forms in complementary distribution (where /s/ occurs, /z/ and /ə z/ cannot occur; where /z/ occurs, /ə z/ and /s/ cannot; and where /ə z/ occurs, /s/ and /z/ cannot):

cats	=	cat + s /kæt + s/
dogs	=	dog + s /dɔg + z/
witches	=	witch + es /wɪč + ə z/

1.22 SYNTAX

In a linguistic description the next higher level of language structure to be described is the syntactic level. In Gleason's words, "SYNTAX may be roughly defined as the principles of arrangement of the constructions formed by the process of derivation and inflection (words) into larger constructions of various kinds" (1961:128).

The early formulations of descriptive linguistics had no separate level of syntax. Bloomfield distinguished between lexical terms and grammatical terms in a description (1933:264). Both lexical and grammatical terms were parallel rather than hierarchical, "lexical" referring to what can be described as combinations of phonemes, and "grammatical" referring to what can be described as features of arrangement.

In a hierarchical description of language (proceeding from the lowest to the highest descriptive level), however, syntax should be described in terms of morphemes and morphemes in terms of phonemes. The method of analysis at the syntactic level involves searching for IMMEDIATE CONSTITUENTS within utterances by comparing samples. "An immediate constituent (IC) is one of the two or a few constituents of which any given construction is directly formed" (Gleason 1961:133). For example, given the utterance *The three men read the new books*, an immediate-constituent analysis, segmenting the sentence into its constituents, would yield cuts in the following way:

1. The three men / read the new books.
2. The three men / read / the new books.
3. The / three men / read / the / new books.
4. The / three / men / read / the / new / books.

The sentence is broken up into its major constituents—here in the first cut consisting of the total subject and the total predicate. The next cut separates the constituents of the subject and of the predicate respectively, and later cuts continue the separation until all the constituents of the utterance have been marked. One may analyze an utterance in terms of its immediate constituents working either from the utterance to the word as in the above example, or from the word to the utterance. To go from the word to the utterance, constituent cuts are progressively erased, forming larger and larger constituents back to the utterance itself; in other words, moving from Step 4 to Step 1 in the above example.

The idea in immediate-constituent analysis is to break up an utterance at a point where a native speaker perceives a "fundamental cleavage" (Gleason 1961:130), as in Step 1. This process is continued until the divisions consist of single words, as in Step 4.

Once constituent cuts have been made, the linguist describes the relationships between immediate constituents. In the example cited here, the constituent *The three men* is an IC of *read the new books*. Both constituents *The three men* and *read the new books* are constituents of the utterance *The three men read the new books*.

The method of IC analysis is to compare samples of utterances from the language being described. For example:

1. The three men read the new books.
2. John ate the fish.
3. Her big black dog died.

As noted above, *The three men* is an immediate constituent of *read the new books*. Similarly, *John* and *ate the fish* are constituents of the utterance *John ate the fish*, and *Her big black dog* and *died* are constituents of *Her big black dog died*.

Further analysis into immediate constituents allows the linguist to describe relationships within the constituents identified in the first cut:

      The three / men   *The three* is an IC of *men*.
            / John   *John* is the smallest constituent here.
  Her big black / dog   *Her big black* is an IC of *dog*.

The words *men*, *John*, and *dog* belong to the same syntactic-order class; that is, they occur in the same place in utterances of this particular language. Further cuts within these data are:

          The / three
      Her big / black

As the analysis progresses, the linguist is able to make statements about the arrangements of constituents.

The method of immediate-constituent analysis presents a number of problems. Gleason notes that "the method as sketched would be useless to a linguist confronted with a language for which he lacked a native speaker's 'feel' " (132). For descriptive linguistics, the problem of syntax was one of attempting to set up methods whereby it would be possible to state the organization of a given utterance in the best way. Also there existed the problem of insuring that results would be comparable, given comparable material.

The discussion of transformational/generative grammar in the following chapter will show that these problems were never successfully solved and that some linguists then approached syntax by relying on the intuition of the linguist rather than that of the native speaker.

1.3   Descriptive Linguistics

We have seen that the method of descriptive linguistics of analyzing a corpus of data into phonemes, morphemes, and immediate constituents is a model used by the anthropological or descriptive linguist in preparing an adequate description of the data. A description of a language in these terms comprises five steps:

Phonology (Phonetics and Phonemics)
1.   Gathering a corpus of data
2.   Transcribing the corpus of data phonetically
3.   Carrying out phonemic analysis
     Result: list of phonemes and allophones
Grammar (Morphology or Word Grammar, and Syntax or Sentence Grammar)
4.   Carrying out morphemic analysis
     Result: list of morphemes and allomorphs
5.   Carrying out syntactic analysis
     Result: an utterance marked off into immediate constituents

In a descriptive model, the discourse level, the next higher level above the sentence, is not as highly developed. Recent work in formal semantic analysis done largely by anthropologists and cognitive psychologists, and studies purporting to deal with the "total linguistic context," are attempting to carry on descriptive analytical techniques. These studies, however, go beyond the realm of anthropological linguistics as defined in this chapter, and move into the area of language and culture and of sociolinguistics, each of which is the subject of a later chapter.

For the descriptive linguist, a language is adequately described by its phonology, morphology, and syntax. Descriptive linguistics has been defined as "the discipline which studies languages in terms of their internal structures" (Gleason 1961:iii).

The descriptive linguist considers meaning as content in language as undiscoverable and therefore unanalyzable. This position is the mechanistic one held by Bloomfield, who holds that a scientist can deal only with observable fact. The only type of meaning which can be dealt with in a descriptive analysis of language is that expressed by form, in other words, the meaning obtained by analyzing the shape and function of sequences of sound apart from their referent.

In a descriptive linguistic analysis, phonemes, morphemes, and constituents from a corpus are listed in a grammar. A lexicon contains glosses for morphemes and their combinations.

1.4 Emics and Etics

Two concepts, emic and etic, emerged from the studies of sound done by descriptive linguists. These concepts have come to refer to two approaches currently widely debated among ethnographers.

In phonology, the distinction between emic and etic may be viewed thus: EMIC units are functionally significant units among the sounds of the system of language (*langue*; see Section 1.6), and ETIC units are the objectively definable entities of speech (*parole*; again see section 1.6). A phoneme is an emic unit. All allophones of a phoneme are etic units.

At successively higher levels of description, the methodology of descriptive linguistics involves isolating emic, or functionally significant, units in a particular linguistic system from the etic data of speech.

Kenneth Pike, whose book *Phonemics* (1947) represents the development of the emic approach as applicable to phonological data, attempted to extend the approach used in discovering phonemes in a corpus of linguistic data to apply to a description of human behavior. The response to this attempt will be seen as influential in such areas as ethnoscience (see Chapter 4 below) and also in sociolinguistics (see Chapter 5). Pike (1965:55), in agreement with Goodenough (1957:173), sees the problem to which the etic/emic approach is directed as one of how to go from the material world which is infinitely variable (an etic view of the world) to the subjective world existing in men's minds (through the discovery of emic units).

Marvin Harris devoted a chapter in his book *The Rise of Anthropological Theory: A History of Theories of Culture* (1968) to Pike's proposed expansion of etics/emics toward developing a theory of culture or human behavior. It should be noted that in Harris's view the approach is termed emic/etic, while in the Pikean interpretation it is etic/emic.

Since etics/emics or emics/etics is an important concept in the area of language and culture, it is necessary to examine its application to descriptive linguistics in comparison with its application to the broader area of language and culture, that is, as used in the "new ethnography," or ethnoscience.

The reversal of the order of the terms as seen in M. Harris (1968:Chapter 20) is of some significance. It is the etic/emic approach as developed by Pike that is used in descriptive linguistics, entailing a description of the functionally significant units of a particular language system—as the phonemes of English, French, Swahili, and so forth—using the observable and recorded sounds in a corpus of data, collected as examples of the speech of an Englishman, Frenchman, or Swahili-speaking person (that is, the phonetics of English, French, Swahili). However, when the analytical approach is applied outside the realm of specific behavior to behavior in general, it might be better seen as an emic/etic one.

According to Pike,

> Through the etic "lens" the analyst views the data in tacit reference to a perspective oriented to all comparable events (whether sounds, ceremonies, activities), of all peoples, of all parts of the earth; through the other lens, the emic one, he views the same events, at the same time, in the same context, in reference to a perspective oriented to the particular function of those particular events in that particular culture, as it and it alone is structured (1967:41).

What is emic is specific to a language or a culture. When the emic units of one language are compared to the emic units of other languages, those units are then etic,

> since they are divorced from the context of the structure of the language from which they have come, and are viewed as generalized instances of abstract stereotypes, rather than as living parts of an actual sequence of behavior events within a particular culture (Pike 1967:41).

For descriptive linguistics, with its goal of analyzing a corpus of data into its functionally significant units, etic/emic methodology is appropriate, that is, to go from the units of speech (etic) to the units of the system of a language (emic).

For anthropology in general, the goal is not to analyze particular cultures into their functionally significant units, just as for linguistics in general (as opposed to descriptive linguistics), the goal is not to come up with a set of functionally significant units for each language known to man. Anthropology is interested in developing a theory of Culture; linguistics, in developing a theory of Language.

Emic analyses in descriptive linguistics and in descriptive ethnographies, when compared each to each respectively, yield etic data which tell us about language in general and culture in general. Such comparisons yield cultural and linguistic universals and may be said to employ an emic/etic approach.

A set of cultural and linguistic universals is both emic and etic in that universal statements represent functionally significant features of particular languages and cultures as well as features of language and culture in general. The remaining differences between languages and cultures are emic to those particular languages and cultures if they are functionally significant in context, etic if not. For example, it is thought that [a] occurs in all or almost all languages—it is emic for each particular language system, and etic when all languages are considered together. An aspirated /k/ ([kʰ]) is an etic unit in English, not being part of the sound system of English since it is not functionally significant in that language. We do not distinguish [kʰaet] from [k=aet] 'cat' in English. However, [kʰ] is an emic unit in Hindi because it is functionally significant in distinguishing sounds in that language; for example, Hindi speakers distinguish [k=aanaa] 'one-eyed' from [kʰaanaa] 'food, to eat'. Thus, [kʰ] is etic in English; /kʰ/ is emic in Hindi.

The anthropologist Marvin Harris views emics/etics as *two* approaches to research. With an emic approach, the researcher can discover the informant's point of view by analyzing an elicited corpus of data "in a descriptively adequate" way based on the informant's judgments:

> In ethnography, an emic approach to purposes, goals, motivations, attitudes etc., is premised on the assumption that between the actor and the observer, it is the actor who is better able to know his own inner state (1968:574).

On the other hand,

> etic statements depend upon phenomenal distinctions judged appropriate by the community of scientific observers . . . an ethnography carried out according to etic principles is thus a corpus of predictions about the behavior of classes of people.

> . . . An emic statement can be falsified if it can be shown that it contradicts the cognitive calculus by which relevant actors judge that entities are similar or different, real, meaningful, significant, or in some other sense "appropriate" or "acceptable" (574).

It might be argued that there is an element of predictability also in an emic approach, as well as in an etic one, for in an emic analysis the researcher strives for specification as to what the actors will or will not do, and how they will behave or will not behave (acceptably or unacceptably).

In summary, the etic/emic distinction is a controversial one which seems valid for the goals of descriptive linguistics, but when it is extended beyond verbal (perhaps even phonological) behavior, it becomes vague in its applicability and embroiled in the theoretical issues of all social sciences—in the war of description versus theory, the universal versus the particular, the general versus the specific.

1.5 Structural Linguistics

For descriptive linguistics, Gleason's *An Introduction to Descriptive Linguistics* is generally thought of as its "bible"; it is so regarded on a practical level in conjunction with its accompanying *Workbook in Descriptive Linguistics* (Gleason 1955) and along with at least three other works, Kenneth Pike's *Phonemics* (1947), Eugene Nida's *Morphology* (1946), and Bernard Bloch and George Trager's *Outline of Linguistic Analysis* (1942). This set of works in part or in full comprised the textual material for courses in general linguistics during the 1950s and 1960s. This codification of the descriptive linguistic method and technique stands today alongside other schools of linguistics.

In 1951, the linguist Zellig Harris published *Structural Linguistics*, which may be seen as a link between the type of American linguistics of the descriptive anthropologists and various offshoots since then both in linguistics and anthropology. Some of these offshoots are the subject of later chapters.

Z. Harris's structural linguistics basically involves a set of operations performed on a raw corpus of speech leading up to or resulting in, "a compact statement of what utterances occur in the corpus" (Z. Harris 1951:361). Harris defined structural linguistics as the "structural methods for descriptive linguistics" (v). Structural linguistics moves more toward the abstract representation of language than does the descriptivism of Gleason.

In the phonology and morphology of Zellig Harris's structural approach, the notion of COMPONENT is introduced. Harris's phoneme is defined as "a unique combination of components" (361). Parts of utterances which are not distinct from each other form classes. These classes, if they occur freely or are in complementary distribution with another class or classes, are called phonemes. The classes of sound (or phonemes) are composed of components. Thus, although the phoneme is still the basic unit in phonology, it is composed of components that may define the distinctive difference between one phoneme and another. In Bloomfield's approach, distinctions were noted between sounds in order to differentiate the sounds, but no attempt was made to identify the distinctions themselves. Gleason does not use the notion of component, but does discuss the idea of morphophonemic changes (for example, assimilation), the idea that sounds may differ in respect to certain sound features, and that sound features may occur singly or in combination (1955:84).

When /p/ and /b/ are seen as two phonemes, the first a voiceless bilabial stop and the second a voiced bilabial stop, each is viewed as a distinct class of sounds. The notion of component alters the situation such that while /p/ and /b/ are still distinct phonemes, their distinctiveness is in the component of voicing. Some phonemes differ from each other in only one component, but others may differ in more than one component. The components of Zellig Harris's structural linguistics are the forerunners of phonological distinctive features, which will be discussed in Chapter 2.

The sharp divisions between level of description in the Bloomfield and Gleason framework become blurred in Z. Harris's scheme. The MORPHO-PHONEME is defined by Harris as a class constituted by "the interchange of phonemes or components in corresponding sections of the variant members of each morpheme" (1951:362). For example, in *knife*, *knives* (from *knife* + plural morpheme), the final sound in *knife* is the phoneme /f/, which occurs as /v/ before the plural morpheme. The phoneme /f/ as it occurs in *knife* and /v/ as it occurs in *knives* may be referred to as the morphophoneme /F/ such that the morpheme #knife# can be represented as /naiF/. The final *-F* indicates that it is realized as /f/ in final position and as /v/ before the plural. "Each morpheme is composed directly of a sequence of morphophonemes, each of which in turn is a class consisting of one or more complementary phonemes or components" (362).

The notion of morphophoneme eliminates the problem of having to decide which phoneme to assign a particular allophone. Instead, morphophonemics allows the statement to be made that /F/ occurs as /f/ in final position and as /v/ before the plural.

The interconnection between Zellig Harris's structural linguistics as an extension of methodology in descriptive linguistics and structuralism in anthropology and linguistics is expounded by Harris:

> It may be noted that there are not just two descriptive systems [in language]—phonology and morphology—but a rather indefinite number, some of these being phonologic and some morphologic. It is thus possible to extend the descriptive methods for the creation of additional systems having other terms of reference. For example, investigations in stylistics and in culture-language correlations may be carried out by setting up systems parallel to the morphologic one but based on the distribution of elements (morpheme classes, sentence types, etc.) over stretches longer than one utterance (1951:365).

Ethnoscience (see Chapter 4 below) is, to a great extent, an extension of descriptive methods to investigations of a system relating language to culture.

The goal of linguistics as seen by Z. Harris is the description of language structure. His break with descriptivists and their insistence on (1) not mixing descriptive levels (that is, keeping phonology, morphology, and syntax distinct) and (2) their minimal unit of sound feature definition of the phoneme, gave more power to his type of analysis. Descriptivism could do no more than present a description of a corpus of data as lists of phonemes, morphemes, and constituents discovered in the corpus. For Zellig Harris, descriptive linguistics embodying the concepts of the morphophoneme and the component allowed for generalizations to be made beyond the corpus.

In Z. Harris's approach, the corpus of linguistic data is considered to be an adequate sample of the language being described. From the analysis of the data, the linguist is able to say that particular sequences of elements occur in the language and other sequences seem not to occur.

> The work of analysis leads right up to the statements which enable anyone to synthesize or predict utterances in the language. These statements form a deductive system with axiomatically defined initial elements and with theorems concerning the relations among them. The final theorems would indicate the structure of the utterances of the language in terms of the preceding parts of the system.

There may be various ways of presenting this system which constitutes the description of the language structure (Z. Harris 1951:372–373).

Z. Harris's view of language as an analyzable system of relatable elements constitutes a structural approach. In the next chapter we will discuss another type of structuralism which has a European origin, but which is also concerned with systems and relations and their analysis.

American structural linguistics as discussed here is a refinement, in a sense, of descriptive linguistics. It emphasizes, unlike descriptive linguistics, the study of the character of language apart from its history. The structural linguist looks at data collected at one point in time as representative of an analyzable linguistic system. The linguist's goal is an analysis of that system rather than a description of data to be used for eventual language comparison or classification.

European structuralism built on this foundation, but went beyond the analysis of surface data. The structuralism of Lévi-Strauss, for example, looks at structures as underlying a particular system's overt manifestation. These underlying structures of linguistic or cultural systems are seen as being unconscious.

A structural linguistic analysis, then, moves beyond describing adequately the discoverable phonological and morphological elements of a corpus. It attempts to describe the interrelationship of elements within language. This view of language as a system with speech as a representative sample of a language's surface system has had a great deal of influence in the area of language and culture. The system of language which the structural linguist seeks to analyze is often referred to as LANGUE; the corpus of speech analyzed is often referred to as PAROLE.

1.6   Langue and Parole

From the work of Ferdinand deSaussure, a Swiss structural linguist, has come a distinction which serves to distinguish the term *language* as used in a descriptive linguistic sense from its use in everyday speech. For anthropological linguistics, the distinction is a necessary one. What the anthropological linguist produces from his corpus of data is a description of the structure of a particular language, that is, of *langue* (language). The utterances in the corpus which are taken as evidence of the structure of the language (the langue) are instances of *parole* (speech).

Ferdinand deSaussure's approach to linguistics may be best seen in *Cours de Linguistique Générale*, a book of his lectures compiled by his students (1916, 1966). His view was:

[Language (langue)] is a storehouse filled by the members of a given community through their active use of speaking, a grammatical system that has a potential existence in each brain, or, more specifically, in the brains of a group of individuals. For language is not complete in any speaker; it exists perfectly only within a collectivity.

In separating language (langue) from speaking (parole) we are at the same time separating: (1) what is social from what is individual; and (2) what is essential from what is accessory and more or less accidental (1966:13–14).

The techniques of descriptive/anthropological linguistics are all means whereby parole is gathered and refined at various levels of description and whereby basic units are analyzed in combination in order to produce an overall description of a langue. Langue is to parole as the English language is to what an individual speaker of English speaks at a given time. The distinction is that of a particular language as a system versus a particular language as uttered.

A corpus of linguistic data is a sample of parole, the language it represents is the langue. An analyzed corpus of linguistic data presented as a description of a language is a description of langue as exemplified by parole.

The idea of language as a *system* of language and this system as the proper area of study for the linguist is credited to deSaussure as the founder of modern structural linguistics. In America, Zellig Harris implicitly used the idea in his book *Structural Linguistics* (see Section 1.5). The concept of parole as actual instances of speech is an important one in descriptive linguistics. The descriptive linguist looks at parole as it represents langue. The structuralist, in the deSaussure sense, makes claims about langue which are borne out in parole.

1.7 Summary

In this chapter, we have seen that anthropological linguistics developed largely in America as a set of descriptive methods and techniques for describing unwritten languages. The procedure consists of identifying units at various descriptive levels of language. Each language can be described in terms of its phonemes, morphemes, and syntax. A grammar of a language describes these three levels and includes a lexicon or list of glosses (translations) for the various morphemes. The description of meaning as content is considered by the descriptive linguist as outside the realm of linguistic science. One can describe the form and function of a morpheme and provide a gloss for the morpheme in a lexicon, but the content of linguistic elements cannot be described in an objectively verifiable manner; the task is, therefore, considered not part of the field of linguistics. Semantics is not considered a part of linguistic description.

The idea that one could discover linguistically distinctive elements (emics) amidst the gross phonetic features (etics) of a particular language became an important notion in the study of particular cultures as well. Certain cultural factors might be seen to have particular (emic) significance for bearers of one culture, whereas those same factors in another culture might be nondistinctive (etic). The anthropologist is often advised to be careful not to impose his own emics on the culture he is studying, but instead to discover the distinctions made in the culture studied by observing the behavior of the culture bearers as they interact with each other.

From an emphasis on describing linguistic units in different languages grew the idea that the units exist in a system and are interrelated within that system. The system of language is known as *langue*, whereas instances of language as speech are known as *parole*. The development of structuralism in linguistics turned the focus of linguistic inquiry from that of describing and isolating units such as phonemes and morphemes in language to one of examining interrelationships among the units within the system. Chapter 2 expands this idea of interrelationships within a system as used in an anthropological context and leads into the development of nondescriptive linguistics and modern linguistic theory.

Anthropological linguistics sought to provide observationally adequate descriptions of linguistic data from various languages all over the world. From that approach evolved a separate goal for linguistics—to describe and understand the nature of language and its acquisition by people.

At this point it is necessary to mention THE PRINCIPLE OF THREE ADEQUACIES, which was alluded to in the Introduction to this chapter. It is a principle having to do with stating the goals of linguistics. An understanding of the distinctions made among the terms OBSERVATIONAL, DESCRIPTIVE, and EXPLANATORY ADEQUACY will be useful throughout the rest of this book.

According to the noted modern linguist Noam Chomsky, a grammar which is *observationally* adequate is one which gives an account of the corpus of data. A grammar that is *descriptively* adequate gives a "correct account of the linguistic intuition of the native speaker . . ." Finally, the goal of *explanatory* adequacy is met by a theory which "aims to provide a principled basis, independent of any particular language, for the selection of the descriptively adequate grammar of each language" (1964:923–924).

The anthropological linguistics discussed in this chapter has as its goal the production of grammars which adequately describe the body of linguistic data; such grammars meet the goal of observational adequacy. In the next chapter, we will see that transformational/generative grammar is aiming toward descriptive adequacy and at the same time hoping to come up with a theory that is explanatorily adequate. It is Chomsky's view that observationally adequate grammars such as those aimed at by the descriptive linguists emphasize the development of procedures for rearranging and reorganizing data economically rather than emphasizing ways of accounting for the knowledge of people who have language.

Chapter 2 Structuralism and Transformationalism

2.0 Introduction

As seen in the preceding chapter, structural linguistics, as the term is used by Zellig Harris (1951), refers to a methodology developed for describing a language using data collected from an informant, that is, using speech, or parole, as data. This descriptive methodology and the concept of etics and emics figured predominantly in the American-based school of descriptive linguistics. Little was consciously borrowed from Europe.

Simultaneously—that is, during the first half of this century—linguistics in Europe was developing in a different direction, but also employing deSaussure's basic distinction between langue (language system) versus parole (speech). The approach that arose in Europe under the influence of deSaussure's Geneva School of Linguistics and French structuralism in the thirties became known as structural linguistics as well—known more generally as the *Prague School of Linguistics*, since many of the leading linguists were followers of N. S. Troubetzkoy of Prague.

Descriptive linguistics and structural methods are today influencing the study of culture in areas such as ethnoscience, but the Prague School has left its influence on anthropology through what is known as a structuralist approach to culture, most clearly seen in the writings of Claude Lévi-Strauss. The structuralism of the Prague School may also be seen as the impetus, along with descriptive linguistics, for the development of transformational/generative grammar.

In this chapter we will look at both language and culture as systems of relational elements. We will discuss this view, known as structuralism, touching upon the influence of the Prague School of Linguistics on both fields. This influence was exerted mostly through the works of two men, Jakobson and Troubetzkoy.

Adequately described data were seen as too narrow a goal. Interest turned toward investigating the nature of language and the nature of culture. It was felt that facts observed and described in a corpus did not reveal any understanding of the nature of the system behind the data. Notable in the new direction as it exists today are the transformational/generative linguists and the structural anthropologists.

Just as the phonology of descriptive linguistics formed the basis of linguistic analogies in the analysis of cultural data through etics and emics, so too the phonology of the Prague School forms the basis for the theoretical linguistics of Chomsky and his followers—through the idea that the sound system of language is composed of relational features.

This idea of the systematic nature of language is also applied to culture, especially to systems of kinship and mythology which may be analyzed through the relationships seen among components.

Structuralism in both language and culture is characterized by a search for linguistic and cultural universals through the formulation of testable theories of language and culture. Structuralism in both language and culture involves theory building; it involves looking at language and culture as systems, and holds that elements within a system exist in relationship to one another.

For each system, the investigator asks (paraphrased from Lévi-Strauss 1967:33):

1. What are the relationships expressed in the system?
2. What connotation does each element of the system express with regard to the relationships within the system? Connotations are expressed as positive or negative values.

For example, in the phonological system of English there is a relationship between /p/ and /b/, /t/ and /d/, /k/ and /g/, and /s/ and /z/. The relationship is one of voicing. For each pair of sounds, one is voiced and the other voiceless; /p/ expresses a negative connotation for voicing with respect to /b/. Therefore, /p/ has the feature [-voice] and /b/ has the feature [+voice]. With regard to the feature of voice in English, /p/, /t/, /k/, and /s/ are all [-voice], whereas /b/, /d/, /g/, and /z/ are [+voice]. Further, /p/ is to /b/, as /t/ is to /d/, as /k/ is to /g/, and as /s/ is to /z/. The only difference in these pairs of sounds is in the feature of voice; they share all other articulatory and acoustic features in common. Thus, [± voice] is a distinctive feature in English. More will be said about distinctive features in Section 2.1 below.

N. S. Troubetzkoy and Roman Jakobson, along with other linguists of the

Prague circle, were able to demonstrate that contrasts such as this one of voicing in phonology form a set from which each language of the world selects its significant sounds. The nature of phonological contrasts such as [± voice] is systemic; the structure of the system is a network of binary oppositions of sound difference. The number of such differences of sound is relatively small. One distinguishes consonants as $\begin{bmatrix} +consonantal \\ -vocalic \end{bmatrix}$ from vowels, which are $\begin{bmatrix} -consonantal \\ +vocalic \end{bmatrix}$. The terms *consonantal*, *vocalic*, *voiced*, and *voiceless* express phonological features of relationships among sounds in language. Often features are distinctive in that their particular plus or minus values serve to minimally distinguish sounds from each other.

This approach to language as a system of relationships in opposition, particularly in phonology, had a profound impact on both linguistics and anthropology. Marvin Harris claims that for Lévi-Strauss this constituted "a scientific revolution comparable to that which flowed from Copernicus or from the development of nuclear physics" (1968:494).

Lévi-Strauss saw that the structural approach of the Prague linguists had a certain appeal in the analysis of kinship systems and systems of mythology. He noted that just as the sounds that are possible for man to make are almost unlimited, so, too, are the attitudes of man to interpersonal relationships. A particular phonological system will select as distinctive only certain of those sounds; likewise, a particular kinship system or social group will select only certain of its attitudes as distinctive in that system. These attitudes may also be seen in structural terms as features of relationships within a system (Lévi-Strauss 1967:38, 43).

The structuralist approach did not stop at discovering the terms within a system (that is, phonemes, kinship terms, and so forth), but instead the goal was to analyze the system, whether of language or culture, as a series of relationships among terms in the system.

The transformational/generative linguists are now moving beyond an attempt to state relationships between and among systemic elements and are attempting to uncover the rules that govern the relationships among features, elements, or terms in a system. For example, generative phonology holds that "the phonological component [of a theory of language] is a system of rules . . . that relates surface structures . . . to phonetic representations" (Chomsky and Halle 1968:14).

The phonetic representation in this approach is a matrix or network of the features that occur in sounds. On a matrix, the rows correspond to the features (voiced, consonantal, vocalic, and so forth) and the columns to the segments (/p/, /t/, /k/, and so forth). The segments occur sequentially; the features within a segment, simultaneously. This matrix notion was used by Jakobson as well, and applied to the analysis of myth by Lévi-Strauss in his discussion of myth as being composed of sequences (diachronic elements) and frameworks (synchronic elements).

The business of phonology in a generative grammar is not to describe the sound system (that is, a phonetic representation on a matrix), but rather to relate the sound system to the rest of language (grammar and meaning) by a system of rules.

On the other hand, structuralism did aim to describe the sound system of language, the kinship system of culture, and the structural system of myth. To Lévi-Strauss, the discovery of the sequences and frameworks in a myth is an analysis of the myth's message; the oppositions uncovered from the interconnections among the diachronic and synchronic aspects of myth reveal the myth's meaning or connotation.

Chomsky, in moving from structuralism to a transformational/generative approach, claims that

> the structure of a phonological system is of very little interest as a formal object; there is nothing of significance to be said, from a formal point of view, about a set of forty-odd elements cross-classified in terms of eight or ten features . . . if we abstract away from the specific universal set of features and the rule systems in which they function, little of significance remains . . . it is the properties of the systems of rules . . . that really shed light on the specific nature of the organization of language (1972:74–75).

In recent cultural anthropology, these ideas of the structuralists and transformationalists may be seen as heading toward even wider applicability: toward a search for cultural universals, a theory of Culture, and an understanding of man's "ideational" world as it applies to the acquisition of behavior.

It is now considered appropriate to ask general questions and test out answers, sometimes arrived at intuitively, relating to complex wholes in social science. Both anthropology and linguistics have moved away from describing exotic languages and cultures toward an attempt to account for Language and Culture. Attention is being focused on the rule systems and the properties of such rule systems underlying the acquisition of language and cultural behavior.

In this chapter, we will look at the distinctive features proposed for phonology by Roman Jakobson and the Prague circle of linguists. We will also discuss the structuralism of Lévi-Strauss, and Noam Chomsky's theory of transformational/generative grammar. We will then briefly examine the application of some of the theoretical notions from structuralism and transformationalism to general cultural anthropology.

2.1   Jakobsonian Distinctive Features

For our purposes here, Jakobson and Halle's *Fundamentals of Language* (1956) is the most influential work introducing structuralism to American linguistics. Their book introduces the idea of *distinctive feature* to phonology. Jakobson's effort was to "dissolve language into its ultimate components, the dyadic distinctive features" (1956:vi).

As early as the 1920s, Jakobson was convinced that it is impossible to evaluate properly any element of a language's system if that element is not viewed in relation to other elements of the system (Vachek 1972:12–14). This view, influenced by Troubetzkoy (1937 and other works), led to the development of relational distinctive features in phonology. The "once a phoneme, always a phoneme" approach of the descriptivists was rejected. An English word such as *water* might be pronounced as [watɜ^r] or as [wadə] "wadda." The phonemicist working on a corpus of data and not knowing English would have difficulty deciding to which phoneme to assign the middle consonant; that is, is [t] a phonetic form of /d/ or /t/ in the first form and is [d] a form of /d/ or /t/ in the second? To Jakobson, the question need not arise. What is important are the features of the consonant in relation to other sounds in the language. This relational approach allows the linguist who observes sounds in context to discover that the feature [-voice] of a sound surrounded by vowels often tends to change to [+voice] in agreement with the vowels, since all vowels have the feature [+voice].

Jakobson felt that linguistic analysis ought to break down speech units into morphemes as the minimal units of language with meaning. Then, the analysis ought to break down morphemes into whatever components allow morphemes to be differentiated from each other. These components which differentiate morphemes are called DISTINCTIVE FEATURES: "Each distinctive feature involves a choice between two terms of an opposition that displays a specific differential property, diverging from the properties of all other oppositions" (1956:4).

Jakobson's view holds that the main function of sound in language is to differentiate semantic units, which is done through perceiving the distinctive features of sound as separate from the other features of sound. That is, /s/ and /z/ in *seal* /sil/ and *zeal* /zil/ are consonants—fricatives articulated at the alveolar ridge; they are not vowels, not stops, not nasals. They have all these positive and negative features in common, but these features, though perceived, do not account for the difference between the two sounds. The feature to note is voice: /s/ is [-voice], /z/ is [+voice]. Thus, [voice] is a distinctive feature distinguishing /s/ from /z/.

The /I/ in *bit* /bIt/ and the /i/ in *beat* /bit/ share the features [+voice], [+front] (articulated in the front of the mouth), and [+high] (articulated with the tongue raised). These common features, again, do not account for the phonological difference in the words. However, /i/ is longer than /I/. It is said that /i/ is [+tense] in relation to /I/, which is therefore [-tense], or lax. Thus, [tense] is a distinctive feature for vowels in English. This feature also distinguishes *pull* from *pool* and *late* from *let* in English. Therefore, /i/ is to /I/, as /u/ is to /U/, and as /e/ is to /E/.

Distinctive features of sound are grouped into BUNDLES that occur simultaneously in speech. These bundles of distinctive features are called phonemes. This definition differs substantially from the "minimal unit of sound feature" definition of the phoneme employed in descriptive linguistics. A /p/ is a minimal unit for the descriptivist, but for the structuralist a /p/ is a bundle of features such as [-voice], [+cons], [-voc], and so forth. One feature or set of features might differentiate /p/ from /b/ in a language, another /t/ from /d/. The descriptive linguist can only state that each of the sounds is distinct despite phonetic similarity. Features provide the linguist with a way to relate sounds according to shared and nonshared values within a system. The features themselves are defined as oppositions largely in acoustic and articulatory terms.

Jakobson and Halle (1956) discuss twelve oppositions as the distinctive features from which each language in the world chooses its sound system. Sounds are defined acoustically and articulatorily by means of the following oppositions (paraphrased from Jakobson and Halle):

1. vocalic—nonvocalic
2. consonantal—nonconsonantal
3. compact—diffuse
4. tense—lax
5. voiced—voiceless
6. nasal—non-nasal
7. discontinuous—continuant
8. strident—mellow
9. checked—unchecked
10. grave—acute
11. flat—plain
12. sharp—plain

We will not discuss here the precise definitions of these features since they have been greatly modified since the time of Jakobson and Halle's writing. It is sufficient for our purposes to note that there were twelve features posited as sets of oppositions. Whereas in phonemics the task was to describe each significant sound in a particular language with reference to its point and manner of articulation in speech in order to list the phonemes of language X and of language Y, the distinctive-feature framework marked an attempt to set up acoustic as well as articulatory correlates for sound in all languages and to designate these correlates as a series of feature oppositions.

Distinctive features, which in bundles make up phonemes, may be influenced by their environment:

A distinctive feature is a relational property so that the "minimum same" of a feature in its combination with various other concurrent or successive features lies in the essentially identical relation between the two opposite alternatives (Jakobson and Halle (1956:14).

The example given by Jakobson and Halle is the English word *tot*, in which the

Table 3.
Feature Composition of Some English Segments*

		Segments								
		i	l	w	p	b	t	d	s	z
Features	sonorant	+	+	+	−	−	−	−	−	−
	vocalic	+	+	−	−	−	−	−	−	−
	consonantal	−	−	−	+	+	+	+	+	+
	high	+	+	+	−	−	−	−	−	−
	back	−	−	+	−	−	−	−	−	−
	low	−	−	−	−	−	−	−	−	−
	anterior	−	−	−	+	+	+	+	+	+
	coronal	−	−	−	−	−	+	+	+	+
	round	−	−	+						
	tense	+	−	−						
	voice				−	+	−	+	−	+
	continuant				−	−	−	−	+	+
	nasal				−	−	−	−	−	−
	strident				−	−	−	−	+	+

*Feature specifications which appear redundant here serve to distinguish other sounds in the system. See Chomsky and Halle (1968:176) for a table of the distinctive feature composition of all the segments of English.

two /t/'s differ from each other acoustically and articulatorily; that is, the initial /t/ is aspirated, the latter unaspirated. However, when considered along with the two /p/'s in *pop* and the two /k/ sounds in *cock*, the two /t/'s are relationally the same. In terms of distinctive features, a phoneme in different contexts is said to retain the distinctive feature which differentiates that phoneme from others in the system. In phonemic terms, one need not state allophonic variation, nor assign allophones to phonemes, nor confront the problem of overlapping phonemes.

Jakobson and Halle's features are now referred to as the "old" features. Table 3 presents the feature composition of some English segments[1] in terms of "new" features, with phonetic representation described on a matrix. Note that the two feature frameworks overlap to some extent. The "new" versus the "old" fea-

---

[1]In the Chomsky and Halle framework, the term SEGMENT is used to refer to consonants and vowels that constitute a FORMATIVE, a formative being a string of consonants and vowels (1968:28).

tures may best be understood through Chomsky and Halle's *The Sound Pattern of English* (1968).

This structuralist approach to language as an entire system, with phonology functioning to differentiate semantic units, is a radical departure from the descriptive approach of building up from phoneme to morpheme to utterance in order to describe a language from a corpus gathered as a sample of the whole.

André Martinet, a French structural linguist, noted that within a framework such as that espoused by Troubetzkoy and Jakobson, one must remember that language resides in the speaker. Corpuses of data can be conceived of as indicators of this fact only through overt procedures involving comparisons of utterances. The physical features of the structure of a language often reflect only what is accessible to observation. He provides this example:

> If I say phoneme A distinguishes itself from phoneme B by a certain articulatory feature, I note thereby a structural feature, which, at one point in the speech circuit, takes the concrete form of a certain movement of the speech organs. But I could just as well have formulated this feature in acoustic terms and, less easily, in terms of hearing or of voice production, at the neuro-muscular level. That is perhaps a simple enough reminder of how much more complex language structure is than the structure of a brick, stone, or concrete building (Martinet, in Ehrmann 1970:8).

Jakobson and Halle caution that they are not concerned with substituting an acoustic classification for an articulatory one as used by the descriptivists, but instead they hope to uncover the most productive criteria of division valid for both purposes (1956:36). Their proposed framework of features may be seen as one of the most significant aspects of structuralist phonology. In the words of Chomsky, this significance lies in the fact that

> A fairly small number of features that can be specified in absolute, language-independent terms appear to provide the basis for the organization of all phonological systems. The achievement of structuralist phonology was to show that the phonological rules of a great variety of languages apply to classes of elements that can be simply characterized in terms of these features; that historical change affects such classes in a uniform way; and that the organization of features plays a basic role in the use and acquisition of language (1972:74–75).

2.2 Claude Lévi-Strauss

The structuralist approach to cultural matters *beyond* the linguistic level is primarily exemplified in the work of Claude Lévi-Strauss. Lévi-Strauss is an important figure in anthropology mainly for his assertion and demonstration that cultural systemic phenomena contain underlying elemental structures. According to Lévi-Strauss,

The human brain has certain formal properties resulting from its structure and its organization. All that we are permitted to do . . . is to lessen the gap that separates what we can assume about the brain's structure and organization from the way in which it actually functions in particular cases (*Psychology Today* 5[1972]:76).

In the approach of Lévi-Strauss, as influenced by both the linguists of Prague and earlier French structural anthropologists, it became respectable in the analysis of culture to go beyond the objectively verifiable data of observed behavior and attempt to describe what lies behind the surface data. Lévi-Strauss believes that empirical data are not sufficient evidence for explanation of cultural systems. The structure of a system described in terms of the relationships of the elements within that system offers a more descriptively adequate model of the phenomena than does a description of the elements alone:

a myth or a detail of a myth is never intelligible by itself. It becomes intelligible insofar as it says the opposite of what the same myth says in another part of the narrative, or of what is said in a different myth from nearby (*Psychology Today* 5[1972]:78).

In Lévi-Strauss's view, the scientist who looks at myth should not just analyze a myth as told to him by an informant or as it appears in written form. Instead, he must analyze myth as it occurs within a group of both similar and different myths and extract from the system as a whole sets of oppositions among and within the different versions. In working this way, according to Lévi-Strauss, it is possible to reveal the meaning of myth.

In both traditional linguistics and traditional ethnography, a focus on empirically discoverable elements of language and culture stood in the way of deeper analyses. The description of such elements was no more than a statement of what the elements are and how they are delimited. From such ethnographies and linguistic descriptions it was not possible to make statements as to how the elements relate in an overall system, thereby explaining how the system "works." A rigorous descriptive method forced the scientist to isolate elements at various levels of description rather than interrelate them within the system as a whole.

To Lévi-Strauss, the structural linguistics of deSaussure of the Geneva School and of Jakobson and Troubetzkoy of the Prague School is a methodological model which may be adapted to certain anthropological analyses. Lévi-Strauss sees social activity and social expression as similar to language in that each is a (1) type of communication, (2) form of expression, and (3) system of behavior structured by unconscious laws. The structure of social activity or expression in these terms may be analyzed somewhat as the linguist analyzes the grammar of a language (deGeorge and deGeorge 1972:xxv).

To apply structural analysis to anthropological data, Lévi-Strauss urges the anthropologist, as Jakobson urged the linguist, to adopt the four operations of the structural method as set forth by Troubetzkoy (paraphrased from Lévi-Strauss 1967:33):

1. to shift from the study of conscious linguistic phenomena to a study of their uncon-
    scious infrastructure
2. to treat terms not as independent entities but instead to analyze the relations between
    terms
3. to utilize the concept of the system
4. to discover general laws

In applying structural analysis to kinship, Lévi-Strauss uses as an example the avunculate relationship—that of the mother's brother. A finite corpus of attitudes is possible with regard to interpersonal relationships in culture, with certain ones used in certain ways in particular cultures. Using a study by Radcliffe-Brown on the position of the mother's brother in South Africa (1924), Lévi-Strauss points out two situations with regard to the son/nephew (1967:39): (1) where the father represents authority and the uncle represents familiarity, and (2) the oppposite, where the father and son have a familiar relationship and the uncle represents authority. For Lévi-Strauss these two situations represent two sets of attitudes constituting two pairs of oppositions with descent determining the choice of opposition. In a patrilineal society the mother's brother is $\begin{bmatrix} +\text{familiar} \\ -\text{authority} \end{bmatrix}$, but in a matrilineal society he is $\begin{bmatrix} -\text{familiar} \\ +\text{authority} \end{bmatrix}$.

To look at kinship terms in this way is to look for attitudes, or unconscious features, of the terms as parts of a system. It also means to begin looking at each particular term as a bundle of attitudes (features) which relate in various ways to other terms, similarly composed, within the system.

In his approach to structural analysis in the area of kinship, Lévi-Strauss examines other relationships as well; for in order to arrive at a general law within a kinship system, it is necessary to go beyond correlating only attitudes such as those between father/son and uncle/nephew (sister's son). He sees such a relationship within a kinship system as a correlation which is "only one aspect of a global system containing four types of relationship which are organically linked, namely: brother/sister, husband/wife, father/son, and mother's brother/sister's son" (1967:40).

From observing a number of different kinship systems, Lévi-Strauss formulates a general rule to the effect that the "relation between maternal uncle and nephew [in cultures where that relationship is distinctive] is to the relation between brother and sister as the relation between father and son is to that between husband and wife" (40). The claim here is that to know one pair of relations is to infer the other. Likewise, in phonology, if we know the relationship between /p/ and /b/, we can infer the relationship between /t/ and /d/.

This example of the analysis of mother's brother in structuralist terms eliminates the problem faced by a traditional ethnographer—that of interpreting how a term acquired significance in the culture in which it occurs. The traditional ethnographer could either simply state that there is a term for mother's brother in culture X or state, as Radcliffe-Brown did, that the mother, an indulgent figure, is identified with her brother.

However, if kinship is seen as a system, Lévi-Strauss believes that there is no longer a need to explain the occurrence of a term for mother's brother. Mother's brother is a part of all kinship systems whether or not the culture in question uses a kin-term for that relationship. Lévi-Strauss postulates the existence of an underlying structure of kinship from which all relationships derive.

In addition to being influenced by the structuralist feature phonology in linguistics, Lévi-Strauss also draws upon deSaussure's langue and parole distinction discussed in Chapter 1 above. Lévi-Strauss contends that language can be analyzed into entities that are both similar and different, an idea that is expressed in the langue and parole distinction. Langue is the structural side of language and belongs to revertible time (is recurrent), whereas parole is the statistical side of language and is nonrevertible. The elements of langue (that is, the systematic elements of language) are finite, but the elements of parole are variable. In addition to langue and parole, Lévi-Strauss maintains that language has a third aspect —time. This time element of language comes into play in forms of language such as myth.

In applying his structural analysis to myth, Lévi-Strauss claims that myth may be looked at as being both revertible (it has recurring systematic elements) and nonrevertible (the words used in telling a myth vary), and also both synchronic (elements of a myth co-occur simultaneously) and diachronic (a myth is composed of sequential events) (Lévi-Strauss 1955:430).

Lévi-Strauss holds that meaning in mythology cannot be analyzed through looking at the isolated elements that enter into the composition of a myth. One must analyze how the elements of a myth are combined. The properties of mythological language are above the ordinary linguistic level, and exhibit more complex features than those which occur in linguistic expression (such as phonology, syntax, and the like).

Assuming that myth is a special case of language and accepting Lévi-Strauss's addition of the time (synchronic/diachronic) element to the langue/parole distinction, we may summarize his view of myth thus: Myth is made up of constituent units which presuppose the constituent units present in language when analyzed on other levels (such as phonemes, morphemes, and so forth). The constituent units of myth belong to "a higher order, a more complex one" than those of language. Lévi-Strauss calls these units of myth GROSS CONSTITUENT UNITS (1955:431).

The gross constituent units or distinctive features of myth are not proposed as isolated relations (just as features are not isolated units of sound), but rather "bundles of relations" (as phonemes are bundles of distinctive features). As bundles of relations, gross constituent units may be combined to produce meaning somewhat as phonemes are combined in morphemes.

This approach analyzes myth such that relations connected with the same bundle (gross constituent unit) may appear throughout the myth at different and separated intervals. The analyst seeks to group these sequentially occurring bundles of relations together. He thereby reorganizes the myth

according to a time referent of a new nature corresponding to the prerequisite of the initial hypothesis, namely, a two dimensional time referent which is simultaneously diachronic and synchronic and which accordingly integrates the characteristics of the langue on one hand and parole on the other (Lévi-Strauss 1967:207–208).

Essentially, the structuralist retells the myth as a series of recurring relationships among its structural units and thereby discovers the structural features of the myth apart from the narrative sequence. One example of Lévi-Strauss's structural approach to myth is his analysis of the Tsimshian myth *The Story of Asdiwal* (Lévi-Strauss, in Leach 1967:1–47). We will consider only a summary of the main points of the analysis here.

Lévi-Strauss maintains in this analysis that myth exists in a culture as that culture's way of resolving certain contradictions between the culture-bearers and nature. Mythology appears to have no logical continuity, yet it has correspondences, much like sequences of sound have one meaning in one culture and another meaning in another culture.

A myth is constructed by employing a number of SEQUENCES and a number of differing FRAMEWORKS (schema). The sequences form the content of the myth. These chronological, meaningful sequences occur within settings or frameworks; for example, the story of Asdiwal has a geographical, an economic, a sociological, and a cosmological framework. These frameworks occur on different levels but are seen as symmetrical. For example, the geographical and economic settings of a myth would be at the level of reality; its sociological context would be at the level of both reality and unreality; and its cosmological framework would be at the level of the unreal.

Each level of a myth's framework has a CODE, and the codes of all levels are used to transmit the myth's MESSAGE. To separate out the codes at the various levels of a myth is to analyze the structure of the myth's message.

The remaining task in completing a structural analysis of a myth is to uncover the meaning of the myth's message through an analysis of the sequences in terms of the relationships expressed among gross constituent units. In analyzing the meaning, the structuralist looks for pairs of oppositions among the situations and the frameworks which need to be resolved. For example, in a myth literally telling about animals, one might discover other levels of meaning by uncovering oppositions at various levels corresponding to oppositions at the literal level. A myth that contains sequences of events about an antelope and a lion, and in a later sequence about a hyena, may be said to contain the opposition:

herbivore(antelope)/carnivore(lion)

This opposition is one which needs to be resolved in the myth. Later the introduction of the hyena may be seen to neutralize or mediate the opposition, since the hyena holds a mid-position, for he eats meat but does not kill it himself. As a mid-point in the opposition, the hyena serves to deny the contradiction expressed in the opposition. At another level of analysis, the myth may be seen as functioning to "mediate the gulf between life and death" (example elaborated from Keesing and Keesing 1971:311):

antelope:life :: lion:death

(The antelope is to life as the lion is to death.)

It is impossible in these pages to demonstrate fully how a structural analysis of a myth operates without recounting a myth and going through the analysis step by step. The important aspect to note is how this approach compares methodologically with that in structuralist phonology. One might envision an analyzed myth on a feature matrix such as that in Table 3 above, with the rows representing the sequences of the narrative and the columns, the feature composition of each gross constituent unit. The rows would then represent the diachronic element and the columns the synchronic element; the pluses and minuses would represent the resolutions and oppositions from which the meaning of the message is extracted.

Myth, to Lévi-Strauss, permits intellectual solutions to events which can be resolved in no other way. The oppositions uncovered in analyzing a myth are paradoxes of which the culture-bearer is unaware. The message of a myth uncovered by such an analysis occurs at all levels of the myth in a symmetrical pattern.

The structuralist argues that the science of man depends upon considering both conscious and unconscious social processes at work in areas such as language, kinship, social organization, myth, religion, magic, and art. The nature of the phenomena is not important; instead, the relations among phenomena and the systems into which relations enter hold the key (Lévi-Strauss 1967:ix).

In concluding this section on structuralism, it must be reemphasized that the term *structuralism* applied to the Prague School of Linguistics, applied yet earlier to the Geneva School, and has later been applied to the work of Lévi-Strauss on kinship and mythology. However, *structural linguistics* refers to the methods of descriptive linguistics developed by Zellig Harris. Both structuralism and structural linguistics formed the background of the development of transformational/generative grammar as developed by Noam Chomsky, taken up in the next section.

2.3 Chomsky: Transformational/Generative Grammar

In 1957, Noam Chomsky's book *Syntactic Structures* introduced transformational grammar to the science of linguistics. Chomsky was trained as a descriptive linguist and was both a student and collaborator of the structural linguist Zellig Harris, sharing his emphasis on rigor in description. However, Chomsky later moved away from descriptive linguistics, and his new goal became an attempt to "construct a formalized general theory of linguistic structure" (1957:5). In his early works, his approach moved gradually from one using structural methods devised to produce adequate descriptions of language data to one using structuralism—an approach holding that the unconscious infrastructure of language as a system is of paramount importance.

Noam Chomsky is an important figure in linguistics much in the way that Lévi-Strauss is a key influence in anthropology. Chomsky made it respectable in linguistics to go beyond the objectively verifiable surface data to attempt to make explicit abstract underlying linguistic forms which could be used to explain surface data. Just as Lévi-Strauss discovered that the kinship system contains underlying relationships, Chomsky demonstrated that relatable elemental structures underlie sentences in language. However, the unique significance in Chomsky's approach to language is that an understanding of language comes not from describing the relationships among structural features, nor from isolating the structural features, but rather from determining and describing the properties of the system of rules that underlies the features and relationships of language. These "rules of grammar" make explicit the principles of organization of a grammar and also of language.

Chomsky's rule-governed theory of language was first known as TRANSFORMATIONAL GRAMMAR and later as GENERATIVE GRAMMAR (which includes a transformational component), or variously as TRANSFORMATIONAL/GENERATIVE GRAMMAR. The term *grammar* to Chomsky refers to a theory; a grammar of language in his view is a theory of Language.

In order to produce a general theory of linguistic structure, Chomsky added in his post-1957 writings a rationalist dimension to linguistic science. He observed, as the philosopher Descartes had seen, that language use has a creative aspect which is an indicator of how man is innovative and of how human behavior is diverse. Thus, a general theory of language, in Chomsky's view,

> requires the postulation of a "creative principle" alongside of the "mechanical principle" that suffices to account for all other aspects of the inanimate and animate world and for a significant range of human actions and "passions" as well (1966:6).

Chomsky's theory aims to account for this "creative principle" of language with the central doctrine of his approach to linguistics—that "the general features of grammatical structure are common to all languages and reflect certain fundamental properties of the mind" (59).

Another important feature of this approach focusing on the creative aspect of language and on the relationship of language to mind, is the assumption that common to all people is an innate capacity to acquire a linguistic system. The structural properties of language, as a skeletal linguistic system, are inborn. The system is a base on which a person builds "those structural details that translate this base into the fully specified system that is used around him" (Langacker 1968:236). That is, the language an individual speaks and hears, in common with others in his linguistic community, derives its particular structure from a set of structural possibilities. These particular structural features are added onto the common/universal innate base.

Aside from its theory about the innateness of man's ability to acquire language, Chomsky's approach diverges from structuralism in its emphasis on a SYSTEM OF RULES which reveal the generative processes in language that allow novel sentences to be created. Language to the transformational/generative linguist is a rule-governed system in which the rules attempt to account for linguistic COMPETENCE, that is, for what people know unconsciously about their language. The linguist's rules attempt to determine the rules that a language learner (for example, a child) uses to move from his innate language structure to an actual speaking and hearing ability with respect to the sentences of his language.

> A grammar of a language purports to be a description of the ideal speaker-hearer's intrinsic competence. If the grammar is, furthermore, perfectly explicit—in other words, if it does not rely on the intelligence of the understanding reader but rather provides an explicit analysis of his contribution—we may (somewhat redundantly) call it a *generative grammar* (Chomsky 1965:4).

This theoretical approach to language differs in one major aspect from both descriptive methods and from structuralism. Both the structuralist and the descriptivist are interested in finding out about language and culture from directly observable data. The descriptivist's main focus is on producing adequate descriptions on the assumption that one may abstract from the data to the language or the culture. The structuralists focus on the systematic nature of language and culture and seek to describe each system in terms of relationships within it, as found in data, assuming that systematic relationships reveal an understanding of the system itself. On the contrary, the transformational/generativists proceed from theory, using data to check the applicability of their rules. The theory aims to account for sentences not yet produced as well as those one might be able to transcribe in a corpus.

A transformational/generative grammar aims to describe formally the competence (knowledge) of an ideal speaker-hearer in a language. The grammar must account for all the sentences a speaker could use, has used, or will use. The rules of the grammar should link the meaning of a sentence with the sounds in that sentence.

The notion of COMPETENCE as that which a grammar describes or accounts for (that is, the unconscious linguistic knowledge of the ideal speaker-hearer) is opposed to that of PERFORMANCE (what the ideal speaker-hearer does with his knowledge or competence). Chomsky defines performance as "the actual use of language in concrete situations" (1965:4). The competence/performance distinction is related to deSaussure's langue/parole distinction. However, Chomsky rejects deSaussure's concept of langue as a systematic inventory of items and recommends that the linguist view underlying competence as a system of generative processes, as a system of rules accounting for language. As we have seen, Chomsky's view of a system as being composed of rules rather than of elements which enter relationships is his point of departure from structuralism.

Chomsky's break with descriptive linguistics is essentially his rejection of the importance of discovery procedures for grammar. In Chomsky's view, the descriptive linguist develops a description of a corpus of data level by level, describing phonemes, then morphemes in terms of phonemes, then constituents in terms of morphemes, and so forth, in an attempt to show how one arrives at a grammar of a language. In his own work, Chomsky disclaims any emphasis on such a search for discovery procedures (1957:60). His goal is not to describe a language by discovering its grammar, but rather to account for the process of language acquisition.

Chomsky sees the grammar of a language as a complex system with many and varied interconnections between its parts. He holds that "to develop one part of grammar thoroughly, it is often useful, or even necessary, to have some picture of the character of a completed system" (60). The descriptivist notion "that syntactic theory must await the solution of problems of phonology and morphology" is, in Chomsky's view, an untenable one. The idea of the separation of levels of grammar (phonology, morphology, syntax), with a prohibition on mixing the levels and the accompanying idea that grammar works from the bottom up (phonology to utterance), is seen by Chomsky as based on a faulty analogy "between the order of development of linguistic theory and the presumed order of operations in the discovery of grammatical structure" (60).

Transformational/generative grammar is an attempt to arrive at a theory of linguistic competence. The generativist assumes that problems of performance and performance theory must necessarily await a theory of competence. In a similar way, the structuralists hold that one must deal with *langue* (system) if one ever hopes to deal with *parole* (variability).

A transformational/generative grammar as a theory of linguistic competence has three components:

1. a phonological component
2. a syntactic component
3. a semantic component

In a generative grammar, language is thought of as a set of sentences "each with an ideal phonetic form and an associated intrinsic semantic interpretation. The grammar of the language is the system of rules that specifies this sound-meaning correspondence" (Chomsky and Halle 1968:1).

The clearest statement about generative grammar is perhaps the following by Chomsky:

> The syntactic component consists of a base that generates deep structures and a transformational part that maps them into surface structures. The deep structure of a sentence is submitted to the semantic component for semantic interpretation, and its surface structure enters the phonological component and undergoes phonetic interpretation. The final effect of a grammar, then, is to relate a semantic interpretation to a phonetic representation—that is, to state how a sentence is interpreted. This relation is mediated by the syntactic component of the grammar which constitutes its sole "creative" part (1965:135).

This statement is set out diagrammatically as Figure 1.

Figure 1.
Transformational/Generative Grammar

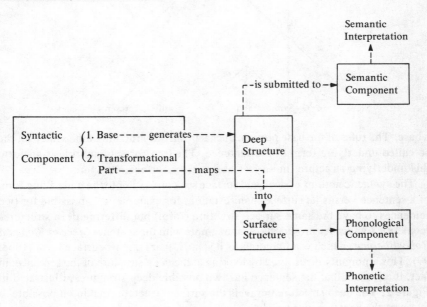

The theoretical model of Chomsky assumes that syntax is the central component mediating the relationship between the phonetic representation and the semantic interpretation of a sentence. In this theory, then, the sentence is the basic unit of language with all other parts of language interpreted in reference to it.

As may be seen from Figure 1, one of the elements in the syntactic component is

Figure 2.
Sample of Divergent Deep Structures for One Surface Structure (from Langacker 1968:99)

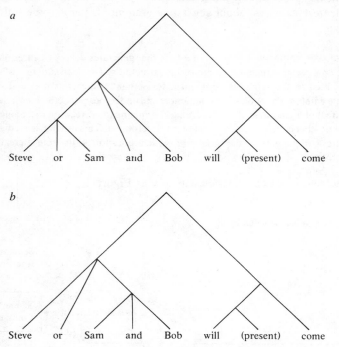

a base. The rules of the base provide the basic phrase structure of the sentence, the so-called underlying form of the sentence. The transformational rules transform this underlying structure into a less abstract, or surface, structure.

The syntactic notions of deep and surface structures refer to the underlying form of a sentence versus its surface manifestation; for example, it is possible for two sentences to have the same surface structure (form) but differing deep structures (content). Langacker provides a clear example with the sentence *Steve or Sam and Bob will come*, which is ambiguous as it stands, that is, in its surface form (1968: 99). This ambiguity is resolved by looking at the deep structure of the sentence; in fact, it turns out that the sentence has two possible deep structures, illustrated in Figure 2. The deep structure unravels the surface structure, making it possible to interpret the sentence properly.

The sentence with the surface structure *Steve or Sam and Bob will come* can be interpreted to mean:

a. Bob will come, and either Steve or Sam will come too.
    or
b. Either Steve will come or Sam and Bob will.

Interpretation *a* corresponds to the top structure in Figure 2; interpretation *b*, to the bottom structure (Langacker 1968:99).

The difference in deep structures for the two interpretations of the sentence *Steve or Sam and Bob will come* is whether or not conjunction is first accomplished by *and* or by *or*. A purely descriptive grammar deals only with surface structure, making it impossible to resolve ambiguities. The notions of deep (or underlying) and surface structures in syntax allow differences in conceptual structure and phonetic output to be made more explicit; one may disambiguate sentences, delete certain parts of sentences, and transform sentences without changing meaning.

The phonological component of the theory of transformational/generative grammar appears in its most complete form in Chomsky and Halle's *The Sound Pattern of English* (1968). According to them,

> The phonological component is a system of rules . . . that relates surface structures . . . to phonetic representations. . . . A phonetic representation is actually a feature matrix in which the rows correspond to a restricted set of universal phonetic features (voicing, nasality, etc.) and the columns to successive segments (14).

The distinctive features proposed by Chomsky and Halle differ substantially from those of Jakobson and Halle (1956) in that new features are added and others altered in an attempt to provide more general and universal applicability. Table 3 above contains these new features. Chomsky and Halle (1968) provide a full explication of their feature framework for phonology.

The semantic component of the theory of transformational/generative grammar is basically undeveloped at this time; indeed, the relationship between syntax and semantics is obscure (see Chapter 4, Section 4.3 below). Furthermore, it has been questioned whether the notion of deep structure is useful in understanding how meaning is attached to a sentence.

In transformational/generative grammar, the sentence is regarded as the given. The following is a simplified elaboration of how the theory proposes a particular sentence be interpreted.

Within the base of the syntactic component, phrase-structure rules generate the sentence's deep structure. The arrow means 'is rewritten as'.

1. Sentence → Noun Phrase + Verb Phrase
2. Noun Phrase → Article + Noun
3. Verb Phrase → Tense + Verb
4. Article → Definite
5. Noun → [−adult] [+human] [+male]
6. Tense → Present
7. Verb → [+motion] [+fast]

To the left of the arrow is the phrase structure, to the right, the deep structure. This example shows only one choice for each rewriting rule, that is, only one of the many possible structures that could be generated. However, many other sentences could be generated from such a base, depending upon how each node (element to the left of the arrow) is expanded. The effect of the rules is illustrated on a tree diagram in Figure 3.

Figure 3.
Tree Diagram

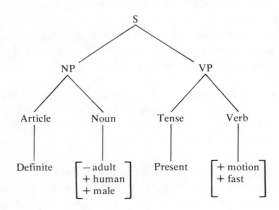

The deep structure generated by the base is submitted to the semantic component for semantic interpretation. The rules of the semantic component might look like the following (to the right of the arrow is the lexical representation of the semantic units; these are stored in the semantic component in terms of their distinctive-feature specifications on a matrix):

$$\text{Definite} \rightarrow \text{The}$$

$$\begin{bmatrix} -\text{adult} \\ +\text{human} \\ +\text{male} \end{bmatrix} \rightarrow \text{boy}$$

$$\text{Present} \rightarrow \text{s}$$

$$\begin{bmatrix} +\text{motion} \\ +\text{fast} \end{bmatrix} \rightarrow \text{run}$$

The transformational part of the syntactic component contains rules which rearrange the elements of deep structure so that as surface structures they may receive the correct phonetic representation. The transformational rules apply to the order of the output of the phrase-structure rules. In the following example, one transformational rule is needed:

1	2	3	4	1	2	4	3
The	*boy*	*s*	*run*	*The*	*boy*	*run*	*s*

Article + Noun + Tense + Verb =⟩ Article + Noun + Verb + Tense

or: 1234 =⟩ 1243

The input to the phonological component is this surface structure to which both the rules of the base and of the transformational part of the syntactic component have been applied: *The + boy + run +s*.

Phonetic representation is accomplished by specifying the distinctive features of the sounds as they occur in the utterance and by applying rules of pronunciation. For example, in this case we need a rule to account for how *run + s* (verb + present tense) receives phonetic representation as [r ə nz]. The rule would be somewhat like this:

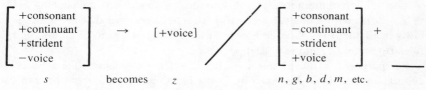

$$
\begin{bmatrix} +\text{consonant} \\ +\text{continuant} \\ +\text{strident} \\ -\text{voice} \end{bmatrix} \rightarrow [+\text{voice}] \Bigg/ \begin{bmatrix} +\text{consonant} \\ -\text{continuant} \\ -\text{strident} \\ +\text{voice} \end{bmatrix} + \underline{\qquad}
$$

| *s* | becomes | *z* | | *n, g, b, d, m*, etc. |

This rule states that the present-tense morpheme #s# is phonetically represented as [z] after voiced noncontinuant consonants in this language, that is, in English. This rule is a general one that applies throughout the language and is part of the phonological component of English. The elements of the sentence can be phonetically represented as features on a matrix, with the output of the semantic component (lexical elements and morphological elements) as the second set of features.

This example has been a simplified representation of how the theory of transformational/generative grammar proposes to interpret a sentence such as *The boy runs*, and demonstrates how each component of a grammar/theory is conceived of as a system of rules.

The advent of the transformational/generative approach in linguistics marks a change and a new direction. It moves away from American descriptive linguistics and its reliance on discovery procedure. It also diverges from the Prague School and its feature-based linguistics and moves toward a view of language as a system of rules.

In a report of the "Chomsky Revolution" in linguistics, John Davy of the *London Observer* makes the following analogy:

It is as though students of cookery were to turn their attention away from analysing various species of cake and time-and-motion studies of pastry-cooks, to discover the principles of cake-making lying behind the activities of cake-makers, the rules they are following, and the complex structure of the concept "cake" which guides their operations. This concept can be transformed by following the rules, into a number of confections, all of which are digestible (August 10, 1969, p. 21).

2.4   The "New" Cultural Anthropology

Influences such as structuralism and transformationalism in linguistic anthropology have begun to have ramifications in cultural anthropology as well. An example is the notion of the ideational order of culture, which, according to Ward Goodenough, is

> composed of ideal forms as they exist in people's minds, propositions about their interrelationships, preference ratings regarding them and recipes for their mutual ordering as means for organizing and interpreting new experience (1964:11).

The field of ethnoscience uses this notion, as we will see in Chapter 4 below, in analyzing terminological sets. In this section, we will discuss some of the ideas beginning to proliferate about the underlying structure of culture and the rules supporting a culture's ideational code.

For purposes of illustration here, it will suffice to examine the approach to cultural anthropology expressed by Roger Keesing in *New Perspectives in Cultural Anthropology* (1971), and then to provide an example of applying notions from modern linguistic theory to cultural data (Burling 1969).

2.41   CULTURE'S IDEATIONAL CODE

As has been seen throughout the discussion so far and as will be seen in the following chapters, linguistic analogies are very tempting to apply in the study of culture. Roger Keesing in his cultural anthropology text (1971) draws a parallel between culture and competence, and behavior and performance. Keesing proposes that certain insights from transformational/generative grammar as to the nature of language might also apply to the nature of culture.

The ideational code of culture is to be distinguished from its enactment in behavior, just as our linguistic competence is distinguished from performance. Keesing urges cultural anthropologists to take up the study of the ideational code, even though it cannot be directly observed, in addition to the traditional pursuit of analyzing the patterning of observable behavior.

A theory of a culture's ideational code aims to account for the creativity of behavior just as a theory of linguistic competence has as its goal an accounting for the creative aspect of language. Such a theory of code in culture is seen as a system of rules. Cultures are expected to vary greatly in content and in particular rules, yet all cultures, like all languages, are expected to be similar in overall design. Keesing suggests that for culture we might hope to arrive at a set of universal distinctive features of behavioral acts which would enter in various ways into the rules governing behavior.

Just as Chomsky assumes that the ability to acquire language is innate, so too the general outlines of cultural design may be partly or largely built in. In culture, humans continually produce behavior sequences, as in language they produce speech sequences, that they have never experienced before. New combinations of familiar elements of behavior are continually being generated.

For culture, as well as for language, the scientist is shifting away from an attempt to show how he arrives at a theory in a systematic way, that is, away from an attempt to make his discovery procedures explicit. More important in the study of the ideational code of culture is whether or not the theory works—whether the theory does "account for the intuition of the people under study" (Keesing and Keesing 1971:81). Discovery procedures in both language and culture fail to provide systematic ways of going from linguistic data to a theory of Language, from behavior to a theory of Culture.

Just as in linguistics a theory of linguistic competence may be criticized for slighting the study of performance, an analogous approach to culture through a theory of the ideational code might be said to slight its use—the actual behavior in cultural context.

Roger Keesing believes that, despite these possible analogies of language to culture, linguistic models have only limited applicability to the study of culture (ideational code and behavior). Culture—seen as that which people know about what they can do or what can be done to or for them (ideational code), and as that which is actually done (behavior)—occurs in a broader framework than that of the behavioral act. Linguists, too, are beginning to argue that the sentence as the basic unit of linguistic theory is perhaps too narrow. Such anthropologists and linguists prefer to see language and culture in context; specific among such scientists are the sociolinguists, whose work will be discussed in Chapter 5 below. Roger Keesing sees a need for a broader science of communication which will "have to be a study of messages, not simply sentences; of nonlinguistic as well as linguistic communications; and of contexts and networks as well as codes" (Keesing and Keesing 1971:85).

The field of sociolinguistics, and the work in communicational anthropology of Gregory Bateson, and of Edward T. Hall and R. L. Birdwhistell in such areas as proxemics and gesture language, deal with the interaction of culture (including language) with the environment. These types of study along with developments in cybernetics and systems theory are pointing toward a broader science which carries us well beyond the scope of this volume. Lévi-Strauss, too, saw this need to go beyond language in the study of social systems, especially in his analysis of myth, wherein he draws on such communicational notions as message and code.

Robbins Burling (1969) applies the approach of transformational/generative grammar to cultural anthropology to data on household composition among the Garo of Assam, India. He enunciates rules that account for the varied composition of the households. Using the linguist's approach to "rules of grammar," he states that "rules of household composition can be said to constitute a theory" (822). The rules do not specify the composition in any particular household, but account for the range of alternatives of household composition in Garo society. The system of rules he sets forth predicts not only what occurs in the data, "but [it] also predicts additional data in the form of other household types that were not included in the original sample" (822). Burling does not justify the rules with reference to any particular method used; that is, he does not make explicit any discovery procedures. The rules of household composition, as rules of grammar, are checked insofar as they account for the data.

Burling has ten rules to account for the composition of all possible households among the Garo (821). His rules are in the form of statements such as (here in paraphrased form):

1. A married couple has common residence.
2. Children live with their mother; if their mother is married, they therefore also live with her husband, usually their father.
3. One daughter, after marriage, *must* continue to live with her parents. (From Rule 1 we also know that this married daughter's husband lives with his in-laws.)

Just as in language a sentence's surface structure may have two underlying deep structures, the application of different sequences of household-composition rules might produce superficially identical households.

These rules of household composition are a kind of syntax of the Garo ideational code. Each particular Garo household conforms to the rules, and so would any new household. Burling maintains that rules which account for the data are more satisfying than traditional ethnographic accounts describing the diversity among households.

2.5   Formal and Substantive Universals

Traditionally, cultural anthropology and descriptive linguistics have focused on noting differences between languages and cultures. The hope was that someday, when enough descriptions had been made, languages could be compared to languages, and cultures to cultures, throughout the world. These comparisons would allow languages and cultures to be classified by their similarities and differences. The comparative method (see Chapter 3) was developed as a means of comparing languages to languages and cultures to cultures, assuming that the data have been described in a way that makes comparison possible.

Phonemics represents a concern with extracting distinctive units of sound in order that each language be described in terms of its own unique sound system. Also, traditional ethnographies, often formulated on a linguistic analogy, stress the uniqueness of the culture being described.

However, the advent of transformational/generative grammar "has cast aside the dogma that each language is a unique conceptual universe. Its quest is for a universal design of which each language is a variant form" (Keesing and Keesing 1971:120).

Universals in language are of two types: formal and substantive. Chomsky holds that a theory of SUBSTANTIVE UNIVERSALS makes the claim that "items of a particular kind in any language must be drawn from a fixed class of items" (1965:28).

Such a fixed class of items constituting a substantive language universal is the distinctive-feature framework in phonology. Phonological theory states that all languages select their distinctive sounds from a universal set of features of sound, including such features as [consonantal], [vocalic], [continuant], and [nasal].

Semantic features such as [male], [animate], [human], [count], and [mass] are part of a class of all semantic features from which lexical items in language are drawn. The set of all semantic features of language, if known in its entirety and if finite, would constitute another substantive universal.

Likewise, all the syntactic categories of language such as Noun Phrase, Verb Phrase, Noun, and Present Tense form a set of items making up the syntactic component of language. The total number of these categories, from which all languages draw their syntactic categories, constitutes another substantive universal.

FORMAL UNIVERSALS involve "the character of the rules that appear in grammars and the ways in which they can be interconnected" (Chomsky 1965:29). The two kinds of universals may be differentiated as universals of content (substantive) versus universals of organization (formal).

Some anthropologists suggest that a great diversity of content within and among cultures builds on an organizational, or formal, framework of culture which is universal. They also suggest the existence of a universal cultural framework from which each culture selects out certain behavioral acts or features for its particular structure. This cultural framework forms a substantive universal. In different cultures, the selected cultural features are combined in unique ways, according to organizational features determining the character of the rules. To Keesing, these notions of formal and substantive universals go far in validating the claims of both the uniqueness and universality of culture.

Formal universals of language determine the structure of grammars and the form and organization of rules. The conventions used in writing rules of grammar are examples of formal universals; and substantive universals of language "define the sets of elements that may figure in particular grammars" (Chomsky and Halle 1968:4).

the theory of transformational/generative grammar proposes certain formal universals regarding the kinds of rules that can appear in a grammar, the kinds of structures on which they may operate, and the ordering conditions under which these rules may apply (4).

These formal universals are the subject of the study of GENERATIVE PHO-NOLOGY, which deals with questions such as how the rules of the phonological component of a generative grammar should work, what rules the phonological component of a generative grammar should include, and so forth.

Substantive universals which might be proposed by general linguistic theory are statements such as,

> the lexical items of any language are assigned to fixed categories such as noun, verb, and adjective . . . phonetic transcriptions must make use of a particular, fixed set of phonetic features (Chomsky and Halle 1968:4).

The field of cultural anthropology needs a general theory of culture and of the formal universals which organize culture. Given such a theory, what appears as diversity, in the form of social and cultural institutions, and as uniqueness in their content from culture to culture (as evidenced by the numbers of ethnographies of different cultures the world over), would reveal underlying similarities masked by descriptive ethnographic methodology.

2.6 Summary

In this chapter we have seen that certain influences from Europe began to alter the nature of linguistics in the post-descriptivist period. The notion that sounds are composed of bundles of distinctive features which occur as binary oppositions replaced the fixed phonemic entity as the unit of phonological analysis. If the sound system of language could be viewed as a system of relational and universal sound features, then perhaps the whole of language, and even the whole of culture, can be seen as systemic.

To describe the data of language and culture it was no longer enough to state the observable facts: it became incumbent upon the scientist to seek an explanation of linguistic and cultural phenomena. Writing grammars and recording the kinship system and myths of a people were noble tasks and useful in their own right, but did not meet the goals of science—such tasks did not lead to an understanding of language and culture and the organizational principles which underlie them.

Proceeding from the ideas of the distinctive-feature phonologists and influenced as well by French structural anthropologists, Claude Lévi-Strauss sought to explain the unconscious logical structures which underlie cultural facts. A myth, which is an orally related sequence of events explaining the behavior or values of a particular culture, may be transcribed and preserved literally, but the myth has meaning only if it is analyzed as part of the myth system in which it occurs and as a set of sequences of events which are related to each other at many levels in explicable ways.

A given myth is composed of categories drawn from a set of categories under-lying myth systems. The categories of myth, like phonological features, are binarily opposed and universal. From culture to culture, myths may be analyzed in terms of relatable categories selected from this universal set, just as from language to language distinctive sounds are composed of relatable features drawn from a universal set of distinctive features, but arranged in bundles in differing ways.

Lévi-Strauss turned the study of kinship systems and systems of mythology away from a focus on surface interpretation toward an understanding of these systems as reflecting the logical structure underlying culture, that is, the logical structure of the mind.

A term in a particular culture for mother's brother is not significant only because the term occurs where the father is authoritarian and the mother familiar. A myth is not significant only as an explanation of complex and nonunderstood phenomena such as "love and death or pleasure and suffering" (Lévi-Strauss 1964:340). Mother's brother is a category of the logical structure of kinship as a system. The literal level of a myth, which may be an explanation of a phenomenon such as love, is related to other levels found in the setting and in the sequences; the various levels together may be attempting to explain the relationship of man to natural phenomena.

> By taking its raw material from nature, mythic thought proceeds in the same way as language, which chooses phonemes from among the natural sounds of which a prac-tically unlimited range is to be found in childish babbling. For, as in the case of language, the empirical material is too abundant to be all accepted indiscriminately or to be all used on the same level . . . . Only a few of its elements are retained—those suitable for the expression of contrasts or forming pairs of opposites (Lévi-Strauss 1964:341).

In linguistics, the influence of distinctive-feature phonology and the American structural linguistics of Zellig Harris led to the Chomsky "revolution." In order to understand the nature of language, Chomsky maintained, it is not enough to de-scribe the facts nor to show relationships among elements of structure. If the structure of language reflects the logical structure of the mind, and if we assume that the logical structure so reflected is innate, then the key for the understanding of language is the system of rules underlying linguistic structure. Transformational/ generative grammar seeks to make explicit the rules governing the combination of linguistic elements.

Both structuralism and transformationalism have had a profound effect on students of language and culture. We saw that the ideas developed are beginning to be generalized in cultural anthropology. In a book popularizing linguistics, Peter

Farb clearly conveys the prevailing notion which is an outgrowth of the ideas presented in this chapter, culminating in the Chomsky school:

> The situation is somewhat like learning to walk. The child possesses at birth the blueprint for the muscular coordination that he will develop later in order to walk. No one tells him how to lift his legs, bend his ankles or knees, or place his feet on the ground. He does not consciously arrive at the skill of balancing himself on his legs, any more than a three-year-old consciously figures out the rules for grammatical transformations. The child walks and the child talks—and in neither case does he know exactly how he did it (1974:245).

Perhaps we are born with a blueprint for culture also. The concluding section of this chapter dealt with the types of universal statements needed to explicate a theory of language, and possibly also a theory of culture based on such a hypothesis. The totality of items on the general blueprint is a substantive universal; the directions or rules for building a particular version by using a subset of the totality of items on the general blueprint are the formal universals.

The anthropologist Robin Fox, in taking up the old question as to whether or not children isolated from human contact would develop language and, if so, what language, made the following observations reflecting the ideas discussed here. According to Fox (1973), children would develop language, but the language would be unlike any known language, yet be analyzable by linguists and translatable into other languages. That is, the language would be composed of sounds that make use of a subset of universal distinctive features and would be governed by a system of phonological, semantic, and syntactic rules.

Fox further observed that such isolated children would also develop culture. That is, they would have laws "about property, its inheritance and exchange; rules about incest and marriage, customs of taboo and avoidance . . ." According to Fox, isolated children would develop both language and culture "because it is in the beast" (1973:326).

Whether or not the structures which Lévi-Strauss proposes for myth or kinship or the rules of grammar proposed by Chomsky do reflect "logical structures of the mind" or "man's capacity for language" is not at issue here. What is significant is the impact that the ideas of Chomsky and Lévi-Strauss have had on approaches to the study of language and culture.

In current linguistics, a point of controversy is the form that rules of grammar should take; many notions in linguistic theory such as deep structure in syntax and rule order in phonology are also at issue. In anthropology, structural analysis is controversial. Yet, it is becoming generally more and more accepted, aside from the details of each approach, that both language and culture need to be examined in their relationship to the mind. Furthermore, language and culture are being increasingly viewed as systems governed by rules of language and rules of behavior.

Chapter 3 The Comparative Method

3.0 Introduction

In Chapter 1, we looked at the development of descriptive methods for analyzing languages, focusing on a concern for rigorous attention to data, for ways to identify units within the data, and for the resulting adequate descriptions of the data. We saw that these concerns also apply to the description of ethnographic data.

In Chapter 2, we saw a shift in focus away from identifying units toward an emphasis on describing the system of which the data are but a sample. Such a system was to be described by analyzing the relationships within it. This structuralist approach attempted to make internal generalizations about a system based on the evidence of relationships observed in a body of data.

Both descriptivism and structuralism are methods of analyzing specific languages and cultures at a specific point in time—the time being represented by the data. A descriptive analysis of a language tells us nothing of the history of that language nor of changes that that language may have gone through that might account for the similarities or differences it has in relationship to other languages.

In the study of language, attempts have been made to reconstruct the history of particular languages by examining earlier descriptions of the languages or by setting up a hypothetical earlier form of related languages through a comparative method known as HISTORICAL RECONSTRUCTION. This type of endeavor is carried out by HISTORICAL LINGUISTS. On the other hand, linguists who compare language descriptions or parts of language descriptions are called COMPARATIVE LINGUISTS. They analyze correspondences in sound, meaning, and other aspects of a set of languages, with the goal of showing relationships among those languages, that is, of producing language classification.

The comparative method is an outgrowth of the development of anthropology in the nineteenth century. Early anthropological studies have been said to be evolutionary in that such studies assumed that present-day primitive cultures represent versions of past cultures. It was thought that many "exotic" societies were in an earlier stage of development than modern "civilized" ones. Observing certain cultural traits, such as marriage and religion, in these "uncivilized" societies, would allow the anthropologist to see how those same traits existed earlier in the "civilized" ones. This form of the comparative method claimed to demonstrate cultural evolution by comparing existing cultures with respect to stages of development of common traits within them. The basic assumption was that all cultural institutions develop by going through the same stages in the same order. In brief, the early comparative method assumed an accepted theory of evolution. As Alexander Goldenweiser noted, the results of the comparative method may be seen only "as a series of illustrations of a postulated evolutionary theory" (1922:22).

This evolutionary bent of the comparative method was largely discredited. It developed in anthropological studies in two directions. First, the comparative method may be seen today in cross-cultural comparison studies in which existing cultures are compared on one or another particular dimension. In such studies no claim or assumption is made that one culture in the comparison represents a "higher" or "lower," "earlier" or "later" form with respect to the others. Such comparison is often used in culture classification. In this sense, then, cross-cultural comparison and comparative linguistics are analogous.

Second, the comparative method figures in what are known as ETHNOHISTORICAL STUDIES. The goal of these studies is to describe and observe culture change much as the goal of historical linguistics is to study language change. Ethnohistory makes use of oral and written traditions that reflect earlier time stages of a culture, and attempts to reconstruct cultures—not in order to demonstrate progress, but rather to note and observe change. Just as historical linguistics has its own method for language reconstruction, ethnohistory employs paleobiological and archeological data, ethnographic and linguistic data, and oral and written records of the culture (Carmack 1972:232). In one sense, ethnohistory is more properly history than comparison, whereas historical linguistics uses comparison as the basis of its method.

The comparative method seeks to make generalizations about sociocultural systems by comparing descriptive analyses of data from different cultures with each other. The generalizations specify what is common to language and what is common to culture wherever found in the world. If a generalization applies to all known instances, it is known as a universal (see Chapter 2 above).

In addition to the goal of discovering cultural and linguistic universals, the comparative method is used for making cross-linguistic and cross-cultural comparisons in order to establish relationships among languages and among cultures. The comparative method is the approach used to establish language family trees; for example, the Indo-European family of languages to which English belongs was established through the comparative method in linguistics.

Along with comparing data from language to language and culture to culture (SYNCHRONIC COMPARISON), it is also sometimes possible to compare descriptions of sociocultural sytems made years apart. This type of comparison allows the scientist to discover instances of change in the system. The comparative method applied to data for the purpose of analyzing change is known as DIACHRONIC COMPARISON.

In the field of linguistics, synchronic comparison is known as *comparative linguistics*, while diachronic comparison is known as *historical linguistics*.

In this chapter, we will not be dealing with the nineteenth-century development of the comparative method except to note that the evolution of the method in Europe coincided with the beginnings of linguistics and of anthropology as sciences. The comparative method predated the focus on descriptive method in both anthropology and linguistics; in fact, the comparative method gave impetus to the development of rigorous descriptive techniques. As cross-cultural and cross-linguistic comparisons were beginning to be made, it became clear that a uniform method of data description for the ethnographer and linguist would facilitate later diachronic and synchronic comparisons of the data.

The evolutionist anthropologists of the nineteenth century noted the need for detailed synchronic studies. They wanted to trace the evolution of sociocultural systems through time, but had at their disposal only "documentary accounts about native cultures written by travellers, missionaries, etc." (Carmack 1972: 227).

In America, Franz Boas's main interest was in language classification. His goal was to set up the language families of North America. However, he soon saw the need for developing a uniform methodology for the gathering of linguistic data. In order to classify the languages of the new world, he would have to compare them to each other. He needed a way to ascertain that the data used in his comparisons were actually comparable.

In Europe, where the problem of unwritten and unknown languages was not as acute, data often existed in a form that was valid for comparison. However, for both language and culture, the results of comparison are only as valid as the descriptions of the languages and cultures being compared.

In this chapter we will describe the comparative method as it developed in linguistics. We will then discuss synchronic studies and diachronic studies—an important distinction in the context of the comparative method. We will look at various systems of language and culture classification as examples of the results of the application of the comparative method. Finally, we will discuss the controversial method of comparison of linguistic data known as lexicostatistics in glottochronology. The glottochronologist, using lexicostatistics as a tool, attempts to discover by means of the comparative method how long ago languages diverged from each other.

3.1   The Comparative Method in Linguistics

In linguistics, the comparative method proceeds as follows: the linguist examines both vocabulary and grammar in the languages to be compared, looking for items that correspond with each other in a systematic way by sharing sounds, functions, and meanings. The scientist makes every effort to exclude from his comparison items which are known to be borrowed into a language and items which correspond by chance. Two branches of linguistic science make use of the comparative method: historical linguistics and comparative linguistics.

HISTORICAL LINGUISTICS is the branch of linguistics which employs the comparative method to look at different time states of the same language. When one hears of university courses such as the history of English or the history of German, the reference is to studies of English and German from the earliest days of written records until the present time. Such studies compare grammatical and lexical data. For example, in the history of English, Anglo-Saxon, Old English, Middle English, and Modern English are compared. The purpose is to uncover regularities and significant relationships among these various time states of English. In this way, much of what seems random or unexplainable about modern English may be explained. The relationships noted between and among elements of English at these various historical periods are stated as generalizations. To state regular relationships, whether changes or similarities, requires a systematic application of comparative methods to the data.

DIACHRONIC LINGUISTICS is an equivalent term for historical linguistics— *diachronic* meaning literally 'across time'. Diachronic linguistics is a study of linguistic data as occurring over a period of time. The history of a language can be studied by comparing a series of synchronic descriptions (done at a particular point in time) representing the language in different periods in its development.

The term *diachronic* refers to historical, dynamic studies. *Synchronic* refers to the opposite approach—synchronic studies of language are static views of language. The descriptivist's analysis of a corpus of collected linguistic data is a synchronic description of a language. Section 3.2 below goes into more detail regarding synchronic and diachronic studies in both linguistics and anthropology.

The field of historical linguistics may be seen in its full form in E. H. Sturtevant's *Linguistic Change* (1917). There has been little change since then in theory or method.

The comparative method in historical linguistics marks the beginning of linguistics as a science. At the turn of the century in Europe, it was generally accepted that linguistic change through time is regular; that is, change observed in language at different periods of history is systematic. If a sound in Old English occurs in Modern English as another sound in one lexical item, the same shift will be observed throughout the language. If one Old English /p/ in a certain environment appears as /b/ in Modern English (for example, between vowels), then all instances of O.E. /p/ = Modern English /b/ between vowels.

It was also observed that if linguistic changes from one language to another are regular in their sound-and-meaning correspondences, then those languages are related. When the comparative method is thus applied to different languages to observe systematic correspondences among them, the procedure is known as COMPARATIVE LINGUISTICS.

The beginning of the comparative method in linguistics predated deSaussure's distinction of synchronic versus diachronic studies (see Section 3.2 below). The beginning of the comparative method also predated the existence of any method for the investigation of significant sounds in language, that is, of phonemics. However, during the nineteenth century, scholars began to observe "that languages which were reasonably suspected of being related, actually agreed in their inflectional systems" (Pedersen 1959:240), and hence they set up agreement in inflectional system as a criterion of linguistic relationship. The two principles significant for language comparison—(1) agreement in inflectional and grammatical systems, and (2) agreement in laws of sound shift—constituted the comparative method prior to 1870 (242).

After the 1870s it became clear that if agreement among languages, and within a language at different stages of history, is controlled by laws of sound shift among the items of much of the vocabulary, then this regular agreement is as much a proof of relationship of the languages or stages as is the existence of relatable inflectional systems. However, in order to prove that different languages are related, the comparative method holds that one must compare them to each other point by point, both in vocabulary and grammar. Also, languages must be compared systematically. For grammatical and vocabulary items to be compared, they must be shown to be identical by pointing back to an original identity of words and inflectional forms (245). In other words, the items must be shown to be COGNATE, that is, descended from a common traceable language (where written records exist) or from a common traceable hypothetical language.

The method of determining the unrecorded form of a language by comparing descended related forms in order to show the identity of the compared items is known as LINGUISTIC RECONSTRUCTION. The linguist attempts to reconstruct items of vocabulary and grammar reflecting the situation existing in all the related languages; the reconstructed forms are marked by an asterisk, *. It is then possible to derive the forms as they exist in the related languages from the common reconstructed form. Reconstructed forms, whether or not attested by historical records, are a means of deriving related forms and showing the nature of the relationship.

They should, therefore, always be considered hypothetical and as formulas. The following example from Pedersen is somewhat of a classic for students of comparative/historical linguistics:

> The formula *ekwo-s* tells us at a glance, for instance, a great many things about the forms of the word for *horse* in the various Indo-European languages; it tells us that there is virtually nothing in the form of the Indian *asva-s* which we can regard as wholly primitive: each of the two identical vowels had originally its own coloring, the first like *e* (cf. *e* in Latin *equo-s*), the second like *o* (which Greek *hippo-s* has best preserved), and both the consonants were at first different in quality from what they are in Indian. In the same way the formula with its five characters tells us many things about the presumable development of the other languages that it would take much longer to express in words. But if we are asked whether *ekwo-s* is identical with the pronunciation of the noun which the linguistic ancestors of our race used thousands of years ago in their original home, we must reply only that we cannot be sure (1959:268).

Figure 4.
The Reconstructed Form *ekwo-s*

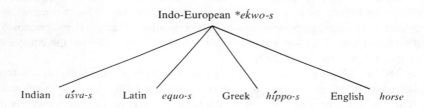

The method of phonological reconstruction (that is, how we reconstruct *ekwo-s* on evidence such as *asva-s*, *equo-s*, *hippo-s*, and *horse*) was developed largely by August Schleicher in the early 1860s. Reconstructed forms of vocabulary and grammar make up a PROTO-LANGUAGE (Ursprache), the hypothetical ancestor language to which present forms may be systematically traced back.

In order to compare languages by reconstructing cognate forms, one makes use of the principle of historical linguistics that "certain kinds of linguistic change (phonetic and phonemic) are regular" (Gleason 1961:446). The observation of regular sound change consists of noting phonological CORRESPONDENCES among languages. For two languages, if change is regular in both lines of descent from a common proto-language, then there should be regular correspondences observable between forms in one language and cognate forms in the other. It should then be possible to make statements accounting for correspondences between sounds in different languages.

One such statement is known as GRIMM'S LAW, so called since it was first formulated by Jakob Grimm, one of the Grimm Brothers of fairy-tale fame. Grimm noted that there were correspondences between consonants in languages such as English and German (that is, in Germanic languages) and consonants in other languages, specifically in Sanskrit, Greek, and Latin.

Grimm observed that a /p/ in Latin and Greek is an /f/ in German and English. The word *piscis* ('fish' in Latin) corresponds to *fish* in English. The voiceless stops /p/, /t/, and /k/ in Greek and Latin appear in English and German as /f/, / θ /, and /h/ respectively. For example:

	Latin		*English*
/p/	piscis	/f/	fish
/t/	tres	/θ/	three
/k/	centum	/h/	hundred

These correspondences show how the Germanic languages differ with respect to stop consonants from other languages with which they are related. The shifts from /p/ to /f/, /t/ to /θ/, and /k/ to /h/ are regular; in the Germanic languages, the voiceless stops of Latin, Greek, and Sanskrit are realized as fricatives (f, θ, and h). The shifts allow the linguist to relate the Germanic languages to Greek, Latin, and Sanskrit; these languages so interrelated are called Indo-European languages. It is said that the phonological system of proto-Indo-European contained the voiceless stops */p/, */t/, and */k/, which are realized as /p/, /t/, and /k/ in Latin, but as /f/, /θ/, and /h/ in English.

3.2   Synchronic versus Diachronic Studies

In discussing the development of the comparative method in linguistics in the previous section, we observed that the comparative method could be used to study a language in terms of its historical development (diachronically) and that the method could also be applied to many languages at once in the interest of discovering interrelationships among them and observing language change. Such diachronic studies are often contrasted with what are known as synchronic studies.

Early twentieth-century linguistics (and anthropology) were primarily concerned with providing adequate descriptions of languages (and cultures) based on data gathered by the scientist. These descriptions as discussed in Chapter 1 are termed *synchronic* in that they deal with a particular *state* of that language (or culture) at some point in time.

In anthropology, the distinction between synchronic and diachronic studies in the comparative analysis of culture is responsible for two different approaches to culture. One approach, a synchronic one, may be exemplified by Clyde Kluckhohn's interest in discovering within varied cultures certain regularities determined by such factors as psychology, biology, and constraints on social interaction. As the scientist studies cultures or systems in culture, perhaps certain universal categories of culture will emerge—cultural elements shared by all cultures. If there are common and universal categories of culture (see Kluckhohn 1953), they will become evident by examining various ethnographies, that is, synchronic studies.

As noted earlier, nineteenth-century cultural-evolution studies in anthropology have been for the most part discredited. Diachronic studies in anthropology no longer seek to show the "progress" of culture, but are diachronic in the sense that they seek to document the history of a culture by using the evidence of oral and written traditions, archeological evidence, and the results of diachronic linguistic studies. It may be that such documented culture histories will shed light on change within the general System of Culture. Attempts to trace the migration of Bantu-speaking peoples in Africa (see Collins 1968:57–113) may be seen as a diachronic ethnohistorical analysis. The researcher used comparative and historical linguistic studies in conjunction with archeological and other types of evidence to reconstruct the likely routes of the expansion of these people throughout sub-Saharan Africa.

Prior to this century, however, diachronic studies in anthropology involved the search for instances of cultural change within and across cultures in the interest of making generalizations about culture. This situation largely parallels that in diachronic linguistics. Diachronic linguistics and diachronic anthropology did differ in one area, though—in the interpretation of the findings. Since diachronic linguistics assumes that language is a system, linguistic change is seen as change within the system. Reconstructed forms are regarded as hypothetical, and are not regarded as "primitive" in any real sense. Although the linguist may note language change through time and recognize that certain forms derive from earlier forms at other time stages, he does not construe the results of linguistic reconstruction as indicating that language has evolved from a "primitive" to a "civilized" form, nor that it has either "progressed" or "regressed."

The distinction between the synchronic and the diachronic study of language was introduced in linguistics by Ferdinand deSaussure. Synchronic description implied that diachronic description would presuppose previous synchronic analysis of the different states or time stages through which the languages have historically developed (Lyons 1969:49). This implication was recognized by Bloomfield, who insisted that adequate descriptive information about languages is a prerequisite for historical understanding. For anthropology the implication may be seen in Marvin Harris's view that the comparative method can be valid only where the ethnographies compared are comparable and adequate (1968:156).

In both anthropology and linguistics, much effort has been applied to improve the observational adequacy of data. The whole of descriptive linguistics had this adequacy as its goal in the interest of making eventual comparisons possible. In anthropology, Herbert Spencer's *Descriptive Sociology* (1873-1933) was an effort to outline the elements which individual synchronic ethnographies should contain (such as morphology and physiology) in order that they might be compared with each other. The comparison would enable one to observe culture change and classify cultures with regard to their interrelated elements.

Later, the Human Relations Area Files (HRAF), developed by George P. Murdock, provided some guidelines to the field worker interested in describing cultures synchronically for eventual comparative purposes. The files contain descriptions of significant portions of hundreds of cultures throughout the world and are located at a number of universities for use by scholars. Ethnographies constructed along such a model were intended to be looked at cross-culturally, as well as in reference to a single culture described at different periods of history.

In diachronic studies, just as the linguist looked for regular sound changes, the anthropologist searched for regular culture changes. Efforts were made to reconstruct hypothetical intermediate and transitional stages of cultural evolution. In the twentieth century, in an effort to insure that the comparative method be applied to adequately described data, there was a deemphasis on the development of diachronic studies through the comparative method, in favor of developing a descriptive method for synchronic studies.

In anthropology, Fred Eggan (1954) made known what is called the METHOD OF CONTROLLED COMPARISON, which combines synchronic and diachronic approaches to the study of cultural phenomena. This method takes into account the idea that a time perspective is needed for synchronic differences to be understood across cultures. Eggan was interested in explaining puzzling variations in kinship terms among a group of southeastern U.S. Indian tribes. The tribes' kinship terms did not consistently fit into particular types of systems in accord with the recognized typology of the world's kinship systems. Kinship systems are generally classified on the basis of parental generation and/or classification of cousins. Each of the tribes in question used what is known as the Crow type kinship terminology, but considerable variation in terminology existed between the different tribes. There was pressure to acculturate to cultures using the Omaha type terminology. Eggan demonstrated that length of time and degree of exposure to pressures for acculturation correlated with differences in the kinship terminological systems. The tribes in question had differences in their kinship terminological systems such that tribes of the Crow type tended toward systems resembling the Omaha type of kinship reckoning.

The method of controlled comparison is used in studies known as CONCOMITANT VARIATION STUDIES. Such studies examine selected traits which occur in geographical, social, or historical wholes (Clignet 1973:597). At the same time, these studies show that variations in irrelevant social variables within the particular context do not alter the relationship between the dependent and independent variable or variables. A classic example of such a study is one done by William Bascom (1962), which examines the traits of size, density, and heterogeneity among Yoruba cities. The variability in these traits among and between Yoruba cities occurs despite geographical and cultural homogeneity and despite a similar socioeconomic context. Thus, cultural, geographical, and socioeconomic variables are held constant while the traits of size, density, and heterogeneity are variable.

All comparisons, such as Bascom's comparison of Yoruba cities, in which certain social variables that are considered insignificant are held constant, are said to "involve the systematic manipulation of constants" and are "controlled" (Clignet 1973:598).

Today much comparative anthropology is of a highly statistical nature and, as such, is tending to blur the synchronic/diachronic distinction; for the data being compared are from vast numbers of different cultures and vastly different periods of time. The advent of cross-cultural survey procedures for the anthropologist permitted the possibility that the data at the base of correlations might contain ethographic flaws. Synchronically adequate descriptions, though desirable, were not considered essential. The feeling developed that if a sample were large enough such flaws would average out. This view, that the larger the sample the more accurate the data, will be seen to have a part in the development of the comparative procedure for language data known as glottochronology, discussed in Section 3.4 below.[1]

It is a sad fact with regard to the comparative method as proposed for both linguistics and anthropology that very often data of scholars other than the researcher cannot be interpreted or relied upon for comparative purposes. Further, outside of areas of the world with long written histories, no early "states" exist of linguistic or ethnographic data—flawed or flawless—which can be used for comparative/historical purposes. In a sense, without written records, the linguist or ethnographer is at the mercy of the archeologist when it comes to evidence of historical reconstruction.

3.3   Language and Culture Classification

Language classification uses the methods of comparative linguistics in order to show the degree of relationship of languages to each other. Three main approaches are assumed to exist in language classification—genetic, areal, and typological. Culture classifications are generally areal and typological. Genetic classifications of language provide data on likely genetic relationship among cultures.

3.31   GENETIC CLASSIFICATION

GENETIC CLASSIFICATION compares languages in order to discover parental relationships among languages and to construct language family trees. The classi-

---

[1]The reader interested in the procedures involved in undertaking a cross-cultural study is referred to Keith F. Otterbein's "Basic Steps in Conducting a Cross-Cultural Study" (1969).

Figure 5.
Family Tree Diagram: An Example of Genetic
Classification Showing the Relationship of
English to Indo-European (adapted from Stur-
tevant 1947:157–158)

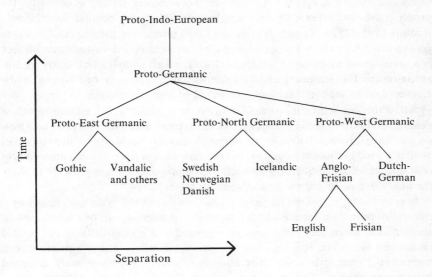

fication is based totally on resemblances arising from a genetic historical connection among the languages, regardless of where the languages are located geographically or temporally. Languages are classified by historical relationship and
descent (demonstrable or hypothetical) from a single ancestor.

In a language family tree representing such a classification, every node or
branching point represents a language, whether or not it is known from written
records. All languages descended from one such node on the tree constitute a
GENETIC GROUP. For example, all Indo-European languages belong to a single
genetic group because they all descend from one node, proto-Indo-European
(Greenberg 1968:121). The Germanic languages within the Indo-European genetic group constitute a genetic subgroup (see Figure 5).

Genetic classifications result from comparing languages in terms of sound and
meaning correspondences in grammar and vocabulary. The findings that the method reveals about linguistic change from language to language establish the degree
of relationship. Comparative linguistics is most valuable not for asserting that
related languages have a common origin, but for being able to define the degree of
divergence between related languages along the variable of time and separation
(Swadesh 1959:27). These variables of time and separation account for the use of
such classifications by anthropologists to infer that migrations have occurred.

In his study of the expansion of the Bantu peoples in Africa, George P. Murdock used evidence from genetic classification. In the absence of any direct historical and archeological radio-carbon evidence, only linguistic evidence and historical inferences could be used to trace the migration of the Bantu. Murdock noted that since the Bantu languages are very closely related genetically, the people must have diverged from a single ancestral speech community relatively recently (1959:272). Various approaches to the problem of the dispersal of Bantu speakers in Africa using a genetic language classification as evidence may be seen in a work edited by Robert O. Collins (1968), which contains articles by the linguists Joseph H. Greenberg and Malcolm Guthrie. Also included are articles by anthropologists such as Murdock as well as by some historians.

All who deal with this particular question agree that the establishment of genetic relationship among languages is one type of evidence that can show how people have dispersed to various culture areas in the world. Other types of evidence used to discern migration patterns are data on crop introduction and, of course, archeological data. Using such migration patterns, it is possible to show the likely degree of genetic relatedness among cultures.

In anthropology, genetic language classification can aid in the understanding of culture by providing facts about a time when speakers spoke one language and about a time when they subsequently separated and spoke different but related languages. When one language was spoken, the speakers shared a single speech community; later, when different languages developed, there were different speech communities. To some extent, different languages imply different cultures, especially in terms of genetic relationship and genetic classification.

Genetic language classifications are also valuable to the anthropologist in that some of the vocabulary items compared may provide an idea as to what physical environment existed where the languages were spoken and what some of the content of the cultural context was (Swadesh 1959:32).

3.32   AREAL CLASSIFICATION

Joseph H. Greenberg gives this definition of AREAL CLASSIFICATION:

An areal classification . . . is based on an estimate that on the dimension of external diachronic process, of which the most easily detectable instances are borrowings, a particular group of languages have through contact developed common features that distinguish them from languages of other geographical areas (1968:122).

Areal and genetic classifications are not rival methods but exist for different purposes. Areal classifications assert nothing about common linguistic origin but do have bearing on time of divergence and geographical separation of languages. An "areal classification deals with the results of the establishment and maintenance of contact among speech communities, even if once remote or independent"

(Hymes 1964:568). In genetic classification, genetic relationship *must* be established with chance and borrowing ruled out as reasons for the existence of similar items among languages. However, in areal classification, borrowing is *the* crucial evidence.

Areal groupings of languages are historical. They are similar to "culture area" classifications used by anthropologists to classify cultures (Greenberg 1968:123).

Speech communities, like cultural communities, interact with their neighbors. Things are transferred back and forth from community to community from time to time. Just as material goods are mutually exchanged, so too are patterns of behavior. Some such exchanged patterns are fashions, ways of producing goods, and rituals. The process is known as diffusion, specifically, CULTURAL DIFFUSION (Bloomfield 1933:445). Diffusion of cultural features can be plotted on a map. When cross-cultural diffusion occurs, the names for the objects or patterns of behavior diffused are likewise spread about, producing linguistic diffusion.

In anthropology, a culture area is an analytical tool for classifying cultures by means of ecological and institutional factors which might shed light on cultural differences and similarities—peoples are classified according to their "primary orientations" (Herskovits 1962:56).

In linguistics, the concept is known as "language area." In North America, Boas noticed,

> in a considerable number of native languages of the North Pacific coast we find, notwithstanding fundamental differences in structure and vocabulary, similarities in particular grammatical features distributed in such a way that neighboring languages show striking similarities. . . . It seems . . . almost impossible to explain this phenomenon without assuming the diffusion of grammatical processes over contiguous areas (1929:6).

Culture areas and areal groupings of languages may coincide, but genetic groupings of languages and areal groupings of cultures need not overlap. This point might seem an unnecessary one to make. However, often the two are confused, because in some cases there is legitimate overlap. For example, Herskovits in numerous publications refers to the culture areas of Africa, that is, to ecological groupings in Africa prior to European influence. The culture areas for Africa are, from north to south geographically: North Africa, Egypt, Desert, Western Sudan, Eastern Sudan, East Horn, East African Cattle Area, Guinea Coast, Congo, Southwestern Cattle Area, and Khoisan Area. According to the Greenberg classification of African languages, there are genetic groups of languages also called Khoisan, Western Sudanic, and Eastern Sudanic. The Western Sudanic group of genetically related languages refers only to certain languages which are related in terms of sound and meaning correspondences. The Western Sudan culture area refers to a geographical area set apart by certain ecological conditions. Western

Sudanic languages are spoken in the Western Sudan culture area, but the classificatory terms used refer to two different methods of classification, the former genetic, the latter areal.

An important difference to note is that the most widely used language classifications are genetic, whereas cultural classifications are usually areal.

For languages, Greenberg distinguishes genetic families, areal groups, and typological classes (1957:67). Languages which share borrowings in sound and meaning, or which share influences in sound and/or meaning as a result of historical contact, form an areal group. Areal groups of languages and culture areas are similar in that they are a result of diffusion, are usually geographically continuous, and usually coincide to a great extent. Conversely, genetic families rarely coincide with culture areas, since they are set up by excluding evidence of borrowing and contact. Areal classifications of language are expressed in terms such as "the languages of Eastern Europe." Languages so classified will have many shared items due to close geographical and cultural contact but need not be related genetically at all.

A by-product of the areal classification of language and culture was the AGE-AREA PRINCIPLE, which is a method of inferring the relative age of cultural traits (including linguistic units) from their geographical distribution. The most widely distributed traits around the center of a speech or cultural community would be regarded as the oldest traits. This conclusion assumes that diffusion moves from the center outward (Harris 1968:376).

G. Bonfante and Thomas A. Sebeok (1944) outline the principles of age and area for linguistics as first presented in the early twentieth century by the Italian neolinguistic school and the work of Matteo Bartoli. The principles are:

1. Isolated areas (such as islands or mountainous regions) conserve older linguistic features than others.
2. Lateral areas preserve older linguistic features than central areas except when the central area is also an isolated one.
3. Of two [linguistic] forms, the older one is spread over the larger area, the innovation over the lesser area except when the lesser area is isolated or the sum of lateral areas.
4. Of two [linguistic] forms, the older one is preserved in a territory later occupied or colonial (1944:383–385).

In anthropology, the work of C. Wissler (1926) and A. L. Kroeber (1931, 1939), students of Boas, exemplifies areal classification as applied to cultural traits. Wissler's "law of diffusion," which held that "anthropological traits tend to diffuse in all directions from their centers of origin," led to the age-area principle (Wissler 1926:372). Kroeber attempted to define culture areas by using lists of shared items to establish similarities between cultures (Harris 1968:376).

Limits exist on the usefulness of areal groupings of languages and cultures in determining boundaries (as one might assume from the principles quoted above from Bonfante and Sebeok) and in determining the position of marginal areas. As Greenberg has stated, "Boundaries between groups may therefore be arbitrary, so that the simultaneous assignment to different areal groups involves no contradiction . . . areal classification lacks the definiteness that is inherent in the genetic model" (1968:123, 124).

3.33 TYPOLOGICAL CLASSIFICATION

TYPOLOGICAL CLASSIFICATION consists of the comparative study and classification of languages on the basis of similarities and differences in structure rather than on the basis of historical relationships or proximity. If seen as classes, typological groups are referred to by phrases such as "tone languages versus non-tone languages," "hunting and gathering societies," and so forth.

In the nineteenth century, languages were classified as belonging to one of four categories: isolating, agglutinative, inflectional, or polysynthetic. Whether or not a particular language belonged to one category rather than another depended on the order and arrangement of morphemes in the language. The notion of BOUND MORPHEME—or, in nineteenth-century terms, the BOUND FORM—figured strongly in so classifying the world's languages. A bound morpheme is a morpheme which is never uttered alone; conversely, an example of a free morpheme is any morpheme which requires no prefixes or suffixes.

Languages classified as ISOLATING contain no bound forms. One such language is Chinese, which is composed entirely of free morphemes. In AGGLUTINATIVE languages, bound morphemes occur one after the other. Such languages will have pre-prefixes and compound suffixes. Turkish is such a language. INFLECTIONAL languages make semantic distinctions by means of single bound forms or closely united bound forms. Latin is an inflectional language in that a single suffix may express many semantic distinctions (Bloomfield 1933:207–208). In POLYSYNTHETIC languages, meaningful elements such as verbal goals (the equivalents of direct objects and adverbial phrases in English) are expressed by bound forms; that is, bound forms make important semantic distinctions. One language where this is the case is Eskimo. Classifications such as these based on structural criteria—the role of bound forms in the language—are known as typological classifications.

In a typology, any criteria may be employed. An example of the use of typology in anthropology was the nineteenth-century work of J. C. Nott and G. R. Glidden, *Types of Mankind* (1854), in which race was used as a criterion for grouping the peoples of the world. Nott and Glidden argued that all races were created separately and that each race possesses both moral and physical characteristics unique to it which are perpetuated with the race through time.

Typological classes "are arbitrary . . . exhaustive and unique" and have no historical implications (Greenberg 1957:67). Since any criteria will do to set up a typology, it is useful to choose criteria which may be assumed significant.

Typological classifications have been most useful in grouping languages according to certain of their structural characteristics as "a heuristic device in formulating generalizations about human language" (Greenberg 1968:130). However, Roman Jakobson, as a structural linguist (see Chapter 2 above), cautioned that a linguistic typology is hard-pressed to produce satisfactory or useful results if the typological traits are chosen arbitrarily. Nott and Glidden's classification using race as a culture trait certainly produced controversial results. In Jakobson's words,

> a linguistic typology based on arbitrarily selected traits cannot yield satisfactory results any more than the classification of the animal kingdom which instead of the productive division into vertebrates and non-vertebrates, mammals and birds, etc., would use, for instance, the criterion of skin color and on this basis group together, e.g., white people and light pigs (1958:20).

Jakobson sees utility in typological classifications of languages as long as the basis of the typology is the system of language. The structural laws of the system restrict the arbitrary nature of typological criteria. Further, the structural units and relationships among units in language restrict what transitions might occur from one language state to another. If the structural laws of the system of language at different states or time stages are uncovered, they would help predict reconstructed forms and provide ideas as to where to begin to look for a genetic relationship among languages (20). Thus, typological classifications may serve as a tool for setting up genetic classifications.

Typologies should establish the one-to-one correspondence between structural elements of languages while preserving the relationship between the elements. For example, as Greenberg points out for Indo-European, French has been losing case markings in nouns (1968:132). French is moving from the class of languages with case systems to the class of languages without case systems. This kind of typological transition has implications for keeping sight of the genetic affiliation of French within the Indo-European family, whose member languages have historically preserved their case systems.

When based on significant criteria, typological classifications require that definitions and procedures of classification be developed which are applicable to all languages, such that any language may be said to belong (+) or not belong (−) to that class, for example, languages with case systems versus languages without.

In conclusion, it must be stressed again that typological classifications have no historical or genetic implications, that genetic relationship rests on sound and meaning correspondences and on the method of historical reconstruction, and that areal groups map languages that are in contact through borrowing and diffusion. Culture areas and culture types are not directly relatable to linguistic families.

3.4 Lexicostatistics and Glottochronology

In this last section having to do with the comparative method, we will discuss glottochronology and the chief technique used in glottochronology, that of lexicostatistics. GLOTTOCHRONOLOGY is the method whereby one may establish approximate dates when modern languages diverged from a common parent stock. LEXICOSTATISTICS is the technique employed in comparing percentages of cognate items retained in pairs of languages. The purpose of glottochronology is to provide a time perspective for genetic classification of languages. The name of Morris Swadesh figured importantly in the development of glottochronology. Swadesh saw the main value of genetic language classification (arrived at through the comparative method) to be in the use of the variables of time and separation.

Our description here will follow that of Sarah Gudschinsky (1956) for the most part. Her article "The ABCs of Lexicostatistics (Glottochronology)" presents the assumptions, techniques, and value of the method for its intended purpose—to date early stages of languages.

It is possible to set up genetic classifications with or without written data as evidence. But, in the absence of historical and written records and prior to the advent of glottochronology, there was no way to determine at what historical period early stages of language existed.

Gudschinsky observes that four basic assumptions underlie the technique of lexicostatistics in glottochronology (paraphrased from 1956:177–178).

1. Lexicostatistics assumes that some parts of the vocabulary of any language are less subject to change than other parts.
2. It further assumes that, in the parts of vocabulary that don't change or which are unlikely to change, the retention of vocabulary items is constant through time.
3. The rate of loss of items in the stable part of vocabulary is 19 percent per thousand years in all languages.
4. If the percentage of cognate items in the stable part of vocabulary is known for any two languages, then the amount of time which has elapsed since those languages diverged from a common parent can be calculated.

The part of vocabulary which is unlikely to change in any language constitutes a basic core vocabulary consisting mainly of assumed "culture-free" items such as pronouns, numerals, body parts, and so forth. The name of Morris Swadesh is linked with the development of the notion of a basic vocabulary list. His idea was that certain objects and situations occur in all societies despite cultural and geographical differences. The words naming these objects and situations are items of basic vocabulary.

To calculate the length of time since two languages separated, it is necessary to rule out factors that might have influenced which cognate basic vocabulary items are shared and which are not. Such influences are those of cultural and linguistic diffusion. According to Gudschinsky, migrations, conquests, or other social contacts could slow down or speed up the separation of two languages. Essentially, lexicostatistics is a genetic technique—in that only cognate items are acceptable evidence for establishing both relationship and time of divergence of languages.

From the four assumptions underlying lexicostatistics, the steps involved in lexicostatistical dating developed as follows:

1. Collect basic vocabulary items in the languages to be compared.
2. Determine which items are cognate in the two languages by establishing both sound and meaning correspondences.
3. Compute the time depth by means of a formula.
4. Compute the range of error by means of another formula.

Alternatively, the data may be computed by degree of lexical relationship (known as "dips") rather than by historical dates.

The formula for computing time depth is

$$t = log\ C/(2\ log\ r)$$

with the instruction to solve for t.

The formula is used to determine when the languages diverged. The letter t refers to the time depth, C is the fraction of corresponding cognates in the two languages, and r is the percentage of cognates assumed to remain after a thousand-year divergence (that is, 81 percent).

The range of error is determined by computing the standard error in terms of percentage of cognates.

Lexicostatistics, with its reliance on cognates and on the exclusion of diffusionary influences, may be seen as a kind of technique of establishing, temporally and genetically, the relationship between languages. As such, it implies, as does any genetic classification, a systematic prior analysis of sound correspondences between the languages compared.

As discussed above, genetic classifications, where reliably set up, are useful as one type of evidence in tracing cultural migrations; they imply cultural genetic relationship as well. Glottochronology, then, which purports to show the time and degree of linguistic divergence, is of particular use in this regard.

In Gudschinsky's words,

by studying a number of pairs of languages or dialects within a related group, or within a dialect area, those pairs which show greatest time depth are assumed to be representative of older splits in the dialects, and those showing lesser time depth show more recent splits so that a progressive splitting is implied (Gudschinsky, 1955). This suggested order of splitting may help in correlating the linguistic data with known or suspected migrations, cultural developments, etc. (1956:207).

Also, the languages or dialects which show little difference in time depth may be assumed to "have been closest geographically and longest in cultural contact" (207).

Glottochronology and the lexicostatistical method of dating language divergence have been controversial topics since their inception. The criterion that cognates be systematically set up (that is, on traceable sound-and-meaning correspondences) is rarely met, the range of error in the statement of time depth is quite large, and the underlying notion of the method that basic vocabulary changes at a constant rate has been often questioned (for example, see Kroeber 1955). Indeed, it is not deemed likely that a list of one or two hundred "culture-free" words could ever be constructed and then applied cross-culturally with validity for comparative purposes. The problems of translation and range of usage of the lexical items would make success in the task unlikely.

Morris Swadesh, who devised the proposed basic vocabulary for lexicostatistical use, saw a need to vary the test list in an effort to attain his goal that "suitable items for a test list must be universal and non-cultural. . . . Moreover, they must be easily identifiable broad concepts, which can be matched with simple terms in most languages" (1952:457). In his article "Towards Greater Accuracy in Lexicostatistic Dating," he saw the need to drop the words *ice*, *snow*, *freeze*, *snake*, and *sea* from his original list (1955:124).

Recently some by-products of glottochronology and lexicostatistics have been observed. Hymes (1964:572) claims that test lists may be used in the comparative study of the semantic aspects of the words, both synchronically and diachronically. Such study may provide insights as to possible "lexicosemantic universals" and provide semantic information about various language groups. Also, the word lists can be used as an aid in the elicitation of linguistic data and also for studies of a sociolinguistic nature. This use of the test list as noted by Hymes will be described below in Chapter 5, "Sociolinguistics."

In his book *Language and Culture* (1966) Herbert Landar discusses glottochronology and linguistic genetic subgrouping by means of lexicostatistics. In Landar's book the Swadesh two-hundred-word basic vocabulary list is reprinted (pp. 186–191) and filled in for English, French, German, and Welsh, providing data with which one might apply the method. Landar gives a word of caution:

> Archaeologists and ethnologists in search of linguistic support for theories of culture history based on nonlinguistic data have sometimes made too much of glottochronology. Various positions have been taken by linguists, from rejection on mathematical grounds (by Lees and later Chrétien), to guarded interest (manifested notably by Hymes), to unguarded devotion (particularly when archaeological data and glottochronological data seem to jibe, as sometimes happens) (1966:186).

Hymes (1960) provides a review of lexicostatistics and the arguments for and against the method of glottochronology, and also sets out the one-hundred-word list, the two-hundred-word list, and supplementary items.

3.5 Summary

In this chapter we have seen that the comparative method carried both linguistics and anthropology into the twentieth century. Nineteenth-century anthropological scientists were adherents to an evolutionary framework, seeking to show the development of cultures from the simple to the complex by comparing "primitive" to "civilized" societies. The discovery that good descriptions of cultural traits were lacking led to a general abandonment of comparison in favor of description, on the basis that such descriptions would facilitate eventual comparison of data. This descriptive era was the focus of Chapter 1.

In current anthropology and linguistics both comparative and historical studies are being pursued. Historical studies are undertaken by two kinds of researchers:

1. Historical linguists carry out linguistic reconstruction in order to come up with hypothetical forms which allow them to show correspondences among languages or within a language through time. By reconstructing forms using written records or reasonable hypotheses of sound change and meaning correspondence, the linguist can demonstrate that languages which appear unrelated or dissimilar actually may have been very closely related in the past.
2. Ethnohistorians make use of the findings of historical linguists as well as other data, including the traditions of the culture-bearers themselves, in order to attempt to reconstruct particular culture histories. We observed that ethnohistory is essentially a historical rather than a comparative study.

Comparative studies in both anthropology and linguistics are concerned with classification. For languages, genetic classification has proven most useful. For cultures, areal classifications have traditionally been most popular since one can safely assume that neighboring cultures interact.

Comparison in anthropology has become quite statistical in nature. For language, the requirement that both sound *and* meaning correspondences need be shown, or that structural units must be compared in both form *and* function, provided a certain amount of control.

However, for culture, of which language itself is considered a trait, the number of variables involved is vast. In order to be able to compare cultural traits in any meaningful way, it was necessary to control certain of the variables that might have altered the calssifications so derived. Today, concomitant variation studies and the method of controlled comparison represent attempts to insure that compared traits are, in fact, comparable from one culture to another.

Glottochronology, with its method of lexicostatistics, has been an attempt to date periods at which genetically related languages diverged. Glottochronology employs the comparative method for the purposes of both comparative linguistics and ethnohistory. Data from existing languages are compared (synchronic comparison) and a degree of genetic relationship calculated. Then, on the basis of this degree of relationship, a formula is applied to calculate how long ago (diachronically) the compared languages diverged. The ethnohistorian may assume that at approximately that same point in time also the speakers of those languages diverged.

Chapter 4 Language and Culture

4.0 Introduction

In the previous three chapters, most attention was directed to parallel and analogous developments in linguistics and in anthropology—to descriptive methodology in both fields, to structuralism and its ramifications for both, and to the comparative-historical method. In this chapter, we will turn our attention to the studies which combine the areas of both fields. Generally this area is known as "Language *and* Culture," but variously as "Language *in* Culture." The goal of such study is to ascertain the relationship between language and culture.

We will investigate the study of language in its context from the perspective of the *world-view problem* (does culture influence language or does language influence culture?), through developments in the relatively new area of *ethnoscience* (the study of folk conceptual systems in order to discover the conceptual world of a people through their linguistic categories), and through various approaches to the development of *semantics* (the study of meaning).

As we have seen in previous chapters, linguists have had little success in semantic analysis or semantic theory. Sapir saw language as a mixture of forms and concepts and suggested a "psychological reality" for the phoneme. The Bloomfieldians abandoned such "mentalist" notions in favor of refining methods for describing directly observable data. DeSaussure's notion of langue as the system underlying speech (parole) typifies the structuralist's attempt to get at "inner" language again. Chomsky's idea of deep structure underlying the surface manifestation of a sentence was an attempt to determine the abstract nature of sentences in language but stopped short of the concept of meaning as content in language.

It appears that attempts to understand linguistic content will likely have to take account of context and experience in the "outer" as well as the "inner" worlds.

4.1 The World-View Problem

The question as to what extent and in what way a language is related to the world-view (that is, thought and reality) of those who speak it has been the subject of much research in anthropology and linguistics in this century.[1] The issue arose from a number of papers and articles including one by Edward Sapir, "Conceptual Categories in Primitive Languages" (1931), and another by Benjamin Lee Whorf, "A Linguistic Consideration of Thinking in Primitive Communities." Whorf's paper was written about 1936 but was first published in the collection of Whorf's writings edited by Carroll in 1956. This paper is said to have been found by Whorf's wife in handwritten form after his death, never having been completed for final publication. Both of these articles by Sapir and Whorf are reprinted in Hymes (1964).

Sapir's paper is very short, pointing out that in his view language "defines experience for us by reason of its formal completeness and because of our unconscious projection of its implicit expectations into experience" (1931:578). It is noteworthy that this view counters any idea of a universalistic nature that reality is the same for all men. Sapir's statement in that short paper has been interpreted to mean that people who speak different languages segment their world differently.

Whorf's view is essentially the same as Sapir's and may be stated as follows:

> The forms of a person's thoughts are controlled by inexorable laws of pattern of which he is unconscious. These patterns are the unperceived intricate systematizations of his own language—shown readily enough by a candid comparison and contrast with other languages, especially those of a different linguistic family. His thinking itself is in a language—in English, in Sanskrit, in Chinese. And, every language is a vast pattern system, different from others, in which are culturally ordained the forms and categories by which the personality not only communicates but also analyzes nature, notices or neglects types of relationship and phenomena, channels his reasoning and builds the house of his consciousness (Carroll 1956:252).

The idea of Sapir and Whorf that a person's language determines how that person segments his world is sometimes referred to as "the Sapir-Whorf Hypothesis."

Sapir viewed the relationship of language to culture somewhat differently than he viewed language in relation to thought. This difference is often overlooked when we think of Sapir in terms of the Sapir-Whorf Hypothesis. For example, in his book *Language* (1921), Sapir insists that language and culture are each independent and there is no causal connection between the two. Culture is *what* society thinks and does and language is *how* people think (1921:218). Language is

---

[1] *Language, Thought, and Reality* is the title given by John B. Carroll to the collected and edited articles of Benjamin Lee Whorf concerned with the question of language and culture.

related to thought in that "language is primarily a pre-rational function. It humbly works up to the thought that is latent in, that may eventually be read into, its classifications and its forms; it is not, as is generally but naively assumed, the final label put upon the finished thought" (15).

It would seem fitting to refer to the whole question of the relationship of language to culture and to thought as the World-View Problem, rather than as the Sapir-Whorf Hypothesis or the Whorf Hypothesis. It will be seen below that this issue of the relationship of language to culture and to thought has also given rise to what is known as the theory of Linguistic Relativity, a modification of the Whorf position, which is also known as the theory of Linguistic Determinism (that is, Whorf's view is one of extreme linguistic relativity). All of these labels may be subsumed under that of the World-View Problem.

Whorf believed that the idea that language influences culture would enable researchers to find out how the peoples of various cultures think. This discovery would be made by investigating the grammar and lexicons of different peoples' languages.

Anthropologists and linguists tend to divide into two camps over this issue, some agreeing with Whorf, others being opposed. Proponents of the Sapir-Whorf hypothesis often cite, as an illustration of the correctness of their position, the word for *snow* among the Eskimo. Since Eskimo languages have many different words for *snow* and most dialects of English have only one word, advocates would say that Eskimos see snow differently. Opponents to the notion that language determines world-view would say that that illustration demonstrates nothing. It is possible to cite English-speaking skiers, for example, who have many words for the substance.

According to the psychologist Roger Brown,

> Whorf . . . notes that the Eskimo lexicon uses three words to distinguish three varieties of snow for which English does not have three single-word equivalents. We should use "snow" for all three. Does this mean that the Eskimo sees differences and similarities among snows that we are unable to see?
>
> There is evidence to indicate that the speaker of English can classify snows as the Eskimo does. If we listen to the talk of small boys it is clear that they pay attention to at least two kinds of snow—the "good packing" and the "bad packing." Whorf himself must have been able to see snow as the Eskimos do since his article describes and pictures the referents for the words (1958:234).

The reason some people have more words for things such as snow is because some people *need* more than one label for certain things because they require additional distinctions within the labeled category in order to carry out certain functions, for instance, skiing or making snowballs.

Roger Brown's position occasioned a modification of Whorf's idea that our language determines how we segment our world. He proposed that a perceptual category which is used by people more often than others is a category which is more "available" than one less frequently used. Brown observed,

> When the Eskimo steps from his igloo in the morning I expect him to see the snow as falling into one or another of his single-word categories. For the American who is only able to name these categories with a phrase, I do not expect such ready categorization of snows. If, however, the American were subjected to a discrimination learning experiment, if he were studying the Eskimo language, or if the perceptual structure were otherwise made worth his while, he could see snow as the Eskimo does (1958:236).

Brown suggested that categories which have short names (more readily codable categories) are more likely to be used and are more available for expectancies and inventions.

This modification of the linguistic determinism of the Whorfian stand is known as linguistic relativity, implying not that one's world-view is determined by one's language, but rather that one categorizes his world by using his language according to his need.

> linguistic relativity holds that where there are differences of language there will also be differences of thought, that language and thought covary. Determinism goes beyond this to require that the prior existence of some language pattern is either necessary or sufficient to produce some thought pattern (Brown 1958:260).

The Eskimo's language does not force the Eskimo to perceive many different kinds of snow; the Eskimo, rather, uses his language to categorize snow according to the needs and uses he has for it.

Brown (1958:235–236), cognizant of Zipf's Law (or the Principle of Least Effort), observed that "the length of a word is negatively correlated with its frequency of usage," for example, *automobile* → *car*, *television* → *TV*.

A perceptual category that is frequently utilized is more available than one less frequently utilized:

1. If you need a phrase to label a category, the category has low codability.
2. If you need a word, the category has high codability.

This tendency may be seen in the observation that some languages have more single-word color terms than others (see Section 4.23 below).

It appears, then, that languages differ in the categories they name and code grammatically as well as in phonology, morphology, and syntax. The more codable a category, the more available it is for general psychological use.

In the Sapir statement quoted on page 75 and in the Whorfian view presented, the idea is implicit that individual languages differ from each other in structure. The assumption of different structures for different languages was also assumed by descriptive linguists (see Chapter 1 above), who used their techniques and methods to describe languages such that their differences could be seen and compared.

Today, the trend is away from such particularism. Cognitive anthropologists, theoretical linguists, and psychologists now tend toward the idea that reality is the same for all people but that some people segment that reality differently. Perhaps language and culture contain universal categories from which all people select categories relevant to their needs.

In summary, the world-view problem is that of the relationship between language and thought and of the relationship between language and thought to reality. Whorf believed that (here in paraphrased form):

1. Each language embodies and perpetuates a particular world-view. The speakers of a language agree to perceive and think of the world in a certain way—but not in the only possible way.
2. The same reality—both physical and social—can be variously structured; different languages operate with different structures.

However, what if the structure of language is universal? Most of Whorf's examples come from American Indian languages (especially Hopi) or at least from non-Indo-European languages. Many of his conclusions are based on literal translations from Shawnee, Nootka, Apache, and Hopi.

Joshua Fishman (1960) questions on a number of levels Whorf's view that language *structure* structures thought; among his points are, in paraphrased form:

1. Language differences with respect to numbers of words for particular items allow speakers to be more aware of aspects of their environment and to communicate more easily about those aspects. Such differences deal with the relationship of cultural elements to language elements but not with their relationship to thought.
2. In some cultures, learning in general and recognition and recall in particular seem to be accomplished more efficiently than in others. What effect does language have on this difference if, in fact, this is the case?
3. What is the relationship of meaning to thought? Concern should not be only about the relationship of structure to thought, or of grammar to thought.
4. What is the relationship of nonlinguistic and nonverbal behavior to thought? For example, how are perception and cognition related to thought?

Some of these questions posed by Fishman are now being asked in tangential areas of linguistics and anthropology.

We will see in Section 4.2 below that the meanings of words and the role of meanings in cognitive systems are the focus of *ethnoscience*. In Section 4.3, we will see that theoretical linguists are attempting to develop a *semantic theory* within the framework of transformational/generative grammar, aimed at explaining how sentences are meaningfully interpreted.

Questions concerning the relationship of meaning to thought, the relationship of the meaning of extralinguistic behavior to thought, and the relationship of learning to language are currently being asked outside the linguistic-anthropological context. Currently much research in the field of cognitive psychology is focusing on the relationship of linguistic and cultural behavior to thought. Some areas where psychological study represents further research on the world-view question are discussed below. The field of *psycholinguistics* particularly deals with these questions.

4.11 LANGUAGE AND THOUGHT

The term PSYCHOLINGUISTICS refers to studies of language behavior, of how children acquire language, and also of how language is "encoded, . . . decoded, produced, and understood" (DeVito 1971:4). Psycholinguists are attempting to develop a theory of linguistic performance; that is, they are trying to show how linguistic competence is used.[2] Competence represents the linguistic knowledge of the ideal speaker-listener. A theory of performance, in contrast, is aimed at explaining *how* this knowledge is used by real speakers and by real listeners. The emphasis in psycholinguistics with respect to the question of world-view is on the psychological relationship of linguistic behavior to thought. In this section, we will touch only briefly on some of the ideas being explored in these areas.

One type of research being done is to examine and compare nonlinguistic behaviors of speakers of unrelated languages to see if they share any conceptual categories underlying different labels and differing numbers of labels for the categories. One of the first experimental studies carried out was that of Roger Brown and E. H. Lenneberg (1954). They first investigated English speakers only and tried to link memory to codability of items in the color lexicon. Subjects were first shown twenty-four color chips one at a time and asked to name the color as quickly as possible. It was found that the longer the color name was, the longer it took the subject to say the name and the less agreement there was among subjects with regard to the name of that color. Such a term was considered low in codability. Agreement among subjects on a color name was interpreted as indicating high codability for that name.

Another group of subjects was then tested with the intent of studying the relationship between codability and memory availability. A subject was shown four color chips from the previous set of twenty-four for five seconds. The chips were taken away and the subject was asked to pick out the four from a set of 120 chips. Correct identification of the four was regarded as recognition. Brown and Lenneberg found a small correlation between codability (agreement on a color name) and recognition. Later a larger correlation was found when the delay period was increased from five seconds and punctuated with distractions. When the delay was

---

[2]See Chapter 2 above for the competence/performance distinction in language made by Chomsky.

reduced from five seconds, the correlation almost disappeared.

Later, however, Lenneberg used a different array of colors and came up with a negative correlation between recognition and codability. He found that the more agreement there was in naming a color term, the lower was the recognition score. These results indicate that a short label for a color, such as *blue*, can be useful for remembering that color when it is surrounded by other distinctive ones (for example, red, yellow, or green). However, the short term *blue* is not useful if the task is to select a particular blue from an array of blues of different brightnesses and saturations.

This study, which hypothesized a relationship between codability and memory, assumed that the subjects "actively applied and stored verbal labels for the test colors" (Cole 1974:49). These experiments support the linguistic-relativity idea that language (labels) has an influence on thought (memory). We will see in Section 4.23, however, that an anthropological cross-cultural study by Berlin and Kay (1969) of color terms and their referents led to a somewhat different conclusion. Berlin and Kay claim that certain basic color terms have a stable focus cross-culturally and that the scientist ought to correlate the "focal color referents" with the labels. Previous studies, such as those discussed above, dealt with color boundaries instead of color foci.

Another well-known study in this area of language and thought is that of John B. Carroll and Joseph B. Casagrande (1958). They studied (1) Hopi-speaking and English-speaking adults, and (2) Navaho-speaking and English-speaking children.

In the Hopi language, verbs are chosen depending upon certain physical qualities of the object. A speaker of Hopi, for example, "uses the same verb for *spilling* and *pouring*, but must use a different verb depending on whether the material being spilled or poured is liquid or non-liquid" (Carroll and Casagrande 1958:22). Carroll and Casagrande wanted to know if such linguistic features which differentiate Hopi from English have correspondences in nonlinguistic behavior. The subjects were asked to sort pictures representing breaking, spilling, pressing, and similar physical activities into groups and to explain why they felt the pictures they chose went together. The results of this study support the view that the form of an object is significant in Hopi nonlinguistic as well as linguistic categories. Carroll and Casagrande concluded that it is the language categories which influence this particular type of nonverbal behavior.

The Navaho language, too, contains the categorization of verbs with respect to the form of the object. Carroll and Casagrande hypothesized that Navaho children would learn to discriminate nonverbally formal characteristics of concrete objects earlier than English-speaking children. The method used in this experiment was to ask children, after being given two objects, to group a third object with one from the previous pair.

For example, one of the pairs consisted of a yellow stick and a piece of blue rope of comparable size. The child was then shown a yellow rope, and the basis of his choice could be either color or the Navaho verb-form classification—since different verbal forms are used for a length of rope and a stick (1958:28).

The hypothesis was borne out by the experiment. That is, the Navaho children did tend to base their choices of matching objects according to form rather than color. However, a sample of white American children, although expected to use color as their basis of grouping objects, also used form; but the white American children were older than the Navaho children and were also from the upper-middle class.

The conclusion reached in this study was that as children get older, they match objects based on form rather than color. This tendency gains impetus if the child is learning a language like Navaho in which form is an obligatory grammatical category that he must use in order to be understood. The tendency is also enhanced if the child is in a cultural setting which reinforces form categorization by providing toys that require fitting forms and shapes, such as puzzles and form boards.

Essentially, Carroll and Casagrande concluded from their research that both culture and language influence the development of perceptual categories. Again, a weak version of the Whorf Hypothesis is vindicated: language does influence thought (perception) but so, too, does culture.

Two psychologists, Patricia Greenfield and Jerome Bruner, carried out some studies which further upheld the hypothesis that linguistic encoding affects cognitive operations such as perception—but with some qualifications, which will be explained below. Bruner, Greenfield, and Olver (1966) carried out an experiment involving French and Wolof-speaking children presented with pictures in sets of three. In each set, two pictures were alike in color, two in form, and two in function of the object pictured. The children were asked to choose the two pictures out of each set that were most alike and to state why they made their choice.

In Wolof, there is no single word for the color *blue*, the colors *orange* and *red* are labeled by a single term, and the color *yellow* is labeled but of low codability (that is, there is a low degree of agreement among Wolof-speakers as to its referent). Both languages, French and Wolof, were judged similar in being able to code the aspects of function represented in the pictures; that is, speakers of either language could express the functions of the objects in their own language.

The expectation in this experiment was that Wolof-speaking children would group the pictures based on function rather than color. Bilingual children would show more color-groupings than monolingual Wolof-speakers, but fewer such groupings than monolingual French-speakers. The results of this experiment went directly against the expectations. Monolingual Wolof children used only color to form their groupings of the pictures! The bilinguals and the French-speakers used color less and function and shape more, and this tendency increased with age. Clearly, the fact that the Wolof language does not have certain color words does not inhibit the Wolof-speakers' perceptual categories of color.

Another experiment was designed to test whether the lack of color words in Wolof affects color discrimination. The subjects were asked to group the two most similar pictures in sets of three on the basis of color. This time each set consisted of two pictures of one predominant color such as orange. Perception errors were counted—instances of grouping orange and red rather than orange and orange. It was found that Wolof monolinguals made the most discrimination errors, bilinguals somewhat fewer, and French monolinguals the fewest. In all cases, errors were relatively infrequent. The researchers concluded that lexical coding (here, color labeling) does influence color discrimination to some extent. Again, age was shown to be an important factor, with errors in color perception decreasing to almost none for the older children regardless of dominant language.

Greenfield and Bruner (1966) noted certain conditions that influence how linguistic encoding affects cognitive operations such as perception. Perceptual representations may be thought of as consisting of a SCHEMA (linguistic label) and a CORRECTION (visual image) as proposed by D. McNeil (1965). Greenfield and Bruner concluded that linguistic labels (schema) used for perceptual representation are important for cognitive tasks of a general nature, such as grouping by color as opposed to shape or function, but that the labels are less important, vague, and less useful if the cognitive tasks involve both the label and the visual image (correction).

In fact, in this experiment there was an implicit assumption that both Wolof- and French-speakers have labeled abstract concepts of color, shape, and function. These abstract concepts can be considered to be at the top of a hierarchical structure in the speakers' lexicon, with the concrete words at a lower level of the hierarchy. A speaker who uses the superordinate words "is operating at the top of the hierarchy and has access to the entire hierarchy" (Greenfield and Bruner 1966:385). A speaker who uses only the individual color, shape, or function names "would be cut off from the top of the hierarchy and its connections with other branches."

Thus, if superordinate and concrete words are hierarchically organized in a lexicon, a speaker lacking a superordinate word would be likely to restrict himself to the lower branches of the hierarchy, to use only the names for specific items included in the concept, but not to use the concept label itself. A speaker lacking the superordinate label *color*, which represents the concept rather than specific instances, would use only labels referring to instances—concrete words with specific referents such as *red* or *blue*. In the experiment described above, a speaker whose lexicon did not have a label for the concept of color would be likely to group pictures only on the basis of the concrete color terms available to him. This tendency was demonstrated by the Wolof-speaking children. Since in Wolof there is no word for the concept of color, the subjects grouped pictures by specific colors for which they had words, rather than by the different concepts represented—form, function, and color.

Greenfield and Bruner concluded that studies of the relationship of lexical items to perceptual categories, in order to say anything significant about the relation of language and thought, will necessarily need to be concerned with the organizational structure of the lexicon, rather than solely with lists of terms from a lexicon:

> We seem to have found an important correspondence between linguistic and conceptual structure. But it relates not to words in isolation but to their depth of hierarchical embedding both in the language and in thought (1966:386).

Greenfield and Bruner maintain that for a domain of vocabulary items to be useful to a speaker it must be organized so that it can be activated as a whole.

The influence of linguistic structure, grammatical as well as lexical, on concept formation is seen by scholars such as Greenfield and Bruner to be of significance not only with regard to the relation of language and thought but with regard as well to the relation of language to learning in schools. The type of learning required in schools is context-independent. The schema (label) and correction (image) of perceptual representations are divorced. The referents to what is said are not present in the classroom. Symbolic rather than iconic representation of thought is required. The school situation helps to separate thought from objects and thus "allows symbolic processes to run ahead of concrete fact, for thought to be in terms of possibility rather than actuality" (390).

Research into concept formation and the notion of the hierarchical structure of thought and language with respect to learning has led to some interesting results in studies on the cognitive nature of educational disadvantage. We have just seen that thought and language tend to go from the iconic (the label and the image are identical) to the symbolic (the label and the image are divorced) and that symbolic or abstract thought is required in the schools. Indeed, writing, on which most learning is based, is an overt change of the iconic into the symbolic. Another way of looking at the situation is to say that schools require an *analytic* approach to cognitive organization.

Rosalie Cohen (1969) investigated the cognitive requirements of schools and the learning characteristics of schoolchildren from low-income homes. Her findings indicate that the schools' requirement of analytic cognitive organization excludes another well-documented type of cognitive organization, one that is common among children from low-income homes.

Types of cognitive organization may be referred to as CONCEPTUAL STYLES: "Conceptual styles are rule-sets for the selection and organization of sense data" (Cohen 1969:828). One such style is the ANALYTIC and the other, suggests

Cohen, is the RELATIONAL. The analytic cognitive style consists of abstracting salient information from a stimulus or situation in a formal or analytic way and by a "stimulus-centered orientation to reality" (830). The relational cognitive style requires abstracting in a descriptive way. This style is "self-centered in its orientation to reality." Those with an analytic style feel that parts of a stimulus have meaning along with and apart from the whole. Those with a relational style feel that a stimulus has meaning only in terms of its "global characteristics."

Cohen examined different modes of reality organization—psychological, linguistic, and attitudinal—with respect to the cognitive styles which emerge from various tests. *Conceptual style* as a construct incorporates the psychological, linguistic, and attitudinal dimensions in the two cognitive styles—relational and analytic. Within the rule-set of each conceptual style—analytic or relational—certain assumptions and relations can be identified as logically possible and mutually exclusive from those in the other rule-set. These psychological, linguistic, and attitudinal assumptions and relations can be thought of as either analytical or relational.

If a child's conceptual style is relational, then he organizes reality in a way that goes against the conceptual style of the school, which is purely analytical: "Highly relational children in the highly analytic school are thus seen as a case of culture conflict, regardless of whether deprivation and culture difference are also present" (Cohen 1969:842).

In tests of language style, Cohen found that lexical abstraction is analytic for those with an analytic conceptual style and descriptive for those with a relational style. To the analytic person, words have formal meanings—for example, *money* "means" coins, cash, currency; and *wine* "means" port, sherry, and so forth. To the relational person, words have meanings specific to certain contexts. Words are concrete and used with "visual and tactile symbols." A person with a relational conceptual style would associate words—for example, *money* "means" green, bundle, trash; and *wine* "means" blood, slop, molasses, and so forth. The person with a relational style "ties actors to actions, causes to results, means to ends." He uses colorful and idiomatic expressions and has a "low level of generality." The analytical person uses synonyms, whereas the relational person tends to use few and to restrict semantic ranges. Some other linguistic characteristics of each conceptual style noted by Cohen are (849–852), in paraphrased form:

Analytic	*Relational*
a. meaning unrelated to social relationships and context of the communication	a. meaning related to time, place, authority, and other social relationships between communicants
b. complex grammar	b. simple grammar
c. varied-length sentences, many adjectives and adverbs	c. short sentences and few adjectives and adverbs
d. pauses for verbal planning	d. high fluency

In Chapter 5, Section 5.32 below, a study of the speech of English schoolboys is seen as a function of social class. Basil Bernstein's concept of elaborated and restricted codes will be shown attributing many of these linguistic characteristics of conceptual style to factors of social class. In Cohen's view, conceptual styles develop in shared-function and formally organized primary groups as socialization settings.

These few examples of the various kinds of research being done with regard to questions raised by the Whorf Hypothesis tend to support the modified version of the hypothesis that it is certainly not language (lexicon or grammar) alone which structures thought, but both linguistic and cultural factors. Further, it is now being suggested that the structure of language and culture may be related to the structure of thought. In the next section of this chapter we will see that in anthropology, the field of ethnoscience has some exponents who are attempting to make cognitive structure explicit. Experiments such as those cited above are attempting to investigate what is the relation of language to cognition.[3] At present such studies are still in their infancy, and much discussion is focused on "the need to put psychological theory and experimentation on a rigorous scientific plane" (Cole and Scribner 1974:200).

4.2   Ethnoscience

The continuing research on the world-view problem in anthropology is focusing in the area of study broadly known as ethnoscience. As defined in the introduction to this chapter, the admittedly imprecise term ETHNOSCIENCE refers to the study of folk conceptual systems in order to discover the conceptual world of a people through their linguistic categories. As such, ethnoscience is the study of language, thought, and reality. In a more narrow sense, ethnoscience is concerned with finding a way to determine the interconnections of language, thought, and world-view. It is concerned with developing the method or methods which were not available to Whorf.

In its methodological sense, ethnoscience shares a goal with descriptive linguistics: to describe data adequately in order to make predictions about behavior. This goal differs from that of modern theoretical linguistics and the new cultural anthropology, both of which seek to develop general theories of the nature of language and culture. These theories hope to account for language and culture.

---

[3]The reader interested in pursuing research that tries to link language, thought, and culture is referred to Michael Cole and Sylvia Scribner's book *Culture and Thought: A Psychological Introduction* (1974).

The methods of ethnoscience hope to describe linguistic and cultural behavior and to develop a theory of descriptions of such behavior.

Ethnoscience arose as a movement within cultural anthropology in the 1950s and aimed for improving methods and techniques of ethnographic analysis and description. The term *ethnoscience* is sometimes used synonymously with the expressions ETHNOGRAPHIC SEMANTICS and ETHNOSEMANTICS. Paul Kay states that these three terms refer to "the systematic study of the meanings of words and the role of these meanings in cognitive systems" (1969:2). Kay distinguishes ethnoscience from THE NEW ETHNOGRAPHY. The new ethnography is synonymous with LINGUISTIC ETHNOGRAPHY and with COGNITIVE ETHNOGRAPHY. All three of these terms refer to an approach to ethnography which includes ethnoscientific study as a part. Although ethnoscientific methods are employed as part of the new ethnography, the new ethnography makes use of other methods as well, such as traditional field-work methodology and participant observation and techniques such as multidimensional scaling and soil analysis.

Additional terms are used to refer to ethnoscience and to the new ethnography. E. Hunn suggests the term FOLK SCIENCE to "shift the emphasis from method to content" (1973:7). In a folk-science study the scientist researches the role of man in nature, rather than nature as something to which to apply a methodological tool. Hunn cites an ethnoscientific study by Metzger and Williams, "Some Procedures and Results in the Study of Native Categories: Tzeltal 'Firewood' " (1966), as an example of a study which "was certainly not motivated by an interest in firewood. . . . Firewood was simply the vehicle for the methodological exercise" (8). Studies which are motivated by a desire on the part of the ethnographer to understand the role of man in nature rather than to understand and apply methodology would, in Hunn's view, be more properly termed *folk science*.

The term *ethnoscience*, which originally seemed to encompass all the other terms, seems now to have come to refer primarily to the methods or tools used in certain studies within the new ethnography. However, all of the studies discussed in this section have at some time or other been referred to as ethnoscientific; hence, *ethnoscience* is here used as a cover term.

There is yet another term, COGNITIVE ANTHROPOLOGY, which appears to encompass most of what the new ethnography does. In discussing the terminological variation in the area of ethnoscience, Stephen Tyler in his book entitled *Cognitive Anthropology* (1969:1) sees such variation as a reflection of the discovery in the field of anthropology of a need to develop new theories to explain accumulated data. This need has arisen because "the descriptive facts" of the science "no longer fit the older explanatory models." His term for the new ethnography, *cognitive anthropology*, has as its goal not a theory of Culture but rather, theories of cultures or a theory of descriptions.

As the results of descriptive linguistic analyses were used, so the results of ethnoscientific analyses may also be used to provide comparative data from which cultural universals might be discerned. In the view of Paul Kay, the semantic universals which would emerge from ethnoscientific analysis would be a step toward an empirically based description of the assumed "psychic unity of mankind."

4.21   ETHNOSCIENTIFIC METHOD

William Sturtevant (1964) provides a survey of ethnoscience as an ethnographic methodological approach. Sturtevant urges that the term *science* in *ethnoscience* be interpreted to mean 'classification'.

The main features of ethnoscientific methodology may be seen as employing six principles or aspects of analysis, many of which have been mentioned in previous chapters in connection with descriptive linguistics (paraphrased from Sturtevant 1964:101–113):

1.   Etics and emics
2.   Domains
3.   Terminological systems
4.   Paradigms and componential analyses
5.   Taxonomies, trees, and the notion of *key*
6.   Discovery procedures

Items 4 and 5 relate to types of data arrangement and analysis.

(1) Etics and Emics

An understanding of a culture and a full description of it in a foreign language requires "the ultimate reduction of the significant attributes of the local classifications into culture-free terms" (Sturtevant 1964:102). In Pike's classification (1967), such culture-free features of the real world are etic. An emic description should ultimately indicate which etic characters are locally significant. Just as for language, the International Phonetic Alphabet (IPA) provided symbols for the recording of all possible speech sounds and phonemic analysis provided a means of selecting those sounds which were distinctive in specific languages, the study of culture ethnoscientifically requires an etic set of descriptive terms from which those significant in a given culture may be distinguished.

For example, in kinship studies, the KIN TYPES *Mo* (mother), *Bro* (brother), *Si* (sister), or *MoBro* (mother's brother) are etic in that, though they often refer to actual KIN TERMS in English (*mother*, *brother*, *sister*, but not *uncle*), they are also features from the set of which all cultures may define their kin types. The particular kin types actually realized as kin terms (that is, etic units which are emic in a given culture) are describable with respect to the etic features which comprise them. For example, *Mo* is an etic type in Swahili and in English, indeed, in all languages and cultures in the world. In English, the etic type *Mo* is realized as a distinctive or emic term, *mother*. The etic type *Mo* is also emic in Swahili, realized in that language as *mama*. Also, *MoBro* is an etic type; it is distinctive (emic) in Swahili as *mjomba* and in English as *uncle*. However, in English, the emic term *uncle* is the realization of the etic type *FaBro* (father's brother) as well. In the same way, a phoneme /p/ in one language may be composed of different etic features in another language.

There are also possible etic types which are not realized in a given culture. For example, *DaHuBro* (daughter's husband's brother), an etic type, is not emic in American kinship. American English does not have a kinship term which refers to one's daughter's husband's brother.

The ethnoscientist's method requires that there be etic units available which account for the cultural system being described. The emic system of the particular culture is then described in terms of which etic units it treats as distinctive.

(2) Domains

To study culture or particular systems within particular cultures ethnoscientifi- cally, it is necessary to be able to determine "in a nonarbitrary manner the boundaries of the major category or classification system being analyzed." The ethnoscientist must be able to discover how a domain is bounded "in the culture being described rather than applying some external, cross-cultural definition of the field" (Sturtevant 1964:103–104). Unfortunately, procedures for unarbitrarily defining domains have not been well worked out.

According to Tyler, a SEMANTIC DOMAIN is one which consists of a class of objects all of which share at least one feature in common which differentiates those objects from other domains (1969:8). He provides as an example the semantic domain *furniture*. The domain is the total range of meaning of the class of objects in it (see Principle 5 below).

One might discover cultural conceptual boundaries by searching for "sets of questions that the people of a society are responding to when they behave in systematic ways, and for the relations existing among these questions and responses" (Black and Metzger 1965:142).

In Tyler's *furniture* domain, an item used to fill in the blank in the statement *a _____ is a kind of furniture* would constitute a member of that domain. Using this approach, however, it is difficult to know when or if one might have elicited the entire membership.

(3) Terminological Systems

A large part of ethnoscientific research involves analyzing terminological systems within a culture. This analysis is done on the assumption that,

> Culturally significant cognitive features must be communicable between persons in one of the standard symbolic systems of the culture. A major share of these features will undoubtedly be codable in a society's most flexible and productive communication device, its language (Frake 1962:75).

Categories within domains are usually named, and such classificatory categories are labeled as LEXEMES. A lexeme in this sense may be contrasted with a word in that the lexeme usually refers to the word and its paradigm set. For example, *man* is a lexeme encompassing the words *man/man's/men/men's*; *man* is the citation form used to represent that set (Greenberg 1968:58).

Lexemes are distinguishable for ethnoscientific purposes from grammatically similar linguistic forms in that they label discrete entities in a domain. Lexemes are analyzed as part of a terminological system in the language of the culture employing that terminological system. One of the emphatic points of ethnoscientific methodology is that the investigator must work within the system being analyzed. If he is analyzing the kinship system of Swahili, he should do so by using the Swahili language. The investigator should not impose on his analysis the categories of his or her own language and culture.

Translation of lexemes into the language of the investigator might result in use of a label which has wider or narrower applicability in the target language. A lexeme in the system being analyzed might refer to no item in the language of analysis. For example, the three Eskimo words for 'snow' translate into only one English word, *snow*. If the investigator were to translate the data from the Eskimo language into English, he would obscure the fact that there is variability in the Eskimo words (Sturtevant 1964:106–107).

Semantic domains may be looked at in terms of their internal structure in a number of ways. Lexemes in a semantic domain may be hierarchically arranged. In such an arrangement, lexemes at successively lower levels in the hierarchy are included in the meaning of lexemes at the higher levels.

Lexemes in a semantic domain may also be arranged by using intersecting features rather than features of inclusion and exclusion. For example, in a hierarchical arrangement of the domain *furniture*, the lexeme *table* includes the lexeme *end table*. In an arrangement according to intersecting features within another domain, *vehicle*, the lexeme *car* falls into the class designated by the intersection of the features *land-operated*, *wheeled*, and *motored*.

Another type of arrangement distinguishes lexemes by the presence or absence of defining features. The lexeme *car* in the domain *vehicle* has the features *+land-operated*, *+wheels*, and *+motor*; thus, it differs from *bicycle*, which has the feature *−motor*, and differs from *stern-wheeler*, which is *−land-operated* but *+water-operated*.

The arrangement of lexemes in a domain by considering features in terms of opposition, inclusion and contrast, or intersection aids the investigator in discovering and describing the principles of organization of that domain. Principles 4 and 5 of the ethnoscientific method relate to types of data arrangement.

Figure 6.
Paradigm of Features—Vehicle (suggested by
Douglas Paterson)

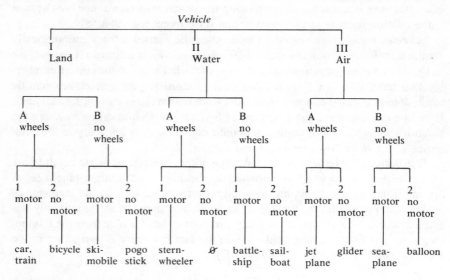

(4) Paradigms and Componential Analyses

As seen above, a domain is defined as the total range of meaning of the objects in it. For example, the domain *furniture* consists of all objects which may fill the frame *a* _____ *is a kind of furniture*. The domain *vehicle* consists of all objects which may fill the frame *a* _____ *is a kind of vehicle*. The words *furniture* and *vehicle* are known as the ROOTS OF THE DOMAIN; they label the field covered.

A PARADIGM can be defined as a type of arrangement of a set of segregates (labeled discrete entities) which "can be partitioned by features of meaning, i.e. a set some members of which share features not shared by other segregates in the same set" (Sturtevant 1964:108). Features of meaning intersect on a paradigm. Ideally, a paradigm should deal with a complete contrast set. It should show the features of shared and unshared meanings among *all* members of the domain of which it is an analysis—with no overlap. However, this stipulation presupposes a prior exhaustive demarcation of the studied domain such that it does not overlap elsewhere in the culture. Further, as noted above, marking domain boundaries continues to be a problem in ethnoscience. Figure 6 provides an example of a paradigmatic arrangement for a semantic domain labeled *vehicle*.

Within the semantic domain *vehicle*, the features are: I. *Land*, II. *Water*, III. *Air*, A. *presence of wheels*, B. *absence of wheels*, 1. *presence of a motor*, 2. *absence of a motor*. A particular lexeme designating an object within the

paradigm falls in the class designated by the intersection of the features. For e
ample, IA1 designates the intersection of the features *land-operated*, *with wheels*,
and *motor-run*; *train* and *car* are examples of lexemes in that class. Note that some
classes may be empty; for example, IIA2, which designates a class of objects
which travel primarily in the water, have wheels, and are not motor-operated.
English has no lexemes referring to such vehicles.

Thus we see that a paradigm is a method of arrangement of data in a terminological set to show relationships within the set. When a domain is partitioned by
features of meaning showing relationships in a paradigm, the method of COMPO-
NENTIAL ANALYSIS is applied to the data. "A componential analysis is an
analysis of a paradigm in terms of the defining features, 'the dimensions of contrast' or 'criterial attributes' of the segregates in the set" (Sturtevant 1964:109).

A componential analysis of the domain *vehicle* in Figure 6 would reveal that the
defining features of the paradigm are at three levels of contrast—primary mode of
travel, presence or absence of wheels, type of power (presence or absence of a
motor). These three dimensions of contrast are called COMPONENTS and are used
to distinguish the lexemes which occur on a paradigmatic representation of the
domain *vehicle*. More will be said about componential analysis in Section 4.22
below.

(5) Taxonomies, Trees, and the Notion of Key

As we have just observed, a paradigm is a type of arrangement of ethnoscientific
data; a taxonomy is another type of arrangement of ethnoscientific data. We will
also look at yet another type of arrangement, that referred to as a tree.

TAXONOMIES are hierarchical arrangements constructed by means of contrast
and inclusion. A domain label is the uppermost category in a taxonomy, for it
includes all its members. The hierarchy then successively sections the domain by
means of contrast and inclusion into its members (objects, lexemes). A taxonomy
of the domain *furniture* is illustrated in Figure 7.

Figure 7.
Sample Partial Taxonomy—Furniture (adapted
from Tyler 1969:7)

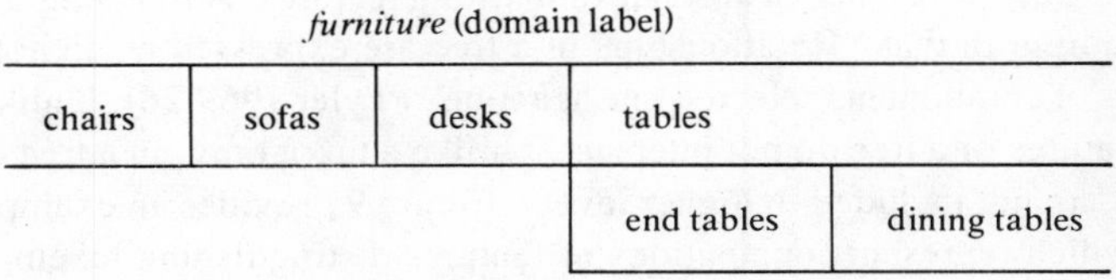

furniture (domain label)

chairs	sofas	desks	tables	
			end tables	dining tables

The domain *furniture* includes *chairs, sofas, desks, tables, end tables,* and *dining tables. Chairs, sofas, desks,* and *tables* contrast with one another at one level of contrast. *End tables* and *dining tables* contrast with one another at another level of contrast. *End tables* and *dining tables,* though they contrast with one another, are somehow similar in that they are included in the higher-level category *tables.* Likewise, *chairs, sofas, desks,* and *tables* (including *end tables* and *dining tables*), though they contrast with one another, are somehow similar in that they are included in the higher-level category *furniture.*

In taxonomies, "categories at the same level contrast with one another while categories at lower levels are included in categories at higher levels. Categories at the same level differ from one another, but when included in the same higher level category are somehow like one another" (Tyler 1969:26).

Taxonomies are less powerful and less interesting for ethnoscientific data than are paradigms, since they do not show the intersection features in a domain from which components of meaning may be extracted. Taxonomies show the hierarchical relationship between categories; the lexemes within each category imply contrast, yet provide no way to observe minimal features of contrast, that is, we cannot establish the components of meaning which minimally distinguish *tables* from *desks* or *chairs* from *sofas.*

An arrangement that may be represented on a taxonomy may also be represented on a branching diagram (see Figure 8).

The next type of arrangement we will look at is that of data arranged on a tree and represented by a key. "Paradigms, taxonomies, and trees are fundamentally different kinds of semantic arrangements. Each semantic domain of a culture may be ordered by one or more of these arrangements" (Tyler 1969:26).

All three arrangements, taxonomies, paradigms, and trees, are kinds of semantic structures. When such types of arrangement can be represented by a key, they become a *representation* of a semantic structure.

Unlike the other types of arrangement, a tree requires representation by a key. A SEMANTIC KEY is a "branching structure . . . where the first node indicates the 'root' or domain feature . . . and each succeeding node represents a selection of a single feature from some particular dimension" (Kay 1966:22).

A TREE primarily distinguishes the lexemes of a domain from each other by indicating the presence or absence of defining features. A tree diagram differs from a paradigm in that "Relationships in a tree are expressed as dichotomous oppositions of components selected one at a time" (Tyler 1969:26). Unlike a paradigm, the features of a tree do not intersect. Unlike a taxonomy, in a tree items at lower levels are not included in higher levels. Figure 9 provides an example of a simple tree which represents oppositions of features distinguishing lexemes which refer specifically to male or female horses.

To represent a tree (or a paradigm or a taxonomy) by a key, Kay states that the key must be one in which "each node corresponds to a lexeme" (1966:22). Usually, paradigms are not represented by keys, and a taxonomy can be represent-

Figure 8.
Branching Diagram—Furniture (adapted from
Tyler 1969:8)

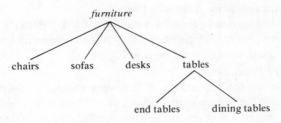

Figure 9.
Tree Diagram—Male and Female Horses

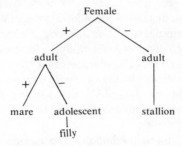

A *mare* is an *adult, female* horse; a *stallion* is an *adult non-female* horse; a *filly* is
an *adolescent non-adult female* horse.

Figure 10.
Tree Diagram—Flowers with and without Spurs
(from Tyler 1969:11, as adapted from Porter
1967:83)

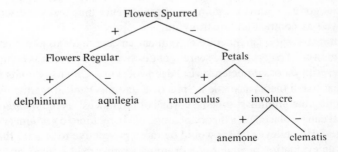

A *delphinium* is a *regular spurred flower*, an *aquilegia* is a *non-regular spurred
flower*, a *ranunculus* has *petals* but no *spurs*. Both *anemones* and *clematis* have
no *petals* and no *spurs*; the *anemone* has *involucre* while the *clematis* does not.

ed by a key only if that key also represents a tree or a paradigm, since keys specify semantic features and taxonomies do not. In the simple diagram of a tree in Figure 9, the root feature of the key is + or − *female*, with the feature + or − *adult* serving to distinguish *mare* from *filly* further.

Tyler provides an example of a tree from C. L. Porter's *Taxonomy of Flowering Plants* (1967), which distinguishes certain flowers on a tree represented by a key. We quote that example here in Figure 10.

(6) Discovery Procedures

The rationale for the importance of discovery procedures in ethnoscience is similar to that used for the importance of such procedures in descriptive linguistics. Sturtevant has stated, "If an ethnography is to reflect the cognitive system of the bearers of a culture, the validity of the description depends on the discovery procedures" (1964:11). It must be possible to check hypotheses about the data in the field and revise them according to the facts of the data.

In descriptive linguistics, discovery procedures are applied to raw data in order to identify phonemes and morphemes. The methods of phonemics and morphemics are actually discovery procedures in themselves, for they provide the steps by which one may identify phonemes and morphemes within a body of data. Somewhat the same situation appears to be the case with the proposed methodology of ethnoscience. The methodology aims to identify distinctive units within various systems of culture by uncovering contrasts which are identified through distributional analysis (Landar 1966:69).

Descriptive linguistics, and its methodology based on such discovery procedures, has recently been termed TAXONOMIC LINGUISTICS because of its "class-discovering" approaches (Landar 1966:69). Such a label might also be appropriate for that aspect of ethnoscience which is interested in showing contrast within domains by representing data on taxonomies.

In the areas of ethnoscience which seek to go beyond identifying levels of contrast, the label "taxonomic" would, of course, not apply. After determining dimensions of contrast, the ethnoscientist may seek to discover which features define categories in semantic domains. Ethnoscience thus seeks to discover meaning as well as contrast and distribution.

The transformational/generative grammarians are antitaxonomic on "grounds of parsimony." They reject the search for discovery procedures as being unrelated to the description of competence (Landar 1966:111). Chomsky holds that the requirement that a theory provide a "practical and mechanical method for actually constructing the grammar, given a corpus of utterances" is the *strongest* requirement that can be placed on a theory of language in relation to grammars of specific languages. He believes that it would be more productive to require that a theory provide an evaluation procedure for grammars rather than a discovery procedure. This more reachable goal for a theory of language would allow the linguist to "focus attention more clearly on really crucial problems of linguistic structure" and provide a means whereby he "can arrive at more satisfying answers to them" (Chomsky 1957:50–53).

If, however, ethnoscience has as its goal a theory of descriptions of cultures rather than a general theory of Culture, that goal would require the development of discovery procedures. Chomsky, with his goal of developing a theory of Language, rather than a theory of descriptions of languages, maintains that the requirement that a theory provide a discovery procedure by presenting and developing a methodology which an investigator might use to construct a grammar from raw data "will lead into a maze of more and more elaborate complex analytic procedures that will fail to provide answers for many important questions about the nature of linguistic structure" (53).

Since ethnoscience places its emphasis on discovery procedures, it may be viewed on that level as somewhat analogous to descriptive linguistics. On the other hand, the new cultural anthropology and nonmethodological aspects of the new ethnography may be seen to be analogous to transformational/generative grammar, emphasizing language and culture as rule-governed systems.

The reliance of ethnoscience on discovery procedures takes the form of determining the right questions to ask the bearers of the culture in order to elicit classes of responses and thereby discover categories and significant environments within a domain (Sturtevant 1964:111). For example, Charles Frake (1961), in working with the Subanun people of the Philippines, noted that in all cultures illness evokes questions such as, "What kind of disease do I have?" and "What caused this disease?" If the answers to such questions had "disease names," he termed them *diagnosis*.

According to Frake, the question "What kind of illness is that?" in the language of the Subanun will always elicit a diagnostic description. Frake suggests that the investigator collect contrasting answers to the questions the Subanun ask when diagnosing disease in order to elicit the significant criteria for diagnosis.

The procedure for an ethnoscientific description of disease concepts is illustrated in Table 4, which shows the contrasts arrived at in distinguishing types of *sores* in the language of the Subanun. The top half of Table 4 is a representation of the category *sore* and the levels of terminological contrasts within that category among the Subanun. The bottom half of the table shows the questions asked about the contrasting lexemes, and the range of answers received to those questions. The questions themselves are the discovery procedures used.

The above six major aspects of the methodology of ethnoscience have so far been applied to a rather narrow set of terminological systems. Sturtevant saw the usefulness of the method of ethnoscience as applicable, perhaps widely, in the area of material culture. An ethnoscientific analysis of material culture would make use of discovery procedures other than questioning. In such a study of material culture, "the possibility of pointing to and manipulating concrete objects may partially replace the use of question frames and the reliance on terminological systems in eliciting significant categories and contrasts" (Sturtevant 1964:112).

Table 4.
Subanun "Skin Disease" Terminology—Levels of Contrast (adapted and modified from Frake 1961:118)

Category →	beldut 'sore'						
Levels of Terminological Contrast	*telemaw* 'distal ulcer'		*baga?* 'proximal ulcer'				
	telemaw glai shallow distal ulcer	*telemaw glibun* deep distal ulcer	*baga?* shallow proximal ulcer	*begwak* deep proximal ulcer	*beldut* simple sore	*selimbunut* multiple sore
Diagnostic Questions (criteria of diagnosis significant in distinguishing sores)	*Range of Answers to Diagnostic Questions*						
How Deep?	sh	dp	sh	dp		
Distality?	distal		proximal			
How Severe?	severe				mild	
What Is Its Spread?	single					multiple

4.22   COMPONENTIAL ANALYSIS

Componential semantic analysis (or formal semantic analysis) to date has interested anthropologists more so than linguists. To understand what the term *componential analysis* means in semantics, John Lyons (1969:470–472) provided the following example using data arranged on a paradigm (see 4.21, #4 above):

The Data

1. man	woman	child
2. bull	cow	calf
3. rooster	hen	chicken
4. drake	duck	duckling
5. stallion	mare	foal
6. ram	ewe	lamb

From the data, it is possible to set up equations in the form of an analogy:

a.   man is to woman is to child *as*
b.   bull is to cow is to calf

Groups *a* and *b* may be said to share a set of semantic components. What *man* and *bull* have in common, what *woman* and *cow* have in common, and what *calf* and *child* have in common are components. Likewise, *bull*, *cow*, and *calf* share a semantic component with each other (they are bovine) not shared by *man*, *woman*, and *child* (who are human). In terms of semantic components, enclosed in parentheses, the analogy may be rewritten as the following proportion:

MAN	WOMAN	CHILD
(male) - (adult) - (human) is to	(female) - (adult) - (human) is to	(non-adult) - (human)

as

BULL	COW	CALF
(male) - (adult) - (bovine) is to	(female) - (adult) - (bovine) is to	(non-adult) - (bovine)

The semantic components that can be extracted from the data (*man*, *woman*, *child*, *bull*, *cow*, *calf*) are (male), (female), (adult), (non-adult), (human), and (bovine), which may also be viewed as a set of oppositions (±male), (±adult), (±human). Componential definitions in the context of these data are:

man   is defined as $\begin{bmatrix} +male \\ +adult \\ +human \end{bmatrix}$

bull   is defined as $\begin{bmatrix} +male \\ +adult \\ -human \end{bmatrix}$

According to Lyons (1969:472), "it is conceivable that, by bringing forward for comparison other words of English and setting up further proportions, we should be able to factorize (human) or (male) into 'smaller' semantic components. . . ."

Much work by anthropologists on componential analysis has been in the area of the analysis of kinship terms in various languages. As mentioned above, a componential analysis is carried out on data arranged in a paradigm. A paradigm differs from a taxonomy in that in a paradigm, semantic distinctions crosscut; for example, the component (male) is applicable to segments both (human) and (bovine). On the other hand, in a taxonomy (for example, of the domain *sore* in Subanun shown in Table 4 above) the semantic distinctions needed for one segment or level of contrast do not apply in other segments; for example, the component (deep) is not applicable to *simple sores* or *multiple sores*.

Robbins Burling provides some relief amidst the plethora of ethnoscientific jargon by telling us,

> Still, the differences between a taxonomy and a paradigm are not profound. To sort terms in either way requires us to search for distinctive features of the observable world and to note how a terminology discriminates among these features and how various combinations of features are assigned to particular terms (1970:42).

Ward Goodenough (1956), viewing componential analysis as a means to describe culture properly, considers the methodological problem of ethnography to be identical with that of descriptive linguistics. Goodenough's view may be summarized by saying that

> the task of the analyst is to derive from a sample of etic data their emic structure and the relationships among the elements of that structure. The adequacy of the emic description is based on the ability to interpret and predict the events (behavioral or otherwise) of the cultural community (Paterson 1973:14,15).

Componential analysis is suggested as a way to accomplish such an emic goal for cultural description. In componential analysis, the terms of a semantic domain such as kinship are distinguished from one another by distinctive semantic features. Thus, in Goodenough's (1965) analysis of English kinship terminology, distinctions made among kinsmen along the semantic dimensions of (1) genealogical distance, (2) consanguinity, (3) self, (4) generation, and (5) generational location of the marriage bond, serve to distinguish *all* the major terms used. Those five semantic components distinguish for Goodenough *all* the terms in his kin system, just as the components (±human), (±male), and (±adult) served to minimally distinguish the lexemes *man*, *woman*, *child*, *bull*, *cow*, and *calf* in Lyons's paradigm mentioned earlier.

However, a number of problems exist in componential analysis. From the work done, it seems that the goal has been to discover and then describe "how the people themselves use their terms to classify the phenomena of their world" (Burling 1970:42–43). Assuming the classification of terminological systems to be an aspect of cognition, componential analysis further assumes that the study of the use of terms is a means of investigating cognition. Burling cautions that "To investigate cognition is a far more ambitious goal than simply to provide a device that chooses the same terms a native speaker would choose without pretending to duplicate his inner mental processes of classification and decision" (42-43).

Componential analysis and ethnoscientific methodology in general are beset with a preoccupation with determining discovery procedures and assigning cognitive status to the resultant analyses. Attempts to delimit domains rarely go beyond sets such as kinship terms, color terms, or botanical terms. How do we know that Frake's data contains *all* relevant types of Subanun words for sores? How can we say that semantic components extracted from a terminological set reveal distinctions in the mind of the native speaker?

Burling sees those problems as peripheral to semantic analysis and expresses the hope that formal semantic analysts and/or componential analysts will continue to work to "try to specify precisely what terms 'mean' and to describe precisely the objects to which terms are applied" (1964:27). He states in his well-known "God's Truth or Hocus-pocus?" article,

> Linguists in referring to attitudes toward grammatical analyses have sometimes made a distinction between the "God's truth" view and the "hocus-pocus" view (Householder 1952). When a linguist makes his investigation and writes his grammar, is he discovering something about the language which is "out there" waiting to be described and recorded or is he simply formulating a set of rules which somehow work? Similarly, when an anthropologist undertakes a semantic analysis, is he discovering some "psychological reality" which speakers are presumed to have or is he simply working out a set of rules which somehow take account of the observed phenomenon (27)?

Burling's attitude is that semantic analysis should be done within the "hocus-pocus" view. He grants the fact that it is tempting for semanticists to attribute more to their work than simply manipulating "operational devices," but he feels that claims of discovering "psychological reality" (God's truth) are unjustified. In his words, "It certainly sounds more exciting to say we are 'discovering the cognitive system of the people' than to admit that we are just fiddling with a set of rules which allow us to use the terms as others do" (27). Burling believes that a realistic goal for the ethnoscientist is to admit that he is coming up with rules that allow others to use terms appropriately, but making the cognitive system explicit is not. He urges the ethnoscientist to "be content with the less exciting objective of showing how terms in language are applied to objects in the world and stop pursuing the illusory goal of cognitive structures" (27).

4.23   BASIC COLOR TERMS AND SEMANTIC ANALYSIS

Ethnoscientific methodology, as we have seen, stresses the importance of gathering data in the language of the culture-bearers and contains the tenet that each culture and language should be dealt with in its own terms. Further, most detailed studies have dealt with recognized delimited and supposed universal domains such as kinship and color terms. The finding of a great deal of variation cross-culturally among terminological systems implicitly argues against the existence of semantic universals (Berlin and Kay 1967:2), just as descriptive linguistics stressed linguistic differences rather than similarities. In the Whorfian sense, ethnoscientific and descriptive linguistic studies tend to reinforce the idea that each language and culture embodies a particular world view.

Brent Berlin and Paul Kay researched the lexical coding of color to determine the degree of arbitrariness in the coding:

> The prevailing doctrine of American linguists and anthropologists has, in this century, been that of extreme linguistic relativity. Proponents of this view frequently offer as a paradigm example the alleged total semantic arbitrariness of the lexical coding of color. We suspect that this allegation of "total arbitrariness" in the way languages segment the color space is a gross overstatement (2, 3).

Their research took the form of systematically gathering data from native speakers of twenty different languages representing unrelated language families, plus the grammars of another sixty languages. Their thesis was that "color words translate rather too easily among various pairs of unrelated languages" and that it is untrue that each language "segments the three dimensional color continuum arbitrarily and independently of each other language" (2, 3). (See the experiments discussed in Section 4.11 above.)

Informants provided the investigators with the basic color words of their respective languages. Only single lexical items referring to colors were used; phrases such as *light blue* or *sky blue* were excluded. Techniques of data elicitation used the discovery procedures developed for ethnoscience as described above; for example, _____ *is a color term in my language.* Each informant, after providing his color terms, was asked to indicate the *focal point* and *outer boundary* of each of his terms among the set of color chips used. Each was asked, for example, which chip represents the truest *blue* and where among the chips or on the color chart does *blue* stop being *blue* and become another color.

The study revealed that in all languages speakers seem to center the foci of their labels for color terms at nearly the same locations on the color chart. Some languages have greater numbers of basic color terms than others, but the focus for each term that a language has is in the same location as the focus for the corresponding term in other languages.

Color has traditionally been a domain used to demonstrate in support of the

Whorf Hypothesis that a person's language forces him to divide the spectrum in a certain way, with each language making "its own distinctions, which need have little to do with the distinctions made by other languages" (Burling 1970:46). Indeed, the method of ethnoscience implicitly assumes that the terminological sets which are the object of analysis are perceptual continua, "and that only by the use of our terminology do we introduce divisions within . . . [each] continuum." Burling states further, "This assumption misses the possibility that common human perceptual abilities might introduce similar distinctions in all languages" (45).

Berlin and Kay's work challenges the assumption of dissimilar color distinctions quite convincingly, and from their research they conclude that,

> Although different languages encode in the lexicon different *numbers* of basic color categories, there exists a total inventory of about eleven basic color categories from which the eleven or fewer basic color categories of any given language are always drawn (1967:2).

It would appear from this study that there are universal perceptual distinctions of color, with each language differing as to how the distinctions are labeled. One might make several analogies: linguists have proposed universal distinctive features in phonology, but allow that languages differ in the bundles of features distinctive in their sound systems (see Section 2.1 above); and the psychologist Roger Brown (see Section 4.1 above) maintains that perceptual categories which are frequently utilized receive labels, while unutilized categories may be seen as universal, "sitting there, waiting for a label" (Burling 1970:48).

4.24   URBAN ANTHROPOLOGY AND ETHNOSCIENCE

Despite some criticism of ethnoscience as being preoccupied with discovery procedures and with attempting to claim cognitive reality for its results (see Section 4.22 above), ethnoscientific studies might make significant contributions to a knowledge of what terms mean and to what they refer. In recent years, some anthropologists have studied subcultures or distinct groups of people in an urban setting by using ethnoscientific methodology to understand social identity. In order to show how ethnoscience might be applied, we will examine an example of one such study, James Spradley's ethnography of "urban nomads" (1970).

Spradley's definition of a subculture is that it is "the symbolic system of knowledge people use to order their behavior as members of a group" (1970:263). Urban entities are often comprised of numbers of subcultures each of which interacts in various ways with the institutions of the larger culture. The subculture investigated by Spradley is a group of men termed "urban nomads," each of whom "has no family, travels from town to town, seldom works, and drinks a great deal" (68). The object of the study was to determine the relationship between urban nomads and urban institutions of law enforcement. Another purpose was to provide non-urban nomads or outsiders with information to help them understand how urban nomads see themselves in relation to the rest of culture. Somewhat passionately, Spradley states:

> The distance between most Americans and urban nomads cannot be measured in miles: they are separated from us by cultural distance. Their style of life is not only strange but also abhorrent to most Americans. They are socially alienated and culturally separated from us but still they are in our very midst! This book is an attempt to build a bridge of understanding by providing a description of their way of life from the insider's point of view (1970:6).

Spradley gathered his data by first listening and observing casually in order to find the right questions to ask informants. He recorded the terms used by his subjects in reference to themselves and to each other, terms used by them to refer to law-enforcement personnel, and terms for where they sleep, for aspects of the jail experience, and for other facets of their lives. Spradley then analyzed the meaning of the terms to arrive at *taxonomic* and *componential* definitions of them.

Spradley also elicited terms by formal questioning and sorting tasks; for example, informants were asked to rank order the terms which best described their group from a list of terms gleaned through conversation, and they "were instructed to include additional words which would better describe the population" (70–71).

Table 5.

Taxonomic Definition of the Domain *Tramp*
(adapted from Spradley 1970:74)

Tramp												
Working Stiff					*Mission Stiff*							
construction tramp	sea tramp	tramp miner	harvest tramp	fruit tramp	nose diver	professional nose diver	bindle stiff	airedale	rubber tramp	home guard tramp	box car tramp	ding

For our purposes here, only one taxonomic and one componential definition will be given. The term *tramp* emerged as a cover term for labels the informants used for themselves and each other. Spradley explains that "informants were asked, 'are there different kinds of tramps?' An affirmative answer to this question was followed by asking 'What kinds of tramps are there?' " (73). The results were arranged on a taxonomy (see Section 4.21, #5 above) which is shown in Table 5.

Informants were then asked to choose from three items in the taxonomy two which were similar and one which was different from the first two in order to arrive at a componential definition of *tramp* and to show what criterial attributes distinguish different terms in the taxonomy. In such a componential definition, components or criterial attributes distinguishing one term from another need not be the total number of features of difference but rather the *necessary* features. Spradley's componential definition of the domain *tramp* appears here as Table 6.

The four components or dimensions of contrast seen in Table 6—*mobility*, *mode of travel*, *home base*, and *livelihood*—distinguish the eight categories of *tramp* listed in the taxonomy (Table 5). Spradley's study contains such componential and taxonomic definitions of a number of other aspects of the subculture of urban nomads from which he draws a number of conclusions. Of his analysis of the domain *tramp*, he states:

> The ethnographic study of identity seeks to find out how people in alien societies organize their knowledge about themselves, but it does not prescribe which criteria should be significant, allowing these to arise from the empirical situation. The present study might have been done with questions derived from the popular, medical, legal, or sociological models of identity; instead, the questions asked were first discovered from informants. They define their primary identity with the word "tramp," and in order to

Table 6.
Componential Definition of the Domain *Tramp*
(adapted from Spradley 1970:76)

Components →	Mobile	Mode of Travel	Home Base	Livelihood
Working Stiff	yes	freight/commercial	job	specialized—works
Mission Stiff	yes	commercial	mission	specialized—mission
Bindle Stiff	yes	freight	pack	generalized
Airedale	yes	walk	pack	generalized
Rubber Tramp	yes	car	car	generalized
Home Guard Tramp	no	∅	town and kinsmen	generalized
Box Car Tramp	yes	freight	∅	generalized
Ding	yes	freight	∅	specialized—begs

understand the meaning of such an identity this word was defined both taxonomically and componentially. The underlying semantic principles for organizing their knowledge about their own identity are intimately related to their nomadic style of life (1970:79).

Such an application of ethnoscientific methods to the study of urban subcultures can provide insights as to how members of particular subcultures regard their position in a group vis-à-vis the culture at large. The results of such studies have some obvious implications. The knowledge that there are many types of tramps and an understanding of some of the differences and similarities among them provide information to the larger culture and its institutions which deal with these people. The information revealed about particular subcultures may be used to understand or affect behavior, or both.

Ethnoscientific investigations of terminological systems within subcultures do not result in statements about how subcultures and their members think or how different people see the world. Rather, such studies reveal the categories within terminological sets which are important to the existence of a subculture as a group. Also, such results represent collective objectivity on the part of the informant population. Rarely would a *ding* refer to himself as a *ding*. In fact, the descriptive statements collected in the Spradley study as examples of the use of the terms were generally objective and of the nature, "I was with a ding one time and he made thirty dollars begging while we walked back to town . . ." (1970:75).

Ethnoscientific methods used in an ethnographic analysis may be viewed as essentially techniques developed for presenting and organizing data in an effort to arrive at an observationally adequate description of the data.

4.3   Semantics

Outside of anthropological linguistics, and specifically outside of ethnoscience, there has been little progress in theory or description in the study of linguistic meaning. As seen in Chapter 1 above, descriptive linguistics of the Bloomfieldian era viewed meaning as the response a hearer makes to a form uttered by a speaker. In this section, we will examine the situation in linguistics with respect to semantics in the post-Bloomfieldian era. Transformational/generative linguists generally see syntax as the main component of grammar with all segments of language (including semantics or meaning) interpreted with reference to the sentence (see Chapter 2, Section 2.3). We noted earlier that the semantic component of a grammar (remembering that grammar is defined in transformational/generative terms as a "theory of Language") is basically undeveloped and that the relationship between syntax and semantics is obscure. Here, we will discuss some views on the relationship between syntax and semantics, look at one proposal put forth for a semantic theory, and mention a relatively recent development known as *generative semantics*.

Chomsky (1965:142) presumed the existence of a universal "alphabet" of semantic features, defining a semantic feature as one "not mentioned in any syntactic rule." Further, he held that there is no way to demonstrate that "semantic considerations play a role in the choice of the syntactic or phonological component of a grammar or that semantic features . . . play a role in the functioning of the syntactic or phonological rules" (1965:footnote 15, 226).

In their proposal for a semantic theory, Jerrold Katz and Jerry Fodor noted that most linguists, in an effort to say where the division between syntax and semantics lies, invariably would propose criteria that

> with apparently equal justice, [can] be regarded as either syntactical or semantic. . . . For example, such markers as MALE, FEMALE, HUMAN, ANIMAL, ANIMATE, CONCRETE, ABSTRACT, and so on, appear to fall in this overlap. But the confusion engendered in the search for a line between grammar and semantics is unwarranted because the overlap exists in name only (1964:517).

Katz and Fodor believe that grammatical and semantic markers may be differentiated "in terms of the theoretical functions they perform"; for example, a grammatical marker would be the label *feminine* for the nouns *ship*, *England*, *fortune*, and *fate* in English, indicating the type of pronoun agreement for those nouns (she, her), whereas these same nouns "cannot receive the semantic marker FEMALE if sentences are to receive the correct semantic interpretations" (518).

Where both syntax (grammar) and semantics seem to have a common marker (feature), Katz and Fodor contend that there are two markers with the same or similar names:

> Thus, grammatical and semantic markers have different theoretical import. Grammatical markers have the function of marking the formal differences upon which the distinction between well-formed and ill-formed strings of morphemes rests, whereas semantic markers have the function of giving each well-formed string the conceptual content that permits them to be represented in terms of the message they communicate to speakers in normal situations (518).

In Katz and Fodor's terms, linguistic description minus grammar equals semantics. From their point of view, linguistic description is a representation of the knowledge of a speaker-hearer. They assume that linguistic knowledge is in the form of rules "which project the finite set of sentences" encountered by an individual "to the infinite set of sentences of the language" (483).

Semantics, in this framework, is the explanation of one's "ability to produce and understand infinitely many new sentences at the point where grammar leaves off." The formulation of grammatical and semantic rules in a syntactic and semantic theory solves what is termed the *projection problem* of language. Transformational grammars explain what a speaker knows about the "phonological and syntactic structure of his language which enables him to use and understand any of its sentences, including those he has never previously heard (Katz and Fodor 1964:483). Then, it is the goal of a semantic theory to explain the rest of an individual's linguistic knowledge—that which is beyond grammar but is still language (excluding the setting, about which see Chapter 5 below). A semantic theory should explain the speaker-hearer's ability to interpret sentences.

The semantic theory proposed by Katz and Fodor must contain (493, paraphrased):

1. A *dictionary* of the lexical items of the language.
2. A system of *projection rules*. The system of projection rules "operates on full grammatical descriptions of sentences and on dictionary entries to produce semantic interpretations for every sentence of the language."

A dictionary entry contains grammatical markers, semantic markers, and distinguishers (see Figure 11).

Figure 11.
Example of a Dictionary Entry in Semantics
(adapted from Katz and Fodor 1964:496)

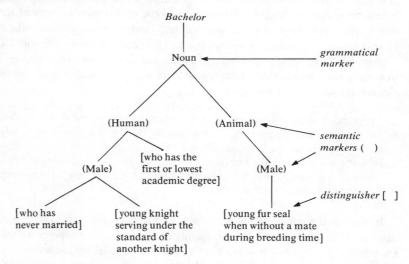

Projection rules would "provide the combinatorial machinery for projecting the semantic representation for all supra-word constituents in a sentence from the representations given in the dictionary for the meanings of the words in the sentence" (Katz 1966:152). That is, projection rules would combine dictionary entries with the appropriate grammatical descriptions of parts of the sentence in such a way that the sentence receives a meaningful interpretation. The input to the projection-rule component of semantic theory is the sentence to be interpreted plus its derivation. The rules unite the various paths of the derivation, working up to the complete sentence: "The projection rules amalgamate sets of paths dominated by a grammatical marker by combining elements from each of them to form a new set of paths which provides a set of readings for the sequence of lexical items under the grammatical marker" (Katz and Fodor 1964:506). The result of applying the dictionary and projection rules to a sentence is its SEMANTIC INTERPRETATION.

Ever since Katz and Fodor put forth this proposal for an abstract semantic theory, which has been generally known as INTERPRETIVE SEMANTICS, a number of issues have come up regarding semantics within the framework of transformational/generative grammar.

In their formulation, Katz and Fodor suggested that within the schema,

Dictionary Entry⟩
Projection Rules⟩ → *applied to* → Sentence → *yields* → Semantic Interpretation,

two types of projection rules would operate:

> *Type 1 rules* would operate on the output of phrase-structure rules (see Chapter 2, Section 2.3) and obligatory transformations of the syntactic component.
>
> *Type 2 rules* would apply to the output of optional transformations.

Without going into detail here regarding the position of transformations in syntax and the differences in point of view among various proponents of differing forms of transformational/generative theory, it is sufficient to observe that Katz and Fodor held that syntactic transformations (to whose result projection rules are applied) should not change meaning.

This view argued for an autonomous position for syntax and is a view shared by Chomsky as well. However, in recent years various critics have taken the position that no boundary can be drawn between syntax and semantics. As stated by Howard Maclay, "Katz and Fodor expanded the empirical domain of linguistics to include semantics with the ultimate result that the autonomy of syntax is now seriously questioned by linguists" (1971:180).

A theory such as that proposed by Katz and Fodor for semantics seems to entail considerable duplication with syntax. Maclay (178) reviewed some such duplications noted by critics of the Katz and Fodor theory, including, in paraphrased form:

1. The semantic component contains a dictionary; the syntactic component, a lexicon.
2. Both deep structure in syntax and semantic representations in semantics consist of labeled trees.

A more recent proposal for a semantic theory has been suggested by George Lakoff and is termed GENERATIVE SEMANTICS. Generative semantics makes the claim that "semantic representations and syntactic phrase-markers are formal objects of the same kind, and that there exist no projection rules, but only grammatical transformations" (Lakoff 1971:269).

The differing positions on semantic theory held by transformational/generative linguists may, however, be seen to share a common denominator which "is a conviction that semantic criteria are at least equal in importance to other factors in justifying solutions to linguistic problems and that semantic problems are an appropriate beginning point" (Maclay 1971:178).

Lakoff calls his proposal for generative semantics, Basic Theory. In his view, grammar is a system of rules which relate sound in language to meaning. Both semantic representations and phonological representations of sentences are provided in a language-independent way. In Lakoff's scheme, the lexicon contains the necessary phonological, semantic, and syntactic information in order for the lexical items to be interpreted in a sentence. With the syntactic structure of the sentence as given, the semantic representation of a sentence must take account of the syntactic string itself, a set of conjoined *presuppositions*, the *topic* of the sentence, and the *focus* of the sentence (1971:234).

The notion of PRESUPPOSITION in semantic interpretation may be illustrated by the sentence *Pedro regretted being Norwegian*. The presupposition is that Pedro is Norwegian. A sentence is true or false *only* if all its presuppositions are true.

The notion of TOPIC, a special case of presupposition, involves "a two place relation having the meaning 'concerns' or 'is about' " (Lakoff 1971:263). For example, in the sentence *John, Mary hates him*, the topic is *John*; but in the sentence *Mary, she hates him*, the topic is *Mary*.

The notion of FOCUS expresses an assertion of coreferentiality. In the sentence *The tall girl left*, the presupposition that the individual is a girl is coreferential with the presupposition that the girl is tall.

Semantic interpretation is accomplished by applying transformational rules (both syntactic rules and rules that insert into the sentence items from the lexicon) which apply to the generated syntactic string, and by using *derivational constraints*. A DERIVATIONAL CONSTRAINT "is a rule of grammar that requires some relation to hold between two or more stages of a derivation, independent of the intermediate transformational steps relating them" (Lakoff 1971:243). The notions of presupposition, topic, and focus are handled by such derivational constraints. Lakoff envisions the semantic representation of a sentence to be a representation of the inherent logical form of the sentence.

Ray Jackendoff, in reviewing the state of linguistic art with respect to semantic theory, reminds us that it is not clear that it is actually possible to construct a formal object to correspond to "the intuitive notion 'semantic interpretation of a sentence' "(1972:14). How can one determine what information is derivable from the sentence in contrast to what information flows from it? As was seen to be the case with ethnoscience, semantic interpretation also faces the problem of how to represent the meanings of lexical items. Jackendoff proposes that semantic theory focus more on how "lexical items are combined to form meanings of sentences and within that focus select out certain discrete aspects of meaning and deal with them coherently" (14). The aspects of meaning suggested by Jackendoff are four (paraphrased from Jackendoff):

1.   the functional structure of a semantic reading
2.   the coreference relations in a semantic reading
3.   focus and presupposition in a semantic reading
4.   the modal structure of a semantic reading

The analysis of the FUNCTIONAL STRUCTURE of a semantic reading would involve answering questions such as, What relationship is there between a verb in the deep structure (syntax) of a sentence and the function of that verb (for example, is it causal? directional?) in the semantic representation?

The analysis of COREFERENTIAL RELATIONS in a semantic reading could be performed through a TABLE OF COREFERENCE independent of the sentence's functional structure or structures. For example, a pair of noun phrases in a sentence would be shown as either coreferential with respect to each other or as noncoreferential.

Jackendoff's notions of focus and presupposition in a semantic reading differ somewhat from Lakoff's. The two linguists agree that both focus and presupposition are essential in semantic representation yet independent of the functional structure of semantic representation. However, Jackendoff defines FOCUS as the information the speaker assumes that is not shared by himself and the hearer; PRESUPPOSITION, on the other hand, is the information the speaker assumes to be shared with the hearer.

The MODAL STRUCTURE of a semantic reading is yet another independent part of semantic representation. The modal structure specifies the scope of negation and quantifiers. Both the functional and modal structures differ in their particular properties. The modal structure also deals with general and specific reference in a semantic reading and with the illocutionary force of the semantic reading; that is, Is the sentence declarative, imperative, or interrogative? An analysis of the modal structure would indicate whether indefinite noun phrases are specific, general, or opaque in reference. For example, the sentence *Fred wants to meet a voluptuous blonde* is ambiguous with regard to specificity since it is not known whether or not the speaker can point out the girl Fred wants to meet (Jackendoff 1972:16).

4.4   New Developments in the Study of Language and Mind

Semantic theory awaits neurolinguistic evidence as to the structure and function of the brain. Toward a broader view, the computational linguist David

G. Hays noted that "the human faculty of language has four parts," each of which may be "the reflection of a single specialized operational capacity in the human brain." The parts are (paraphrased from 1973:2, 3):

1. A sensorimotor skill which enables one to produce and interpret complex sound sequences.
2. A semantic aspect of language which allows one to correlate "sense impressions and bodily movements with verbal expressions."
3. A syntactic aspect of language which allows one to "identify with abstract symbols the roles that different objects play in a single activity."
4. A metalingual aspect of language which allows one "to compare two composite symbols, each consisting of symbols in syntactic relation and act on the comparison," for example, the ability to transform sentences and argue logically.

In these terms, one might look for a semantic theory to evolve through an understanding of the metalingual, as well as semantic, aspect of language.

Chomsky has stated that it is his belief that the study of language "can clarify and in part substantiate certain conclusions about human knowledge that relate directly to classical issues in the philosophy of mind" (1972:194).

Work currently being carried on dealing with information-processing activities and human and artificial intelligence is attempting to make progress in the development of semantic theory, taking advantage of the availability of the vast storage capacity of computers to develop memory models and store data of the "dictionary entry" form generally agreed to be a requisite in a semantic theory.[4]

Working from ideas developed in transformational/generative grammar, various computational linguists and cognitive psychologists are currently beginning to make advances in the understanding of the relationship of language, thought, and reality.

Research is also being done in other areas, such as psychological studies of hemispheric dominance in the brain and psycholinguistic studies of language acquisition by children. In man, it appears that language specialization is "primarily localized in the left hemisphere" (Lenneberg 1967:66) and that this localization is greater in adults than in children. However, the right hemisphere also has certain language functions. A study by Critchley has shown that lesions in the right hemisphere may be followed by (1962, in Lenneberg 1967, paraphrased):

1. difficult articulation
2. impaired creativity in literary work

---

[4] A sample of the type of work being done can be found in Feigenbaum and Feldman, *Computers and Thought* (1963).

3. hesitations
4. difficulty in finding words
5. difficulty in learning new linguistic material

The conclusion drawn is that the right hemisphere of the brain has to do with verbal aspects which are intellectually (perceptually and cognitively) significant but not related to speech in general. On the other hand, lesions in the left hemisphere interfere primarily with verbal activity and less often with "verbal perceptual and cognitive functions" (Milner 1962, Weinstein 1962, reported by Lenneberg 1967).

According to Lenneberg, hemispheric dominance increases with age and is closely tied to growth and development. Language development may be seen to be "related physiologically, structurally, and developmentally to two typically human characteristics, cerebral dominance and maturational history" (1967:174–175).

In view of psychological experiments such as those discussed above in Section 4.11, and in view of data from studies of hemispheric dominance and language acquisition, Lenneberg proposes that properties of natural language have very little to do with memory functions. The fruitful questions to ask, it would seem, are not only, How does language influence thought? but also, What cognitive processes are influential in acquiring and using language? In a sense, the transformational/generative linguists are asking this question as they seek to come up with a theory of linguistic competence, that is, to make explicit what we need to know to acquire language. A descriptively adequate transformational grammar would account for the intuition of a native speaker. Similarly, the relationship of culture to thought might be seen in discovering what people need to know to acquire culture—in discovering what cognitive processes are contained in a culture's ideational code.

4.5 Summary

We have seen in this chapter that the study of the relationship of language and culture was given its impetus from the world-view problem and that the methodology of ethnoscience for analyzing terminological sets attempted to determine how individuals categorize their world. Components of meaning extracted from terminological sets were termed *semantic components*. Experimental psychologists have been carrying out experiments on the relationship of perception and memory to labeled linguistic categories to see what influence language has on thought. Linguists, however, began to view semantics as the interpretation of sentences and attempted to elaborate what a semantic theory ought to be and how such a theory fits into a general theory of language. Ultimately, Richard Thompson (1968) has suggested, it might be possible to pool some of the methodology of ethnoscience with some of the constructs of linguistic theory—given the maintenance of the requirement of a lexicon or dictionary in linguistic theory, with some of its content coming directly from the investigation of speech.

The semantic markers—for example, (ANIMAL) or (MALE)—and distinguishers—[who has never married] or [who has the lowest or first academic degree]—of Katz and Fodor, "representing primary semantic distinctions between words and the completed characterization of each word, respectively, DO NOT DIFFER IN PRINCIPLE from the semantic rules derived in formal semantic analysis" (Thompson 1968:77).

Componential analysis may constitute an ethnographic tool for eliciting semantic markers and distinguishers. However, neither the ethnoscientific nor the linguistic approach to semantics (whether theory or analysis) can claim to reach an understanding of cognition. We are no nearer through anthropology or linguistics to an understanding of the relationship of language to thought (cognition) or culture to thought (cognition), and we are reminded that the area of investigation known as "language and culture" has as its purpose the investigation of language, thought, and reality.

The discussion in Section 4.11 alluded to an increasing interest by psycholinguists in solving the world-view problem dealing with language and thought. Results indicate that language may well have some influence on perception and memory but certainly does not seem to be a determining factor of cognition. In essence, a weak version of linguistic relativity may hold. That is, language may be a factor in thought but not *the* factor. For example, the obligatory grammatical category of form in Navaho may be seen to influence the perception of form among Navaho speakers, but other evidence has shown that cultural factors are also influential, especially when similar results are obtained for speakers of a language such as English, which has no obligatory category of form.

Eric Lenneberg observed that "cognitive processes studied so far are largely independent from peculiarities of any natural language and, in fact, that cognition can develop to a certain extent even in the absence of knowledge of any language" (1967:553).

Theories of cognition (thought) at the moment seem well outside the admittedly expanding boundaries of linguistics and anthropology, even in light of proposed semantic theories and descriptive techniques.

Chapter 5 Sociolinguistics

5.0 Introduction

This chapter will survey the relatively new field of sociolinguistics. Whereas the study known as "language and culture" is concerned with the relationship of both language and culture to thought, cognition, or meaning, sociolinguistics looks outward to examine the social context in which linguistic and cultural activity occurs. In fact, sociolinguistics is often referred to as the sociology of language. As one sociolinguist put it, "A sociolinguist is defined not by formal criteria of training or method but by his interest in a subject matter which falls between traditional academic boundaries" (Darnell 1971:viii).

Sociolinguistics is concerned with the interaction of language and setting. Much work focuses on the relationship of language and social organization by examining linguistic evidence of class and status. Other work investigates individual variability among speakers as related to the sociological context. Areas of investigation such as multilingualism, bilingualism, and the development of national language policies fall within the purview of sociolinguistics.

Joshua Fishman claims that sociolinguistics is concerned with the "patterned co-variation of language and society" and attempts to see if rules can be written for the co-variation of different aspects of language such as geographical dialects, social dialects, and stylistic differences. Fishman also notes that sociolinguistics is the only discipline concerned with language in its behavioral context (1968:5–13).

John Gumperz and Dell Hymes see the central notion for sociolinguistics to be "the appropriateness of verbal messages in context or their acceptability in the broader sense." Fishman's term for the subject matter of sociolinguistics as "patterned co-variation of language and society" is supplemented by the view of Gumperz and Hymes that sociolinguistics studies "communicative competence" defined as "what a speaker needs to know to communicate effectively in culturally significant settings" (1972:vii).

This chapter will examine sociolinguistic methodology, research in areas such as bilingualism, multilingualism, diglossia, and code-switching, the study of social dialects, the area of ethnicity, and language as seen through the study of language planning and the choosing of a national language.

5.1   Sociolinguistic Methodology

In the field of sociolinguistics, much stress is placed on procedures for eliciting data and on a necessary interdependence between linguistic data and the procedures which elicited the data. In sociolinguistics, "The basic elicitation method can be regarded as an extension of the linguist's practice of studying the same linguistic forms in different linguistic environments" (Gumperz and Hymes 1972: 24). The constant factor is the basic message and the varied one is the social relationship.

The sociolinguist needs criteria for defining the various significant contexts for his study. The basic unit of analysis in a sociolinguistic study is the speech community and not a given language (or dialect) or language which may crosscut speech communities. A particular language may be only a part of the resources of a particular speech community. Different languages and social dialects may be used within a single speech community. This co-variation in a speech community is the object of sociolinguistic study.

Hymes has outlined a proposal for a methodology of description in sociolinguistics in the belief that a specific and explicit descriptive model "can guarantee the maintenance and success of the current interest in sociolinguistics" (1972:52), since,

> It was the development of a specific mode of description that insured the success of linguistics as an autonomous discipline in the United States in the twentieth century, and the lack of it that led to the until recently peripheral status of folklore, although both had started from a similar base, the converging interest of anthropologists, and English scholars, in language and in verbal tradition (52).

Hymes' suggestion for a descriptive model of sociolinguistics has been called by him the "ethnography of speaking" (Hymes 1967:8–28) and aims to make explicit a set of notions or components. The components of a descriptive ethnography of speaking are (paraphrased from Hymes 1972:52–70):

1.   *Speech Community*: This component is the unit of sociolinguistic analysis which may be defined as a community that *must* (a) "share rules for the conduct and interpretation of speech" and (b) share rules for the interpretation of at least one "linguistic variety" (language).

2.   *Speech Situation*: This component refers to the context which may act as the environment for rules of speech events to operate.

3.   *Speech Event:* This component is the activity or aspect of activity "directly governed by the rules or norms for speech use."

4.   *Speech Act*:This component is the minimal unit of a speech event. A speech act "mediates immediately between the usual levels of grammar and the rest of a speech event or situation in that it implicates both linguistic form and social norms."
5.   *Speech Style*:This component involves the description of the quality, expression, and intensity of speech as style and the "co-occurrence within each [style] . . . and contrastive choice among [styles]."
6.   *Ways of Speaking*: This component refers to the communicative rule-governed behavior of a diversified speech community as compared to the communicative behavior of other diversified speech communities. "The point of it is the regulative idea that the communicative behavior within a community is analyzable in terms of determinate ways of speaking, that the communicative competence of persons comprises in part a knowledge of determinate ways of speaking."
7.   *Components of Speech*: These are the features of speech acts, which themselves are the minimal units of speech events. Hymes, on a linguistic analogy, expresses the aim of arriving at a universal set of speech features from which all communities choose bundles to comprise speech acts (see Chapters 2 and 4 above regarding bundles of features in phonology and semantics). Hymes provides the mnemonic, SPEAKING, for the components or speech acts:
     *S*etting and scene
     *P*articipants
     *E*nds: goals and outcomes
     *A*ct sequence: message form and message content
     *K*ey: tone, manner, spirit; for example, mock or serious
     *I*nstrumentalities: channels and forms of speech; for example, written, spoken, mutually intelligible, pig latin
     *N*orms of interaction: for example, taboo or not, possible to interrupt or not
     *G*enres: for example, poem, myth, letter, commercial communication, conversation
8.   *Rules of Speaking*: Little work has been done toward the actual formalizing of rules, but Hymes proposes that "a shift in any of the components of speaking [items *S* through *G* above] may mark the presence of a rule (or structured) relation, e.g., from normal tone of voice to whisper, from formal English to slang, correction, praise, embarrassment, withdrawal, and other evaluative responses to speech may indicate [sic] the violation or accomplishment of a rule." (See Section 5.34 below for suggestions as to possible sociolinguistic rules.)

Thus, a descriptive sociolinguistics may be seen as a description of speech events (which have been defined to take place in speech situations of a speech community) in terms of speech acts which are made up of speech components. The rules of speech proposed by Hymes, unlike rules of syntax in transformational/ generative grammar, would describe the presence or absence of and types of components of individual events.

A further exemplification of the methodology of descriptive sociolinguistic analysis and an extension of it can be found in Joel Sherzer and Regna Darnell's "Outline Guide for the Ethnographic Study of Speech Use" (1972:548–554).

The guide indicates (here in paraphrased form) that the ethnography of speaking involves,

1. an analysis of the use of speech (compare with Hymes' speech components and rules of speaking)
2. a description of attitudes toward the use of speech
3. knowledge of the acquisition of speaking competence, that is, how the ability to speak and use language appropriately is acquired
4. a description of the use of speech in education and social control
5. typological generalizations (compare with Hymes' ways of speaking)

Hymes' descriptive method appears to be chiefly concerned with parts 1 and 5 above. It is generally assumed, as Sherzer and Darnell indicate, that sociolinguistics also goes beyond descriptive analysis of speech events in context to a concern with attitudes of the speech community toward speech use (#2 above) and away from description altogether toward developing a theory of communicative competence (#3 above).

As seen in previous chapters, description and descriptive methods in the areas of study dealing with language and culture share a concern for discovery procedures and a common goal of observational adequacy. The methodology being proposed for the new field of sociolinguistics shares such goals and a number of techniques with descriptive linguistics and ethnoscience. The extension of sociolinguistics to a concern with attitudes of speech use (as proposed by Sherzer and Darnell) moves beyond description to the understanding of thought as attitudes, just as ethnoscience proposed to understand thought as cognition.

It may be that sociolinguistics, as Burling suggested for ethnoscience, ought to be content with the more modest goal of observational adequacy (see Chapter 1, Section 1.7 above) in analyzing speech events in the absence of any demonstrable cognitive reality to ascribe to such an analysis.

Likewise, any proposal for a knowledge of the acquisition of communicative competence requires a theory of communication, just as for Chomsky knowledge of the acquisition of linguistic competence requires a theory of language (1965:4). The competence/performance distinction made for language by Chomsky rests on competence defined as "the speaker-hearer's knowledge of his language" and performance defined as "the actual use of language in concrete situations." The communicative competence of the sociolinguist is defined, as stated above, as "what a speaker needs to know to communicate effectively in culturally significant settings." Communicative competence, then, in one sense, is a type of performance concerned with how language is used (or performed) in context. One aim of descriptive sociolinguistics is to describe the various aspects or components of speech events as they occur (or are performed) in context. Another is to describe the acquisition of the ability or knowledge (competence) to communicate.

Sociolinguistics so far has been mainly descriptive and is aiming toward developing a theory meeting the requirements of descriptive and explanatory adequacy. Currently, sociolinguistics seeks to *describe* the what (performance) and the how (competence) of language use in context. The current period of descriptivism is bringing in a sociolinguistic data base and a number of descriptions and analyses of language use. It is justifiable and necessary to attempt to meet the goal of adequate descriptions of observable data in areas awaiting investigation. It is also justifiable and necessary to deal with the issue of explanation. Without the descriptions as data with which to test the theories, the goal of attaining adequacy with an explanation could not be met. The field of sociolinguistics is so new that the descriptive methodology suggested for an ethnography of speaking cannot be judged even observationally adequate until it has been judged applicable to a wide variety of data on speech use in speech communities.

In the rest of this chapter we will look at areas of sociolinguistic study to which a sociolinguistic descriptive methodology may be applied.

Fishman cautions that for sociolinguistics and the broad range of issues to which it is addressed, "It would be foolhardy to claim that one and the same method of data collection and data analysis be utilized for such a variety of problems and purposes" (1972:453). The ethnography of speaking just outlined in this section is essentially a proposal for a general methodology to apply to the integration of language and society. As problems of sociolinguistic inquiry take form, various and differing methods of investigation are likely to develop. As Fishman says, "It is one of the hallmarks of scientific social inquiry that methods are selected as a *result* of problem specifications rather than independently of them" (453).

5.2   Bilingualism, Multilingualism, Diglossia, and Code-Switching

Sociolinguistics so far has frequently dealt with studying speech communities where more than one language is spoken. Such a situation may be referred to as LANGUAGE IN CONTACT: "two or more languages will be said to be *in contact* if they are used alternately by the same persons. The language-using individuals are thus the locus of the contact" (Weinreich 1954:1). There are various in-contact situations which may result in (paraphrased from Weinreich):

Bilingualism, "the practice of alternatively using two languages" (1).
Multilingualism, "the practice of using alternatively three or more languages" (1).
Diglossia, the practice by some speakers of using "two or more varieties of the same language . . . under different conditions" (Ferguson 1959:325).
Code-Switching, the practice of alternatively using two or more languages or dialects in one speech situation.

The term *language contact* is used here to refer to the study of the alternation among or between languages in the speech of individuals in context. We are excluding the study of linguistic borrowing in accord with William Mackey (1968).

All of these language situations which result from language contact involve deviation from the norms of each language (or dialect) involved. Such deviation results from familiarity by members of the speech community with one or more other languages or dialects, and is termed INTERFERENCE. According to Weinreich, "It is these phenomena of speech, and their impact on the norms of . . . language exposed to contact, that invite the interest of the linguist" (1954:1).

Studies of languages in contact aim to describe the differences and similarities between the two or more languages with respect to their structural variations. In Weinreich's words, "The forms of mutual interference of languages that are in contact are stated in terms of descriptive linguistics" (2). In addition to being described in linguistic terms, interference is also examined with respect to, and from the point of view of, the speech community. According to Mackey, the description of interference in bilingualism requires three steps (paraphrased from 1968:573):

1. the discovery through descriptive linguistic method of what "foreign element is introduced by the speaker into his speech"
2. an analysis of what the speaker does with such a foreign element introduced into his speech
3. a "measurement of the extent to which foreign elements replace native elements"

Studies of interference in language-contact situations aim to describe factors involved in linguistic choice through SITUATIONAL ANALYSIS (Fishman 1972: 444–445). With regard to multilingualism, Fishman urges that language behavior be looked at in terms of domains (see Chapter 4 above) of language behavior such as family, employment, or education, which can be "differentiated into role relations that are specifically crucial or typical of it [the particular domain]" (443).

The study of language choice among multilinguals seeks to describe which language is used in which domain and, within a domain, considers the locale of speech, with whom one speaks, and what the topic of conversation is.

The study of language interference and of factors of language choice in terms of domains is not restricted only to situations in which an individual speaks one or more languages, but may be carried out in situations where varieties of the same language are used in different situations. In this latter case, situational analysis seeks to describe how the varieties relate (that is, to describe the interference) and to describe the domains (noting topics, setting, speakers) in which the different varieties are used. Charles Ferguson termed this particular result of language contact, DIGLOSSIA. According to Ferguson,

> Perhaps the most familiar example [of diglossia] is the standard language and regional dialect as used, say, in Italian or Persian where many speakers speak their local dialect at home or among family or friends of the same dialect area but use the standard language in communicating with speakers of other dialects or on public occasions (1959:325).

A description of diglossia may be carried out by referring to one of the varieties of the language as *High* (*H*), the other as *Low* (*L*). In all situations of diglossia known to Ferguson, *H* and *L* differ in function and appropriateness in various situations. Usually *H* is considered to have more prestige, *H* has a written literary tradition, *L* is the language of conversation within the family, and *H* is usually acquired formally and often through grammatical study.

The sociolinguistic description of diglossia involves taking into consideration the following factors of the linguistic situation:

1.   function of each language variety
2.   prestige of each
3.   the literary tradition of the society
4.   the method of acquisition of each language variety
5.   the situation in the society with regard to language standardization
6.   the grammatical structure of the language varieties (for example, the relative simplicity of *L* with respect to *H*)
7.   differences in the lexicons of the varieties
8.   the phonological systems of each variety

The description of CODE-SWITCHING, that is, using more than one language in one situation, presents somewhat different problems than those encountered in descriptions of other in-contact situations. Code-switching occurs within the context of multilingualism, bilingualism, and diglossia. The description of it involves the analysis of linguistic choices or code-switches made within speech situations which occur among individuals who share languages, dialects, or language varieties.

Jan-Peter Blom and John J. Gumperz observe that to understand code-switching (for example, between a dialect and a standard language or between different languages), it is necessary to analyze the particular speech events in which switching occurs (1972:433). Descriptions of code-switching must include a statement as to the (1) setting, (2) social situation, and (3) social event in which the switching occurs. This detailing represents, "an attempt to explain the natives' conception of their behavioral environment in terms of an ordered set of constraints which operate to transform alternate lines of behavior into particular social meanings" (433).

Blom and Gumperz distinguish two types of code-switching (paraphrased from 424–425):

1.   *Situational switching* occurs within the same setting when the participants redefine the social event. For example, when two businessmen meet in New York City and begin a conversation in English, they may discover in the course of the conversation

that they are both native speakers of French. The situation is then redefined as one in which two Frenchmen meet on foreign soil. They might then switch to French while keeping the topic of conversation the same.

2. *Metaphorical switching* refers to a language switch which occurs in relation to "particular kinds of topics or subject matters rather than to change in social situation."

Brock Beardsley and Carol Eastman (1971), in an analysis of conversation between individuals bilingual in Swahili and English, also found that for metaphorical code-switching, the topic influences language choice. They observed further that the speakers' notions as to how relevant a particular topic is to one of their languages (as opposed to the other) influence their choice of language for that topic. For example, education was discussed by the bilingual individuals using a relatively high number of Swahili words, but they used more English to discuss racial prejudice, which the speakers regarded as not a problem to Tanzanians (1971:24).

Perhaps the most significant tendency noted by Beardsley and Eastman was that overt code-switches are accompanied by both markers and pauses in the utterance. MARKERS are words in an utterance which are meaningless in that context and cannot be considered part of either or any of the languages of the speaker (18). The markers may or may not, in other contexts, have meaning in one or other of the speaker's languages. In English, *like*, *let's see*, or *uh* are examples, as in, "It was, *uh*, a bird or a, *let's see*, plane but it was not superman." It might be that markers and pauses can be used to predict the likelihood of code-switches as well as anticipate predictors such a topic, speaker, setting, or position in the utterance where a metaphorical code-switch occurs.

In summary, the description of in-contact language situations of various types has involved psychological and sociological as well as linguistic factors. Descriptions of multilingualism, bilingualism, code-switching, and diglossia entail certain special notions such as interference, topic, setting, social situation, and social event in conjunction with components of descriptive sociolinguistics as outlined in the previous section.

Descriptions of differential language usage in a cultural setting containing in-contact linguistic results (bilingualism, multilingualism, diglossia, and code-switching) provide ethnographic information of a complexity not possible in a purely linguistic or purely ethnographic description of the same set of data. A linguistic or ethnographic description of a conversation between bilinguals, for example, would not include any statement of the sociolinguistic factors which might have influenced the description of the conversation, such as topic choice, linguistic variation, or code-switching. The strictly linguistic description would be restricted to an analysis of the transcribed phonology and grammar (morphology, syntax, lexicon) alone.

5.3   Social Dialects and Urban Dialectology

The study of social dialects is essentially the investigation and description of the use of speech *appropriately* in context (see Gumperz and Hymes 1972:11–14). Within a speech community, the study of social dialects investigates linguistic differences which may act as indicators of social class or ethnic identity. Social-dialect studies investigate the function of such socially related linguistic differences within a culture as well.

An early view of the importance of social dialects was the late Nancy Mitford's humorous and biting essay (1955) noting that British society has basically two linguistic divisions, "U" (upper class) and "non-U": "Dentures" are "non-U for false teeth . . . Britain: non-U for England" (Mitford 1956:27, 28).

Social dialects are to be differentiated from geographic or regional dialects, which are popularly referred to in the United States, for example, as "East Coast accent," "Southern accent," or "Chicago accent." Regional or geographic dialects such as these may be mapped according to phonological and morphological differences. The study of geographic dialects is called LINGUISTIC GEOGRAPHY. The study of social dialects may be referred to as URBAN DIALECTOLOGY.

Urban dialectology refers to that aspect of sociolinguistics which through "the adaptation of dialect survey techniques" studies "language usage in modern urban settings." Urban dialectology, then, is the study of social dialects in an urban setting, whereas the more general term SOCIAL-DIALECT STUDIES has a reference not so restricted (Gumperz and Hymes 1972:11).

In this section we will discuss a few well-known social-dialect studies done in a sociolinguistic framework: Labov's work in New York City as a speech community, Bernstein's controversial "elaborated" and "restricted" codes in England, Emeneau's report on the "Todas," and Ervin-Tripp's suggestions for writing rules for social dialects. These examples show the broad range of types of data used in the study of social dialects. Many other situations as well could have been included here as proper areas of sociolinguistic concern in social dialectology. Examples are studies of: glossolalia (speaking in tongues), the function and appropriateness of gesture and body movement in social speech (kinesics), the use of trick languages such as pig latin by children, the use of narrative events (tales, proverbs, myths) in particular cultures, situations wherein men's speech differs from women's speech, and specific situations such as the differential use of the definite article in French as spoken by speakers in Montreal.

Many other situations exist in which social dialects operate to assert ethnicity, class consciousness, and other aspects of identity such as religion, age, peer-group status, privilege, and seniority. Many examples of studies of social dialect including those mentioned here may be found in Gumperz and Hymes (1972), Hymes (1964), and Fishman (1968), and in more recent edited collections of sociolinguistic articles that appeared as this book went to press.

5.31   SOCIAL DIALECTS IN NEW YORK CITY

In 1964, William Labov completed his doctoral dissertation entitled "The Social Stratification of English in New York City." In an article published later (Labov 1968), he summarized some of his results, which will be noted here. Labov's dissertation is now published, and provides an example of a thorough-going sociolinguistic social-dialect study in an urban setting (see Labov 1966).

The survey carried out by Labov investigated the relationship of phonological variation among speakers of English in New York City to social variation among the same speakers. One of the variables investigated was the use of *r*, traditionally dropped in final position and before consonants (for example, /gɒːd/, homonymous with *god*, for /gard/ *guard*), which has led to the popular belief that "New Yawkahs have no ahs." It was found that recently it has become prestigious to pronounce *r* rather than drop it finally and before consonants. Labov surveyed a large sample of native New Yorkers to find out who—in social and socioeconomic terms such as occupation, education, and income—uses *r* and who does not, and in what situations *r* is dropped or retained. His hypothesis was that "any groups of New Yorkers that are ranked in a hierarchical scale by non-linguistic criteria will be ranked in the same order by their differential use of *r*" (1968:245).

Labov's hypothesis was borne out. He examined *r* in casual speech, careful speech, in reading, as pronounced in citation forms (in words in a list), and as elicited in minimal pairs of words with and without *r*. He found that all informants as they attempted to be more careful in speech tended to use *r* more; in other words, they tended to speak what they considered to be more prestigious English.

In a summary of Labov's findings with respect to *r*, Burling noted, "people who are relatively high in the social scale use *r* a good deal more readily than do those lower down. To the extent that the higher classes set the standard, it is obviously prestigious to use the *r*" (1970:94).

In casual speech only the upper-middle class (the highest class) used *r* with any regularity. Surprisingly, the lower-middle class in careful or formal speech used the prestigious *r* with more frequency than the upper-middle class. Labov sees such "hyper-correct" behavior of the lower-middle class as a "synchronic indicator of linguistic change in progress" (1968:245). Burling points out with respect to this finding, "Sociologically, members of the second highest group [lower-middle class] are the ones who are classically supposed to be uncertain of their own position. In their uncertainty they may overcompensate in trying to demonstrate prestigious forms" (1970:94).

All subjects under forty years of age agreed that *r* is prestigious whether or not they use it in daily speech, whereas among those over forty, some who used *r* thought it was prestigious and some did not (Labov 1968:247). The prestige-linked reintroduction of *r* in the speech of New Yorkers is a post-World War II development (that is, those under forty uniformly value its use), being carried forth as linguistic change largely through the values of the lower-middle class.

It appears that with respect to this particular phonological variable and others investigated by Labov, New York City represents "a single speech community, united by a uniform evaluation of linguistic features, yet diversified by increasing stratification in objective performance" (247).

Just this one example from Labov's broader study of linguistic differences within a speech community serves to indicate that "a speech community is not defined by any marked agreement in the use of language elements so much as by participation in a set of shared norms" (251). Thus, changing norms may be looked at as influencers and effecters of linguistic change.

5.32   ELABORATED AND RESTRICTED CODES

The study of the implications of the structuring of society for social-dialect differences constitutes another area of urban-dialect study. Best known for his work in this area is the British sociolinguist Basil Bernstein, who developed the notions of ELABORATED and RESTRICTED CODES. He distinguishes these terms by means of differences in range of alternatives available to speakers of each:

> These two codes may be distinguished on the linguistic level in terms of the probabilities of predicting, FOR ANY ONE SPEAKER, which structural elements will be used to organize meaning. In the case of an ELABORATED code the speaker will select from a relatively extensive range of alternatives, therefore the probability of predicting the pattern of organizing elements in ANY ONE SEQUENCE is considerably reduced. If a speaker is using a RESTRICTED code then the range of these alternatives is severely limited and the probability of predicting the pattern is greatly increased (1961, in Hymes 1964:259).

A restricted code *par excellence* would be a situation in which speech is totally predictable, as in some rituals or, as Bernstein states, in a play where all the actors have learned their parts. To the actors the play is a restricted code; to an audience, never having previously seen or read the play, it is an elaborated code; that is, the audience cannot predict what will be said, but the players are operating on cues (259).

To Bernstein, the word *code* involves the regulation of three communication processes: ORIENTATION (the hearer scans the message sent by the speaker), ASSOCIATION (the hearer matches the "signals" to those in his "signal store"), and ORGANIZATION (the hearer "integrates" the signals in order "to produce a sequential reply"). Bernstein holds that social structure determines whether the principles of orientation, association, and organization will result in elaborated or restricted codes in specific situations. He postulates, "The form of the social relationship acts selectively on the type of code which then becomes a symbolic expression of the relationship AND proceeds to regulate the nature of the interaction" (259).

In 1964, Bernstein published a study in which he investigated conversations of groups of English schoolboys in their teens in London from both the middle class and working class. He matched the boys in groups according to results on tests of verbal and nonverbal intelligence. Burling summarizes the differences found between the middle- and working-class boys as follows,

> Bernstein concludes that the working-class boys used short, grammatically simple sentences, often unfinished and having poor syntactical form. Working-class boys stressed the active as opposed to the passive voice. They used simple and repetitive conjunctions, and he believes that their limited variety of subordinate clauses made it difficult for them to break down the initial categories of the dominant subject. They were, he claims, unable to hold a formal subject through a speech sequence, and this brought difficulties in conveying information clearly. Their use of adjectives and adverbs was rigid and limited, and they used many statements where the conclusions were confounded. They used many phrases such as "wouldn't it?," "you see," "just fancy," which Bernstein interprets as reinforcing the idea of the preceding sentence (1970:164).

The working-class boys in Bernstein's study were seen to use a restricted code, whereas the middle-class boys used an elaborated code. To Bernstein, membership in the working class determines that working-class people speak with a restricted code; middle-class speakers have both the elaborated and restricted codes available to them. He sees the restricted code as a limiting factor for working-class people.

In Bernstein's view, his study has four major implications, each of which makes learning difficult and each of which points out that an elaborated code entails more complex verbal planning than a restricted code. The implications are (paraphrased from 1961:324):

1. A restricted code reinforces social relationship and group membership "rather than increasing the tension to signal individualized intent."
2. A restricted code limits the "range and type of others" with whom one can communicate or mutually understand.
3. A restricted code limits the ability of the speaker to "change the quality of the environment" through orienting oneself through speech or problem solving.
4. A restricted code prohibits lengthy "delay between impulse and signalling" and "does not facilitate the toleration of anxiety and the reduction of anxiety by appropriate signalling."

This study of Bernstein's has caused a good deal of controversy because of the magnitude of its implications. If it is the case that social structure does determine the type of linguistic code available to members of differing segments of society and that one's linguistic code affects one's ability to learn, it would appear, as Burling has noted, that, if we want to provide all children with equal opportunities, we will have to catch them very early so that we can give them enough enriched verbal experience to let them rise above the restricted code to which their own family and social class background would condemn them (1970:166).

Burling cautions that the conclusions drawn by Bernstein are based on rather limited observations. It is possible that the differences in code noted between his groups of working and middle-class boys might reflect differences in prior educational background and opportunity rather than imply likely causes of educational difficulty to come. In Burling's words again, "Bernstein has not effectively ruled out the possibility that he is measuring the EFFECT of educational deficiencies rather than their cause" (167). Burling also cautions that the possibility exists that the conversations elicited as data in the study presented a situation colored by middle-class expectations and might have inhibited the freedom of the working-class boys to respond freely and creatively.

Further, there are problems in defining social class such that it is difficult to see what constitutes working-class and middle-class membership. Bernstein's reliance on I.Q. tests of verbal and nonverbal skills as a means of matching his groups of speakers so as to rule out individual differences also leaves unaccounted for any differences which do not show up in such tests.

In a more recent study, Bernstein further develops his distinction between elaborated and restricted codes as part of "a general theory of the processes by which fundamental properties of social systems . . . are linked and maintained (or changed)" (1972:465). He believes that if one were to examine the relationships of a social group at work, in the community, and in its system of family roles, one could argue that "the genres of social class may well be carried not through a genetic code but through a communication code that social class itself promotes" (472). Bernstein reinforces his earlier views and claims that a child's communication code often directs him in ways that do not coincide with the communication code of the school system.

Much ethnographic research on the notions of elaborated and restricted codes is still needed. The idea of the two codes provides a rich testing ground for the development of sociolinguistic method and theory.

5.33   ORAL LITERATURE IN A SOCIAL SETTING

Another area which may be included in the study of social dialects in sociolinguistics is that of oral literature in relation to society. The study of the use of such oral genres as proverbs, tales, songs, and myths in social context falls into the general category of social-dialect study. How do proverbs influence such areas as social control? Who are the narrators in a society? What social events are accompanied by oral literary events? Folklore studies which attempt to integrate the lore within a social context may likewise by viewed as sociolinguistics.

Hymes refers to oral literature in a social setting under the term "Speech Play and Verbal Art," noting that studies in this area are relatively rare (1964:291–294). We have knowledge of word games and other aspects of oral literature often only from collections which ignore context, or as illustrative examples within ethnographies.

The study of oral literature in a sociolinguistic sense seeks to answer questions about the linguistic traits of the genre, the relationship of the verbal aspects of the literary language used to the ordinary use of language in the society, the function of the oral literature, the relationship of the oral literature to the society as a whole, and the cross-cultural occurrence of instances of various types of speech play and verbal art. It is outside the scope of this work to consider to any great extent the study of folklore as such. For our purposes here, the oral literature of the Todas, notably their songs, will be described as an instance of the type of oral literature in a social context which constitutes sociolinguistic subject matter.

Emeneau (1958) reports that while on a field trip to India in the 1930s in order to investigate the nonliterary languages of South India, he began his investigations among the Todas, known to speak an atypical language of the Dravidian language family. Early in his field work, Emeneau found that the Todas were very interested in their own songs: "I found that the utterances of greatest interest to the Todas themselves were their songs, and that here was a new example of oral poetry" (1958:316).

This aesthetic use of language through oral poetry in the form of songs was seen by Emeneau to function socially within Toda culture. His notice of this phenomenon and his decision to describe the relationship of Toda oral poetry to their culture mark an early form of sociolinguistic research.

Emeneau found that the subject matter of Toda songs reflects the culture and interests of the people and that "every theme in Toda culture and every detail of the working out of every theme have been provided with one or several set patterns of words and turns of phrase for use in song" (318). The songs of the Toda essentially comprise a "stereotyped two dimensional poetic language." The two dimensions are (1) the syntactic construction made up of sung units which consist of three syllables each, and (2) the fact that no syntactic construction may be sung "without being paired with another sentence exactly parallel to it in syntactic structure and in number of units" (317). Many things are sung of only in pairs. People's clan affiliations may have special three-syllable names for use in song.

The most common Toda songs are associated with funerals and review the life of the deceased. Also, Emeneau singled out weddings and wife-stealing as frequent subjects for songs, along with other domestic ceremonies and ceremonies associated with the seasons of dairy farming. Songs in Toda culture are so pervasive that every Toda is a composer. All events of significance are remembered in a highly formalized way in the traditional phraseology of their songs.

Emeneau reported that the culture of the Todas may be referred to as "closed." "The total impression given by the Todas is that in the course of centuries they have produced a culture marked by extreme elaboration of a smallish number of basic terms and that little of the detailed elaboration is not obligatory" (316). Their songs, as seen by Emeneau, reflect this closed nature of the society in that the song technique is limited. The songs are devoid of "accent, quantity, alliteration, rhyme" and rest on syllable-counting alone. The songs deal solely with the themes of the culture and are extremely formulaic in nature. Moreover, "If the culture is as nearly closed as I have said earlier, one of the factors making for this situation, perhaps only a minor one but still worth identifying as such, is, in all probability, the role that songs fill as censor" (322).

In addition to possibly reinforcing the closed nature of society, the songs of the Todas have the function of providing entertainment within the society.

The poetic technique of Toda songs is seen as "enigmatic-allusive," with each song dealing with a "single situation spoken of in terms of a generalization of Toda culture themes" (319). As an area of sociolinguistic concern rather than of chiefly literary concern, the Toda songs as oral poetry are interesting in that their technique "has as its aim a generalization of all that makes the Todas Todas." Emeneau makes the distinction that poetry with literary intent, on the other hand, aims at "universality" or "at the poet's individual expression of his own psyche" (324).

5.34   RULES IN SOCIOLINGUISTICS

Underlying all studies which may be construed to involve social dialects, and for that matter sociolinguistics, is the idea that speakers of a common language may have differing rule systems. We have seen that within the speech community of native New Yorkers some speakers have a rule for pronouncing *r* before consonants and in final position while others do not. We have seen that in differing social classes some speakers use the active voice more than the passive.

One of the consequences of differing sociolinguistic rule systems both within and among communities may be that speakers "misread each others' intentions" (Ervin-Tripp 1972:214). In social interaction, such misreading of intentions may cause serious problems, especially in urban areas, in schools, and in interaction between minority groups and society at large.

Ervin-Tripp suggests two types of rules for sociolinguistics: ALTERNATION RULES and CO-OCCURRENCE RULES. Alternation rules set out the sociolinguistic choices an individual has before him when he makes a decision or interpretation for appropriate verbal behavior. A case where alternation rules function is in the decision-making process involved in deciding whether or not to call another person in social intercourse by his title (and if so, which title), by his first name only, by his last name with title, and so forth.

Figure 12.
An Alternation Rule: Knowledge of Address of a
Competent Adult Member of a Western
American Academic Community* (from Ervin-
Tripp 1972:219)

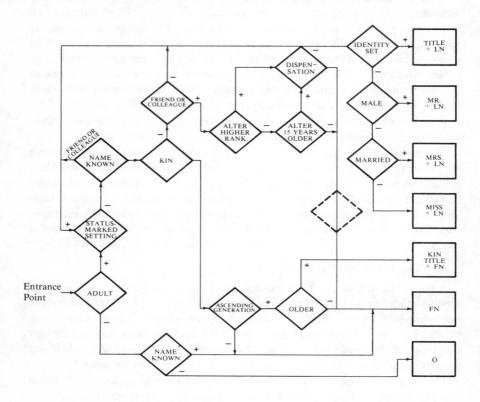

*FN = first name; LN = last name.

Ervin-Tripp dramatically shows the effect of the operation of alternation rules in a quotation from a report of an incident involving a black psychiatrist and a policeman (223):

"What's your name, boy?" the policeman asked. . . .
"Dr. Poussaint, I'm a physician. . . ."
"What's your first name, boy? . . ."
"Alvin."

This exchange represents an insult by the policeman to the physician which has its impact due to shared sociolinguistic alternation rules. Both the policeman and the physician "were familiar with an address system which contained a [social] selector available to both blacks and whites for insult condescension, or deference as needed" (223).

The decision sequence used by a speaker to choose which form of address to use or which way to interpret a form used in relation to him has been schematized by Ervin-Tripp and appears here as Figure 12. Each path leads to an alternative through a series of conditions of choice to be met (social selectors). In Figure 12, "The entrance point is on the left, and from left to right are a series of binary selectors. Each path through the diagram leads to a possible outcome, that is, one of the possible alternative forms of address" (219).

Despite such a wide range of alternatives in this chart, a shared language does not necessarily imply a shared set of alternatives. Indeed, for some speakers there is a broader range of alternatives and for some a narrower one. Much depends on the identity of the speaker-hearer. Every path has on it selectors, each of which marks where social categories present alternatives.

For our adult member of a Western academic community illustrated in Figure 12, social categories such as ±*status-marked setting*, ±*name known*, ±*kin*, ±*older*, ±*male*, and ±*friend or colleague* determine his range of alternatives as to what to call another person. For example, a person named Bobby Jones may be called *title Jones*, *Mr. Jones*, *Mrs. Jones*, *Miss Jones*, *kin title Bobby*, *Bobby*, or no name—depending upon the social relationship of the speaker to the Jones person.

Ervin-Tripp refers to the diagram as a rule, and states that it is "like a formal grammar in that it is a way of representing a logical model" (219). She suggests for sociolinguistics that alternatives, especially with respect to address systems, be compared cross-culturally. Eventually it may be possible to typologize systems of address with reference to universal social selectors (compare with universal phonological features and universal semantic features, discussed in previous chapters), options allowed, types of outcome, and so on. The development of rules of alternation in sociolinguistic contexts (such as situations calling for decisions as to appropriate terms of address) involves the "selection of lexical items, pronouns, or inflectional alternatives" in decisions about "social selectors" (1972:233).

Another example of language alternation within a changing context is the use of the familiar second-person singular pronouns *tu* and *du* (symbolized as *T*) in French and German versus the polite forms *vos*, *vous*, and *Sie* (symbolized as *V*). Originally, in Latin *tu* referred to the second-person singular and *vos* to the second-person plural. The original use of *vos* in the singular was only when speaking to the emperor. Today, both the *T* and *V* terms are used to refer to the second-person singular in accord with an alternation rule with reference not to status (as was the original case using *vos* to address the emperor) but to solidarity. Brown and Gilman (1960) interviewed fifty Parisian students studying in the Boston area, in order to see what factors governed both the wide and narrow use of the familiar second-person singular pronoun *tu*. They found out that the more radical the social and political ideology of the students, the more widely *tu* (familiar) rather than *vous* (polite or formal) was used. The radical social and political view was characterized by denial of any distinctions among people based on such factors as religion, race, nationality, ownership of property, and the like. Such a person, on Eysenck's Social Attitude Inventory (1957), "disapproves of any absolute line separating the solidary, the 'in-group,' from the nonsolidary, the 'out-group' " (Brown 1965:67).

According to Brown, the use of a single pronoun *tu* to refer to all people is an expression of solidarity among those who share such an ideology and is, in fact, an expression of that ideology. It is interesting that the pronoun generalized is the familiar one. In Brown's view, the extension of the pronoun which is used between brothers, sisters, and close friends, to a usage between all people "expresses the radical's intention to extend the in-group, solidary ethic to everyone" (1965:61).

In addition to rules of alternation in sociolinguistics, there are also rules of co-occurrence. Co-occurrence rules deal with the predictability of later occurrences in context of a selection made by means of an alternation rule. Horizontal co-occurrence rules specify "relations between items [lexical or structural] sequentially in the discourse." Vertical co-occurrence rules specify "the realization of an item at each of the levels of structure of a language" (Ervin-Tripp 1972:233).

For example, for a person who is bilingual in German and English such as a speaker of Pennsylvania German, a syntactic co-occurrence rule might reflect German while the lexicon is English. As Ervin-Tripp states, the structure is predictable independent of the lexicon, as in, *Di kau ist over di fens jumpt.*

The code-switching by speakers of more than one language discussed earlier in this chapter often involves the retention of horizontal co-occurrence rules of word-order (syntax) for one language while lexical items are plugged in from another language.

In the same discussion, Ervin-Tripp exemplifies vertical co-occurrence rules with the following example in which the rules are violated:

> "How's it going, Your Eminence? Centrifuging o.k.? Also have you been analyzin' whatch 'unnertook t'achieve?''

The main violation in this example is the co-occurrence of casual speech such as *how's it going?* with the deferential address form used only to a cardinal of the Church. Other violations are the pronunciation of the /g/ of the *-ing* on *going* in *how's it going?* while the /g/ of the *-ing* on *analyzing* is dropped. One would expect the reverse. In addition, Ervin-Tripp notes further violations:

   b.   An elliptical construction is used in the second utterance, which contains only a participle, but the formal "-ing" appears again ["centrifuging ok?"]

    c.   A technical word, "centrifuge," is used in the elliptical construction [where in an ellipsis technical words are not expected]

    d.   The "-in" suffix is used with the formal "analyze"

    e.   Rapid informal articulation is used for the pedantic phrase "undertook to achieve" [ordinarily expected to be articulated carefully] (234)

The example, showing violations of co-occurrence rules, represents a "sociolinguistically deviant utterance":

> Like ungrammatical sentences, sociolinguistically deviant utterances become normal if one can define setting and personnel to locate them . . . wherever there are regular co-occurrences, deviant behavior is marked and calls attention to its social meaning (234).

The deviant behavior of the utterance cited may be seen as normal if "one pictures a cardinal in a microbiology laboratory addressed by a janitor who knows technical terms but cannot fully control formal syntax and phonology" (234).

    These suggestions for viewing sociolinguistic data as representing rule systems provide a means of noting differences in speech style. Co-occurrence rules and alternation rules apply to the speech of monolinguals when they use different social dialects in different situations. There are rules to be defined for how to address a public meeting, rules for dealing with one's employer, and rules for speaking during a bridge game. Co-occurrence and alternation rules may be seen to operate as well in the speech of bilinguals and multilinguals in varying contexts. Indeed, both code-switching and diglossia involve the use of such proposed sociolinguistic rules. Diglossia, as discussed earlier, is the co-occurrence of two versions of one language within one speech community, wherein rules for the use of each or a combination of both play an integral role.

5.4   National-Language Policies

    Another area in which sociolinguistic study plays an important role is LANGUAGE PLANNING. Language planning may be viewed as "the activity of preparing a normative orthography, grammar, and dictionary for the guidance of writers and speakers in a non-homogenous speech community" (Haugen 1959:8).

    Very often language planning involves decisions regarding the development of national languages and, in effect, acts to standardize languages. A number of factors of a sociolinguistic nature must be considered in the area of language planning; indeed, there are various sociolinguistic situations from which a particular one or a particular combination of situations is chosen as the norm.

    In a nonhomogenous speech community, some or all of the following ten situations may prevail (1951 Report of the UNESCO Meeting of Specialists, "The Use of Vernacular Languages in Education," in Fishman 1968:689–690):

1. *Indigenous Language:* "the language of the people considered to be the original inhabitants of an area."
2. *Lingua Franca:* "a language which is used habitually by people whose mother tongues are different in order to facilitate communication between them."
3. *Mother or Native Tongue:* "the language which a person acquires in early years and which normally becomes his natural instrument of thought and communication."
4. *National Language:* "the language of a political, social and cultural entity."
5. *Official Language:* "a language used in the business of government—legislative, executive, and judicial."
6. *Pidgin:* "a language which has arisen as the result of contact between peoples of different language, usually formed from a mixing of the languages."
7. *Regional Language:* "a language which is used as a medium of communication between peoples living within a certain area who have different mother tongues."
8. *Second Language:* "a language acquired by a person in addition to his mother tongue."
9. *Vernacular Language:* "a language which is the mother tongue of a group which is socially or politically dominated by another group speaking a different language."
10. *World Language:* "a language used over wide areas of the world."

The linguistic diversity represented by these ten sociolinguistic situations involves the interrelationship of language for wider communication purposes with what may be looked at as an aspect of ethnic identity, one's mother tongue. Language planning aims to reconcile mother-tongue loyalty with the need of a speech community to operate efficiently and uniformly; but all planning must be sensitive to the cultural diversity reflected in such sociolinguistic situations when decisions are made as to what language is to become a national language, a lingua franca, official language, or the like.

In a given speech community the particular sociolinguistic situations (of the ten) which exist may be seen to comprise a system of language types. Decisions about standardization in such a community ideally seek to arrive at a "common national norm" (Guxman, in Fishman 1968:778). However, often linguistic diversity is so broad that the ideal is beyond reach. Language planning then must be directed toward designing "a rational language policy which is both just and flexible" (Darnell 1971:28).

In some cases, choosing a national language may involve a choice between or among languages already standardized. English has long had an orthography, grammar, and dictionary which is standard along with many spoken dialects quite different from the standard in many parts of the world. Swahili, an East African Bantu language, has been under a program of standardization for much of this century under the aegis of the Inter-territorial Language Committee established in East Africa in 1930 on a formal basis (Whiteley 1969:82). For example, in Kenya Swahili was chosen as the national language in the late 1960s and implemented in the early 1970s following a period when English had been the official language there. Swahili had long been a lingua franca in the area, and a number of vernacular languages were spoken throughout the country. In fact, Kikuyu and Luo, the former a Bantu language as is Swahili and the latter non-Bantu, were spoken widely in the capital city and its environs as indigenous languages by the country's politically most significant groups.

When Kenya achieved independence on December 12, 1963, it faced three problems simultaneously:

1.   developing a feeling of ethnic identity as Kenyans among her people
2.   legitimizing her government's authority
3.   justifying the authority of the Kenyan government over the Kenyan people

The authorities became convinced that a uniform national and official language for both the people and the government would help solve these problems. The Ministry of Education and the Ministry of Community Development and National Culture were designated by the government to develop Swahili as the national language. A number of problems were encountered, many having to do with a simultaneously national cultural revival of traditional dances and songs as part of the new nationalism.

The greatest strength of Swahili in pre-independent Kenya was that the language was not associated with any tribal unit; the culture associated with Swahili as a mother tongue was that of an Islamic coastal community. However, of the fifty-six or so local languages of Kenya in addition to Swahili, each represented its own regional culture and each was encouraged as part of the cultural revival. Coastal speakers of Swahili as a mother tongue felt that up-country speakers of Swahili as a lingua franca would corrupt their language. Urban Kikuyu and Luo speakers were reluctant to use the language as their national language, which for them would have to be learned as a second language, only to be ridiculed by their rural countrymen, for whom it was a mother tongue.

On July 26, 1969, the *Daily Nation* newspaper of Nairobi, Kenya, quoted the Attorney General of Kenya as saying that about 40 percent of the people in Kenya did not even know a word of Swahili and that it would be impossible to compel this number to speak it. On contentions that Kenya was an independent nation and ought to discontinue using English because it was a foreign, and moreover a colonial, language, the Attorney General stated to Parliament:

> Let us all agree and not deceive ourselves that Swahili is an African language. It is Arabic and if I had to do away with all foreign languages, then Swahili would be one of them. . . . If I had to speak Swahili in this House tomorrow then a lot of problems would arise. Nearly every MP has his own way of speaking Swahili and to use it in Parliament

would make this House like that of Babel, where nobody would understand what the other said (*Daily Nation*, July 26, 1969).

The position of Swahili as the national language of Kenya is now a fact, and this sociolinguistic situation alters the linguistic diversity in Kenya. Such a situation is rich in data for the sociolinguist. One might now ask regarding Kenya: Is the national language standard changing as a result of Swahili having been both a mother tongue and a lingua franca? How is Swahili being "planned" as a tool of communication for Kenyans who have another mother tongue and no knowledge of Swahili beyond some acquaintance with it as a lingua franca? How has Swahili as the national language come to terms, as an official language as well, with English, the replaced official language?

Such questions arising from changes in language policy form an area of legitimate sociolinguistic inquiry, in addition to the areas discussed above of bilingualism, multilingualism, and social or urban dialectology. The inquiry entails the study of sociolinguistic situations within a speech community which determine the identity of the speech community as such.

Language-planning research examines linguistic diversity and the development of language policies within social and political contexts. Many situations exist in the world where this type of sociolinguistic research has relevance; for example, the case of French and English in Canada, the situation in Belgium, and the phenomenon of language riots in India.[1]

In conclusion, we will look at one further example of linguistic diversity where such research is needed—that of New Guinea, which has considerable linguistic diversity and whose national language is Melanesian pidgin English. With approximately 700 languages spoken in New Guinea and with a pidgin as the national language, feelings of nationalism, patriotism, and a common goal are extremely hard to inculcate. This lack of an adequate national language and the problems relating to it, both political and social, provide a situation standing to benefit greatly from language-planning research.

R. F. Salisbury (1962) has noted, however, that New Guinea has "cultural and interactional homogeneity" in sharp contrast to linguistic diversity. He worked with speakers of the Siane language of the Siane-Gahuku-Bena language family. Specifically, Salisbury's work was with the Emenyo tribe. The Emenyo speak the Komunku dialect of Siane. Villages bordering on those of the Emenyo, however, speak the Dene language (of the Chimbu-Dene subfamily of the Chimbu-Hagen family) and Kamfau, another dialect of Siane. Thus, many Emenyo can speak not

---

[1]See Fishman's edited *Readings in the Sociology of Language* (1968), especially Section VII, "The Social Contexts and Consequences of Language Planning," for a number of articles reporting on this type of research.

only Siane dialects, but also dialects of Dene from a totally different language family.

The following situation is reported by Salisbury to occur on formal occasions involving Komunku speakers and those from another speech community:

> In such situations, each formal speech would be followed immediately by a translation of it into the other language. The same pattern is followed when Administration officials speaking only Pidgin, or when Lutheran missionaries speaking only the coastal Kate language are present (1962:3).

Salisbury cites a church service which he attended in a Siane-speaking area conducted by a Dene-speaking catechist who had learned also to speak Kate, a coastal language not indigenous to the Highlands. The Lutheran missionary delivered his sermon in Kate. The catechist translated it from Kate to Dene, and a Siane-speaking Emenyo translated the Dene into Siane. In the catechist's translation into Dene, some pidgin was thrown in for the benefit of the Europeans present who understood pidgin but spoke English with one another. Such frequent translations made in public social contexts from language to language provide "a linguistic means of emphasizing the importance and public nature of the discourse" (4).

Salisbury interprets the use of diverse languages among the Emenyo and their neighbors as a ploy "used in the competitive oneupmanship involved in most spheres of social relationship"(4). The ability to translate from language to language ascribes to the translator varying degrees of status dependent upon which languages the individual has at his command. The New Guinean sociolinguistic situation also creates a showplace for displaying an "intensity of local patriotism and ethnocentrism regarding the local dialect." The situation is one in which "Linguistic differentiation and change would be given added impetus by political rivalries between groups, while existing speech barriers are encouraged by individuals wishing to prove their ability to learn difficult, exotic languages" (11).

The Emenyo who knows his own local language and can translate the languages of nearby villages has a high status and, as long as his neighbors do not know his local language, that status is maintained. If one of the neighboring languages were to be ascribed political prestige, again the status of the Emenyo would be in contest and a rivalry would develop. This situation is just one of many in New Guinea, which provides a rich research area focusing on the problems of language and politics, linguistic diversity, and sociolinguistic attitudes.

5.5   Summary

We have examined the field of sociolinguistics with respect to its study of how language is used in a variety of social settings. The sociolinguist may be seen as a scientist who is interested in the use functions of language. He studies language "as human communication sensitive to the social contexts in which it is carried out" (Cole and Scribner 1974:60).

Sociolinguistics, in its concern for what speakers of languages or dialects need to know in order to communicate effectively in their cultures, is contributing toward an answer to the question of the relationship of language to culture at the level of performance. The field of sociolinguistics studies questions such as, What do we say when we do X and what do we do when we say Y? Currently, sociolinguistics is concerned with observational adequacy, attempting to describe the data of language in context. Eventually, the sociolinguist hopes to be able to account for what underlies the use of language in context, to meet the criterion of descriptive adequacy through setting up rules such as those proposed by Ervin-Tripp, and others more recently, for linguistic choices made in various settings.

Certain areas of sociolinguistic investigation are complementary to psycholinguistic investigation, especially with regard to Bernstein's sociolinguistic study of elaborated and restricted codes (Section 5.32) and Cohen's study of analytic and relational conceptual styles (Section 4.11). Cohen found, in her attempt to delineate cognitive style, that sociocultural factors influenced the development of ways of thinking. She concluded that cultural factors, including language, influenced conceptual style. In his attempt to relate speech style to social structure, Bernstein found that cognitive factors entered in, and concluded that social factors determined the linguistic code available to his subjects. Both studies, however controversial, point out certain problems of learning as reinforced in the schools. The conceptual styles used in schools present difficulties for many learners, whether for linguistic, social, or psychological reasons.

Perhaps of all the areas of the investigation of language and culture surveyed in this book, sociolinguistics is the most practically applicable. Results of sociolinguistic inquiry can immediately be seen to contribute to a clearer understanding of people interacting with people. Labov's work on the type of phonological differences which people within a speech community recognize among members of their own cultural milieu provides an understanding of notions such as prestige in language. Bernstein's study of the language differences among schoolboys has turned much attention toward developing programs to effect learning in schools despite language problems. Emeneau's study of the context of songs in the Toda culture has shown how the form, function, and content of a people's lore reflect cultural values.

It is becoming increasingly more necessary for all folklorists to study and analyze their data in context. Many of the recently published works of folklore employ the method of the ethnography of speaking in their data analysis. Today, few and far between are collections of tales being published as such. Genres of folklore are seen as oral events and are described in the context of the performance of the work—whether myth, tale, proverb, story, or song. A description also takes into account the setting, the participants, and the audience. The oral literary event so transcribed and described is then further analyzed in terms of how the lore functions in the larger ethnographic context of the culture. A recent study of narrative events among Mayan-speaking peoples in Yucatan (Burns 1973) further exemplifies the sociolinguistic analysis of folklore.

The sociolinguistic study of choices available to speakers in terms of style, the use of more than one language, and the phenomenon of code-switching, along with the investigation of methods of language planning and developing language policy, all represent new areas of investigation which show great promise in making contributions to education, government, and to society in general.

Afterword

"Language and Culture" as the anthropological context of linguistics has been shown to be a very broadly defined area. Yet, certain questions have guided most of the theoretical and practical approaches to the great variety of research that has been conducted:

1. How can languages and cultures be described adequately?
2. How can languages and cultures be classified in order to demonstrate relationships among them?
3. What is the history of language, of different languages, of culture, and of different cultures?
4. What does the structure of cultural phenomena (including language) tell us about the underlying logical structure of consciousness?
5. How are language and culture acquired?
6. What are the rules of language and culture acquisition?
7. What relationship does language and culture acquisition have to the development of the mind, of thought?
8. What is meaning?
9. Does language structure structure thought? Does thought structure structure language? How are language and thought related to "reality"?
10. What is thought? How are perception and memory related to language? How is language related to perception and memory?
11. What part does social context play in linguistic and cultural behavior?
12. How is language use and cultural behavior to be described in context?
13. What effect do bilingualism, multilingualism, and governmental language policy have on society?

Throughout the book, my focus has been to view these questions mainly from the linguist's vantage point within the context of the anthropologist's milieu. In so doing, some areas of inquiry and research on the problems raised by these questions have been slighted or altogether omitted. In large part I did not consider the psychological approaches to these questions, notably the contributions of Jean Piaget. I mentioned only a few experiments designed to test the Whorf Hypothesis. Work on neurolinguistics was not reviewed, and I mentioned only briefly studies of hemispheric dominance in the brain. I included no discussion of Sydney Lamb's stratificational grammar, little discussion regarding specific studies of child language acquisition, and none at all regarding language loss through aphasia. I touched only slightly on the field of artificial intelligence, which is also considering many of these same questions using the computer to simulate both verbal and nonverbal behavior. In fact, in this review of the various aspects of language and culture in the anthropological context, I have ignored for the most part cybernetic modelling of the phenomena at issue. The field of communications (including general systems theory and information theory) and the philosophy of science are also addressing these same questions.

I have attempted in the preceding pages to show which linguistic theories and approaches have been and are still being applied to the study of cultural data and to indicate certain directions along these lines that continuing research might take.

Bibliography

Bach, Emmon. *An Introduction to Transformational Grammars*. Holt, Rinehart and Winston, 1964.

Bascom, William. "Some Aspects of Yoruba Urbanism." *American Anthropologist* 64(1962):699–708.

Beals, Ralph L., and Harry Hoijer. *An Introduction to Anthropology*. 3rd ed. Macmillan, 1965.

Beardsley, R. Brock, and Carol M. Eastman. "Markers, Pauses and Code Switching in Bilingual Tanzanian Speech." *General Linguistics* 11(1971):17–27.

Berlin, Brent. "A Universalist-Evolutionary Approach in Ethnographic Semantics." *Current Directions in Anthropology* [Bulletin of the American Anthropological Association] 3(1970):3–18.

Berlin, Brent, and Paul Kay. "Universality and Evolution of Basic Color Terms." Working Paper #1, Laboratory for Language-Behavior Research, University of California, Berkeley, 1967; and in *Basic Color Terms: Their Universality and Evolution*. University of California Press, 1969.

Bernstein, Basil. "Aspects of Language and Learning in the Genesis of the Social Process." *Journal of Child Psychology and Psychiatry* 1(1961):313–324.

———."Elaborated and Restricted Codes: Their Social Origins and Some Consequences." In John J. Gumperz and Dell Hymes (eds.), 1964, pp. 55–69.

———. Postscript to "Aspects of Language and Learning in the Genesis of the Social Process." In Dell Hymes (ed.), 1964, pp. 259–260.

———. "A Sociolinguistic Approach to Socialization: With Some Reference to Educability." In John J. Gumperz and Dell Hymes (eds.), 1972, pp. 465–497.

Black, Mary, and Duane Metzger. "Ethnographic Description and the Study of Law." Special Publication of the *American Anthropologist* 6(1965):141–165; and in Stephen Tyler (ed.), 1969, pp. 137–164.

Bloch, Bernard, and George L. Trager. *Outline of Linguistic Analysis*. Linguistic Society of America, 1942.

Blom, Jan-Peter, and John J. Gumperz. "Social Meaning in Linguistic Structure: Code Switching in Norway." In John J. Gumperz and Dell Hymes (eds.), 1972, pp. 407–434.

Bloomfield, Leonard. *Language*. Holt, Rinehart and Winston, 1933.

Boas, Franz. *"Classification of American Indian Languages." Language* 5(1929):1–7.

————. *Handbook of American Indian Languages*. Bulletin #40, Bureau of American Ethnology, U.S. Government Printing Office, 1911.

Bonfante, G., and Thomas A. Sebeok. "Linguistics and the Age and Area Hypothesis." *American Anthropologist* 46(1944):382–386.

Brown, Roger William. *Social Psychology*. The Free Press, 1965.

————. *Words and Things*. The Free Press, 1958.

————, and A. Gilman. "The Pronouns of Power and Solidarity." In T. A. Sebeok (ed.), *Style in Language*. M.I.T. Technology Press, 1960.

————, and E. H. Lenneberg. "A Study in Language and Cognition." *Journal of Abnormal and Social Psychology* 49(1954):454–462; and in Sol Saporta (ed.), 1961, pp. 480–492.

Bruner, Jerome S., and Jeremy M. Anglin, ed. *Beyond the Information Given*. Studies in the Psychology of Knowing. W. W. Norton, 1973.

————, R. R. Olver, P. M. Greenfield, et al. *Studies in Cognitive Growth*. John Wiley, 1966.

Burling, Robbins. "Cognition and Componential Analysis: God's Truth or Hocus-pocus?" *American Anthropologist* 66(1964):20–28; and in Stephen Tyler (ed.), 1969, pp. 419–428.

————. "Linguistics and Ethnographic Description." *American Anthropologist* 71 (1969):817–827.

————. *Man's Many Voices: Language in Its Cultural Context*. Holt, Rinehart and Winston, 1970.

Burns, Alan F. "Pattern and Style in Yucatec Mayan Narrative Events." Unpublished Ph.D. dissertation, University of Washington, Seattle, 1973.

Carmack, Robert H. "Ethnohistory: A Review of Its Development, Definitions, Methods, and Aims." *Annual Review of Anthropology* 1(1972):227–246.

Carroll, John B., ed. *Language, Thought, and Reality: Selected Writings of Benjamin Lee Whorf*. M.I.T. Technology Press, 1956.

————, and Joseph B. Casagrande. "The Function of Language Classifications in Behavior." In E. E. Maccoby, T. H. Newcomb, and E. L. Hartley (eds.), *Readings in Social Psychology*. 3rd ed. Holt, Rinehart and Winston, 1958, pp. 18–31; and in Alfred G. Smith (ed.), *Communication and Culture*. Holt, Rinehart and Winston, 1966, pp. 489–514.

Chomsky, Noam. *Aspects of a Theory of Syntax*. M.I.T. Press, 1965.

————. *Cartesian Linguistics*. Harper & Row, 1966.

————. *Language and Mind*. Enlarged ed. Harcourt Brace Jovanovich, 1972.

————. *Syntactic Structures*. Mouton, The Hague, 1957; Humanities Press, 1957.

————, and Morris Halle. *The Sound Pattern of English*. Harper & Row, 1968.

————. "The Logical Basis of Linguistic Theory." In *Proceedings of the 9th International Congress of Linguists*. Mouton, The Hague, 1964, pp. 914–978.

Clignet, Remi. "A Critical Evaluation of Concomitant Variation Studies." In Raoul Naroll and Ronald Cohen (eds.), *A Handbook of Method in Cultural Anthropology*. Columbia University Press, 1973, pp. 597–619.

Cohen, Rosalie A. "Conceptual Styles, Culture Conflict, and Nonverbal Tests of Intelligence." *American Anthropologist* 71(1969):828–856.

Cole, Michael, and Sylvia Scribner. *Culture and Thought: A Psychological Introduction*. John Wiley, 1974.

Collins, Robert O. *Problems in African History*. Prentice-Hall, 1968, pp. 57–113.

Daily Nation, The. Nairobi, Kenya. July 26, 1969.

Darnell, Regna, ed. *Linguistic Diversity in Canadian Societies*. Linguistic Research, 1971.

————. "Sociolinguistic Perspectives on Linguistic Diversity." In Regna Darnell (ed.), 1971, pp. 15–29.

Davy, John. "Chomsky Revolution." *London Observer*. August 10, 1969.

deCourtenay, Baudouin. *Versuch einer Theorie der Phonetischen Alternationen*. 1895.

deGeorge, Richard, and Fernande deGeorge, eds. *The Structuralists from Marx to Lévi-Strauss*. Doubleday, Anchor Books, 1972.

deSaussure, Ferdinand. *Cours de Linguistique Générale (Course in General Linguistics)*. (1st ed. 1916) McGraw-Hill, The Philosophical Library, 1966.

DeVito, Joseph A. *Psycholinguistics*. The Bobbs-Merrill Studies in Communicative Disorders, 1971.

Dunnell, Robert C. *Systematics in Prehistory*. The Free Press, 1971.

Eggan, Fred. "Social Anthropology and the Method of Controlled Comparison." *American Anthropologist* 56(1954):743–763.

Ehrmann, Jacques, ed. *Structuralism*. Trans. by Thomas G. Penchoen. Doubleday, Anchor Books, 1970.

Emeneau, Murray B. "India as a Linguistic Area." *Language* 32(1956):3–16; and in Dell Hymes (ed.), 1964, pp. 642–650.

————. "Oral Poets of South India—the Todas." *Journal of American Folklore* 71 (1958):312–324; and in Dell Hymes (ed.), 1964, pp. 330–340.

Ervin-Tripp, Susan. "On Sociolinguistic Rules: Alternation and Co-occurrence." In John J. Gumperz and Dell Hymes (eds.), 1972, pp. 213–250.

Farb, Peter. *Word Play: What Happens When People Talk*. Alfred A. Knopf, 1974.

Feigenbaum, Edward A., and Julian Feldman, eds. *Computers and Thought*. McGraw-Hill, 1963.

Ferguson, Charles A. "Diglossia." *Word* 15(1959):325–340; and in Dell Hymes (ed.), 1964, pp. 429–439.

Fishman, Joshua A. "Domains between Micro- and Macro-Sociolinguistics." In John J. Gumperz and Dell Hymes (eds.), 1972, pp. 435–453.

————, ed. *Readings in the Sociology of Language*. Mouton, The Hague, 1968; Humanities Press, 1968.

————. "A Systematization of the Whorfian Hypothesis." *Behavioral Science* 5(1960): 323–339.

Fodor, Jerry A., and Jerrold J. Katz. *The Structure of Language: Readings in the Philosophy of Language*. Prentice-Hall, 1964.

Fox, Robin. *Encounter with Anthropology*. Harcourt Brace Jovanovich, 1973.

Frake, Charles O. "The Diagnosis of Disease Among the Subanun of Mindanao." *American Anthropologist* 63(1961):113–132; and in Dell Hymes (ed.), 1964, pp. 193–211.

————. "The Eastern Subanun of Mindanao." In G. P. Murdock (ed.), *Social Structure in Southeast Asia*. Quadrangle Books, 1960.

————. "The Ethnographic Study of Cognitive Systems." In T. Gladwin and W. C. Sturtevant (ed.), 1962, pp. 72–85, 91–93; and in Stephen Tyler (ed.), 1969, pp. 28–39.

Fried, V., ed. *The Prague School of Linguistics and Language Teaching*. Oxford University Press, 1972.

Gladwin, T., and W. C. Sturtevant, eds. *Anthropology and Human Behavior*. Anthropological Society of Washington, 1962.

Gleason, H. A. *An Introduction to Descriptive Linguistics*. Rev. ed. Holt, Rinehart and Winston, 1961.

————. *Workbook in Descriptive Linguistics*. Holt, Rinehart and Winston, 1955.

Goldenweiser, Alexander A. *Early Civilization*. Alfred A. Knopf, 1922.

Goodenough, Ward. "Componential Analysis and the Study of Meaning." *Language* 32(1956):195–216.

————. "Cultural Anthropology and Linguistics." *Monograph Series on Language and Linguistics*, #9. Georgetown University Press, 1957.

————. "Introduction." *Explorations in Cultural Anthropology*. McGraw-Hill, 1964.

————. "Yankee Kinship Terminology: A Problem in Componential Analysis." In Eugene Hammell (ed.), 1965, pp. 259–287.

Greenfield, Patricia Marks, and Jerome S. Bruner. "Culture and Cognitive Growth." *International Journal of Psychology* 1(1966):89–107.

Greenberg, Joseph H. *Anthropological Linguistics: An Introduction*. Random House, 1968.

————. *Essays in Linguistics*. University of Chicago Press, 1957.

Gudschinsky, Sarah. "The ABCs of Lexicostatistics (Glottochronology)." *Word* 12 (1956):175–210; and in Dell Hymes (ed.), 1964, pp. 612–622.

Gumperz, John J., and Dell Hymes. *Directions in Sociolinguistics: The Ethnography of Communication*. Holt, Rinehart and Winston, 1972.

————, eds. *The Ethnography of Communication*. Special Publication of *American Anthropologist* 66(1964).

Guxman, M. M. "Some General Regularities in the Formation and Development of National Languages." In Joshua A. Fishman (ed.), 1968, pp. 766–779.

Hammell, Eugene, ed. *Formal Semantic Analysis*. Special Publication of *American Anthropologist* 67(1965).

Harris, Marvin. *The Rise of Anthropological Theory: A History of Theories of Culture*. Crowell, 1968.

Harris, Zellig. *Structural Linguistics*. University of Chicago Press, 1951.

Haugen, Einar. "Language Planning in Modern Norway." *Scandinavian Studies* 33 (1961): 68–81; as "Planning for a Standard Language in Modern Norway," *Anthropological Linguistics* 1(1959):8–21; and in Joshua A. Fishman (ed.), 1968, pp. 673–687 .

Hays, David G. "The Meaning of a Term Is a Function of the Theory in Which It Occurs." Unpublished paper, State University of New York, Buffalo, 1973.

Herskovits, Melville J. *The Human Factor in Changing Africa*. Alfred A. Knopf, 1962.

Hunn, E. "Tzeltal Folk Zoology: The Classification of Discontinuities in Nature." Unpublished Ph.D. dissertation, University of California, Berkeley, 1973.

Hymes, Dell. "The Ethnography of Speaking." In T. Gladwin and W. C. Sturtevant (eds.), 1962, pp. 13–53; and in Joshua A. Fishman (ed.), 1968, pp. 99–138.

————, ed. *Language in Culture and Society: A Reader in Linguistics and Anthropology*. Harper & Row, 1964.

————. "Lexicostatistics So Far." *Current Anthropology* 1(1960):3–44.

————. "Models of the Interaction of Language and Social Life." In John J. Gumperz and Dell Hymes (eds.), 1972, pp. 35–71.

————. "Models of the Interaction of Language and Social Setting." *Journal of Social Issues* 23(1967):8–28.

Jackendoff, Ray S. *Semantic Interpretation in Generative Grammar*. M.I.T. Press, Studies in Linguistics Series, 1972.

Jakobson, Roman. "What Can Typological Studies Contribute to Historical Comparative Linguistics?" In *Proceedings of the 8th International Congress of Linguists*. Oslo University Press, 1958, pp. 17–25.

————, and Morris Halle. *Fundamentals of Language*. Mouton, 1956.

Katz, Jerrold J. *The Philosophy of Language*. Harper & Row, 1966.

————. "Semantic Theory." In Jerrold J. Katz, 1966, pp. 151–175.

————, and Jerry A. Fodor. "The Structure of a Semantic Theory." In Jerry A. Fodor and Jerrold J. Katz (eds.), 1964, pp. 479–518.

Kay, Paul. "Comments on Colby." [From Paul Kay, "Comment," on B. N. Colby, "Ethnographic Semantics: A Preliminary Survey." *Current Anthropology* 7(1966): 20–23.] In Stephen Tyler (ed.), 1969, pp. 78–89.

————. "Some Theoretical Implications of Ethnographic Semantics." Working Paper #24, Laboratory for Language-Behavior Research, University of California, Berkeley, 1969.

Keesing, Roger, and Felix Keesing. *New Perspectives in Cultural Anthropology*. Holt, Rinehart and Winston, 1971.

Kluckhohn, Clyde. "Universal Categories of Culture." In A. L. Kroeber (ed.), *Anthropology Today*. University of Chicago Press, 1953, pp. 507–523.

Kroeber, A. L. "The Culture-Area and Age-Area Concepts of Clark Wissler." In S. Rice (ed.), *Methods in Social Science*. University of Chicago Press, 1931, pp. 248–265.

————. "Culture and Natural Areas of Native North America." *University of California Publications in American Archaeology and Ethnology*, vol. 38. 1939.

———— "Linguistic Time Depth Results So Far and Their Meaning." *International Journal of American Linguistics* 21(1955):91–104.

Labov, William. "The Reflection of Social Processes in Linguistic Structures." In Joshua A. Fishman (ed.), 1968, pp. 240–251.

————. *The Social Stratification of English in New York City*. Center for Applied Linguistics, 1966.

Lakoff, George. "On Generative Semantics." In Danny D. Steinberg and Leon A. Jacobovits (eds.), 1971, pp. 232–296.

Landar, Herbert. *Language and Culture*. Oxford University Press, 1966.

Langacker, Ronald W. *Language and Its Structure*. Harcourt, Brace and World, 1968.

Langness, L. L. *The Study of Culture*. Chandler & Sharp, 1974.

Lehmann, Winfred P. *Descriptive Linguistics: An Introduction*. Random House, 1972.

Lenneberg, Eric H. *Biological Foundations of Language*. John Wiley, 1967.

———. "Language and Cognition." In Eric H. Lenneberg, 1967; and in Danny D. Steinberg and Leon A. Jacobovits (eds.), 1971, pp. 536–557.

Lévi-Strauss, Claude. *The Raw and the Cooked*. Harper & Row, 1964.

———. "A Sort of Pope." Interview, *Psychology Today* 5(1972):76–78.

———. "The Story of Asdiwal." In Edmund Leach (ed.), *The Structural Study of Myth and Totemism*. Association of Social Anthropologists Monograph, 1967, pp. 1–47.

———. *Structural Anthropology*. Trans. from French by Claire Jacobsen and Brooke Grundfest Schoept. Basic Books, 1967.

———. "The Structural Study of Myth." *Journal of American Folklore* 68(1955):428–444; and as Chapter 10 in Richard deGeorge and Fernande deGeorge (eds.), 1972, pp. 169–194.

Lyons, John. *Introduction to Theoretical Linguistics*. Cambridge University Press, 1969.

Mackey, William F. "The Description of Bilingualism." *Canadian Journal of Linguistics* 7(1962):51–85; and in Joshua A. Fishman (ed.), 1968, pp. 554–584.

Maclay, Howard. "Linguistics Overview." In Danny D. Steinberg and Leon A. Jacobovits (eds.), 1971, pp. 157–181.

Mandelbaum, David G., ed. *Selected Writings of Edward Sapir in Language, Culture and Personality*. University of California Press, 1949.

Martinet, André. "Structure and Language." In Jacques Ehrmann (ed.), 1970, pp. 1–9.

McNeil, D. "Anthropological Psycholinguistics." Unpublished Manuscript, Harvard University, 1965.

Metzger, D., and G. Williams. "Some Procedures and Results in the Study of Native Categories: Tzeltal 'Firewood.' " *American Anthropologist* 68(1966):389–407.

Mitford, Nancy. "The English Aristocracy." In Nancy Mitford (ed.), *Noblesse Oblige*, Harper & Brothers, 1956, pp. 21–52.

Morton, Samuel George. *Crania Americana*. J. Penington, 1839.

Murdock, George P. *Africa: Its People and Their Culture History*. McGraw-Hill, 1959, pp. 271–274, 290–291.

Nida, Eugene. *Morphology*. University of Michigan Press, 1946.

Nott, J. C., and G. R. Glidden. *Types of Mankind*. J. B. Lippincott, 1854.

Observer Review, The. London. August 10, 1969, p. 22.

Otterbein, Keith F. "Basic Steps in Conducting a Cross-Cultural Study." *Behavior Science Notes* 4(1969):221–236.

Paterson, Douglas. "The Linguistic Analogy in Anthropology." Unpublished Seminar Paper, University of Washington, Seattle, 1973.

Pedersen, Holger. *The Discovery of Language: Linguistic Science in the Nineteenth Century*. Trans. by John Webster Spargo. Indiana University Press, 1959.

Pei, Mario. *Glossary of Linguistic Terminology*. Doubleday, Anchor Books, 1966.

Pike, Kenneth L. *Language in Relation to a Unified Theory of the Structure of Human Behavior*. Mouton, The Hague, 1967.

———. *Phonemics*. University of Michigan Press, 1947.

Porter, C. L. *Taxonomy of Flowering Plants*. W. H. Freeman, 1967.

Principles of the International Phonetic Association, The. The International Phonetic Association, 1949.

Radcliffe-Brown, A. R. "The Mother's Brother in South Africa." *South African Journal of Science* 21(1924):542–555.

Romney, A. Kimball, and Roy Goodwin D'Andrade. "Transcultural Studies in Cognition." Special Issue of *American Anthropologist* 66(1964):Part 2.

Salisbury, R. F. "Notes on Bilingualism and Linguistic Change in New Guinea." *Anthropological Linguistics* 4(1962):1–13.

Sapir, Edward. "Conceptual Categories in Primitive Languages." *Science* 74(1931):578; and in Dell Hymes (ed.), 1964, p. 128.

———. "The Grammarian and His Language." *American Mercury* 1(1924):149–155.

———. *Language: An Introduction to the Study of Speech*. Harcourt, Brace and World, 1921.

———. "La Réalité psychologique des phonèmes." *Journal de Psychologie Normale et Pathologique* 30(1933):247–265.

Saporta, Sol. *Psycholinguistics: A Book of Readings*. Holt, Rinehart and Winston, 1961.

Sherzer, Joel, and Regna Darnell. "Outline Guide for the Ethnographic Study of Speech Use." In John J. Gumperz and Dell Hymes (eds.), 1972, pp. 548–554.

Spencer, Herbert. *Descriptive Sociology*. D. Appleton, 1873–1933.

Spradley, James P. *Culture and Cognition: Rules, Maps, and Plans*. Chandler, 1972.

———. *You Owe Yourself a Drunk: An Ethnography of Urban Nomads*. Little, Brown, 1970.

Steinberg, Danny D., and Leon A. Jacobovits, eds. *Semantics: An Interdisciplinary Reader in Philosophy, Linguistics and Psychology*. Cambridge University Press, 1971.

Sturtevant, Edgar Howard. *An Introduction to Linguistic Science*. Yale University Press, 1947.

———. *Linguistic Change*, University of Chicago Press, 1917; Phoenix Edition, 1965.

Sturtevant, William C. "Studies in Ethnoscience." In A. Kimball Romney and Roy Goodwin D'Andrade (eds.), 1964, pp. 99–131.

Swadesh, Morris. "Lexico-Statistic Dating of Prehistoric Ethnic Contacts." *Proceedings of the American Philosophical Society* (1952)96:453–462.

———. "Linguistics as An Instrument of Prehistory." *Southwestern Journal of Anthropology* 15(1959):20–35; and in Dell Hymes (ed.), 1964, pp. 575–583.

———. "Towards Greater Accuracy in Lexicostatistic Dating." *International Journal of American Linguistics* 21(1955):121–137.

Thompson, Richard A. "Transformational Theory and Semantic Analysis." *Journal of Linguistics* 4(1968):73–78.

Troubetzkoy, N. *Grundzüge der Phonologie*. Travaux du Cercle Linguistique de Prague, VII, 1937.

Tyler, Stephen, ed. *Cognitive Anthropology*. Holt, Rinehart and Winston, 1969.

"Use of Vernacular Languages in Education, The." Report of the UNESCO Meeting of Specialists, 1951. In Joshua A. Fishman (ed.), 1968, pp. 689–690.

Vachek, Josef. "The Linguistic Theory of the Prague School." In V. Fried, 1972, pp. 11–28.

Weinreich, Uriel. "Languages in Contact." *Language in Contact*. Linguistic Circle of New York, 1954, pp. 1–6; and in Sol Saporta (ed.), *Psycholinguistics*, 1961, pp. 376–381.

Whiting, J., and I. Child. *Child Training and Personality: A Cross Cultural Study*. Yale University Press, 1953.

Whiteley, Wilfred. *Swahili: The Rise of a National Language*. Methuen, Studies in African History, #3, 1969.

Whorf, Benjamin Lee. "A Linguistic Consideration of Thinking in Primitive Communities." In John B. Carroll (ed.), 1956, pp. 65–86; and in Dell Hymes (ed.), 1964, pp. 129–141.

Wissler, C. *The Relation of Nature to Man in Aboriginal America*. Oxford University Press, 1926.

Index

Page numbers for definitions are in *italics*.